The Lives of Beryl Markham

Also by Errol Trzebinski

The Kenya Pioneers
Silence Will Speak

ERROL TRZEBINSKI

The Lives of Beryl Markham

W. W. Norton & Company
New York • London

For my husband, Sbish and our
children of Africa, Bruce, Tonio, and Gabriela.
With love and gratitude.

Copyright © 1993 by Errol Trzebinski
First American Edition 1993
First published as a Norton paperback 1995

Printed in the United States of America

Manufacturing by the Haddon Craftsmen, Inc.

ISBN 0-393-31252-6

W. W. Norton & Company, Inc., 500 Fifth Avenue, New York, N.Y. 10110
W. W. Norton & Company Ltd., 10 Coptic Street, London WC1A 1PU

1 2 3 4 5 6 7 8 9 0

Contents

Acknowledgements   ix
Swahili Glossary   xiv
Maps: East Africa Protectorate *c.* 1900   xvi
   Cape to Cairo Air Route *c.* 1933   xviii
Foreword   xixx
1   The Birth of a Life (1902–4)   1
2   Africa (1904–6)   10
3   Life as *Lakwet* (1906–12)   18
4   Lessons at Home, and in the War (1913–19)   35
5   Life as Beryl Purves (1919–22)   59
6   Life at Mbogani (1922–4)   73
7   Life (1924–7)   97
8   Life as Beryl Markham (1927–9)   113
9   Life with Denys (1929–31)   139
10   Life as a Pilot (1931–2)   162
11   An Ocean Flyer in Embryo (1932–5)   179
12   The Waterjump (1936)   199
13   Life without Direction (1936–8)   218
14   West with the Night (1938–42)   233
15   Life as Beryl Schumacher (1942–9)   247
16   Life in Kenya Colony Once More (1950–64)   274
17   Life in South Africa (1964–70)   301
18   A Phoenix from the Ashes (1970–86)   314
Notes   338
References   347
Bibliography   383
Index   385

Who knows not Circe
Daughter of the sun, whose charmed cup
Whoever tasted, lost his upright shape,
And downward fell into a grovelling swine?

Milton, *Comus*, 50–3

Acknowledgements

My first thanks are to James Fox, whose practicality was generous in providing the key by which to unlock several mysteries in Beryl Markham's life, thus greatly enriching my task, and in allowing me to have copies of original draft material for the memoir which Raoul Schumacher used in the writing of *West with the Night*. I am also grateful to George Gutekunst who kindly provided me with transcripts of *A World Without Walls*; it is primarily through his effort, not to mention sacrifice, that republication of Beryl's memoir has scaled the heights, therefore to 'Georgy Porgy' I also offer my apologies for shattering a dream. I am indebted to Muffet Bennett for providing photographs and facets of Arthur Orchardson's childhood with Beryl; and to the late 'Ginger' Birkbeck who granted interviews which ran into many hours in the course of the last twenty years – her contribution has proved invaluable. And to Doria Block who will recognise the underpinnings of our pioneer research shared for five years, and who must surely comprehend the value of her role at last. I am grateful to John Cole, for coming forward with photographs of Denys Finch Hatton's crash in 1931; and to the late Scott O'Dell, and the late John Potter, both of whom did not live to see the fruit of their contributions and recollections of Beryl and Raoul published. To their widows I offer my thanks; Dr Elizabeth Hall O'Dell took up where her husband left off, displaying diligence and, like Carmen Potter, has shown kindness that has been heartwarming. Thanks also to Pat O'Neill for her support and encouragement; Andrew Maxwell-Hyslop for enthusiasm and favours granted when he is always so busy himself; Bill Purdy for generously handing over his collection of memorabilia on Beryl, not least the Lenare portrait for the dust jacket, and for granting access to his own unpublished work on Beryl. To Marian Sharpe my gratitude for bringing to my attention, in particular, the Adele Breaux study of Antoine de St Exupéry and for constant encouragement. To Jorgen and Gisela Thrane special thanks for many informative days spent at Kamwaki Farm. Thanks to Claire Warren, who typed and retyped the even heftier first draft uncomplainingly. To my friends who have put up with my preoccupation I probably owe gratitude and apologies in about equal measure. And last but by no means least my family who had the worst of it; their tolerance is astonishing.

I am also very grateful to three women — Rachel and Sarah whose wisdom and patience and faith combined with that of my agent, Vivienne Schuster, have sustained me with spiritual energy in completing what I set out to do when the going got tough.

Of the hundreds of interviews conducted for any biography, every contribution, no matter how small, provides a facet of recon- struction of the life under scrutiny. To those who asked that their names be withheld, for reasons of discretion, having laid bare their own lives when they did not wish to, I would like to say that their forebearance is all the more appreciated. The divergences of opinion over Beryl Markham are inseparable from the cultural, personal, social and educational prejudices and principles which have inspired them. Without such judgements and recollections biographers would not be able to work. I am indebted to each contributor listed below in a variety of ways and would like to express my sincere thanks not only for advice and help in providing reminiscences but often for hospitality as well: Ann Addly; Tonni Arnold; Bunny Allen; the late Jimmy Algar; Petal Allen; Richard Allen; Warren Austin; Joan Bagehot; Teddy Baring-Gould; Betty Beatty; Muffet Bennett; Alan Bobbe; David Bowden; the late Pat- ricia Bowles; Peter Bramwell; Barney Brantingham; Paul Brooks; Nancy Brown; the late Sonny Bumpus; Desmond Buxton; Juanita Carberry; Lord Carbery; the late Rose Cartwright; Richard Chew; Sally Christensen; Christopher Clarkson; Joan Considine; Eliza- beth Clutterbuck; the late Lady Diana Cooper; Philippa Corse; Humphrey Cottrill; Jack Couldrey; R. Dear; the late Dermott Dempster; Jan Dickinson; Kit Dickinson; the late Winifred Disney;

the late Dickie Edmondson; the late Margaret Elkington; Mary Epsom; Philip Evans; Victoria Eyre; Lady Maureen Fellowes; Jean Fenci; Renzo Fenci; Kathleen Fielden; the Hon. Robin Finch Hatton; Tana Fletcher; Haley Fiske; Major Tim Fitzgeorge-Parker MC; Lucile Flagg; 'Flip' G. D. Fleming; Martha Gellhorn; Nancy Gilbert; Raleigh Gilbert; Stan Gilbert; Melda Gillespie; Mary Gillett, Janice Gott-Kane; the late Dr J. R. Gregory; Douglas Hall; the late Jacko Heath; the late Doris Harries; Patrick Hemingway; Jan Hemsing; the late Robin Higgin; Sally Higgin; the late Cockie Hoogterp; the late Hilary Hook; the late Margot Hudson-Caine; G. M. Hughes, Record Agent; Peter Hughes; Elspeth Huxley with special thanks for the Margaret Elkington mss; Pat Imperato; Betty Kiggan; Ndungu Kigoli; Jan Knappert; the late Cyntha Kofsky; the late Christopher Langlands; David Laws; Hilbert Lee; the late Ingrid Lindstrom; Robin Long; Vicky Nancarrow; Jeremy Needham-Clarke; Vicky Needham-Clarke; Freddie Nettlefold; Sylvia Nettlefold; the Hon. Doreen Norman; Lucy W. Mbugua; Rosemary MacDonald; Shelagh McCutcheon; Hugh McGregor Ross; the late Jimmy McQueen; Diana Guest Manning; the late Beryl Markham; Sir Charles Markham, 3rd Bt; Fleur Markham; Michael Markham; the late Viviane Markham; Sir Peter Masefield; the late Dickie Mason; Philip Mason; David Mathias; the late A. T. Matson; Annabel Maule; Air Commodore H. W. Mermagen, CB, CBE, AFC; Mickey Migdoll; Paddy Migdoll; Bonnie Miller; Iain Miller; Maeve Mitchell; Mary Mitford Barberton; Maddie de Mott; Myra Oates; Jill d'Olier; the late Arnold Paice; Audrey Palmer Neville; Christian de Pange; Julian Phipps; Royston Powell; Tristram Powell; Peter Rand; Joyce Raw; Sylvia Richardson; Mike Richmond; Dr Alistair Robb-Smith; Edward 'Roddy' Rodwell; Olive Rodwell; the Captain and crew of M. V. *Royal Star*; Molly Ryan; Karl Ruedin, Dr Peter Schiller; Fleming Schoidt; the late Pam Scott; the late Sheila Scott; Veronica Scott-Mason; Clara Selborn; Roland Sharpe; Michael Shyne; Sylvia Simpson; Xan Smiley; Michael J. Smith; the late Aldo Soprani; the late Connie Sorsbie; the late Malin Sorsbie; Diggy Spyratos; Dora Stevens; Almira Struthers; the late James Struthers; Michael Taub; Kit Taylor; Barbara Thorpe; Pip Thorpe; Judith Thurman; Ken Towner; Gisela Thrane; Jorgen Thrane; the late Dan Trench; Jack le Poer Trench; John de Villiers; Jasmin

Wali Mohammed; the late James Walker; Dolly Watts; the late Bill Waudby; G. F. Webb; Alex White; Sir Osmond Williams; the late Sir Michael Wood; Robert Young; Maxine Zanacchi.

In addition I would like to thank those members of staff working for the following organisations who obtained information, granted permission to use material submitted, and dealt with correspondence and formalities on my behalf: Academy of Motion Pictures Arts & Sciences; Aerlingus in-flight magazine; the Aero Club of East Africa; *The Aeroplane* (1936); *The African Standard* (1906); the *Argus* (Australia); Associated Press; Australian Archives; Australian Jockey Club; Australian National Library; Bettman Archives, Bettman Newsphotos; *The Blood-Horse*; British Airways (Historical Aviation Service); British High Commission (Nairobi); The British Library (Newspaper Library, Colindale); British Woman Pilots' Association; California Magazine; *Carlisle Express* (1891); Civil Aviation Authority; *Colliers*; *Country Life*; Cunard Archives (Univ. of Liverpool); the *Daily Express*; the *Daily Mail*; the *Daily Mirror*; the *Daily Nation* (Kenya); the *Daily Sketch* (1932); the *Daily Telegraph*; the *East African Annual*; the *East African Journal*; the *Evening Press* (1898); the *East African Standard*; the *Evening Standard*; Fairchild Publications (S.A.); *The Field*; *Flight*; *Flight International*; General Medical Council (Disciplinary Division); Gloucester County Records; the Grosvenor Hotel; *The Guinness Book of Records*; *Harpers & Queen*; Houghton Library (Harvard Univ.); Houghton Mifflin Company; Huntington Memorial Hospital; the *Independent*; *Jambo*; The Jockey Club of Kenya; The Jockey Club of South Africa; The Jockeys' Association of Great Britain Ltd; *Kelly's Yellow Directory*; Kenya National Archives; Kenya Racing (Bendell); *Kenya Official Gazette* XXIV No. 535; the *Kenya Weekly News*; *Ladies' Home Journal*; the *Leader* (BEA) 1910; Leicester County Records; Leicestershire Museums, Art Galleries and Record Service; the *Observer*; the *Illustrated London News*; Lord Chamberlain's Office; Melbourne Public Library; Mitchell Library; Nairobi Library; the *New York Times*; the Rungstedlund Foundation; *Santa Barbara News Press*; *Style*; the *Sunday Express*; the *Sunday Mail* (Rhodesia); the *Sunday Telegraph*; the *Sunday Times*; *Vanity Fair* magazine.

My thanks to Tom Weldon and Emma Rhind-Tutt for editorial guidance and help at Heinemann.

Photo acknowledgements: 1, 29, 30, 49, 50: The late Viviane Markham; 2, 8: Muffet Bennett; 3. Camilla Pelizzoli; 4, 20, 28, 42: Trzebinski collection; 5. Dorothy Vaughan; 6. McGregor Ross collection, Rhodes House, Oxford; 7. Aero Club of East Africa (Trzebinski collection); 9, 15, 34, 37, 39: British Library; 10, 13: Sir Osmond Williams, Bt.; 11. Lord Carbery; 12, 23: The late Ingrid Lindstrom; 14. Paddy Migdoll; 16. Peter Bramwell; 17. Hilda Tofte; 18, 33, 35, 38, 59: William K. Purdy; 19, 21: The late Cockie Hoogterp (2nd Baroness Blixen); 22. the late Viviane Markham; 24. John Cole; 25, 53, 55: The Hon. Patricia O'Neill; 26, 27: The late Chris Langlands; 31. Popperfoto/Reuter; 32. Popperfoto/Reuter; 36. UPI/Bettmann; 40. Michael Taub; 41, 58, 60: Associated Press; 43. The late John Potter; 44. Elizabeth Hall O'Dell; 45. Douglas Hall; 46, 48: Audrey Palmer Neville; 47. Renzo Fenci; 51. Jorgen Thrane; 52. Victoria Eyre; 54. Graham Viney; 56. Peter Colmore; 57. The Nation Group

Swahili Glossary

askari = guard;
ayah = nanny;
bao = board or also the Kenya name given to the African game played on a board;
baraza = meeting, often festive, or dance;
boma = enclosure or corral;
daktari = doctor or vet;
damu = blood;
dhobi = laundry;
donga = gulley;
dudu = insect;
duka = store;
duka wallah = Indian storekeeper;
farazi = horse;
fundi = artisan;
hapa = here;
hapana = no;
hawezi = cannot;
hii = that (object);
huko = there (direction);
jikoni = kitchen;
jua = sun;
juu = on top;

kabila = sort or type;
kabisa = completely or absolutely;
kali = peppery or fierce;
kanzu = long white robe;
kaross = skin cloak;
kata = cut;
kengele = bell;
kiboko = rhino-hide whip;
kikapu = basket;
kitu = thing;
kuni = firewood;
kwangusha = fall;
kwenda = go;
lakini = but;
lakwet, lakwan, lakwani = very little girl (Nandi);
layoni = pre-circumcision (Nandi);
maji = water;
maridadi = pretty or beautiful;
memsahib = madam or Mrs;
mlevi = drunkard;
moja = first or number one;
moran = warrior;
mpishi = cook;

mshara = pay;
mugumu = indigenous tree;
murram = dirt (road);
mungu = God;
mutu = person;
mzungu = white man;
neapara = headman;
ndege = bird, aeroplane;
ndimu = lemon or lime;
ndito = virgin or young girl;
ngini = again;
ngoma = dance;
ngonjwa = sick;
nyama = meat or game;
nzige = locust;
panga = machete;
pesa = money;
pole pole = slowly or gently;
posho = maize meal (staple diet);
reims = zebra hide thongs or reins;
rondavel = the classic African red mud hut;

rungu = club;
saa = hour;
saa moja = seven o'clock;
shamba = garden or estate;
shauri = problem;
shauries = problems;
shauri ya mungu = God's will;
shifta = Somali bandits;
shuka = shift or toga;
siko = day;
simi = sword;
suferia = pan or tin bowl;
syce = groom;
takkies = plimsolls;
tembo = beer;
toto = boy child;
terai = hat;
twende = to go;
ugali = maize meal porridge;
unga = flour;
vlei = grassland;
wapi = where;
wazungus = white people;
yote = all

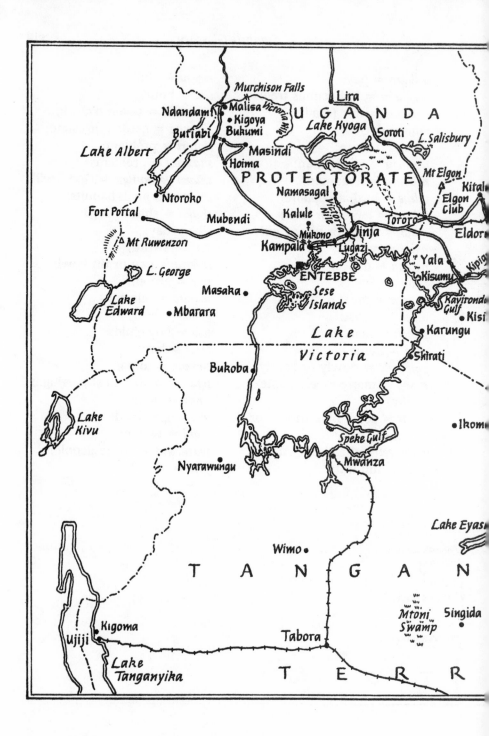

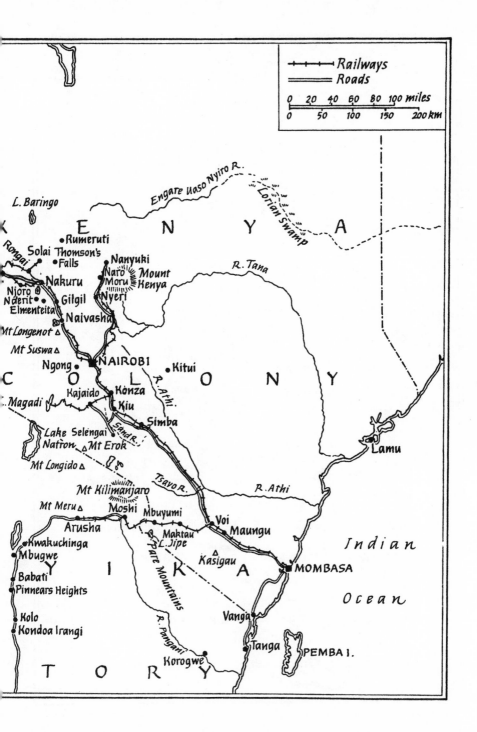

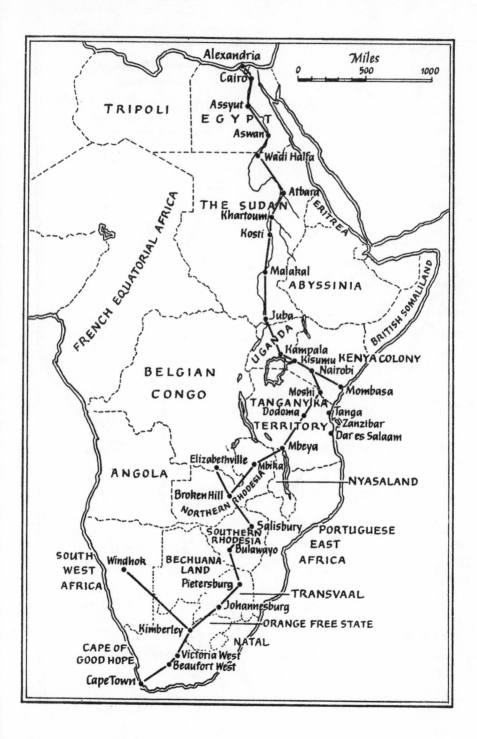

Foreword

I planned *The Lives of Beryl Markham* eighteen years ago, during a series of interviews undertaken with Beryl Markham for my first book *Silence Will Speak*. My quest had been to glean as much information on my subject, Denys Finch Hatton, as I could. Beryl confirmed that she had known this elusive character yet, after two interviews, I required still more detail than she had yielded. Her answers had been arcane when I had tried to establish, somewhat impertinently, whether she had had an affair with Karen Blixen's lover.

To overcome my diffidence I decided that it would be more conducive to broach the subject over a meal; we met at The Bistro, Alan Bobbe's famous restaurant in Nairobi. Thus, in March 1974, we sat upstairs enjoying delectable food, talking about this and that. Gradually I steered Beryl in the direction of my question. She accepted a Cognac with her coffee, as I had hoped, and lit one of her favourite cigarettes; as the smoke spiralled lazily upwards, she appeared sublimely relaxed, the brandy glass cupped in her hand. I phrased my question mentally, but in that split second before I could utter it, Beryl's face altered; as if some stunning interior light had been switched on, she was smiling, radiant, responding to someone else beyond me. 'Fweddy dahling,' she cooed. (Beryl did not have a speech impediment exactly but did not always sound the 'r' so that Nairobi sounded like Naiwobi.) 'How wonderful to see you.' And rising from the banquette, she picked up her handbag, joining her friend on the other side of the room. Minutes later summoning me, she introduced me to Freddie Nettlefold, heir to a nuts and bolts fortune, a Kenya settler who had once trained steeple-chasers in England.

I will never know just how much Beryl's intuition played its part in thwarting my intention all those years ago although I believe now that it was paramount. Had Freddie Nettlefold not walked in, Beryl would have deflected me on some other pretext. She was skilled at pre-emption and at avoiding questions under all circumstances.

This display made such an impact, that I decided that if my Finch Hatton biography was published, I would like one day to write about her, still a seductive woman aged 73.

To understand how different Beryl was from most people, one must realise that she rarely talked about herself and never about her achievements. She was a product of the pioneering era in British East Africa which in itself was interesting enough; she was a racehorse trainer of note. Less known is that Beryl was also one of the first women in the world to hold a commercial pilot's licence; she had learned to fly in 1930 when aviation was dominated by men, capping her own success ultimately by crossing the Atlantic in 1936 solo, from east to west, the difficult way against the wind, becoming the first person to achieve that too.

I was curious as to how so self-effacing a woman had succeeded in a man's world without losing a jot of her femininity, which, judging by her numerous love affairs was never in question, yet the enigma repeated itself. Her ability to turn heads increased rather than lessened over the years. As I had witnessed to my chagrin over the question I wanted to pose, she was still as effective and beguiling; weeks later, I heard that she was training for Nettlefold.

Typically, it was not Beryl but someone else who told me about her memoir *West with the Night*. I managed that year to acquire a first edition. After reading it, I could not understand how the book had escaped me before. I tried to get it republished for her, but reaction from both the head of Heinemann and Hamish Hamilton was identical: nobody but a handful of readers in Kenya would be the least bit interested. I was disappointed, wanting to thank Beryl in some practical way, in return for her help over Denys, when she was ekeing out an existence and short of money. Little had I realised that I had joined a platoon of would-be supporters.

Three years later, an American restaurateur, George Gutekunst, succeeded in getting her memoir republished by Northpoint Press. It was he who produced a TV documentary *A World Without Walls*, upon which I worked both as researcher and interviewee. After it was transmitted *West with the Night* crept into the paperback best-seller lists in America. Everybody who knew Beryl was delighted; at last, though perhaps a little too late for her really to enjoy the financial rewards which had escaped her all her life, she was a star again . . .

In 1986, seven months before the release of *A World Without Walls*, I was commissioned unexpectedly to write Beryl's biography. To be honest, the timing was premature: I had no intention of undertaking such a project while she was alive. I admired her and did not wish to hurt her in any attempt at being objective.

Before long my sleuthing led me to telephone an American, John Potter, living in Bidart who had known Beryl and her third husband, Raoul Schumacher a ghost writer, in the forties in Montecito, California. John Potter volunteered his disappointment in Beryl. With so much success to her credit, her brilliance as a flier and trainer he questioned her failure to 'set the record straight . . . admit that Raoul, rather than she, had written the memoir.' Now that *West with the Night* had been republished to fresh critical acclaim, Potter realised that Beryl would have needed a great deal of moral courage to deny her own authorship but 'how marvellous it would have been, had she come clean at last and confessed.' In no sense was Potter's criticism mean; nor did he begrudge Beryl new-found royalties, feeling it right and proper now that Raoul was dead that she benefit, even if Raoul ought to have been given credit for the writing.

In truth, John Potter had placed me in a real dilemma. For years I had defended Beryl, arguing that her memoir was not the work of one who had never set foot on Kenyan soil. Friends in Kenya had often voiced their doubts but here was the first genuine argument in favour of Schumacher as author. Within a month or so, the documentary *A World Without Walls* was scheduled for transmission in America. In the interview I gave I had been adamant that only Beryl could have written the book, but this disquieting discovery led to greater research into the character of Schumacher.

It was essential to find corroborative evidence of what I had been told. The questions arising from John Potter's revelation were endless and if Potter was right, how was I to handle my own volte-face? My opportunity to challenge Beryl on the subject never arose. Again she cheated me of the chance to confront her. Just four days before my return to Nairobi in 1986, Beryl died.

Unexpectedly, the following March fresh evidence in support of John Potter's claim was published in the American *Vanity Fair* in a letter writen by the celebrated author of children's fiction, Scott O'Dell. Now that Beryl was no longer alive to be embarrassed by him, he had decided to explain his friendship with Raoul Schumacher, to recount how he had introduced Beryl and Raoul to each other at his home in California; how he had advised Schumacher to approach Houghton Mifflin – O'Dell's own publishers – directly, who subsequently published 'Beryl's book'.

Most readers regarded Scott O'Dell's letter as a bombshell. For me, it was a breakthrough. Within eight months, two people, neither knowing of the other's existence, had decided to unburden themselves after keeping quiet for forty years.

Trying to piece together the life of so intricate and secret a woman, one whose cultural background was as diverse as the lovers who populated it, may be likened to reassembling fragments of the Portland Vase without knowing what the classic whole looked like originally with its contrasting images of triumph and pain. Beryl Markham never gossiped yet people never ceased to talk about her. Thus the legend grew. Even after her death, questions proliferate still. Some of the answers, it is hoped, will be found in this book.

1

The Birth of a Life

(1902–4)

'As far as I'm concerned, I was more or less abandoned by my mother,' Beryl Markham conceded in her eighties.[1] Her antipathy was certainly understandable, for Beryl was just four years of age when Clara Clutterbuck walked out of her life.

Even Beryl's birth certificate in 1902 bore a hyphen where her christian name should have been. In a way, this blank was to symbolise one persistent trait in her nature – women were to be little more to her than that hieroglyphic dash, a means to an end. For seventy years, Beryl had remained silent over her mother's defection; then in 1984 she relaxed her admirable discretion with sporadic comments, only volunteering information when pressed, and in her down-to-earth manner she would then utter a few condemning words.

Hitherto she had presented her arrival in Africa as she preferred others to see it: her father, Charles Clutterbuck brought her alone as a small girl to British East Africa in 1906; her mother had remained in England so as to school Beryl's older brother.

It was easier to believe this version of events than to pry any further. The year 1906 was significant, but the circumstances of her abandonment by her mother very different from Beryl's account of them. Beryl's resulting psychological scar was never articulated, but fortunately Beryl was a born survivor, and her mercurial instincts were to be fostered by a pagan habitat. Though she was born in Great Britain of English parents, it was Africa that shaped Beryl's character and beliefs. Her parents spent less than two years together in BEA, the land that forged her destiny, so the bush became Beryl's nursery, her playground and her school.

It is not impossible to gauge how altered she would have been had she remained in colder climes, cossetted within the heritage of the upper classes, reaping the benefit of those privileges that the late Victorian era bestowed upon girls, or how different her disposition, had she occasionally been caressed by a loving mother and influenced by the conventions and Christian repressions of the early Edwardians.

But Beryl was denied these influences, just as she was denied the traditions of a well-to-do household, a proper education and the security of numerous relatives from the vast Clutterbuck family. Childhood insecurity may account for the fact that Beryl's many achievements did not bring her happiness. No matter who or what Beryl won, victory was not enough, a flaw in an otherwise courageous spirit. From the time she took her first steps, there were few opportunities of forming an enjoyable impression of her own sex. Within two years of her parents separating, Beryl had no idea what her mother had looked like. With a lack of maternal affection she learned early on to take love when it was offered: experience taught her that one never knew when it could be withdrawn. Her mistrust of women, despite their kindness to her, arose from the threat Beryl felt from any female who might fracture her one steadfast relationship – that with her father. Thus Charles Clutterbuck became a sheet anchor in her divided world of black and white. She strove for perfection to please her father, which led to her taking a defensive stand when things went wrong, indeed when anything created disappointment. She could never accept responsibility for sorrow, the losses in life; these were always someone else's problem. Instinctively she seemed to grasp at anything that wrenched her emotionally, to push her beyond herself to new heights.

Little is known about the ancestry of Beryl's mother except that they were the titled Alexanders of County Carlow. Of Charles Clutterbuck's genealogy there is more detail: he was the tenth-generation descendant of a Flemish merchant, Thomas Clotterbooke, engaged in the wool trade, one of the many foreigners to come to England from the Low Countries at the time of the Duke of Alba's persecution.[2]

By the time his grandson, Thomas Clotterbooke, married the daughter of the Burgomaster of the Briel, the family was established in Gloucestershire, as one of the 'first makers of Clothe in the county, spinning one thread at a time, in their spinning houses of Miserdine.'[3]

The Clutterbucks prospered within the irregular escarpment of the Cotswold Hills which gave the finest view imaginable over the Golden Vale of Gloucestershire. Sharing the staple industry of Stroud, they had contributed to its affluence by their own effort and prudence. Gradually a series of 'respectable vicars, doctors, administrators and colonels' emerged from the clothier family 'with a high point of the Archdeacon of Winchester' in 1698.[4]

Though they never used it, they next acquired a country seat, Newark Park, Ozleworth, near Wootton-under-Edge, which had been built from the ruins of Kingswood Abbey by Sir Nicolas Poyntz; perhaps it was too decrepit for it was occupied only by the Reverend Lewis Clutterbuck who commissioned James Wyatt to bring the house up to date. During renovations a stained glass panel, edged with a chain of oak leaves in which the Clutterbuck crest was set, was fitted into an oriel window overlooking the main staircase. By now their name was spelled as Beryl would spell it, arising from the old weaver's tag of the sixteenth century:

Clutterbuck small and Pharoah Webb
Of dirty chain made golden Abb.

Their coat of arms, containing four lions rampant, is crowned by a stag sejant. As it happens, the predominating shades of blue and gold matched those of the Markham racing colours.

By the turn of the century many of the Clutterbuck sons had turned their backs on the wool industry. Beryl's great grandfather was an 'attorney-of-law at Painswick and Stroud' whose ghost still haunts the house in Painswick today, the present owner claims. His wife Charlotte, née Weber, a London girl, produced Richard Henry Clutterbuck, Beryl's grandfather who, upon coming of age, broke altogether with tradition. He moved away from his birthplace and went north to Cumberland. He was admitted to Hilary in 1861 and became a solicitor, forming a partnership with the

Town Clerk of Carlisle, John Nanson, but, after this dissolved, practised from his residence on his own account at Durran Hill House in Carlisle. He married Beryl's paternal grandmother, Mary Rose, the daughter of George Baldwin Fakenham of Norfolk, and in doing so, aged thirty-two, introduced his father-in-law's name to the Clutterbuck family tree. Mary Rose Clutterbuck bore three children in quick succession: Helen Baldwin (1868) who died within two months; followed by Henry Baldwin, Beryl's uncle, in 1869; and finally Charles Baldwin Clutterbuck, Beryl's father, born at Durran Hill House on 25 April 1870.[5] Their mother died three months later. Undoubtedly Beryl's father's spartan ideas of child-rearing were influenced by the treatment meted out by the nurse and nanny who cared for himself and his brother for eight years until their father re-married in 1878. Maria Louisa Edwards produced five children of her own so that when Beryl's grandfather was fifty-six, he was stretched financially to maintain seven dependants.[6]

Henry and Charles Clutterbuck attended Repton school in Derbyshire, Beryl's father following her uncle as a boarder in 1885. Neither excelled. The register of their minor public school reveals only that Beryl's father was a pupil for three years. No records exist to suggest that he distinguished himself in the class-room or on the playing fields. Nor did he merit prizes for any quality of character.[7]

In February 1889 Beryl's father was admitted as a gentleman cadet to the Royal Military College of Sandhurst. At almost eighteen, he stood five foot seven: 'Clutterbuck small' on their wool tag indicates that the family were not renowned for height. His eyes were blue, rather too close set; his mouth small and stern and when young partly hidden by a neat military moustache. His conduct was 'exemplary' but, just as at school, Beryl's father was unremarkable, as the Sandhurst Register implies. Charles Clutterbuck's passion for horses was passed on to his only daughter, and Beryl's mother was also an accomplished horsewoman. Her father's love of steeple-chasing and hunting may well have manifested itself as a cadet; before the First World War, cavalry officers were required to take leave from their regiments to keep in trim with the hunt. At any rate, for the rest of his life horses were his abiding interest, be they for sport, pleasure or professional purposes, so much so that one criticism was levelled at him – 'all Captain Clutterbuck cared to talk about was the racing, training and breeding of horses, to the point of being a bore.'[8]

On 1 March, shortly before his nineteenth birthday in 1890, he took up his commission with the 1st Battalion of the King's Own Scottish Borderers, going with his regiment to Rangoon. As a 2nd Lieutenant, he served the last six months in Burma before returning 'home' to Devonport.

In summer 1891, just after Beryl's father came of age, her grandfather, who suffered from a weak heart, succumbed to an epidemic of influenza in Carlisle, dying on 29 June.[9] His widow, Maria Clutterbuck, inherited whatever benefits there were. Once the debts of Beryl's grandfather were paid off, Charles Clutterbuck received the residue of the sale of a modest London property, some shares in the County Hotel Company, three silver salt cellars and two silver candlesticks. As Beryl's father had expensive tastes in horses, this was barely adequate for a budding army officer.[10]

Charles Clutterbuck probably met his first wife, Clara Agnes Alexander, Beryl's mother, at one of the regimental balls in York – where he was stationed for three years, having been promoted to Lieutenant – though possibly the long hack home after hunting provided their prelude to romance. Clara was a beauty; perched on her hunter, and turned out in silk hat, veil and habit, her Munnings-like figure presented an elegant picture. The advantage of riding side-saddle was that the gentlemen of the field gave way at fences and opened gates, affording ample opportunities for flirtation. Beryl's parents would pass on to her, in double measure, a weakness for the opposite sex.

Clara Alexander had recently returned from India, following the death of her father, Josiah William Alexander. He had been attached to the Civil Service at Indore. In bereavement, Clara and her mother were taken under the wing of close family friends, Mr and Mrs Alfred Cholmley, and lived with them at Place Newton, Wintringham, a village outside York. It was here that Clara would marry Beryl's father.[11]

Very little is known about Clara in her youth, apart from her ability as a fine horsewoman, her glamour and her competitive spirit. Clara was always ahead in the field, soaring over hedgerow and fence, cutting a fine figure among the fashionable set just as, one day, her daughter would. She too was tall, slender, flirtatious and bold with a wandering eye. She had blue eyes, as blue and hard as Fabergé enamel. She had Irish colouring – dark hair and an exquisite complexion – and she bore herself with an elegance beyond her years.

Clara accepted Charles Clutterbuck's proposal of marriage but, between 1896 and 1898 something went badly awry with his military career once he returned to Aldershot. Whether it is significant that he was cashiered while engaged to Clara is unknown. Under a general heading of 'Casualties', the Army list states: 'Removed from the Service for Absence without leave, Lt. C. B. Clutterbuck.'[12] However his disgrace did not effect his betrothal. Clara's mother apparently found it no impediment, for in less than three months they were married with Mrs Alexander's blessing, at the Church of St Peter, next door to the Cholmley's home in Wintringham.[13] The event caused a sensation, since no fashionable wedding had occurred there for over a century and 'the spell was broken by Miss Clara Alexander of Place Newton and Mr Charles Clutterbuck of Knaptoft House, Rugby'.[14]

Beryl's maternal grandmother was clearly able to afford Clara's lavish celebration. No expense was spared from her duchesse satin gown 'appliqued with Brussels lace, trimmed with chiffon orange blossoms and diamond ornaments'.[15] Crimson cloth was laid from the gateway to the door of the tiny Gothic church. It was filled with palms, exotic ferns and lilies reminiscent of India. On 6 August 1898 Clara arrived from Place Newton by carriage on the arm of Alfred Cholmley, who gave her away. The sun shone as the couple left the church; the village school children 'all the girls in white . . . with pink sashes flanked the red carpet, strewing flowers in their path . . . Lord Middleton's huntsmen . . . their whips and twenty-three couple of hounds' added a sporting touch. A lavish wedding breakfast followed, given by the Cholmleys. Clara Clutterbuck left for Knaptoft House to become a farmer's wife, wearing 'a large mauve picture hat'.[16] Her first son was born two years later in Scarborough where Clara had joined her mother in July 1890 at the thriving summer resort on the north-east coast. Beryl's older brother was always known as Dickie and required coddling from the outset.[17]

Beryl was born eighteen months later on 26 October 1902, by which time her parents had moved from Rugby to Ashwell in Leicestershire. Westfield House, her birthplace, was three miles from Whissendine and Oakham, a peaceful market town set in a wide Midland vale, among trees full of rooks. Charles Clutterbuck would continue to farm from this modest, red brick, Georgian dwelling with six bedrooms for two more years. Little had changed in the county for over two centuries. Life had a slow, familiar rhythm; cows yielded their milk for Stilton cheese and farming was an intricate part of the preservation of the finest hunting country in England. The Clutterbucks were spoiled for choice where Clara's passion for fox-hunting was concerned. The Belvoir alone met four times a week during a four-month season; they hunted also with the Quorn and occasionally Mr Fernie's Hounds.

As a baby, Beryl was surrounded by the comforting sounds and smells that were subsequently to provide her with a sense of security – the loose-boxes, the whinnyings and snortings, the reek of manure, sweat and litter, mingled with linseed, fodder, leather and fragrant hay. As an adult, whenever she sought refuge, for whatever reason, Beryl was always to make for the stables.[18]

The running of her parents' household in Ashwell was pivotal to fox-hunting, steeple-chasing and the Hunt Balls to mark the close of each season. Clara, who returned to the pleasures of the chase as soon after her confinement as she was able, was regarded as one of the more immaculately turned-out women in the field. On their powerfully haunched hunters, the Clutterbucks were reputed to be 'the best looking couple and hardest riders to hounds in the Melton district'.[19] And, several mornings a week, they thundered across the countryside, their mounts throwing up clods of mud, leaping fences and ditches, relishing the convivial company, stopping for the occasional reviving glass of port. Always in at the kill, at dusk they hacked home to hot baths and a brandy, weary from physical exertion but replete.

An entry in *Kelly's Yellow Directory* for 1904 reveals the first signs of erosion in the marriage of Beryl's parents, as well as insolvency, and this before she was even a year old. There can be no other reason for an advertisement disclosing that Clara was running a 'Tea and Refreshment Room' at 11 Burton Street, Melton Mowbray. Obviously they needed extra funds though the standard of life they led belied their situation.[20] In later life too, however, Clara was often to find herself in dire circumstances and was never disdainful of the most menial of occupations to get her through a bad patch. She would even mind children and sell flowers from her garden so as to pay for gin.[21]

Estranged or not, the Clutterbucks appeared together on 18 March 1904 at the Belvoir Hunt Steeplechase. Also at the event were the Hon. Rupert and Charles Craven and Jim Elkington, who were about to settle in British East Africa – unfortunately because their well-to-do families wanted them out of England. All three had been at Eton together and now were on the brink of becoming what were known as 'remittance men'. They may have been regarded as black sheep, but their enthusiasm fired Beryl's father, who decided to explore the opportunities of pioneering for himself. His departure was planned with military precision, coinciding, six weeks later, with the end of the local hunting activities.

In 1904, the British Government was offering vast acreages cheaply, having taken over the country as the East African Protectorate in 1895, and that was the lure. Africa had hit the headlines when the average reader still found it necessary to look at a map to establish exactly where Mombasa was. Britain, not to be outdone by Imperial expansion when the Germans began building a railway inland from Tanga, constructed their own 'iron snake', as the Maasai called the track running from Mombasa to Port Florence* on Lake Victoria, 508 miles away. The Uganda Railway, being her one link to Nairobi, which passed for civilisation, was to play a vital part in Beryl's life until she was sixteen and married for the first time.

In 1901, 'the Lunatic Line' which had cost £10,000 per mile to lay and had taken five and a half years to construct, was less of an achievement than an uneconomic backbone, traversing the wilderness. It had to be made to pay for itself; so Sir Charles Eliot, the Protectorate's first Commissioner, recruited European settlers from

* See Notes following text.

all over the world. His conviction was that such people would transform unbroken bush into valuable farms with their varying expertise. However impressive the quantity of land on offer, it was virgin, mostly unsurveyed, with no roads by which to reach it, as Beryl's father would shortly discover. As for her mother, Clara had not imagined such isolation possible. Contracts were strict. Clutterbuck needed £1,000 for investment over each of the five coming years; unless he could adhere to this, the Government could confiscate land.

Beryl's father steeple-chased for the last time in England during the series of fixtures that brought the Melton season to a close.[22] By the end of May, whatever chattels the Clutterbucks did not need had been sold and the rest shipped to Mombasa. Dickie was four, Beryl not yet two. When she returned to the county of her birth three decades later it was as Beryl Markham, racehorse trainer, royal courtesan, pilot, and most definitely a child of Africa.

2

Africa

(1904–6)

When Beryl's feet touched African soil, it was as though that moment was her real beginning. The quiet, lovely rhythms of the bush at dawn became integral to her life, as reassuring and as meaningful as the throbbing of distant drums. Whereas their sound and the immense space unnerved her mother, these were as natural to Beryl as to the wild creatures whose habitat she shared. Beryl's entry into the twentieth century was closer to the Africans' experience of it than their European Colonisers'.

Beryl's earliest recollections at the age of three were of being 'more at home on a horse than on my feet and with just the Africans to run around with all day, killing things and hunting with the *totos* because Daddy didn't have time for me'.[1] Beryl's father was establishing his flour and timber mills. Luckily he had secured a contract with the Uganda Railway soon after he bought Ndimu Farm at Njoro. Supplying off-cuts by which all rolling stock was powered, from 1906 onwards he sold thousands of tons of lumber, destined also for the lake steamers. The income paid for two old railway engines, which were converted to power the mills.[2] And gradually the name Ndimu Farm would give way to 'Clutt's Mill'.[3] Beryl's father was called 'Clutt', she explained, 'by all the *wazungus* – white people', lapsing into Swahili as she always did to find the right word. But to the Africans he was known as 'Cluttabucki'. On account of the siding on the farm, they believed that he owned the railway; as the engine hauled the wagons up their slow incline, they simulated its rhythm, chanting:

Cluttabucki kata kuni
Cluttabucki kata unga
Chuff, Chuff, Chuff!

And to their delight, the solitary, golden-haired child joined in.[4]

From their arrival in Mombasa, Clara Clutterbuck had had no illusions as to what was expected of a pioneer farmer's wife. There was no proper social life so a resilient nature was called for, not to mention a sense of humour. In June 1904, after a thirty-six-hour train journey, Beryl's father abandoned his wife and children at Wood's, a crude hotel near Nairobi station (the Norfolk Hotel was still under construction), while he walked thirty miles to inspect land at Thika. He bought purely for investment, deciding not to live there. There was no proper road, nor was a railway planned, and the lion population would have presented an overwhelming threat to horses.

The foray made him realise how many problems he faced. Wisely Clutt chose to gain first-hand experience at someone else's expense before tackling anything on his own account. Lord Delamere needed a dairy manager so he took the job. Delamere, or 'D' as everyone called him, was passionate about Kenya, and already regarded as the father of white settlement in the Colony. His first estate, Equator Ranch at Njoro, 100 miles up-country from Nairobi in the Rift Valley, was beyond Nakuru. In due course Njoro would be looked upon as the cradle of white pioneering, thanks to this tiny knot of settlers.

Thus, Clara and her two young children found themselves spending Christmas in 1904 in a thatched mud hut behind Delamere's dairy. The African *rondavel*, similiar to that which Lord and Lady Delamere occupied seven miles distant as the vulture flies, and their nearest neighbours, stood in 10,000 acres of bush. One visit to Florence Delamere's homestead had mapped out Clara Clutterbuck's future; while Lady Delamere was prepared to waive such niceties as doors and windows, Beryl's mother was not enamoured of the way in which the Delamere cows and oxen poked their faces inquisitively through sacking-covered apertures; nor did she find the non-existent plumbing amusing. The trek to the long-drop to answer nature's calls was not compensated for by

any vista of African plain, no matter how spectacular. To sleep
with a loaded revolver under her pillow, as Lady Delamere did,
was not Clara's idea of safety when Clutt was absent. Lady Delamere was interested in horticulture and poultry which Clara was
not.[5] The loneliness for some women was undeniable and Florence
Delamere was certainly grateful for Clara's unexpected company.
Tom Cholmondeley, the Delameres' only son, had been left in
England to be cared for, so great was the risk thought to be for
young children. Since Beryl's brother was a weak child, Clara
worried constantly therefore that the nearest doctor lived 100 miles
away. In Nairobi Dr Ribeiro, a Goan, rode a tame zebra to his
sickest patients and his rooms, amid the squalor of the bazaar, were
made from old packing cases.

The quarterly jaunts to Nairobi were pinned to the racing calen-
dar. The bush came to town to enjoy itself. Women wore their
prettiest hats, caught up on gossip, replenished supplies, made the
rounds of tailors, lawyers or the dentist. Clara took Dickie but
Beryl was left with the house-servants, who clearly doted on her.
Curiously, unlike other white progeny reared in BEA, Beryl had
neither a European nanny or African *ayah*. Many families brought
out young girls from England when they settled. In spite of advice
not to leave Beryl alone, irrespective of her age, in the company
of indigenous male employees, the Clutterbucks ignored the supposed possibility of sexual molestation.[6]

Beryl's parents were criticised by contemporary settlers for their
negligence and for subjecting her to the ministrations of a handful
of primitive domestic staff. Sometimes she was left with house-boys
for a week at a time. Yet Dickie, clad in a white sailor suit, was
always taken along.[7] Beryl bore no resentment, claiming proudly
that she was only ever looked after by Africans – 'my friends' –
whom she saw first in the morning when she opened her eyes and
last thing at night as the barefoot house-boy padded softly into her
room to turn the hurricane lamp low.

Clutt's role at Delamere's dairy was to supervise cream production and butter-making, driving supplies twice weekly to Njoro
station early in the morning in one of D's fleet of black and yellow
buggys, painted in his racing colours. This task was hardly onerous
to a man of Clutt's energy so he took a second job – temporary

manager to Lords Hindlip and Cardross, founders of the Fawcus and Hindlip Estates. While he was occupied all day long in the bush, local tribal unrest from the Nandi robbed Clara of her peace of mind. Njoro in those days was something of a Tom Tiddler's ground, argued over continuously by the Nandi and the Maasai.[8] Though culturally affiliated, they descended upon Njoro to raid one another's cattle – tribes torn by deeper hatreds than any settler could comprehend. These were fuelled by ancient rivalries within intricate clan systems; the tortuous network of brotherhood survived Colonial rule and persists. To the nomadic Maasai, cattle were currency and therefore the raiding and stealing of them constituted honourable sport. Nandi children were taught to cadge, helping themselves to any small trifle which took their fancy. Such practices caused misunderstanding; to the European eye cadging is no better than petty pilfering.[9] Warriors were trained rigorously to fight, steal and run: song and rhyme in their oral culture perpetuated pride in battle, revenge and death, upholding a ruthless ideology – an ideology incomprehensible to most Westerners, particularly Beryl's father.

Clutt fell out over the Maasai with D, whose trust in them irritated him. Beryl's father regarded them as incorrigible thieves. D's indulgence of them was as unacceptable as the excuse that stock-raids justified theft just because the Maasai believed that every cow and bull in the world was rightly theirs.

In vain Clutt tried to bring D round to his point of view, but D had had beneficial experiences with the Maasai. Born stockmen, they had pin-pointed the problems when D's cattle turned to skin and bone, insisting the fault lay in the grazing. They had been proved right scientifically (soil analysed from Equator Ranch was deficient in cobalt) and D consequently bowed to Maasai judgement on all livestock matters henceforth, seeking their opinion first.[10]

Beryl's father regarded the Maasai as robbers, plain and simple. As a military man, he found D's attitude lax, therefore intolerable, dismissing him as 'a Maasai maniac'. Clutt reached the point of exasperation when D was away and sixty cattle disappeared over the course of one week. Beryl's father sacked all D's Maasai herdsmen, replacing them with Wangmweze. D's outrage at his cavalier action (Beryl was to be as inexorable) was such that there was nothing for it but to go their separate ways.[11] Clutt's penchant for organisation, his training in military tactics, helped him gain his own ends (a talent Beryl shared) with D when matters came to a head. Weeks before their *contretemps*, D had sent Clutt to buy land on his behalf from some 'South Africans who lived off black beans in huddled huts at Molo'. They turned out so impoverished that the requisite investment of one thousand pounds was doing duty for all of them – the same thousand pounds securing different property over and over. During these negotiations for D, Beryl's father bought 5,000 acres at Molo so as to experiment with a sheep farm on the Mau Plateau, when he also bought Ndimu Farm.

As a homestead Ndimu Farm was nothing more than three ugly corrugated iron huts, each with a tank for catching rain water and surrounded by 1,500 acres of bush. It took its name from a newly planted citrus orchard, *ndimu* being Swahili for lemon. Clutt moved his family in during the long rains of 1905.[12] Beryl's father had acquired the property cheaply after Mr Knapp, charged with shooting a native, was forced to sell it off quickly.[13] Clutt had not wasted his first seven months in Africa, paying for these properties by selling off the first land at Thika to the Craven brothers, his old friends from the Quorn. Clutt's financial balancing act enabled him to buy another thousand acres – Brickfields – outside Nakuru, their nearest *dorp*, so as to grow wattle, and to purchase also sixteen thousand acres of sisal plantation at the coast.[14]

Differences of opinion between Clutt and D were forgotten, as Beryl's father became responsible for training the Delamere horses, and for Florence's brothers the Honourable Galbraith and Berkeley Cole, who had recently settled at D's urging, Galbraith at Elmenteita, Berkeley on the slopes of Mt Kenya between Nyeri and Nanyuki. The Coles, Delameres and the Clutterbucks would meet every four months for the races in Nairobi, staying now at the Norfolk Hotel, where trains from Njoro halted, so as to save guests the ride from the station.

Beryl was only three and a half years old when Clara Clutterbuck fell in love with Major Henry Fearnley Kirkpatrick, whom she called Harry. Like so many of the first settlers, he was an old

Etonian; he happened to be visiting his commanding officer, Colonel E. G. Harrison of the King's African Rifles, in 1905. Clutt was riding Harrison's Damfine on the July afternoon that Clutt brought the mare in second. Finding themselves dining in a group in the Officers' Mess of the KAR, Kirkpatrick and Beryl's mother partnered one another during the dance that followed. Both were ripe for an *affaire*. Beryl's mother was thoroughly bored. She missed fox-hunting and the social life that went with it. Had she been truly happy with Clutt, she might have been able to adjust to the bizarre lifestyle she was expected to cope with on Ndimu Farm. There were excitements, such as the time she had gone with Clutt who was out to bag ivory on the Molo land: Beryl's father had wounded, but failed to bring down, an elephant. They followed its tracks but lost it. Next morning they came across it in a small stream, where it had fallen in, trying to reach water; its corpse succeeded in damming the stream and within eighteen months had forced the water-course underground 'where it . . . flowed in this fashion for one mile'.[15] Women acted as nurses and midwives to livestock as well as humans, butchered their own meat having shot it first, played dentist if necessary and hostess too, to each passing white stranger. Clara just found it too difficult to roll up her sleeves, as Lady Delamere and so many other women did, in an environment devoid of social pleasures where her husband was preoccupied with making a go of the farm.

As for Kirkpatrick, Harry had been in Kismayu, Jubaland, deprived of the company of white women for three years; he was in transit for 'home' leave and would not have been in Nairobi at all except for needing to replace his false teeth, having lost them in a violent storm at sea.

Kirkpatrick was regarded as an outstanding soldier, and a fine horseman, excelling at polo and envied as 'the most outstandingly handsome man in the KAR and no wonder Beryl's mother had been attracted' as one reflected. 'Harry was very tall and she . . . very beautiful; they must have made a memorable couple when married.'[16]

Harry and Clara apparently lost no time in organising their future together, for when Harry went back to England, Clara immediately began to scheme her own departure, inviting the Cholmleys of

Place Newton for a three-month holiday in May 1906, bringing
Violet, her former bridesmaid, in order that they could see things
for themselves. Clara's ploy worked perfectly; the three months
the Cholmleys spent at Ndimu Farm proved how unsuited the
Colony was for a child of Dickie's constitution, and how incompatible Clara's marriage was. Finally on 4 August they met Harry
Kirkpatrick when, with the Delameres and Clutterbucks, they
attended the Turf Club Ball. Beryl's parents were seen in public
for the last time together yet Clara seemed 'radiant' in 'a perfectly
lovely frock of pink chiffon which suited her to perfection.'[17]
Within three weeks, Clara saw off 'Master Richard Clutterbuck'
who sailed with the Cholmleys on the SS *Natal*, northbound for
Brindisi and Trieste.[18] When they waved Beryl's mother a temporary farewell, her scheming indicates that she would have taken
the line of least resistance in the matter of divorce from Clutt,
stalling the issue and departing on the grounds that medical check-
ups for Dickie could delay her. There is no evidence of wrangling
over custody of either child. Such tactics would have ensured an
equable departure for Clara but must remain open to conjecture.
The break was clean. Beryl's mother left Ndimu Farm two months
later, taking passage on the SS *Djemnah*, bound for Marseilles, and
would not meet Beryl again until she was twenty-one, and married
at that. Clara's exit effectively orphaned Beryl.

The Africans on Ndimu Farm took Beryl unto themselves after her
mother left. They tied a cowrie shell, the Kipsigis' symbol of the
female genitalia, on a leather thong around her wrist to ward off
evil spirits, as they did for girls within the tribe at birth. They called
her *lakwet* (meaning very little girl), *lakwani* or occasionally *lakwan*
as a special term of endearment, though they were not given to
showing emotion: in their culture to display feelings was impolite.
   Abandoning a normal healthy child was something no African
mother would do. European settlers as far as Molo also thought it
shameful that Clara Clutterbuck had left Beryl, 'running off with
an Army Colonel of the KAR, sending off Beryl's brother so she
could follow'.[19]
   But Beryl never criticised her father. 'I admired the way he raised
me. People go round kissing and fussing over their children. I didn't

get any of that. I had to look after myself . . . Funnily enough, it made me.'[20]

So Beryl was left with her father to love, then the servants, and after them the horses. Until Emma Orchardson appeared.

3

Life as Lakwet

(1906–12)

In those months before Charles Clutterbuck found the 'house-keeper' Mrs Orchardson to help care for Beryl, the *enfant sauvage* was born. With ease Beryl began to straddle two worlds: one where stoicism was cultivated, and 'she thought more like a Kip' (Kipsigis), indoctrinated with the threat of permanent disgrace if she so much as flinched when she hurt herself, and where loss of face is regarded as almost as bad; the other, where to break with European convention was scandalous. She refused to conform to either.

Although we know that the expectations of her father propelled Beryl, a natural competitor, forward, if only to please him, the next eight years of Beryl Clutterbuck's development survive only in glimpses. Some are observations of her father's contemporaries whose recollections are of Beryl as a *pied noir*, fobbed off on any far-flung neighbour willing to have her. The women who took her intermittently into their homesteads were usually childless themselves.

Swahili was already her first language; she had toddled into a tradition of indigenous custom and belief, that was unlike anything she could experience in the Western world. Fortunately pages of material that were not used for *West with the Night* throw light on her father's yard: the African stable routines, the railing of race-horses, the excitement of paydays on the farm, her hatred for 'the governesses' and her propensity to escape them in favour of gambling and catching moles before the *kengele* – the bell – tolled, summoning the African labourers, and so Beryl might get away from that 'bloody woman who was trying to teach me'. But for such vehemence in this material we should know nothing of the things that caught her childish imagination, angered her, or left clues as to what became important to her and how she learned to be fatalistic about death, drought, famine or tribal rebellion. These unembellished reports make clear the more unique aspects of her childhood.[1]

These templates mirror Beryl's unloquacious nature and pre-requisite for privacy; we need only be glad that she hoarded rather than destroyed them. She does not mention Arthur Orchardson, nor his mother or her own. What these excerpts uphold is her determination to re-invent her youthful circumstances; her passion for horses, especially Pegasus, the first colt she delivered; how she backed and broke him to become her favourite hack, and some of her adventures on him. They confirm her strong antipathy toward women; her respect for physical prowess, the power her father wielded on Ndimu Farm. She touches on tribal fraternising, her trust and presence among the Africans, arising out of friendship with her favourite, Kibii – a relationship which was to endure until middle age.

Few, if any, other white girls of Beryl's day would have experienced a cult where the more wives a man had, the better he was respected as was the case in Kipsigis lore. And where unmarried girls were traded for a bride-price – perhaps as many as one hundred goats. The cultures of the Kipsigis and Maasai affected Beryl deeply. Her barefoot start became a habit of a lifetime, as was her upholding of Africa's traditions and harsh expectations for survival.

As *lakwet* Beryl was comforted by the families of the Africans who worked on Ndimu Farm, a trust founded on complicity, establishing security: 'I knew the natives well enough to know that they would never give me away and . . . looked upon me as one of their own children.'[2] She became accustomed to amulets, taking for granted the powers of leaves and bark, even tiny pouches of bones, beads strung along her bedstead to ward off devils while she slept. She came to rely much more on the sky than the carriage clock in her father's house. After the *totos* – boy children – had driven their fathers' livestock into the safety of the thorn *boma* at sundown, they were not sent off to bed; they stayed up late, listening to the grandmothers telling stories, proverbs and riddles of which they had an inexhaustible supply. Beryl did not want to be stopped from playing with the African *totos*.

She was only four and a half when Emma Orchardson began trying to exert control over her. In the six-month interim since her mother had left, Beryl had erased memories of Clara and Dickie, even of what either had looked like. The pretty dark-haired woman with a small boy, Arthur, in tow, took charge. Emma soon became 'Mummy' in name as much for Beryl as for Arthur, and Beryl was never corrected. No one bothered to explain that Emma was not her mother, just their housekeeper, in 1905. And complicating matters further Arthur likewise addressed Clutt as 'Papa',[3] and nobody corrected that either. Possibly Clutt never faced the problem. He was a busy man, an enforcer of laws, rigorous, uncompromising; Blue Coat Boy, 'a good foal getter', was at stud; mares came and went; the yard had to be run, the mills too.[4] Beryl's father was an unsqueamish Colonial master and executant of punishments with power over many men's destinies. He held his own court, made his own rules, meted out his own fines. With 1,500 acres to oversee, all he wanted was someone else to look after Beryl so he could be in the *shamba* from dawn to sundown, freed from anxiety. She had spent so much time with the *totos* that she preferred to speak their language, rejected proper clothes in favour of a *shuka*, ate with her hands.

Emma Orchardson had seemed to Beryl's father to provide the perfect solution. While she 'mothered' Beryl, Arthur would grow into an ideal European playmate for her.* Her estranged husband, Ian Orchardson, stayed in Lumbwa. The couple had emigrated there from Lancashire with baby Arthur and Ian's brother Gordon to seek a better climate for Ian's ailing lungs. Emma had not been put off by the unrest and insecurity of pioneering life in Nandi country, but her husband's attraction to Nandi women she could not tolerate. Captain Clutterbuck's needs for 'a housekeeper' coincided with Emma's determination to get away from Lumbwa. When Arthur became inquisitive about arrangements at Ndimu Farm, Emma would allay suspicion, telling him about the unrest at Lumbwa.[5] Neighbours were scandalised when Beryl's father began openly living with his housekeeper; she was given two pseudonyms, 'Lady O' or 'Mrs O', to protect young ears from the focus of gossip. Settlers refused to speak Emma's name as a sign of their disapproval of the immorality of the set-up. Other European children, far-flung as they were, never came to stay the night with Beryl and Arthur; it was feared that Emma's dubious status would contaminate the morals of their offspring, and it was generally recognised that there were no such things as Pentecostal rebuke or Episcopalean watchwords at Clutt's Mill.

The fact that Emma was pretty, with flawless skin, violet eyes and a trim figure, did not help her reputation and other pioneer women dismissed Clutt's 'fancy woman' for looking like a chorus girl.[6] Others claim she was 'exceedingly kind to Beryl' though 'no one but her father could control her'.[7] Beryl's first jealousy over her father was sparked by Emma, whom Clutterbuck adored, when he deferred to her wish that Beryl wear shoes. His daughter was to wage a fourteen-year battle against his mistress. However, Beryl accepted 'Little A', who took the place of Dickie, becoming a surrogate brother. She was loving and protective and in her dotage admitted how 'my father more or less adopted Arthur . . . took him over', how he became 'a perfectly marvellous jockey'.[8] An air of permissiveness lingered at Ndimu Farm. Beryl rebuffed criticism of her father and although she was to be a victim of the arrangement to a degree, it was Emma who took the brunt. But Beryl learned to defend her and when someone suggested that Emma was 'one of the naughty things your father got up to', Beryl's defence was firm: 'I'd say NATURAL things, NOT naughty'.[9]

The hapless role of this absurdly fetching young woman was to try to exert control over Beryl for her own good: improve her table manners, her courtesy, coax her into a dress, into shoes, into a double terai – the hat worn between 8.30 and 4.30 – and to wean her on to a governess.

Had Clutterbuck sought to impose some limitation himself on Beryl she would have accepted that, beyond the fence of childhood, the world was not simply hers to command. He seemed not to notice that she was all limbs, wilful strength and defiance. Because her outer display was of action, she appeared straightforward; it took years for friends to come to grips with her complexities and some never did. The duality caused by the two different cultures to which she was exposed when most impressionable was continually to baffle people; just as they imagined they had worked her out, some extraordinary inner compulsion led her to behave in such a way that she completely floored them.

Emma battled with her for about a year before domestic arrangements were re-shuffled; Beryl's independence was furthered by moving her from the main dwelling into the *rondavel* which had been occupied by Violet Cholmley. It was customary on Colonial farms to build an extra mud and wattle hut whenever extra accomodation was needed. Arthur occupied the one that had been used by Violet's parents; the two thatched huts stood some twenty yards distant from where Clutt and Emma slept, making it easier, once the time came, for Beryl to creep out at full moon and stay out all night with Kibii.[10]

Inside her hut Beryl was safe, behind heavy wooden shutters with bolts. Glass had not yet been imported. The monastic furnishing had cost nothing: paraffin boxes used by all who bought oil for their lamps were converted into shelving, dressing tables and stools. Beryl's attitude toward her domestic surroundings, best described as casual indifference, stems from this spartan room. She would always be frugal when it came to accoutrements, paring her needs down to an absolute minimum. Her bed was a simple wooden frame, strung across with *reims*, narrow thongs of zebra hide, made by the Maasai after her father shot zebra for dog-meat. Her coverlet of black and white Colobus monkey skins had been traded by a Nandi forest dweller in return for a bag of salt. The simplicity of Beryl's room did not make it uncomfortable, despite its cracked red mud walls which harboured lizards and skinks, mason flies, wasps and hornets. *Dudus*, as insects are called in Swahili regardless of species, busied themselves nest-making all day long, holding no fear for her. As an adult Beryl was able to transform the most unpromising of rooms with dexterity into a welcoming abode. Though her fortunes wavered she never needed trappings or labels to prove her worth, nor felt any need to apologise for the humble way in which she lived. So long as she had water with which to wash, a fire for warmth and cooking, and somewhere to lay her head, she was cheerful. Towards the end of her life, when fame overtook her, one neighbour was startled to see that Beryl's mattress frame stood on four sawn-off tree trunks and offered to replace them, but she could not have cared less; such oddities never bothered her.[11]

Beryl's lullaby was the susurration of crickets, cicadas and tree frogs. Bush babies and hyrax vied at night with fiercer creatures. Beryl never forgot the excitement of baiting for leopard, perching on top of a water-tank watching her father trap and shoot them. The leopard's delicacy is domestic dog, and when Storm and Sleet, two of Clutt's greyhounds, were taken, Clutt was determined to nip the habit in the bud; the exercise was not for the squeamish but became 'a regular necessity and for bait we tied a goat to a tree nearby and that never failed but I always felt so afraid and so sorry for the little goat as I watched it cower with fear as the leopard approached and shuddered to think what would happen to the poor thing, should my father fire too late . . . or his aim be poor . . . He always got one leopard and sometimes two or three.'[12]

Like Beryl's own room the *jikoni*, or kitchen, stood some distance from the main house, with other shacks; one for *dhobi* – the laundry where clothes were pressed with a charcoal iron; another the pantry where charcoal coolers stood, primitive contraptions to store haunches of Thomson's gazelle and other game. The legs of this type of fridge stood in tins filled with paraffin so as to ward off invasions of ants.

The wilderness continued to present new challenges, which Beryl found far more fascinating than anything she might learn from being read fairy-tales by Emma. Elephant raided crops, crushing all in their path, but Beryl learnt from her father that 'The African elephant are afraid of a horse and will turn back or alter their direction . . . if they scent them.' When she was older, she helped her father 'drive the horses downwind' to deflect a herd. The Wanderobo tipped Clutterbuck off, in return for a bag of salt, when elephant were marching in the direction of Ndimu Farm, which proved 'an easy way to save our crops and fences'.[13] Buffalo – the most dangerous of all big game – were trickier. If they wandered onto the farm, 'The brood mares could not be turned out' until they dispersed of their own accord.[14]

Relationships between *Bwana* and employee were archaic, certainly paternalistic, yet the painstaking progress of farming in

Kenya before the First World War allowed black and white children to get to know one another intimately in isolation and, in Beryl's case, unsupervised.

As often as possible she would leave her father's homestead, skirting the stables, heading off toward Kibii's hut before breakfast, while the sky was pale still, before the sun was right up and clouds had formed to float like galleons on the intense blue. The long wet grass soaked her legs and body; she would warm herself by the fire of Kibii's mother, at the farm village.

Before going hunting the Kipsigis fortified their courage with a traditional brew that contained the bark of a local acacia tree which gave the drinker 'a small lift'.[15] It also helped the *totos* to jump; Beryl's earliest example of sustained effort is the way in which she was taught to elevate herself and 'to jump higher than myself.' 'All Nandi boys are supposed to be able to jump over their heads (sic) – as they grew taller, so they were expected to jump higher. When I left the farm at Njoro I could still jump higher than my head.'[16] She learned to wrestle 'the Nandi way. Kibii never liked to pick me up and throw me down with the force that he was supposed to but he took the greatest possible delight in teaching me to do the same to the other *totos* and there were many times when a row started over this . . . rough wrestling – a fight would begin and Kibii would always take my part against the other unfortunate *toto*.'[17]

These traditional games give a fair idea of why Beryl developed with unusual strength for a girl of her age and they encouraged her to take pride in her body from when she was quite small. Had she been an *ndito* – girl or virgin of the tribe – she would never have been allowed to infringe masculine preserves. Hunting was for boys preparing to be warriors or *moran* (as they were called after circumcision). But she would do what they did, her hair shielding her face as she leaned forward with stealth, heel first, then toe, placing each foot soundlessly, copying Kibii, so as not to alarm the quarry.

Beryl developed like a Goliath heron, all legs, a wading bird, moving through a sea of grass. Virtually daily she crossed new cultural boundaries, enjoyed a series of pagan encounters, which Europeans seldom had the chance to share.

Back at home, Clutt educated Beryl in concerns of the yard. Each night he sat poring over stud books, pipe in hand, beer at his elbow, under a dim light, scribbling the names of mare, foal and stallion. 'Entries were made for the next . . . fixture, the position of each runner at the last start, whether a horse was rising in class or failing'.[18] Early observations of her father as a breeder, the struggles, the books, the accounts and the losses, convinced her that 'breeding was a mug's game' which she would ultimately dismiss. Meanwhile, there was still Beryl's formal education to consider and Clutt decided that the time had come for lessons at home; she was about seven years old when Bo Fawcus's fiancée, Miss Le May, became Beryl's first governess.[19] For lessons, Beryl sat at a table in a living room with hunting trophies adorning the walls and floors – Ostrich eggs, lion skins, buffalo horns, leopard pelts, porcupine quills, hooves and claws, bric-à-brac intrinsic to Africa. Beryl without doubt would have preferred to be outside stalking a wart-hog, and from her description Miss Le May seems to have been quite the wrong type of teacher for her, succeeding only in reinforcing mistrust. She could not control her pupil and took to hitting her; Beryl, employing the same tactics as with Emma, escaped by diving into the loose-box of the most ferocious stallion, creeping under its manger in the furthest corner of the stall. Miss Le May did not dare attempt to go beyond the half-door, past a snapping horse with its ears laid back and teeth bared.[20] These tactics unequivocally ended lessons for the day.

The situation worsened. After six weeks when Miss Le May could not get results by bringing down a ruler, hard, on Beryl's knuckles, she resorted to a rhino-hide whip, more appropriate for disciplining oxen in 1910. With pride, Beryl would not allow a groan to pass her lips, no matter how painful the beating: 'she beat me with a *kiboko* until I was raw and bleeding but I became more defiant and more disobedient.'[21] There were permanent psychological scars: 'I certainly have nothing to do with women . . . EVER, because I don't think they ever wanted to have anything to do with me.'[22]

At one point, Clutt was away for several days supervising felling in the Mau Forest, going on to inspect a sugar plantation at Kibigori. Since Emma was also absent, Miss Le May gave Beryl the worst flogging she had ever had, overstepping the limit of acceptable punishment; realising this, she became fearful that Beryl would report her. Her solution was to lock the child in her hut with the shutters barred. Beryl found it 'dark and horrible. I waited until (she) . . . gave me some dry bread and water, the wonderful old fashioned idea of feeding a child when naughty. At nine o'clock . . . I pulled the tusk out and slowly hammered down the wooden window.'[23] It is evident from Beryl's reference that Clutt had hidden illegal ivory under her bed, an indication that he had no permit for these trophies. He was probably waiting to bury it so as to age it falsely, a trick taught to European settlers by the Wanderobo. The minimum weight then was about forty pounds a tusk, showing Beryl's strength and determination. She was terrified that Miss Le May would hear the pounding of the tusk against the shutter and that it would wake her. Luckily a downpour of rain muffled activity for six hours: 'At two in the morning I succeeded in tearing out one of the panels. I was very slim and able to creep out of this opening.'[24] Clad only in flimsy cotton pyjamas, Beryl ran into the Rongai Valley, taking refuge down a pig-hole.[25] The short rains were on; the deluge did not let up for four days. Miss Le May sent staff out to look for Beryl but she was nowhere to be found. Meanwhile on the second night, Beryl was so hungry that she crept from her lair to go in search of food: 'I slept in a native hut after they promised me they would not tell anyone where I was.'[26]

Clutterbuck was understandably frantic with worry to discover that Beryl was missing: 'after riding all night while returning to the farm to change horses . . . he saw a small figure running through the long grass . . . ten miles from home . . . galloped up . . . caught me with my whole body down a pig-hole with two little bare feet sticking out'.[27]

Beryl did not let on what had caused the situation. Only weeks later did Clutt learn what had occurred to make her flee: 'I was struggling over an arithmetic lesson . . . the governess had a heavy, black ruler which she used to rap over my knuckles . . . my hands were so sore that I could barely hold a pencil.' The ruler came down again, 'for not doing a sum correctly, I yelped loudly purposely to attract his attention', taking Miss Le May unawares because 'throughout the beatings she had given me I never uttered a sound. Somehow it seemed impossible for me to cry from physical pain as a child. The howl had the desired effect as my father came rushing in to see what had happened. When he saw the condition of my hands . . . he was so angry that he dismissed the governess there and then.'[28]

Stoicism is cultivated by the Maasai and Kipsigis from childhood, and Beryl had learned a lot under the influence of Kibii who set great store by physical power, refusing to acknowledge pain under duress, emulating the warrior maxims of his father, *arap* Maina. Preparation for circumcision for a *toto* to graduate to the next phase – a *layoni* – was careful. Failure of nerve during this painful operation, or any manifestation of physical suffering, would brand Kibii a coward for life. And this rule extended to emotional display too. Clutt's expectations of Beryl, Arthur and Kibii, schooling them in their riding lessons as if they were English military cadets, were scarcely less demanding. Kibii was probably the finest African rider in Kenya as a result and the first of that quality. The results spoke for themselves and 'there was no finer sight than Beryl Clutterbuck and Arthur Orchardson in the pair classes'.[29]

Beryl agreed: 'I served a hard apprenticeship . . . never got any sympathy if I fell off.' Once while 'day-dreaming' she forgot that one should 'never ride too close to another horse's heels' and the mare in front of her suddenly let out. 'She was plated . . . her hooves split both my shins wide open'. Beryl was older then, of course, than the time of the incident with the *kiboko* yet it was 'one of the most painful things that has ever happened to me'. Her father's reaction was not to comfort her but to express relief that the horse she happened to be riding 'had not been injured'.[30] His rationale, 'every time you come off . . . hurt yourself you will learn something' was as tough on her as was *arap* Maina's attitude toward flinching. The result was that later, Beryl never could accept physical help and found it demeaning. It was instilled into her that she should never let go of the reins if she was thrown, of vital importance with costly thoroughbred stallions when 'to let go would have been terribly dangerous'. But she carried her father's orders to the limit and was 'dragged for seven miles' on one occasion: 'My body was suspended by my leg while my head bounced over the rough ground . . . the two-year-old's hoofs (sic) . . . missed my head by inches. When he pulled up at the stable yard, I hardly had any clothes left on my body, also I was minus a good deal of skin'.[31] In not allowing a moan to escape her lips, by degrees Beryl was to achieve an Amazon-like capacity for control.

Life on an African farm did nothing to foster a child's interest in the dull confines of the school-room. Several more governesses and a tutor tried to teach her. For the latter Beryl behaved marginally better. However they all succumbed eventually to her campaign of attrition; finding a dead snake in bed usually forced resignation.

Until 1910 Beryl remained innocent of her real relationship with Emma, but she was not to remain so for much longer. Clutterbuck was elephant-hunting in the Congo with the Craven brothers. Emma and Arthur had proceeded on home leave with Ian Orchardson, an exercise in keeping up appearances for the sake of their respective families; neither realised that the couple had been estranged for four years.[32] Beryl was eight, yet again left behind. She undoubtedly would have preferred to stay with Lady Delamere in the absence of those whom she assumed were blood relatives. Lately she had taken to riding Wee Macgregor over to Equator Ranch regularly. However, Edward Lidster, the Australian manager in charge of cultivating different strains of wheat for D on Florida Farm, was going with Beryl's father,[33] and Lidster's wife, Wilhelmina – Billie for short – insisted that Beryl come to stay, where the company of her own four young children would be more appropriate. Everything was arranged. Beryl went with Lady Delamere to wave her father off at Nakuru, eight miles away. The safari party of five was completed by Francis Morris, a carpenter who worked for rich Bostonians, the Sewells, at Molo.

At Florida Farm the routine was very different from that at Clutt's farm. Beryl was not used to being made to rest between luncheon and tea-time, when a children's encyclopaedia was produced in the hope that looking at its pictures would encourage the youngsters to read. This is the first known instance of Beryl being presented with the written word, apart from Nelson's *The Crown Readers*, a series to be found on the desk of every Colonial child, which was recommended for teaching purposes in areas where there were no schools.[34] Also Beryl was taken on social calls (Emma Orchardson's status had precluded the custom of 'calling') dressed in a white frock and tying ribbons in her hair. On one of these occasions Billie Lidster took Beryl to Molo to meet the wife and son of Francis Morris, on the farm of the opulent W. G. Sewell. He and his wife Baba were a source of fascination because they employed Chinese servants, said only to remain with the Sewells on condition that coffins were kept in the rafters, lest they die away from their Chinese ancestors.[35] Young Langley Morris, being of Beryl's age, remembers her visit because she was the first white girl he had laid eyes on and she confounded him with her knowledge of bush-craft.[36] Whether Billie Lidster took her to see her uncle, Henry Clutterbuck, is not certain; Henry's wife Annie was expecting their second child. Beryl's father had been instrumental in getting his brother to leave India to settle in 1908 on Clutt's sheep-run at Molo. Beryl's cousin, their first son Jasper, had come with them, but although they had been in Kenya for two years, Beryl hardly knew them. Once more the ostracising effect of Emma may have been the cause. Suffice it to say that Beryl's uncle and aunt were not considered close enough for Beryl to be left with them while Emma and Clutt were away.

Also staying at Florida Farm at the time was Jim Elkington's seventeen-year-old daughter, Margaret. She was the most likely candidate to have disabused Beryl of the illusion that Emma¹ was her mother. Her nickname was 'the shrimp' – a flaxen-haired beauty whose mental age was that of a child of seven, she had a tendency to repeat whatever she overheard, parrot fashion. It seems probable that she innocently apprised Beryl of the facts in this manner. For Beryl the news was a great trauma. We will never know exactly how she was told, only that she received such comfort that she was prompted to say that Lady Delamere 'meant more to me that my own mother'.[37]

Her young life shifted focus: the mother she imagined was hers was a stranger whom Beryl had mistaken for someone wearing the same hat. Only Lady Delamere understood the depth of misery Beryl underwent.

For the next four years, D's wife became important as a white stabilising influence in Beryl's shattered world. As soon as she had been able to manage her half-Shetland, Wee MacGregor, Beryl had hacked regularly to Equator Ranch but from now until the First World War, she was to ride through the bush 'almost daily' seeking out this Irish gentlewoman with whom she now struck an exceptional rapport. When Beryl had arrived so agitated from Florida Farm, having learnt that Emma was not her mother, she had stayed on Equator Ranch until her father returned from the Congo. Beryl developed early an uncanny knack of knowing who would be able to help her – Lady Delamere was the only person to have been aware of events and consequences since the arrival of the Clutterbucks in Kenya. It is significant that she is one of the only two women named in Beryl's memoir.

The Delameres' home became a haven – 'Two poor mud huts, which would have been condemned . . . by any Housing Authority in England.'[38] The floors of beaten earth were strewn with Persian Carpets; a huge stone fireplace dominated one corner of the hut in which they lived and slept. D's four-poster stood in another corner of the room which also housed a large mahogany table, with eight matching chairs. Meals were monotonous: Thomson's gazelle chops, vegetables from the *shamba*, followed by blancmange and tinned peaches prepared by their Goan cook – D's one concession to luxury. In the evenings, six or more Maasai came to crouch, on their haunches, besmeared in sheep fat, to 'talk about those things they wanted Delamere to hear' – D had always believed on consulting the Maasai.[39] Meanwhile Beryl enjoyed Florence's light-hearted, witty Irish humour.

Even as a child, Beryl called Florence's husband D; more formally, he was Hugh Cholmondeley, 3rd Baron Delamere. In a sense D became a surrogate father to Beryl, giving her hand in marriage, in the absence of Clutt, to her second husband. D was eccentric but courageous; his temper matched his red hair and reputation for intolerance, yet he seems not to have overwhelmed Beryl. D's great 'asset was . . . a soft, extremely attractive voice . . . with it . . . he was able to win people over'.[40] Even when he was grossly annoying, others became malleable in his hands when he made his typical apology, 'Ought to be crucified. Ought to be crucified.'[41] He was ugly, with piercing eyes and 'small, stiff, nervous hands, a poor horseman'.[42] As for racing, D saw it merely 'as a way of improving good horse blood'.[43] Whenever he was caught up with any new scheme, it was always to the point of obsession. During this watershed in Beryl's emotional growth, he was experimenting with wheat: obsessed with visions of mile upon mile of golden harvest but fighting canker and 'rust' in mouldering stooks. All D's money and energy for the improvement of stock and crops was channelled, just as Clutterbuck's went into horses, into the country of his adoption.

D had reached Kenya on foot from Somalia with camels through the desert; he had fallen in love with the highlands in 1897 after a formidable 2,000-mile trek. From the time he laid eyes on the thickly forested Mau – Beryl's hunting ground, where she was to spend so much time with her father's *syces* – D's vision of 'a white man's country' haunted him to the extent that he could not settle for his tame estate, Vale Royal, in Cheshire, such was his obsession with Kenya's potential.

Two years later he married Lady Florence Cole, the daughter of the Earl of Enniskillen, and they honeymooned in the Protectorate, in 1889, to see if Lady Delamere shared D's enthusiasm. The couple settled in 1903, a year before Beryl's parents arrived.

Like Clara Clutterbuck, Lady Delamere had loved 'fox-hunting, dancing . . . every form of society' but she had been prepared to sacrifice all that England could offer for the benefits of freedom in Africa, sharing an 'existence of the utmost discomfort . . . with the utmost cheeriness' and a very lonely life.[44] Lady Delamere encouraged Beryl to help with the poultry, experimenting, attempting to breed and fatten turkeys for the Christmas table.

Beryl's first puppy, Buller, was sired by the Delamere's bull terrier, the unbecoming result of mating with the Old English sheepdog dam left behind by Clara Clutterbuck. Buller shadowed every move Beryl made, sleeping on the foot of her bed, trotting at her heels, unless out hunting with the *totos*. Then, according to her description, he took the lead, leaving 'us very much behind . . . we hunted together through thick and thin', chasing wart-hogs. 'He would lie there and bark until I came up to spear it . . . every two minutes he would bite a piece out of the pigs (sic) stomach, the only place soft enough for a dogs (sic) teeth'.[45] These were bloody encounters often culminating in Beryl preventing him 'from being torn to ribbons' or tossed by a wart-hog boar, 'high into the air ... by a vicious ... determined pig on its tusk'. On one occasion she and Kibii were attacked by Wanderobo dogs: 'I was torn to pieces while Buller fought off seven.'[46]

Wee MacGregor was sturdy enough to pull the trap for shopping excursions to the *duka* Ebrahim Karimbux in Nakuru and to take Clutt's weight when necessary for hacking about the farm. Clutt used Beryl as a courier for taking notes to neighbours or to his European foreman, Christian Aronson, 'a fine Norwegian' experienced in logging and timber. Then in 1908, an influx of Afrikaners, *en route* for the Uasin Gishu Plateau where they would establish Eldoret, encamped outside Nakuru and altered Clutt's fortunes, easing at last some of the transport difficulties in Kenya. They had sailed up from Cape Town on the SS *Windhoek* – two hundred and fifty of them led by Jansen van Rensberg. The significance for Beryl's father was that he culled the men from these invaluable settlers. Ploughing problems eased thanks to their skills and, under Clutt's jurisdiction, the expertise of the Boers enabled him to offer a service to farmers for miles around; raw bullocks were sent to be trained at Ndimu Farm, providing another source of income for Beryl's father.[47] Aronson was responsible too for designing wooden houses for newcomers with cedar from Clutt's Mill.

It was decided between Emma and Clutterbuck that Beryl and Arthur would be better off at boarding school. Arthur was obedient and loved lessons but all Beryl cared about was competing with Kibii: 'She became impossible to control. So frightfully strong that she could do what young Africans could do.'[48] She could hurl a spear just as well as Kibii, with deadly accuracy. When intending to kill for food or in self-defence, missing her aim would have been fatal. She had learned to straighten her arm in a backward arabesque, as if to hurl a javelin, sending out a thrust to impale. The grace, the strength of her backward stretched arm manifested all the simplicity and ease of a cave painting. Africa is many things to many people of many races; but a child nurtured on its red, inhospitable soil carries those lessons for ever. So to be wrenched away, dispatched to school in Nairobi, can only have given Beryl a feeling of alienation, as though she had been exiled to another land. It would have been easier for the Biblical camel to pass through the eye of a needle than for her to steer a clear course through this or the next school she attended. Both were to expel her. But the link with her childhood realm of wonder and magic was not finally sundered. Beryl ensured that.

She and Arthur were sent first to the Nairobi European School in 1911; Beryl was listed as 'Clutterbuck' and, according to the register, lasted out for nearly three terms whereas Arthur dutifully remained there until Emma removed him.[49] The school cost 75 rupees per term for boarders and had been founded to educate the children of employees of the Uganda Railway. Known as 'the little school', like most wood and iron buildings, it stood on stilts, on Nairobi's 'Hill' commanding a fine view over the Athi Plains and the tin-pot town itself. Uniforms were non-existent because the parents of most pupils could not afford to pay for 'anything other than basic education'.[50] The few day-children would travel by rickshaw, rode or walked to school accompanied by an *ayah*. Jimmy McQueen, son of the famous blacksmith, one of Nairobi's earliest inhabitants, sat opposite Beryl in class. He was nicknamed 'Syrup' on account of his insatiable appetite for treacle pudding – one of the culinary delights of school meals.[51] 'Syrup' McQueen remarked of Beryl that she was 'taller than everyone else – though a year younger. She was a bit of a tomboy. A wild, unruly sort-of-a-girl'.[52] Another classmate, Mary Pitt, remembered how Beryl rearranged the cumbersome wooden desks into a steeplechase course, over which she made everyone jump. 'She was always leaping over everything she came across.'[53] The first stirrings of female envy over her looks and her physical grace were experienced then. Her eyes, like blue glass beads, were clear, far from limpid, steady for all her shyness, a gaze that could undermine already, never chaste, timid or obedient. She carried herself proudly with the promise of a fiery temperament that might turn to ice. But she always broke tension with infectious laughter. Her long fair hair made everyone wish to be blonde.[54]

It is not surprising that the blackboard-and-chalk hours held no joy for Beryl. Lessons began at 8 a.m. and continued until 5 p.m. with the usual breaks for lunch and tea. Miss Rigel, Beryl's class teacher, insisted that 'books be kept out of sight' under the heavy lids of their desks. Monitors regularly refilled the white porcelain ink-wells set in the desk lids. 'Hours were spent in the perfecting of joined-up writing . . . covering page after page with pot-hooks so as to develop a good hand'.[55] The exercise may have bored Beryl, but Miss Rigel achieved sterling results in that the effect was lasting upon her most reluctant of pupils. Even at the end of her life, Beryl's handwriting was as legible as it was distinctive. She was taught with a classic 'nib and pen-holder' which encouraged a clear script and, in Beryl's case, one which hardly altered. Each letter was forward slanting, angular, with long down-strokes and seldom joined to the stem. For the graphologist, Beryl's wilfulness was all there to interpret.

Games were played in the cool late afternoon; where other girls played rounders, Beryl loved cricket, gravitating naturally to the boys' games. She excelled as a bowler, her very accurate aim so practised. But she thought the other pupils 'rather awful' 'because they were white'.[56] She understood only African *totos*, lacking experience of any white children apart from Arthur. The children who went to school with Beryl insisted that she created a drama deliberately to get herself expelled after two and a half terms. She ran away, disappearing over the Athi Plains, and one of the girls 'split' on her. Beryl regarded this the worst possible disloyalty. Miss Rigel and most of the staff went out and brought Beryl back, to face what the staff imagined was 'disgrace'. But Dos Harris, her closest friend at her next school, understood from Beryl, that 'all she craved was to be allowed to be with her beloved horses and . . . father'.[57]

The upshot was that Beryl was sent home, free to wander the harsh, elemental terrain of Africa again. Alone with Kibii. But for holidays, Arthur remained at this school for three further years.

4

Lessons at Home, and in the War

(1913–19)

Once more life proceeded at a sleepy pace; once more men dominated her existence. Men surrounded her in the house, silent,
obediently waiting at table, padding barefoot to close and open
windows, men in white *kanzus*, the Colonial robes of servitude;
the dogs were cared for by dog-*totos*, boys like Kibii fed them,
removed blood-bloated ticks daily, kept coats shining; *totos* chopped
kuni for fires, to heat *maji* for the baths; men carried water to its
destination, prepared food in the *jikoni* from *saa moja*, the first hour
of the day when morning tea was made, until dinner, rounded off
by over-boiled coffee. Men, in the *shamba* tilling the soil, wielding
whips, driving patient, humped oxen; *syces* grooming horses, muck-
ing out, saddling up, polishing tack; always men, hovering, anonymous voices, to wait upon her and please her, vying to engage
Beryl's attention.

The result was that as an adult, it became impossible for Beryl
to act without a man on whom she could rely totally to steer her,
as her father and *arap* Maina had, in the direction of her own
needs.

In the shifting language of need, the daughter of a rampant
Colonialist identified with the Colonised. Beryl sought comfort within her African family, away from the web of white
deceit, looking to *arap* Maina; he showed Beryl and Kibii how
to make bows, but to begin with would only allow them blunted
arrows. According to Beryl 'Kibii . . . taught me to shoot with a
bow . . . We would practice on wood pigeons . . . dark blue star-
lings . . . wax-bills with delicate red beaks . . . at other times targets
. . . We were never able to kill . . . bushbuck or larger animals as

the Wanderobo refused to let us have any poison for our arrows saying we were too young to be trusted.'[1] Gradually *arap* Maina allowed them real ones. The more brilliant the plumage in their quest for feathers, the more *maridadi* (beautiful) Kibii's circumcision head-dress would be; it had to be the best in his age group or circumcision set.

Beryl regarded herself one of the boys and African at that. She referred to her father as a *mzungu* (a white man) as if she were an *ol morani* (young warrior) not of the same *kabila* (sort) herself.[2] She and Kibii were virtually inseparable: 'When we wanted to relax, we played a funny game with a sodom apple (a small poisonous yellow ball which grows on a bush). It is difficult but Kibii was considered more intelligent than the others of his age because he could play it. He taught me . . . we would gamble over it with our small salary or with money we got from my father for catching moles or killing snakes. I have now quite forgotten how to play it but I remember we had two rows of holes in the ground . . . its nearest equivalent to Western games is backgammon it is well known in Africa and involves such complicated feats of mental arithmetic that few Europeans can play it'.[3] Beryl and Kibii's gambling was enhanced by the happy African illusion that fortune *must* smile upon them; usually *bao*, as it is known in Kenya, is played on a board in which a series of hollows take marble-like balls, substituted by sodom apple in their case.[4] The moles they caught were the Kenya species, the size of a large water-rat, considered by certain tribes a delicacy, especially by coast people, the Giriama. Kibii would have roasted their catch over embers; the mole's dark flesh is said to taste like liver. Trapping them was an art in itself; Beryl and he stuffed one of its two holes in the ground with grass. Then, by placing an ear to the ground, they could locate the creature. They then brought their *rungus* into play, banging the earth directly above until the thunderous noise drove the creature out of its only exit. They caught it by hand, ending its life before submitting their trophy to Beryl's father for money.[5] Wart-hogs were similarly provoked from their holes by scrumpling newspaper at the entrance, until the animal charged forth.[6]

While Clutt, who had a reputation for 'very polished exhibitions of high-class riding', trained them as cavalry cadets,[7] Kibii's father developed their physical skills as *morani*. These lessons were taken as seriously by Beryl as by *arap* Maina. Combat studied early in preparation for adulthood in the bush could one day make the difference between survival or death; where Clutt used guns, *arap* Maina taught them bare-handed courage, to protect themselves with *rungus*, the equivalent of a European knobkerrie. Each had fashioned one for himself from olive wood, the knot forming a sort of club; this weapon is still carried by Maasai today.[8] Beryl killed her father's pet with hers, defending her surrogate brother, who was so much smaller than herself, and afraid of Kima, 'a huge . . . vicious baboon'. Taking the incentive and showing no mercy, one day when Beryl had had enough of its terrorising, with two blows of her *rungu* she ended Kima's life.[9]

Inhabiting a prehistoric realm in the green gold grass, Beryl met enemies daily from the animal kingdom where survival is all that counts. In savage places there are savage rules; to ignore these could easily be to perish. Life in Africa is harsh and shocking. There lion stalk wildebeeste as they migrate toward better grazing, instinctively, before giving birth; but the lioness needs to feed her pride too. As Beryl and Kibii understood things, books and pencils could never protect one from predators. They had smelled the putrid meat of the kill together and witnessed bloodied jaws from a hide at such proximity: the daring in youngsters of ten or eleven is chilling in itself.

She became imbued with an unnerving sense of fate, belonging to a brotherhood where natural law seemed far superior to anything imposed. In her respect for the harsher alternative she seemed drawn to danger for the sake of it. Beryl's longing to be as brave, as fleet and as strong as *arap* Maina's son is as evident as their closeness: 'Kibii and I were great friends. We were about the same age. We rode my father's gallops together as we were about the same weight and could hold any horse at speed. He knew that if he told either of us to take that horse a mile and a quarter, half-speed, and this horse, five furlongs, three-quarter speed, his orders would not be ignored.'[10]

An incident recorded in Beryl's memoir gives us added insight into her bravery: Beryl had a close call with the Elkington lion, Paddy. Her own relating of it underlines a purer courage; how she actually played down the incident, not merely through modesty but because of what she regarded innately as extenuating circumstances: her scar, 'No more than a slight scratch', was prevented from being more serious because Harry Weston, Clutt's jockey, had 'rushed out' to her rescue: 'it was a tame lion you see'.[11] She did not think of herself as brave, 'I wasn't frightened of anything in those days . . . I am sure he (Paddy) didn't mean to hurt me. Luckily the owner (Mrs Jim) came and got rid of it. It was just me running around barefoot that caused it . . . I was hardly touched . . . well, I was *touched*. . . because I was pulled down.'[12] For all Beryl's nonchalance, in 1913 in Nairobi, Paddy was reputed to be so 'enormously powerful . . . no one in their right senses, went near on foot', Jim Elkington included. Paddy hated men.[13] Mrs Jim (the Shrimp's mother) had been given Paddy as a cub by Lord Kingston; once Paddy was fully grown, he roared 'in a very savage way' and could be heard right across Nairobi. After what the Elkingtons considered an alarming but lucky escape for Beryl, Paddy was caged and exiled to their Naivasha property.[14]

However Beryl 'had a truly wonderful gift of understanding and handling of animals . . . adored them . . . was quite fearless',[15] was never less than sympathetic toward them, even the most ill-tempered horse, like her father's valuable stallion, Camciscan, that went for her.

Camciscan's influence on Kenya breeding was enormous; his sire, Spearmint, won the English Derby in 1906. His ferocity and his size – all of seventeen hands – can only have been imposing to a slip of a girl; Beryl agreed that he was 'impossible' when mares were about. She could never mount him with a stirrup: his refusal to have his head held meant that she had to vault on. He once threw her 'on the worst bit of ground he could find'. The daughters of a neighbouring settler watched Beryl in awe one day in Camciscan's 'huge loose-box . . . as Beryl groomed a large . . . beautiful but reputedly savage imported stallion. He was squealing and snapping but never touched her'.[16] Whenever he was railed to Nairobi, Beryl slept between his forelegs; anyone else he 'would bite . . . very hard who came near his head'. If Clutt muzzled him she removed the device as soon as he turned his back.[17] In her own words Camciscan, 'was one of the loves of my life . . . I would willingly have died for him.'[18] More telling still is her admission, 'his faith in me was what I loved – if anyone . . . happened to be looking when he was being . . . sentimental, he would be enraged – he hated . . . people so much that he would rather die, than let me see his feelings.'[19] In Beryl's view Camciscan was behaving naturally; she accepted that she was merely in his way and unequivocally sided with the rebel. Beryl admired the same qualities in men and horses. She forgave Camciscan's 'ungentlemanly' behaviour: 'he would go to the other corner of his box . . . look very ashamed and tremble all over, breaking out in a white sweat, as if to say, "I'm sorry, I lost my temper" . . . He was a lovely companion with much character and a great deal more brains than most humans . . . more than anything else his hard and relentless character always getting what he wanted and with all the spirit and courage in the world – I had learned to mix in with that characteristic . . . perhaps that's why we got on so well together . . . it was terrible . . . to watch that horse in pain, he felt so much . . . he had a delicate constitution . . . if he got worried or upset he would lose condition in a few hours . . . that condition took weeks to get back – . . . he would rest his lovely clean-cut head in my chest, as if to say, "I feel badly, please do something for me" . . . I always thought what a strange thing life is . . . a great big more than powerfuly (sic) beautiful beast – who could crush me with one foot – behaving like a small child.'[20] Often enough he 'had picked Beryl up . . . shaken her like a rat' adding to the 'many feint scars she . . . carried . . . for life'.[21] Those scars she bore with pride just like the *totos*: badges of recognition for courage of the highest order which they showed off as *moran*.

Any girl of Beryl's equivalent in Europe would have been punished for unseemly behaviour. At Njoro among her African friends, being 'ladylike' had no place. So long as Beryl remained invincible, had 'a good fight', she could emerge honourably. This superiority became immensely important to her. By 1913 Beryl's running skills like Kibii's were almost fully developed; with the *layoni* (pre-circumcision group) she had striven for what amounts to Olympian performance. (Athletes of renown today such as Kip Keino, Kiprotich and Kikemboli Kimeli – all Kipisigis – have triumphed in modern stadiums and owe much to evolution, their heritage in

Nandi games.) Beryl's account of a tussle in overcoming a *layoni* who went for her with his *simi* sums up her Nandi attitudes: 'One day a large *toto*. . . almost ready for . . . circumcision waited for me a few miles from the farm . . . he knew Kibii wasn't with me. He had nursed a grievance . . . for months after I had given him a beating. This time he got hold of a native sword and came for me – luckily I had a *rungu* and won in the end, but he succeeded in slashing open my thigh. I have the scar to this day.'[22]

Clutt had aspirations reminiscent of the stage-struck Mrs Worthington, propelling a daughter relentlessly into the limelight. Beryl was expected to outshine Kibii and Arthur, the latter becoming as competitive. Tiny though 'little A' was for his age, Beryl loved and grew to respect him for holding his own with her on equestrian terms, forging a strong sense of family during the course of fourteen shared years. Though they were fundamentally different – Arthur showed no trace of rebellion – he too possessed 'wonderful hands', controlling his champion show-jumper, Totem, in a sheepskin nose-band. At the early gymkhanas in Nakuru, none of his horses was ever ridden with a bit and, like Beryl, Arthur won numerous cups which were displayed in cabinets; Beryl was never to have more than her latest trophy on any mantlepiece.[23]

Beryl modelled herself on her father in the way he handled his staff when she was an adult and had her own employees – a time when females commanded no authority and scant respect in African eyes. Retaining respect in others' eyes was to become vital to Beryl. The European notion of impartial justice is incomprehensible in Africa where revenge is all: blood money must be paid to balance any catastrophe, whether to compensate for cattle theft, a dog bite, or loss of a limb, wife or child. Indemnification is the only satisfaction. Beryl remembered her father's arbitrations, how he 'spent hours trying to draw *shauries* (problems) to a happy conclusion' holding a court daily 'at a certain time to judge the crimes committed by the natives or some had hit the others (sic) or knocked all his (sic) teeth out, teeth always had to be paid for in Africa or because the witch-doctor had willed him to die or if the Dutch (one of the Boers) hit a native and the native hit back then my father nearly always took the side of the white man unless he was too much in the wrong, otherwise it would have been hopeless. The Natives are funny people, they simply hate taking orders from anyone except the man who pays them . . . their great saying is "he doesn't pay me, why should I do that for him?" '[24]

By now Clutt's office was constructed; here he would sit and, through a high window, dole out *mshara* (pay) and punishments: 'the arguments were unbelievable – and I have seen more than one grand fight – my father always had a short knobkerry (sic) by his side was often obliged to rap a troublesome native over the fingers with (sic) – once I saw him lose his temper at this window (with very good cause I may say) he hit at the native who ducked. The knobkerry hit my fathers (sic) hand against the edge of the window – split it open and blood poured in every direction – blood to a native is always fear – so they scattered in thousands with my enraged father making a flying leap out of this narrow window onto the boy who was giving trouble – this boy was rather insulant (sic) and fought back – however my father laid him out good and proper and returned to his office looking rather ashamed of himself – bound up his hand and went on with the paying.'[25] Clutt's rationale, just as Beryl's was to be, stemmed from a time when corporal punishment was justified and 'there were no District Commissioners to keep law and order', elaborating, 'my father even had a prison of his own, where he would . . . lock up a boy for however long he felt fair and just'.[26]

By 1912 Clutt's old *kengele* had been replaced by a factory hooter to summon the labourers to get their weekly wage. One of Beryl's favourite events on the farm was payday, 'a wonderful sight' she tried always to watch, an exercise which took a minimum of 'four hours' as his labour lined up for their *pesa* (money). While a child's admiration for its parents' wealth is commonplace enough, oddly it is the power her father exerted over so many men that touched Beryl, rather than the piles of gleaming coins themselves. In her childhood, there was little regard for the coin and no value attached to paper money at all. Since Beryl mishandled money all her life, even when she had plenty, it is significant that she and Kibii believed in cattle as currency. District Commissioners, well into the 1940s, spent many days paying out for cattle to more primitive tribesmen; 'many had never seen bank notes before and could not understand it at all. The white ants got many notes and

the price of camels soared.'[27] Beryl prefered coins to notes, spending rather than saving them, seeming to have no notion of their
worth. She never learnt to budget. Her written observations seem
doubly relevant, *'mushara* (sic) day was a great day . . . with over
a thousand natives – Dutchmen – Indians – and white men – he
would hand out the money – every native had a ticket . . . showing
how many days he had been at work how many he was sick –
how many . . . he hadn't bothered (there were many of the latter)
a native only seems to work if he feels that way or if he is hungry'.[28]
Labourers were paid in coins minted with a hole in the middle,
ready to be threaded on string so as to carry them more easily. But
they blamed money for taxation which, in their opinion, ruined
barter and the tradition of exchange.

Beryl's father preferred employees to work overtime to redress
any misdemeanor; Beryl was to follow suit for all that she
recognised how Africans hated this form of punishment and would
rather undergo the passing discomfort of a 'flogging'.

The death of Lady Delamere the following May compounded in
Beryl a feeling of deprivation that cannot be overestimated. D's first
wife fell ill unexpectedly at their other estate, Soysambu, although
Beryl had seen less of her confidante since D had moved, for the
sake of his cattle, to a ranch overlooking Lake Elmenteita, where
in her early twenties Beryl was to train for him. For two years, talk
about Lady Delamere's mental state had been circulating; for two
years, rumour was rife that she and Dr Atkinson were in love and
that she was intending to leave D for him. She and D were often
guests at Government House – usually only one at a time, while
the other attended the farm. Gossip had it too that the real reason
Clutt had fallen out with D in 1905 was over her, not the Maasai.
Be that as it may, in 1913, aged only thirty-eight, heart failure was
given as the cause for her untimely death, with little reason to
doubt since her brother, Berkeley Cole, suffered a weak heart too.
But apparently there were other difficulties; D was summoned
more than once at short notice back from Nairobi by her other
brother, Galbraith. One cable read, 'Florence serious nervous
breakdown.'[29] On one occasion during race-week , 'after all the
other ladies had gone to bed . . . dressed . . . up in motor-scarves

(nothing else) she came downstairs and danced the Salome dance to the men!'[30] The majority, like Beryl, and even critics, regarded her as 'plucky, clever and amusing'. Out of devotion to D and the farm she had neglected herself working 'like a galley slave on that lonely farm'.[31] Her death deprived Beryl of a powerful, rare and loving influence at a crucial adolescent stage. The impact of this deprivation sealed in Beryl a singular admiration for Florence; to a degree her memory was hallowed. She was widely known and loved throughout the Colony, but was missed by none more than D and Beryl, who was now bereft of her pillar of former trust. Given Beryl's antipathy to her own sex, her admiration of Florence is all the more remarkable.[32] Unable to express emotional loss, having already learned to screen from others grief, anger, love or joy behind a disciplined Kipsigis mask, Beryl was to be enclosed in her dramas; dramas more diverse than those of other white girls of her day and class.

She took to stealing out at night, under cover of darkness, as soon as she could safely escape the notice of the grown-ups. Arthur knew; he never split on her, though, as she crept past Clutt's man-made mountain of sawdust smouldering with the glow of coals when she should have been tucked up in bed, fast asleep, like Arthur. But if her teens were bleak from the European perspective, from the African they were rich with culture and amusement, unlike anything in the white world. The Mau forest was one of Kibii's and Beryl's favourite haunts. Little grey vervets, and larger Colobus monkeys lived in the tapestry of branches; by day, if the youngsters made a sudden movement, the monkeys would swish through the tree-tops, with a ripple of leaves the only evidence of their route. There were many secret glades for privacy.

By night, the farm became peaceful, windless, when *dudus*, making their fitful drowsing sound from the forest, vied with a thousand tree frogs and cicadas in their shrill chaotic chirping. The stars shone all the brighter in moonless skies, casting no shadows as the youngsters left or entered the village. The edge of a fuller moon, however, rose often enough over the Green Hill to light their way. On such nights Beryl would become impatient yet controlled, feign loss of appetite and sleepiness, wait for Emma and Clutt to finish their meal, so she could retreat to her hut, ostensibly to sleep. Confession was not Beryl's speciality; but she was to give Raoul Schumacher, her lover, whom she was to marry after publication of the memoir, her motive for wanting to get to bed: 'Often I had to appear at dinner with my father otherwise he would wonder where I was but then I would eat nothing so that I could go and eat with Kibii later.'[33]

The chapter entitled 'And We be Playmates, Thou and I'[34] in *West with the Night* appears to explain the basis for her relationship with Kibii in 1914, in the year that war broke out. Beryl was twelve in October. 'Kibii and I did what children do when there are things abroad too big to understand; we stayed close to each other and played games that made no noise.'[35] This is as near to confession as anyone could persuade Beryl to come, inspired by those nocturnal adventures with Kibii which continued regularly from her first expulsion (if not before) and were only interrupted by going to board at Miss Seccombe's School in 1915, to be resumed once she returned to Ndimu Farm. Beryl's adult inclinations suggest that she would have been sexually aware when the outbreak of the First World War was announced, especially since afterwards she would never settle for a sexless union again.

Beryl's upbringing continued to be commented on by neighbours: 'She was left most of the time in the care of her father's syces' or, the Clutterbuck girl 'had such a sad upbringing, lived the life of a stable-boy', yet, miracle of miracles, 'had such charm . . . brains and courage when she grew up'.[36] 'The trouble was that Beryl spent far too much time alone in the forest with the syces.'[37]

It is fact that the criticisms levelled at Clutt for his negligence as a father were not without foundation, partly because he lived openly with Emma but also partly because Beryl had not been chaperoned properly from babyhood. In 1904, the Kavirondo (by now Beryl's father had hundreds in his employ) were prey to the ridiculous myth that penetration of a European virgin cured impotence, infertility and venereal disease. The younger the girl the better according to tribal custom: in this culture a female was seldom virgin after the age of nine.

A contemporary of Beryl's insisted, 'up-bringing was entirely to blame for her character . . . her "immorality", her inclination to slip into bed with any man she fancied.' Her own mother, by contrast, though 'terribly busy', 'took the greatest care . . . only one or two *totos* were ever allowed to accompany us on picnics.'[38] Beryl on the other hand had been 'allowed to hunt . . . go and live with [the fashionable euphemism for sexual congress] those young *morans*, who had slept with and tampered with her from a very early age' in keeping with the way 'Africans molested European children'.[39] There was 'nothing innocent about Beryl's hunting in the forest . . . I know of many dreadful cases.'[40] One concerned the daughter of a Kericho DC whose wife was 'an ardent and regular bridge player for years'. When asked who looked after the girl in her absence, the mother replied, 'Our cook, who has been with us for fifteen years. We trust him.' The daughter became ill. 'Poor girl . . . Her doctor diagnosed . . . incurable syphilis. The cook had black-mailed her, threatening to kill her, should she mention what was happening.'[41]

Initially Beryl crept out to join Kibii at night probably so as to listen to the telling of tales by his family; stories that thrived in the world of the spear and the darkened hut, where oral history prevailed. There were no books, nor any electricity by which to read. Legend was handed down by the old women in the glow of dying embers after eating: myths such as the one which alleged that the paw paw tree would consume anyone who slept under its branches – not a total myth as the juice of its leaves will tenderise the toughest goat-meat. Beryl knew a good deal about the properties of indigenous herbs and bark.[42]

She had progressed, aged ten, with her African friends, to taking part in Kipsigis 'love-games' which were only likely to have increased with the onset of adolescence. Kibii and his age-group (Africans had no idea of how old they actually were; years of birth were approximate then) before the outbreak of the First World War had already performed a small operation on themselves to make the forthcoming circumcision less painful. They cut the light cord joining the foreskin to the head of the penis, using a sharp piece of bracken. The test – not to react to pain – had been passed. Kibii must not budge during circumcision itself; the slightest tremor, even blinking, would brand him a coward for life. In Kipsigis etiquette, absolute control of facial expression was expected. Even 'affection before other adults must *never* be shown. Reticence and repression affect nearly all characteristics . . . sorrow and anger.'[43] In any case it would have been strange had two youngsters, who saw each other daily and who were obssessed with physical excellence, had not compared bodies, found interesting differences, played the time immemorial trading games of youth: 'I'll-show-you-mine-if-you-show-me-yours.' That Kibii was her first sweetheart would have been natural. Sexual awareness in *totos* was quite normal; the notion of sex being sinful could not have entered Beryl's mind. The way in which she was to take lovers as lightly as she discarded them, is also ample proof of how Kipsigis attitudes robbed her of inhibition, a loss that perpetuated her legendary promiscuity. Africans attach no shame to losing virginity; the politics of sex were overtly patriarchal and the strongest principal of organisation in the tribe affected the women of the tribe directly. Females were taught to drop whatever they were doing in favour of sex. Such influences on Beryl cannot be passed over, since she was immersed in Kibii's culture. She even broke the taboos of his tribe by mixing exclusively with the boys. Caught in a time warp, wedged between two disparate cultures, she experienced two different yet parallel lives.

At full moon, she would go to Equator Ranch 'to attend Kikuyu *barazas* held by D's labour, over the next ridge. Dancing continued until early morning.' Kibii who 'had great contempt for the Kikuyu way of dancing' was begrudging – 'their singing was good.' He preferred 'the physique of Nandi *murani*' (sic) which 'are far more impressive and their songs and dances fascinating . . . of a less frivolous nature.'[44] During her first stint of schooling Beryl feared that she would lose all this, and that while she was away, Kibii who '. . . knew still that he was an uncircumcised boy' would abandon her just as 'after they became Morani (sic) – fighting men' he must cast off all thoughts of childhood for those of the *layoni*, whose priorities are clear-cut – sport, bravery, wealth (in cattle) and sex, regarded henceforth as the only things that mattered. As a *moran*, Kibii's proof of manhood would come with the killing of a lion with his spear; his name would change to *arap* Ruta. Already he was skilled enough to bring down a bullock single-handed. Shortly sex games were to commence, new games, games where Kibii's *rungu* was thrown, with those belonging to the other youths of his age set, into a pile. Like a sexual lucky dip, the girls chose one from the pile at random to go off with its owner to a bachelor hut, where the uncircumcised girls joined them for the night.

Slinking back at dawn, so as not to be caught, Beryl developed a sense of total complicity with Kibii, providing a strong sensual fulfilment between two fiercely independent friends, which affected both of them. Beryl was to puzzle European friends with her 'expressionlessness', particularly at dramatic moments, when she gave no clue as to what might be going on in her head. This phenomenon had established itself before she attended school, thanks to *arap* Maina's teachings and, like Kibii's, her facial control was already total and her mannerisms non-existent; later her minimal animation was generally put down to lack of interest or shyness; she remained shy but her reticence was never born of indifference though, mistakenly, many imagined so. Stillness was not only cultivated but was to become part of the key to her allure, enticing men when she was grown up; they longed to disturb her mill-pond calm.

Four different lovers of Beryl's have commented on her sexual behaviour; two opinions were proffered by men whom, as usual, she had kept in ignorance about her adolescence, which had played such an influential part in her adult behaviour. A suitor in her thirties, Chris Langlands, was besotted by her but found her strangely incompatible with his own values, and broke off their engagement because 'Beryl though white, was an African at heart (stemming) obviously from her closeness to the Kipsigis in childhood, which made her so different from other women then, especially her contemporaries.'[45]

Another love, another decade, another continent away, an American doctor was struck by the way time left Beryl untouched. In her forties, in front of this much younger man, Beryl totally lacked inhibition, preferring to go without clothes around the house. 'She walked naked with untouchable arrogance by the physical mobility of "walking tall". She was as thin as a rail, so that clothes hung well on her – even borrowed clothes.'[46]

Another, preferring to remain anonymous, claimed 'The reason why I got on so well with darling Beryl was [as] . . . a blood brother of the Kipsigis myself. She could have walked all over me with her

high-heeled shoes on. I mean that, and all that it implies,'[47]
implying that Beryl understood the hairline border between pain
and exquisite pleasure, developed during the 'heightening process'
undergone to reach warrior status.

In 1914 when the Great War broke out in Europe that August the
common reaction of settlers in BEA was disbelief. Beryl's father
and Emma could only wait for news to trickle through to Njoro
providing glimpses of life in the trenches on the other side of the
world.

The peaceful cluster which Beryl, Kibii and Arthur could see
from the Green Hill, their strategic look-out on the farm, was to
change almost overnight and awaken from its slumber into a garri-
son town. Nakuru stands in Menengei's shadow, a volcanic crater
eight miles across, the largest in the world. Beryl and her friends
had seen flamingoes fly in great pink swathes at sundown over
Menengei each evening. Suddenly Nakuru was transformed. The
racecourse which had been established the year before was to be
turned into a remount depot for horses for the troops. The theatre
of war in BEA would alter the course of Beryl's life – for it was at
Nakuru that she would meet the Scots captain who was to become
her first husband.

When Nakuru race-course was founded in 1911 activities of the
East Africa Turf Club had extended up-country for the first time.
The course was now presided over by the Colony's Chief Veterinary
Officer, Captain Edmondson of the East African Force Remount
Depot at Nakuru. Edmondson was to have 15,000 horses and
12,000 mules in his care. Beryl's father, as an expert on horses,
was called upon to advise on conscripted mounts.[48] When news
of war reached D's ears, he had been loading cattle for auction.
His reaction was to march up and down Elmenteita platform cursing loudly.

On the eve of hostilities in the Colony His Majesty's armed forces
numbered 1,900 *askaris*, commanded by five dozen European
officers. Kenya's white population now numbered 7,000, half of
whom were able-bodied men for whom war was 'a glorious
adventure'.

Martial law was declared in Nairobi; the town was in turmoil.

As shock waves reverberated from Mombasa to Lake Victoria, settlers left their farms, descending from up-country on Nairobi in droves. German nationals were placed under arrest. With no organised reserve force, it was hardly reassuring that one battalion of the KAR was the sole means of the Colony's defence.

D, dismissed once as 'a Maasai maniac', took a group of volunteer *moran* to Kajiado to patrol the border in the bush. His knowledge of them was to be as invaluable as their loyalty and co-operation to the British.

Nairobi Racecourse became a transport depot, HQ for the Carrier Corps.* Emma, fearful of German invasion there, whisked Arthur back to the farm so that he could attend a newly opened day school in Nakuru. That Christmas, Beryl and he received bicycles as gifts; every horse was requisititioned into the East African Mounted Rifles; each homestead was allowed just one mule. Throughout term-time, Arthur cycled to Nakuru daily until the war ended.[49]

Aside from his expert knowledge of horses, Clutt's other contribution was the supply of *posho* and wood-fuel to the army. Meanwhile contact with the remount depot also brought him streams of officers from Nakuru to replenish mounts for their troops; animal mortality was high.[50]

Enlistment fever took over; *arap* Maina was one of the first Kipsigis to be conscripted; Beryl, Arthur and Kibii, and his stepmother, the youngest wife Jebbta, watched him marched off to the KAR to become an *askari*. Jebbta was scarcely older than Beryl, and was soon to become a widow. Beryl was indignant, recalling that they found *arap* Maina's mortality unacceptable. As a warrior he had seemed invincible. 'A great sadness came into Kibii's life . . . I too was very unhappy, as Arab [sic] Maina had been more than a father . . . I had hunted with him night and day, played and laughed with him . . . thought that no one with his skill and courage could ever die'.[51] Beryl's anxiety for Kibii was intense: 'he became thin and would not eat and said he would wait until he became a *murani* would then go and avenge his father's death.' They were consumed by the tragedy, yet at the same time, Kipsigis manners forbade mention of Kibii's loss. 'It would not be right for him to talk to his elders of such things. So he and I used to talk about it. Night and day we would talk about it. I would go with him to Jebbta's hut ... she would prepare meals of *ugali* and nettles ... we would sit over the fire wondering what the war was all about ... Kibii ... only waiting for the day ... when he could eat blood, mixed with curdled milk and rosted [sic] meat ... Jebbta would only smile ... say that he [had] many things to learn before he became a *Murani*.'[52] Beryl took on Kibii's sense of outrage. 'Kibii would get angry ... he and I would go out into the night for long walks. We both loved the night . :. neither of us wanted to go to bed. We would sit on the edge of the forest ... listen to the sharp cry of the hyrax ... to crickets ... watch ... fireflys [sic] ... when we were so sleepy that we could talk no more we would wander back ... Kibii would go to his hut ... I would sneak into my hut so that no one knew how late I had come home.'[53]

Where, once upon a time, Clutt's visitors had been restricted to those whom he invited or employees, now he and his mistress opened Ndimu Farm to convalescent officers. Beryl's husband-to-be was among those tended by Emma, whose nursing experience was harnessed to the war effort.

Captain Alexander Laidlaw Purves claimed to have 'fallen head-over-heels' in love with Beryl when she was 'only thirteen or fourteen'.[54] He was known as 'Jock', was a brawny Scotsman, and was the eldest of the three sons of Dr William Laidlaw Purves, founder of the Royal St George's Golf Club. Jock was a rugger blue; he was convalescing from acute bacillary dysentery in 1916 following an outbreak of epidemic proportions, affecting his regiment and all those who had come from India. Captain Purves was one of the Madras volunteers who, together with officers from the Punjabis and Karputhelas, suddenly dominated Nairobi. They swarmed through Muthaiga Club (barely opened a year) and the Norfolk and New Stanley Hotels, grumbling over the absence of anything *pukka* – the sahibs, bearers, polo, cricket and curry they had left behind.

Rumour abounds in Kenya still over arrangements of Beryl's betrothal before she was sixteen, how her father 'got rid of Beryl to the first man who would take her off his hands'.[55] The myth that Clutterbuck repaid a debt to Purves contained only a grain of truth, in that a deal was struck; the irony is that Beryl was bartered for, in much the same way as *arap* Maina would have acquired another wife. The only difference was that instead of exchanging several hundred goats as Beryl's bride-price, Purves offered to pay for her schooling in return for her hand in marriage. Jock was almost twice Beryl's age (a high preponderance of the men she was to be involved with were balding). This freckle-faced twenty-nine-year-old became obsessed by her. Clutt regarded Beryl as five years under marriageable age. Jock's feelings were to herald the extraordinary effect that Beryl had on men which lasted until she died. Jock wanted to mould her to his dream of her potential. He was 'one of a small company of sick tired men' who stayed at Njoro for about six weeks;[56] during which time, we learn from neighbours and relatives, Jock taught Beryl and Arthur to shoot kongoni when they went riding together in the Rongai Valley. They had known only about shooting with bows and arrows until Jock showed them how to handle European weapons.[57]

In Jock's extreme case of love, it is doubtful if he laid eyes on Beryl again more than a couple of times after his convalescence and before the end of the War.[58] We do not know whether she was aware of the marriage arrangement, but she was acutely observant as well as intuitive, finding it impossible to be romantic about love. The betrothal may even have coloured already fatalistic views. She was never to be sentimental about any of her marriages.

When she was enrolled at Miss Seccombe's in the second term of 1916, as might be expected, she was as much of a misfit as before. She was pressed into a gymslip, as traditional as the iron restrictions of the curriculum and the school rules, which were based upon an English high school, imposed by her headmistress and founding owner, Blanche Lowe (née Seccombe).[59] Miss Seccombe's School was what might be termed Clutt's last desperate attempt to educate Beryl in the European model. These half-hearted attempts – a total of five terms at most, divided by a year on the farm and between two schools – left in Beryl a distaste for paperwork; she would always view it a chore. In later life, when confronted with figures and bills, she would flinch and ignore as much of them as she could for as long as she could.[60] At school, instruction fell upon deaf ears, leaving her with no gift for words, nor any apparent liking for the world of books. Most pupils were affectionately disposed toward her and envied the ease with which she excelled in front of the wicket, outshining the boys. Her strength was awesome: on one occasion Beryl 'picked up little Miss Milton, our matron, a dear person . . . carried her out of the "dorm" amid helpless laughter from the rest of us. Beryl did not like authority . . . Miss Milton had been trying to quieten us down.'[61] Beryl 'disliked rules and regulations but she was always great fun to be with'[62] and could not help but offend the 'great sense of orderliness' of the headmistress, who concerned herself with individuals only if there were problems. Beryl she met all too often for systematically disobeying those in charge.[63]

'Dos', the pet name for Doris Waterman, a daughter of the Manager of the New Stanley Hotel, was Beryl's closest friend in a dormitory of eight other girls and, like her, rebellious: 'I nearly got myself expelled for standing on my desk showing how a girl had ridden a horse in a circus', trying to outdo Beryl who could 'stand on one leg for hours, like a Maasai warrior, resting, stork-like' with an equally impregnable expression. 'We were inseparable. We always walked together in crocodile, went on long walks down over the Athi Plains where today the marshalling yards of Nairobi Station stand. We had to pass the old cemetery and we always used to wonder about the graves of all the old people buried there.' All her life Beryl could not accept the ritual of European death and was accustomed by now to the way in which Africans place the aged and dying outside the hut, in order that the undertakers of nature, the hyena, silver-backed jackal and vultures, dealt finally with human remains. Death was all around those school-girls in 1916 when the Nairobi military hospital stretched several hundred yards beyond the graveyard; row upon row of tents sheltered the wounded. Every time another soldier died 'the sounds of the Last Post drifted up to our class-rooms'.[64]

Even a hundred miles away at boarding school, Beryl found Emma's existence irksome. Beryl rarely gave out secrets but she confided about Emma to Dos, who subsequently took a dislike to the woman even before having met her because 'she was unkind to Beryl . . . Beryl's real mother was never discussed . . . she just told us she'd been left.'[65] Emma was beginning to show signs of stress at the judgements weighed against her, and had already taken to the bottle. The Watermans would not countenance Dos and her sister Ruby accepting invitations to stay on Ndimu Farm for the holidays. Clutterbuck was 'living in sin' and Beryl's association with Kibii was notorious. Dos and Ruby Waterman led protected lives, untainted by immorality[66] and yet Beryl never gave any outward signs of the distress this censorship might have caused her.

Even in her youth, all the boys called her beautiful. It was impossible to keep track of the number of small boys who wanted to marry her. Dicky Edmondson, the Veterinary Officer's son, thought her 'the most beautiful girl I'd ever seen and *so* kind'.[67] Returning after one school holiday, Beryl told those in the 'dorm' after lights-out, how 'the European guard had tried to kiss her on the journey'. The matter was brought to Blanche Lowe's attention, who let forth with a sigh, 'Oh dear . . .'[68] Here was the first public hint of how men of all ages and class would find her irresistible. Only Sonny Bumpus at Miss Seccombe's remained impervious, who, because she bullied him, never fell entirely under Beryl's spell but even so had a lifelong friendship with her: 'She was bossy with Kibii and that Arthur . . . she was a bit of a gawk . . . a bit of a bloody headache [at] a school for young ladies . . . a tough sort of a person . . . paddled her own canoe; no one but her father and Kibii had any influence . . . she tried to organise cricket which never interested me so I . . . kept out of her way. She was a great big, gangling girl, nothing to write home about – no chocolate-box beauty.'[69] Sonny became an outstanding gentleman jockey early on and was to ride for Beryl many times, including the famous race in the memoir when Wise Child breaks down, but wins the Kenya Derby on three legs. Sonny was ultimately sympathetic to Beryl's inadequacies, 'the result of an unhappy childhood . . . growing up overnight . . . into an adult', finding her 'serious-minded', seeing her as 'beautiful rather than pretty'.[70] Beryl the star, the local hero with an inability to knuckle down, was then chosen for Alice in the school's play of Carroll's classic, pin-tucked skirt and all, evidence that she was pardoned for infinite devilment. What a beguiling Alice she made.

Beryl crossed the chasm of adolescence into womanhood without breaking her stride, free of any sense of shame. For her sex was to be spontaneous, a pleasurable form of exercise, like dancing, and with as many changes of partner. She was proud of her developing breasts, her widening shoulders, her slim, boyish hips, an attitude that never changed. There was pride in her carriage. Her hair was unevenly bleached by the sun, unruly, long, and her eyebrows arched in vague and intermittent wonder. Her sweet, casual loveliness was enhanced by her lack of animation. She listened carefully, appeared rapt. When enraged, her eyes gleamed like cold, blue steel without glitter in a long, oval face with a determined chin, the lower jaw inclining toward heaviness later. Her mouth broke easily into laughter, the lips parting, showing slightly wide-spaced teeth. Whenever Beryl felt excited, because she repressed such feelings, only a small vein betrayed them standing out of her forehead.[71] Yet in all that strength was vulnerability, the tremor of her lower lip, a hesitation that touched people with its frailty.

In her third term Beryl made no bones about skipping class: 'I didn't learn much there . . . I wasn't very popular . . . I couldn't stand them [the teachers]' apart from 'one . . . male who I think I took some notice of'.[72] In accordance with French leave Beryl took off, pedalling furiously over the Athi Plains: 'I got the sack for being too rowdy and too gay. I just got on my bicycle and all the other children followed me.' Beryl had set off alone yet Blanche Lowe accused her of inciting rebellion.[73]

Being sent home held no disgrace for Beryl. Early unhappiness had taught her endurance. Already her gift for staying afloat in the most dangerous of seas can be detected. Her almost limitless capacity for manipulation was already evident in the way she had overcome the hidden reefs of school rules and would soon deal with the rocks of European morality.

In December 1917, acting as midwife for the first time, Beryl helped into the world a leggy individual to be called Pegasus: 'My father bent down over the sturdy baby to see whether I had made a good job of tying and cutting the cord, "Very nicely done old girl", then patting me on the shoulder . . . pointed at the foal . . . "There is your Christmas present." '[74] Coquette's colt was the first pony Beryl could call her own and since Coquette 'had won more races than nearly any horse in Kenya since 1911', Pegasus inherited her stamina and was to become Beryl's prize hack.

When Beryl returned to the farm for good, like most pubescent girls, she still had no real sense of the power of her beauty. But Kibii, mistrusting white men's rules and books, knew he would need to edge his way round her. Forbidden to touch the white *memsahib*, he walked three paces behind her. Beryl, however, was thrown entirely by his *moran* status: 'Kibii had become Arab [sic] Ruta' shook hands with men as an equal.[75] She was unsettled when their familiar balance was reversed. Beryl found herself outside Ruta's circumcision set and sensed an inferiority she rarely felt in his company. As Clutt's daughter and as a white person, Beryl had always assumed the superior role of doing anything she liked. Now she must address him formally as *arap* Ruta; she was both confused and frightened of losing him and forfeiting their closeness. 'His weight had shot up from 8 stone to well over 10' which meant he was never again light enough to share gallops with her.[76] Beryl defined the radical changes for the memoir: 'His stature and the calves of his legs seemed to have developed in an unusually short space of time – but then I forgot that he had been living on sour milk and raw blood drawn fresh from the jugular veins of . . . Nandi cattle. His sharp features and high cheekbones had not altered, but his eyes seemed more alert and he gazed at people in a proud and even hostile way. He wore the warrior's *shuka* of ochre. Round his waist was a bright bead belt which held his club. He wore anklets of Colobus monkey, making his calves look larger than they were. He carried in his right hand a long spear with a round ball of black ostrich feathers on the tip . . . A single chain hung loosely round his neck, to which was attached a small horn containing a charm, and a pair of tweezers with which to pluck out any hair on his body'.[77] Recalling his long, satiny but muscular limbs, Beryl was reminded, when looking at Ruta, of *arap* Maina's decree, 'A young man is a piece of God.'[78]

Beryl had turned sixteen as the war entered its fifth year. In October 1918 the defeated but gallant General von Lettow Vorbeck embarked on his final skirmish with the British in Portuguese East Africa, neither side realising that war had ended elsewhere, remaining in ignorance for another month. In Nairobi, the euphoria of victory evaporated with the dying laughter of parades, balls and bonfires, and a period of stark readjustment began.

Captain Purves, ready to claim the hand of his child-bride, was forced to wait another year for her; Beryl was happy and aware of her future as his wife, as is shown by a note to a former class-mate, announcing she had 'become engaged to an orfly [sic] nice man'.[79] The Coming-Out Turf Ball, in August 1919, to be held at Nairobi's New Stanley Hotel, was deemed the most suitable function for Beryl's debut and engagement celebration. The event started off entirely on the wrong note, as Dos Waterman recalled, because Beryl had to share a room with Emma. When Beryl went to dress '. . . Mrs Orchardson had had too much to drink and she wouldn't let her in so I went upstairs and banged on the door until she opened it. I then collected everything for Beryl and I helped her to get ready. How Beryl loathed that frilly frock, hating the wreath of rosebuds in her hair she made her wear and that was the reason Beryl dressed in our flat'.[80]

During the interim before their wedding day, Purves had applied for a Soldier Settlement farm, to which all who had served in BEA were entitled. All land surveyed for alienation could be purchased on easy terms. The mapping out of the Soldier Settlement Scheme had been strategic rather than philanthropic, providing an ongoing insurance for safety in the increased number of European residents. Africans, having observed white men fighting one another, no longer regarded them invincible. The indigenous `were embittered by being called upon to pay taxes, provide animals for slaughter and had acted as human porterage; their death toll had been considerably higher than that of their colonisers – 50,000 perished, 90 per cent of which were black, on both sides. Settlers had come back to find *shambas* in ruin; the sight of rusting machinery, derelict buildings, the loss of fencing and animals was as devastating as the fact that cultivated land had reverted to bush. In June 1919, at Nairobi's Theatre Royal, a draw took place (similar to the one in London) determining the future of some 1,500 hopeful ex-soldiers. Purves drew land on Laikipia, selling it off immediately and, with the proceeds, bought 600 acres adjoining Ndimu Farm. Until October he ran Clutt's saw-mill. In 1919, however, the rains failed, and when Spanish influenza broke out, the epidemic contributed to the great difficulties the Colony's new Governor, Sir Edward Northey, faced as he struggled to put Kenya's economy back on a solid footing. An outbreak of rinderpest killed many cattle, leaving the rest to die from a devastating drought. The scant grazing that was left was consumed by cut-worm or the game. The countdown for Clutterbuck's bankruptcy had begun, though it is doubtful if Beryl realised how severe the situation was.

Anyone who has lived through an African drought can never forget the experience. The sight of carefully bred herds with nothing to eat makes killing of the newly born an essential act of desperation. The land becomes a husk of itself, appears to have turned to stone. Bladeless roots of grass are reminders that the earth yields nothing. Farmers scan the horizon, hoping to detect a rain cloud, but as days pass, the sun returns anew to punish life further. Even the scrubby bushes disappear. Dust devils spiral upwards, reddish into the sky, and vultures circle overhead, waiting for the last heartbeat. The thorn trees blacken as the farmer is condemned to watch livestock die slowly. Prehistoric-looking ribs appear where once sleek coats glimmered with health. Scruffy mealie patches surround the huts of the luckless Africans, their villages grow quiet as everything dries out and becomes brittle.

Beryl's father could ill afford the expenses of a wedding; Muthaiga Country Club would have cost less, but as he and Emma were not legally married, it would not be acceptable to hold the wedding there for the Committee were strict when it came to morals. Photographs from the late Arthur Orchardson's albums, believed to have been taken by Jock Purves, provide a unique look at Beryl Clutterbuck, just before leaving the farm for her wedding in Nairobi in 1919 with Arthur and their parents.[81]

Beryl married Captain Jock Purves at All Saints Cathedral on a Wednesday afternoon, 15 October 1919, eleven days before she turned seventeen. Local reporters made much of the fact that racing and Rugby were enjoined in their union, calling it 'A Sporting Wedding'. At the conclusion of the service by Reverend Thornton Brown, Captain Lavender of the KAR as Best Man ushered the couple into Jock Purves's motor car and drove them to the Norfolk Hotel where 'the spacious dining-room had been tastefully laid out

for the reception' of one hundred guests, including the Acting
Governor, Sir Charles Bowring, and D. Beryl's gown bears Emma's
touch; its corsage of veiled ninon trimmed with pearls was far
from the tailored style Beryl would have preferred. The wedding
photograph reveals a stolid bride, her veil tossed back over a wreath
of orange blossom crowning her head. Her bridesmaid was little
Elizabeth Milne, daugher of Nairobi's Chief Medical Officer for
Health, Dr Milne. The small blonde child appears weighed down
by yards of bridal train 'adorned with roses and thistles' as it folds
about young Mrs Purves's ankles. Her long shapely legs encased in
white stockings look deceptively thick, in satin shoes which seem
uncomfortable. At the entrance to the Norfolk Hotel the couple
are flanked by Delamere and Charles Clutterbuck. The pioneer
farmers look as if they have donned the first suits that came to
hand. Most surprising of all, Jock Purves is holding a cigarette
while posing for the cameraman.[82]

None the less Beryl's contradictory personality can be detected
in that blank façade, as enigmatic as the Mona Lisa with the hint
of a smile. There is little promise of 'the creature' to whom men
would so often refer, as though she were not so much a *femme
fatale* as a wild thing trapped in a white skin. On her wedding day
Beryl is far less alluring than the picture of her with Arthur,
relaxed, in old farm clothes, where all her loveliness is there, waiting, like a fan, to unfold.

Mr and Mrs Jock Purves spent the first night of their honeymoon
at Muthaiga Country Club. Next day, leaving for India, they were
seen off by well-wishers as they embarked on the boat train at
Nairobi station.

5

Life as Beryl Purves

(1919–22)

The odds for the *enfant sauvage* really were against achievement in the 'civilised' world. For in savage cultures there are savage rules; and Beryl to whom European 'manners' and the niceties of her class were anathema, was bound to break Western rules. Many many times Beryl's European friends were to be pulled up short, uncomprehending of her, as she was of their criticisms.

However, if one can measure the success of a life by the length and quality of the journey taken, then Beryl's was epic. It was not merely ambition that led her to victory upon victory; if it were that, she might have given up or, like millions of other women, had that dream driven out of her. She had been moulded by Africa where to be seen to win counts for much in so hostile a terrain; a place where failure cannot be confessed. A matter can only be dropped where it is taboo.

Africa is liable to make one callous. If one lives there long enough one must harden oneself: to dwell too deeply on the sheer hopelessness of massive humanity in the face of drought and famine, or retarded technology, is to perish in the spiritual sense.[1] 'Mat' Matson was an exception in remaining unsurprised by Beryl's behaviour: 'It would have been strange if Beryl had not had a callous, ruthless side to her nature. From her lonely early life, background and good looks . . . lack of inhibitions, sexual successes and other achievements. One can see the grounds for selfishness, for wanting to have her own way and for acting outrageously if thwarted or if her gifts were not fully appreciated'.*[2]

Beryl's charisma, her ability to withstand pain, her stamina, physical prowess and her courage cannot be disentangled from less pleasing or unconventional traits. Her relationship with the truth was a complex one; a certain amount of concealment was often the only way to protect herself. Beryl's honeymoon is a perfect example. Her visit to India with Jock was a disaster. He drank heavily and she steadily lost respect for him. No *moran* would have risked the scorn of his bride, nor his reputation as a lady-killer by approaching her once a drop of alcohol had touched his lips. Drink reduced staying power, to which great kudos was attached, almost as great as the number of lovers one could command. Beryl called Jock 'hopeless', in other words, impotent; and was disappointed he did not meet the sexual demands that she had expected of 'a real man'.[3]

So as to prevent others from realising how bad things really were she gave different impressions to several people. None were detailed, most dismissive. Conflicting reports of Beryl's happiness in 1920 vary in strength, making it virtually impossible to define how well or badly things really stood between herself and Jock Purves: 'We went to India for a bit, then THANK GOD, we came home' hinting at homesickness and miseries untold.[4] She could be more emphatic: 'I couldn't bear India. I nearly killed myself.'[5] Such vehemence can, in part, be explained by homesickness pure and simple. Apart from schooling in Nairobi, which could hardly be called extended, Beryl had never been away from her home or parted so long from Ruta. And yet she also claimed that her honeymoon was 'great fun . . . very glamorous'. In two postcards sent to Dos Waterman, Beryl crowed of how happy she was in her marriage to Jock.[6] However the fact that it was to men she claimed it was unbearable and to females just the opposite must not be overlooked. Jock had taken Beryl to Bombay in order to show her off to relatives and friends before severing ties for good there. The city itself was hardly the cultural shock that London was later to represent to a Colonial girl from the bush. The topees, the *ayahs*, the dust, the sudden nightfall, the balmy nights, the smell of spices, the sound of the sitar were as familiar to Beryl as were the flocks of Indian house crows (imported to Kenya to assist disposal of human remains; the Hindu funeral pyres during the construction of the railway). The architecture was reminiscent of Nairobi – Parsi bungalows encrusted with fungus, all shuttered with columns and little balconies. Shady neem trees flanked the roads in Parklands also, where Beryl had ridden beside her father across Nairobi from the Elkingtons to the racecourse ever since she could remember. She might have been alarmed by the grandeur of members of the Turf Club below Malabar Hill, beyond the atmosphere intrinsic to racing anywhere. The Willingdon, further along Racecourse Road, with its massive entrance in its encircling wall was positively intimidating after the informality of Njoro Club where Beryl had recently taken up polo. Jock played polo with the elite at the Willingdon which had been founded by the Viceroy with mixed Indian and English membership, thriving in an atmosphere of unusual tolerance. The Willingdon had impeccable servants and formal entertaining carried out on such a scale, it was incomparable. Whether or not Beryl enjoyed her first experience of such grandeur in India, this was to be but a foretaste of the style of the men of privilege who would be drawn to her and whom she handled with the consummate skill of a chameleon. She was a shrewd judge of character, taking seconds to sum up any person, directing her responses accordingly. Jock Purves, 'a brawny farmer', the tall, charming, ex-Captain from the London Scottish Regiment, far from teetotal, felt the full force of her dissatisfaction and consumed tumblers of whisky from sundown, sinking into repetitive self-pity. In India this had gone unobserved; but on African soil, Beryl was ashamed of what could not be hidden from Ruta. To her African friends, Jock was nothing but an old *mlevi* and, humour being the enemy of authority, they laughed. Beryl had no respect for him whatsoever.

Neighbours thought Jock 'too coarse for her'. He could not face her in bed without alcohol and she quickly tired of him. None was surprised that the marriage barely lasted six months.[7] These difficulties early in 1920 cannot have been helped by living at Ndimu Farm until their own house was ready.

In addition to Beryl's disaffection with Jock, another jolt came when Dickie Clutterbuck, stranger and long-lost brother, re-appeared to take his rightful place, having followed Clutt's footsteps through Sandhurst. Beryl felt herself and Arthur usurped by the unknown heir. But she took secret pleasure in Dickie's ignorance of Africa, particularly when it came to racing.[8] Dickie's re-emergence further complicated relationships between Beryl, her father and Emma. Now that Beryl was married, the abrasive relationship she had with Emma was apparently less marked, although in actual fact it was simply hidden beneath a mask of female guilelessness. Arthur tried to ease any hostilities, but Beryl continued to need her father's approval and often tried to gain his loyalty at Emma's expense, a task which became more and more competitive. Clutt naming a filly after Emma caused more complications of jealousy. But Arthur's mother did try to steer as clear a course as was possible. Meanwhile Beryl thought of Dickie as a cuckoo, occupying the wrong nest. Only her friendship with Ruta remained unsullied by all events.

The difficulties, however, were not confined to awkward relationships, as it became clear at this time that Clutt was facing an uncertain future. He had established an extremely impressive yard, representing the epitome of success in the eyes of an august, new settler in 1920, who went there to buy horses: 'Mr Clutterbuck has 84 (horses) . . . it took quite some time to go round . . . racehorses, brood mares, foals, Somali ponies . . . a good-looking lot . . . beautifully cared for . . . coats shining like satin.'[9] The irony was that Clutt, for the second year running, won the Kenya Steeple Chase Cup and the War Memorial Cup, rounding off in triumph with the Naval and Military Cup when the first hint of bankrupcty leaked out. Three days before Beryl's nineteenth birthday, barely had Clutt drunk the toast from the Myberg-Hiddell Trophy than the rumour circulated, 'Clutterbuck was leaving the Turf'. The press noted 'the ball failed to strike the usual vivaciousness'.[10]

Once Beryl realised what bankruptcy meant, her faith and pride in him lay in potsherds around her; the shame she felt cannot be overstated. Fate now assumed the weight of a landslide against him, when the exchange rate of Kenya's currency changed. The ignominy of watching her father lose all that he had struggled to build up since she could remember had an almost paralysing effect on Beryl. Nothing seemed to make sense any more; the East Africa Turf Club continued to flourish, monthly fixtures kept him extremely busy now the quarterly routine was done away with and, compared to other victims of failed rains, Ndimu Farm had seemed not too badly off with dams to provide water. But his crops were affected by cut-worm; his Government contract to supply hundreds of tons of grain, the price of which had been pre-fixed could not be fulfilled and there was no escape clause to cover extenuating conditions pinned to drought. Clutt looked to other farmers for maize but they could only offer dribs and drabs and for these uncertain amounts he was forced to pay more than he could sell it for, even before milling it. Beryl's understanding of the disaster was limited.[11]

But the key factor in her father's bankruptcy was far more radical and complex. Before the war, the value of the dollar had soared while the rouble and German mark were swamped. Gold disappeared from circulation so that silver rose in value, affecting the rupee which, in Nairobi, stood at 1*s* 4*d* legally. But in exchange it rose to 2*s* 6*d*. The finance men rubbed their hands, receiving 15 rupees to £1 sterling, having paid the overseas rate, namely 8 rupees to £1. Government framed taxes at 1*s* 4*d* but collected at 2*s* while banks housed rupees at the official value and sold at 50 per cent above par. During 1919 when the rate had flickered, farmers and storekeepers almost came to blows. The farsighted tried to prevent what happened but as was so often the case the decision was made 4,000 miles away from those it affected. Immediately before Beryl and Jock's return from India in February, the Colonial Office in Whitehall decided that the rate of exchange be pegged to 2*s* and the rupee abolished. We have no idea of what Clutt's liabilities amounted to. Suffice it to say that a man going to bed one night with a £5,000 overdraft was in debt by breakfast the following morning to the tune of £7,500. The unhappy man with a mortgage, having borrowed at 1*s* 4*d*, was expected to pay it back at 2*s*. Anyone buying property for £2,000 now owed £1,000 more. D, for example, dogged for years afterwards by exchange difficulties, had his liabilities increased overnight by £20,000. The Governor, Northey, faced with reducing a deficit of £412,000, tried to swell revenue by raising customs duties; but the worst aspect was the crippling burden of overdrafts that fell upon invaluable pioneers such as D and Clutt, men who had struggled hardest and risked the most. Clutt had always done business on the chit system, so was hit especially badly. Beryl avowed he was affected permanently: 'Afterwards my father was terrified of having an account anywhere and everything was paid for in cash. He could not bear the thought of it happening again . . . until he died.'[12]

What followed were some of the unhappiest months in Beryl's life as Ndimu farm was auctioned. Her father decided to leave for Cape Town. To lose all that he stood for was to throw away sixteen years of effort, to turn his back on all within Beryl's horizon that had seemed immutable. The father she adored now clearly had feet of clay, which made her feel isolated beyond physical separation. Ruta remained the one confidante among the ruins. Ever after, like a desert nomad, Beryl took the view that everything was disposable. Her father's retreat as the racing pioneer in the Colony could scarcely have been more ignominious, worse he was being jeered at:

> They speak of a trainer named Clutterbuck,
> Who enjoyed the most absolute an' utter luck,
> Now he's turning his tables,
> And selling his stables,
> In fact he is putting his shutter up.[13]

Beryl was so private an individual that such exposure of her father's frailties in local newspapers was horrific. She loathed the press from now on. Daily she was confronted by advertisements for the sale of the farm and editors exploiting the story of Clutt's demise in racing for their lead columns.[14]

War altered many facets of life in Kenya, though none perhaps as much as transport in an onslaught of Model T Fords and Harley Davidson motor-cycles, not to mention aeroplanes in the skies. The bush, hitherto untouched by sounds of engines, was affected permanently. For years such changes wrecking the fragile balance of nature went unrecognised. Those sounds from which Beryl had taken her cues, voices of the wild, human and animal, had predominated the plains. The valleys had been filled with drumming from distant villages, warnings – the snap of a twig as buffalo passed, the twitter of birds against a snake, the ventriloquist call of a lioness to her pride while on the hunt – but now these could be obliterated by the sound of an encroaching engine. The game began its retreat as roads were improved to take vehicles, forfeiting its realm in the name of man's progress. The shift in habitat wrought by the wheel went unnoticed until almost too late. The tribes and all each stood for in Kenya suffered the same fate. Beryl would ride a motor-cycle, drive a car, and fly an aeroplane herself before the end of the decade.

Once she and Jock moved into the house he had built for them, no longer having any need of him for transport and with no one else for company to buffer their abrasive moments, the refrains of married life palled to the extent that neither could exist under one roof without scenes of physical violence. Rose, née Buxton, a young English woman whose farmer husband, Archie Cartwright ranched cattle thirty miles away at Naivasha, described Beryl during this phase as 'very wild and unhappy'. Her marriage 'beyond repair', she made no effort to hide her adulteries. Unlike her critics, who were mostly women, to whom she was immune anyway, Beryl saw nothing wrong in pursuing her desires.[15] She flirted outrageously in front of Jock, and he reacted by drinking all the more, which sometimes made him violent, but always self-pitying which Beryl could not stand. Her answer was to ride off on Pegasus at any hour of the day or night, staying away for two or three days with mere acquaintances; over the next eighteen months she frequently sought asylum temporarily in this way. She pitched up on Soysambu in the middle of the night on one such occasion, and finding D's son, Tom Cholmondeley, out for Christmas from Eton, relieved him of his virginity in the hay-loft of D's stables.[16]

Beryl found brief comfort in marriage, but now it only made her wary. Anyone colliding nervously for the first time with the African side of Beryl's nature would encounter the kind of uneasiness in her which defined the chasm between African and Western cultures. Jock found himself despised in the troubled course of their relationship; uncomprehending that the only things Beryl saw were his faults to the point where she was blinded to everything else. The greatest offence to her was his drinking: 'I got awfully bored with that'.[17] As a bride of only a year she was humiliated by his impotence. He became 'very *kali*' (fierce) when drunk, from which we may conclude, that his drinking usually led to violence.[18] However he grew accustomed to Beryl's infidelities and was not totally devoid of a sense of irony about them. He installed a typically carved Arab door from Lamu in the house. The next occupants, Patience and 'Mackinlay Mac', who took on Jock's *posho* mill, had Kathleen Fielden, a new settler, to stay. She had 'never seen an Arab door before . . . rich . . . dark . . . polished wood, studded all over . . . hundreds of glowing brass nails in the most intricate pattern . . . Mac had the most lovely sense of humour . . . when asked, "What is the history of that lovely door?" Mac's answer came out pat, "Oh, those were hand-forged by . . . Purves. Every time Beryl committed an indiscretion he would hammer in another nail". . . . There were rows and rows of them. There had been nothing salacious, bitchy or leering in the way he said it . . . one saw the international Rugby player in the mind's eye, perched on a ladder, his head on one side, busy with a hammer and a box of brass studs, concentrating on the arrangement of his next nail, wondering whether he would find a place to put it in.'[19] Though Jock realised Beryl's duplicity, nothing had prepared him for the discovery that while he lay sodden with alcohol, snoring, she stole from their bed to be with Ruta.[20] 'Ruta took me to Nandi *ingomas* [sic] I have always enjoyed them he would take off his working clothes and shoes and with only a *shuka* and Nandi head-dress on take part'. She seldom returned before dawn.[21] 'I would ride Pegusus to the scene and stay until the early hours . . . It was nearly always the cold that drove me home from Molo.' African dancing excited and never offended her. Lack of sexual restraint in tribal dances shocked Europeans in general if they had the chance to watch; all the dances focused on the drumming, throbbing rhythm of sex as torsoes moved suggestively. From the age of six, children performed the same tempo, jumping, running, swaying to a frenzy reaching a climax. The only Western equivalent was the tango which caused public outrage when it was first introduced, as the dancers' bodies are pressed together in a flagrantly sensual series of movements. Significantly the tango was to become Beryl's favourite Western dance.

On 11 December, every asset itemised by the Nakuru auctioneers on Ndimu Farm was sold under W. J. Beeston's hammer but for sixteen horses reserved for sale after the New Year fixture in Nairobi on 2 January 1921. Fetching a total of £4,514.00 (see

Appendix to Chapter 5, p. 339) 'Some good prices were realised . . . one or two purchasers obtained bargains.' Horses, the contents of the twelve-roomed house, outbuildings, stud groom's cottage, five fenced paddocks and 123 looseboxes went to the highest bidders. Beryl felt abandoned, once again, by her father's move to Cape Town although allegedly he did give her the choice of going with him but she preferred to remain in Kenya. How matters were left between Clutt and Emma can only be imagined but she did not go with him either. With so uncertain a future, and no money for her passage perhaps Clutt felt he could offer no future; maybe she intended to join him once he had re-established himself in Cape Town and never did; nor did she divorce Orchardson, moving instead to Nairobi (later emigrating to Australia). She lived in Nairobi with Arthur who was apprenticed meanwhile to the Uganda Railway, continuing to ride for Beryl as a gentleman jockey.[22] After Clutt left Kenya, Arthur alleged that none of them exchanged letters. This does not indicate that they were on bad terms; after a gap of seven years, Clutt was to take up with Beryl, Arthur and Ruta in Kenya as if there had been no separation. None the less, if there was correspondence, none survives.

Although all Clutt's earnings were destined for the Court Broker, he now took on a new owner, the soldier settler, Major Benedict Birkbeck at Rongai, whose farm, Mugunga, adjoined Purves's land.[23] The Birkbecks would become important figures in Beryl's future; she was to train for Ben and his first wife Cockie, née Alexander, who was a distant cousin of Beryl's mother. Cockie witnessed the protracted break-up of Beryl's marriage to Jock, as did Ben's second wife, Penelope, better known as 'Ginger', while both observed Beryl, aged twenty, fall irretrievably for Baroness Blixen's lover of some two years, the Honourable Denys Finch Hatton.

Beryl had already met this legendary and most determined of bachelors – 'terribly tall, terribly good-looking man, wearing a blue bowler' – 'at the races', according to Margaret Elkington when she was staying with Beryl, who first spotted him after the outbreak of war. Whatever girlish comments took place 'at the age of eight',[24] Beryl would actually have been about twelve when Denys volunteered. The high-domed 'Captain Finch Hatton' was not an army man, but he visited the Nakuru remount depot. Nor was he interested in things equestrian beyond necessity and since racing was suspended for the duration of the war anyway it is more likely that Beryl's and Denys's paths would have first crossed in 1915 at Nakuru. What is certain is that when Beryl, aged twenty, was introduced to him properly, for her 'it was a *coup de foudre*'.[25] Within the next twelve months, Beryl was either at a party or staying at Muthaiga Club when the engaging Denys was present too. Thereafter Beryl would stalk this old Etonian relentlessly. She was to move to Soysambu to train for D on account of D's connection with Denys; at Muthaiga Country Club the two men shared a *pied à terre*, and Beryl, in the hope of meeting him, was to spend more and more time at Muthaiga for the same reason. She undertook more journeys in the dark, under pretext of escaping scenes with Jock, in the hope of finding him at her destination than will ever be known. She befriended his circle of friends, watched him from a distance, never taking a step too near, so as not to alarm him. Ironically, in Beryl's pursuit of her quarry, the elusive, patrician hunter became the hunted. She was heedless that Denys was moving into Mbogani – Karen Blixen's coffee farm – so as to be with the Danish Baroness as often as his nomadic life allowed. She was deaf to warnings that 'Denys was very much Karen Blixen's own'.[26] Against all reasonable argument, something in Beryl's blood urged her at every opportunity to take any chance to be with him: her African instinct, decoy tactics and patience upheld her and her mind was made up – she had to have Denys.

'Ginger', who was to be responsible for introducing Beryl to her second husband, Mansfield Markham, explained, 'Lots of women were in love with Denys. Rose Cartwright only married Algy when she got to Kenya and found that Denys was involved with Tania [Karen Blixen]; there were at least eight . . . who, like Tania, absolutely adored him'.[27] Cockie Birkbeck corroborates that 'Beryl fell hopelessly in love with him' and, being fourteen years younger than her rival – Karen Blixen was older than Denys – assumed that she could win Denys easily. But Beryl had never met such resistance to her charms from the opposite sex and, as time went on 'became mad for him'.[28]

According to Ginger Birkbeck, 'If only Pegasus could have talked, there was a book to be written on Beryl's adventures on this gallant hack, alone'.[29] One of the stories would certainly have been one rash and desperate ride across the Aberdares. During that summer Beryl had an affair with Boy Long, a debonair farmer, who lived on Soysambu as D's manager. When Jock got wind of it he was humiliated and infuriated by the role of cuckold. He appeared one night at Soysambu and 'blacked D's eye for stealing my girl', accusing him of harbouring his wife's lovers.[30] Beryl, loathing scenes, simply saddled Pegasus, leaving in the middle of the night for Solio, the Hon. Berkeley Cole's estate on the far side of the Aberdares, beneath Mount Kenya. Berkeley was Lady Delamere's older brother, therefore Beryl had known him for some time. He was also Denys's closest friend, which leaves little doubt that she chose to ride to Solio in the hope of finding Denys there.

Riding the sixty miles that night was a wantonly dangerous act. But even if Beryl did not think consciously of the risks, she did have an instinctive sense of her own ability to survive in perilous conditions. She believed that Pegasus was 'as sure-footed as a cat', and that they would arrive in one piece. One of the more hair-raising moments of the journey occurred when she was half-way there and met a river with very steep banks.[31] She dismounted so as to lead Pegasus, 'over a flimsy *dorobo** bamboo bridge'. While congratulating herself for reaching the far side, she heard 'a nasty creaking and crackling . . . all four of the pony's legs went through the structure. There the poor beast hung, resting on his stomach, with . . . a 20 foot drop and raging river beneath.' It was typical of her to ignore her own danger and concern herself only with Pegasus; 'His usual courage and calm saved him. He did not struggle like nine horses out of ten'.[32] Beryl always carried a hank of rope on her saddle in case of emergencies. She lassoed him near his cheekbone and neck so that the rope could not slip over his head, drawing the other end round a tree, praying that there was enough leverage to prevent Pegasus from falling until 'by some miracle a *dorobo* (sic) might find us'. Instead 'came a crashing . . . breaking of trees . . . a large herd of elephant had got my wind . . . I would have welcomed an elephant at that

* Ndorobo – a tribe

moment!'³³ Beryl coaxed Pegasus toward her, 'he reacted gallantly getting one foreleg onto the bank, though he left huge pieces of skin on the cross-rails.' Fortunately they had been near enough to the far side when they had come to grief, and, using every ounce of remaining strength, she hauled him to safety. She alone knew that her goal had imperilled them, but she confessed, 'I would never have forgiven myself if I had lost Pegasus that day',³⁴ and if she had she would have faced a walk of thirty miles in either direction. As it was she rode on in the small hours to find Berkeley and Tich Miles but no Denys.³⁵ Beryl returned to Jock a few days later.

In 1921, Beryl's ambition was to redress her father's reputation. She began her new life as a trainer without him, with an impressive display of zeal and a self-discipline which were envied by many in one so young, venturing out alone for the first time. In choosing this profession, Beryl had instinctively found a way to avoid female destiny. Her own mother and Emma might have been examples of formidable Victorian industriousness but such preoccupations had passed her by completely. Beryl understood horses and she chose to be independent and go it alone in Kenya instead; that decision brought months of unremitting labour, anguish and exhilaration as she got the most unpromising of horses on form. Her reputation as a trainer of note now began its ascent. Using Clutt's gallops on Mugunga, and his former jockey Harry Walters, Beryl's sacrifice, her unfaltering effort as a trainer, eventually gained her the status of 'genius'. Because the East Africa Turf Club, the original governing body of racing in Kenya, did not provide the names of winning trainers, however, her earliest successes are lost in time. It is little known that Beryl was the first and the youngest female in the history of the Turf to gain recognition. This would never have happened in England where women were not recognised as trainers until 1966. Kenya's space, its raw growth, was responsible for such latitude, offering a different dream (as it has for many other women), allowing Beryl to mature with relatively unfettered ambition in its abstraction of human endeavour; through necessity, pioneering has always dictated that the best person for the job gets it, regardless of sex.

The two-year period to follow saw the formation of a determined will, one that was to become nearly intractable in maturity. Aged nineteen, her fulfilment had to be within herself; she had so little regard for Jock, it was with Ruta that she achieved a symbiosis where there was no need for words. Upon such firm foundations Beryl improvised when required – that was her freedom and her genius. If she had no chair she used a bale of hay just as she would use logs for bedstead legs; when she spoke of 'we' she referred to Ruta, as naturally as her right hand worked with the left. Kenya could not by any stretch of the imagination be described as a major racing country, but competition during Beryl's early triumphs over Gerry Alexander, B. F. Webb and Spencer Tryon was intense. Domestic difficulties notwithstanding, in 1921, Beryl (between Nakuru and Nairobi) won the Trial Stakes for two-year-olds as well as the Produce Stakes with Cam, for his new owner, Major Wac Conduitt* leading in three more winners next day, proving in six months that she was someone to be reckoned with.[36]

Within four weeks, however, her luck changed. Having got Cam on peak form, Beryl expected victory in the East Africa Derby; with Harry Walters up, Cam's win was guaranteed over Dickie, who was riding stablemate Camargo for Ben Birkbeck. But the unthinkable happened: Cameo, ridden by Joey Mulholland for Ann Greswolde-Williams, and Cam were beaten by Camargo by two lengths. The press suggested that Cam had been 'got at'.[37] The accusations caught Beryl entirely off-balance. For whatever reasons, with an incisiveness which was to become characteristic when she lost face, she cut her losses, putting her horses 'on the ease list'.[38] Explaining nothing – for which she was to become renowned – she made rearrangements connected with her permanent move to Soysambu. She was taking the opportunity to leave Jock for good that February.

Jock had created a number of rumpuses in connection with her work, prompting Beryl's decision in a busy racing season. Her allegiance now was to her principal owner, Ben Birkbeck, a congenial ex-army officer, who was the son of a Norfolk squire.[39] Cockie, Ben's first wife, was pert, vivacious, worldly wise, ever loving toward Beryl and always practical.[40] She was the one who calmed Jock down when he created scenes. Jock was finding Beryl's need for freedom and his own inability to cope with a beautiful headstrong wife, 'exasperating'.[41] Beryl had also had enough. Saddling up one day, 'I left never to return and I rode Pegasus and carried nothing more in the world than would fit into my small saddle roll. I had no other possessions in the world. I was on my way to Delamere's at Elmenteita to work and to look after his stud and Ruta was with me next day as he had to walk thirty miles.'[42]

It was Cockie Birkbeck (on the point of leaving Ben), Rose Cartwright (a childhood friend of Denys's), Karen Blixen (his lover) and 'Ginger' (Ben's second wife) whose fortunes were to march parallel with Beryl's own from 1922. Each saw her through different crises, turning points we would scarcely know about were it not for their individual involvement during the next decade. But Rose Cartwright, being shy and discreet, having known Denys since she was seven, was pivotal and often entrusted with secrets, just as Denys was. He too knew a great deal because each friend confided in him, knowing that he could be depended upon not to allow whatever was burdensome to go any further. These submerged bonds of loyalty ran deep. According to Cockie, Ginger and Rose, Beryl's love for the second son of the 13th Earl of Winchilsea and 8th Earl of Nottingham, the Honourable Denys Finch Hatton was her first, possibly unique, experience of all those sensations attributable to romantic love. For Denys alone Beryl underwent a mixture of agonies, ecstacies, fears, insecurities and entrancements. But she had a rival in Karen Blixen.

6

Life at Mbogani

(1922–4)

Baron and Baroness von Blixen Finecke had settled at Ngong in 1914 as newly-weds, intending to pioneer coffee growing. They happened to be second cousins; Karen Christentz Dinesen had actually been in love with Bror von Blixen's twin brother, Hans; but Hans had not cared enough to marry her so 'Tanne' as her Danish family called her, opted instead for the title and to emigrate to BEA. Within a year she had discovered that Bror was an incorrigible philanderer, contracting syphilis from him. It is believed that Maasai women infected him with the venereal disease, while Bror was helping D to patrol the Kajiado border. Karen Blixen sought help medically in Denmark, believing herself cured with Salvarsan (arsphenamine), mercury-based and in wide use since 1909. By the time she returned to their coffee estate, Mbogani, understandably the stigma and mistrust of her Swedish husband brought untold private humiliation. When she met Finch Hatton, in 1918, he was on leave from Mesopotamia, having just qualified as a pilot and helping to defend the French front. She wrote of his effect upon her to her brother, 'In my old age, I have had the good fortune to meet my living ideal in him.'[1] Finch Hatton had not yet based himself at Mbogani with Tania, his pet name for his mistress, but the arrangement was imminent.

By 1922, Denys and Tania, Bror her estranged husband, Cockie and Ben Birkbeck, Rose and Algy Cartwright, D, Berkeley Cole and Tich Miles, as well as Beryl, formed a distinct coterie, though Beryl was still peripheral to its core. Things could hardly have been more intricate, especially since Denys and Bror both used Farah, Tania's Somali major-domo, for their individual safaris and Cockie and Bror were to instigate divorce so as to marry one another. Meanwhile Beryl, the only working female, was also the youngest, the most beautiful and the most sought-after, and yet not by the man she really wanted – Denys Finch Hatton.

Beryl's decision to train from Soysambu took her into the mainstream. Berkeley Cole's brother, Galbraith, owned the neighbouring estate, Kekopey, where Denys often stayed with D's brother-in-law and his wife, Nell. Galbraith suffered crippling arthritis and was restricted to his farm largely; at the Coles' fireside Denys shared 'the divine art of conversation', treating him to discussion on Shakespeare and Homer, which Galbraith regarded as 'merely a charming accessory' to his all-important occupation, the raising of fat wethers for market.[2] Some evenings, his manager, Dermott Dempster joined in their singing, while Denys strummed to a guitar. Before dawn, he and 'Dempey' would set off to go duck shooting. It was Dempey who arranged the annual duck shoot for Galbraith on Boxing Day over on Lake Naivasha.[3] Between Kekopey and Soysambu, the network of old Etonians among the flow of mutual friends from Nairobi or London ensured that Denys's name and whereabouts cropped up frequently and, by serendipity, kept Beryl informed.

According to Ben Birkbeck's next wife, Ginger, Jock's reaction to her moving to Soysambu, was to nurture the dream that 'Beryl would sow her wild oats and come back to him'.[4] This was not an entirely ludicrous notion, given that by the end of 1922 the exchange of spouses among mutual friends resembled a Colonial version of musical chairs. For example, Ginger and Cockie Birkbeck both knew Tania, whose husband would marry Cockie, but Ginger would never meet Ben's former wife. Now that Cockie had moved to live in Nairobi, it was Ginger's turn to cope with Jock's 'boring' behaviour.

In 1921, Ben had engaged Baron Bror von Blixen as their white hunter; during that safari, Cockie and Blix had fallen for one another seriously. Tania was not amused to discover that Blix and Cockie were passing *billets doux* to one another concealed in the barrel of one of Blix's guns; Tania's affair with Denys notwithstanding, she asked Blix to leave Mbogani. Cockie left Ben and ran a dress shop to make ends meet, hiring out Fancy Dress costumes.

Miss Penelope Mayer, Ben Birkbeck's future wife, saw a great deal of Beryl, who continued to train Ben's horses. Ginger, as she was nicknamed, was dressed by Lanvin and Worth. She was as sophisticated as Cockie, and equally understanding of Beryl's youthful whims, just as Ben was. Jock, however, never took into account that her sexual impulses blinded her to everything but their gratification. Beryl had strong masculine traits that Ruta's society had engendered in her and which she saw no reason to forfeit. Ginger now found herself bombarded by Jock's invitations which she dreaded almost as much as Ben's groans of protest against 'having to listen to the same old stories and that same bloody record'. Attempts to console Jock, who was desperately upset when Beryl ran off, proved embarrassing: 'He wept and wept . . . tears running down his face',[5] playing one tune on his gramophone over and over after dinner, 'The hours I spent with thee dear heart, are as a string of pearls to me.' One night, unable to take this refrain once more, Ben smashed the record.[6] Meanwhile, secure with D as a surrogate father, Beryl trained from Soysambu until 1924 and, apart from drunken outbursts occasionally from Jock, life was pleasant and interesting with few problems.

Soysambu, lying in the floor of the Rift Valley, took its Maasai name 'brindled rocks' from the mass behind D's homestead and stables, overlooking Lake Elmenteita. The spartan comfort of D's mud and thatch *rondavels* was in keeping with Beryl's preferred lifestyle. Each individual hut, with its familiar oils framed in grand gilt, complemented the tradition of open-house Kenya hospitality. D's home was run by his butler, Alfred Hyland, whose wife Hannah had replaced the Goan cook. Parties, spawned by an ever-changing rota of pioneers and politicians out from 'home'[7] were made more fun for Beryl by D's handsome manager, Boy, who presided over the dips and woolsheds. His swashbuckling image was added to by one gold earring, bright shirts, ivory and gold bracelets. He looked 'marvellous in his black stetson, mounted on the black stallion he always rode' – with a Somali shawl flung over his shoulders, 'to great effect'.[8] Boy was diverting enough for Beryl to continue their discreet and casual affair into the 1930s. No aimless rake, however, she was kept busy from morn till dusk; her first task was always to rid the land of sodom apple (*Solanum incanum*), the juice of which she swore by to rid horses of warts. The sodom apple is a perennial felt-haired shrub with tiny purple flowers and thorny stems, a scourge related to the deadly nightshade family, requiring diligence to uproot it if it is not to propagate itself during the next rainy season.

Soysambu is puff adder country. Succulents like the aloe and red-hot pokers bloom among the scrubby vegetation, with collections of spikes, razor edged leaves, thorns and other barbs of nature. The lake, gleaming, dark and as smooth as gun steel, is made more dramatic by flat-topped acacia thorns, umbrellas of emerald, encircling its shore of chalky pale soda. Most astonishing of all is a swathe of pink, created by massed flamingoes. These thrive on the algae just below the surface of the waters, bitter from soda and where fish cannot live. Yet hippo can: their grunting, distinct from the steady mutterings of the birds, provides a constant murmur. The wind blows hot off Elmenteita, carrying particles of soda fiercely at times to coat the skin; its not unpleasant acrid smell hangs on the air. And below D's house in 1922 all manner of game cropped the grass down to the lake; 40,000 acres of the ranch was fenced and D had installed irrigation from its only river, the Mereroni.

The Colony was passing through strange political upheavals. With the traditional desire for domination, D was promoting self-rule which was sustained by an upper-class society abundantly presided over by aristocrats and a number of ex-army officers since the 1919 wave of settlement. The white community had now swelled to 10,000. D, as a member of Legislative Council, Kenya's local governing body, was unofficial leader. Legco had 23,000 Indians and two and a half million Africans to consider as it embarked upon an embittered battle to block Indian immigration.

The British Government would shortly publish a Kenya White Paper making clear that African interests were paramount, and just as it proclaimed that settlers of all races were subordinate to indigenous people, so immigration problems known as 'the Indian Question' escalated. D, taking the radical view, prepared to resist any invasion of what white settlers regarded as their rights and formed an Ulster-like movement, a Vigilance Committee, involving Europeans of power, with himself at the helm.

Beryl meantime concentrated on D's horses, doing well in the 1922 season, winning seven times for him, including the Jubaland Cup and his own presentation, the Delamere Gold Cup. Her preparations for race week show just how busy she was kept, 'manes had to be clipped, hooves had to be pared, teeth had to be rasped, saddlery, minerals put in the feeds, iron each day for all those horses in training, carefully measured and watched'.[9] Three days before fixtures, she and Ruta measured up feeds for 'on average fifteen horses, crushed oats, bran, maize (very little), barley for boiling, linseed, rock salt'. Ruta sewed this into bags, seeing that everything was stacked, bales of lucerne and hay, checking and counting the racing tackle again, and putting it in a leather saddle bag making sure that everything was ready for loading. Beryl's colours were ironed, packed in a tin uniform case 'with my own clothes'.[10]

At the last minute odds and ends were added, 'mane clippers and cord for plaiting, hoof-kit, resin for pulling tails . . . On the morning of the last night I order an ox-cart from an Indian with two oxen and we put everything on it to be taken to the ramp near the station – rugs, buckets, saddles, blankets, the syces kit and their food. We quickly lift the heavy doors and bolt them fast.'[11] Having loaded the highly strung runners, 'now comes Pegasus – I just hang the reins over his neck, pat him on the hind quarters . . . he walks in on his own . . . tucks himself into position in his tight-fitting stall.' Shunting the boxes on to the engine unsettled her runners; only when they were calm and fed did she sup herself: 'Ruta unwraps his and mine . . . he and I eat in the stall next to Pegasus'[12] and beside him 'retiring for the night, I spread out my blankets on some new sweet smelling grass bedding and fall asleep'.

By daybreak, the train had hauled itself up the Rift Valley's precipitous escarpment to Kabete; half an hour later, Beryl and Ruta were jostling with owners and trainers 'from all parts of the country – Nyeri, Nanyuki, Molo, Eldoret . . . Nairobi itself' claiming that her only competition was from Sir Northrup and Lady MacMillan, millionaires, whose yard at Chiromo (another home frequented by Denys) was run by Frank Bramwell and whose standards matched her own, with as many runners.[13]

Nairobi had grown beyond recognition since 1904, the year of

Clutt's arrival. Hitching posts were giving way to parking for motorised traffic and tall groves of Australian eucalyptus trees, the fast-growing blue gum, marked the town's raw frontier quality. Beryl was to live to see its dusty thoroughfares tarmacadamed, the open drainage trenches disappear, shacks on stilts replaced by skyscrapers, and Nairobi's racecourse shift to Ngong. The course itself Beryl regarded as picturesque; when the sun shone, its newly painted stand and its view over Donyo Sabuk and Mount Kenya enchanted her. During the rains, however, the soil, as dark as coffee grounds, split when its crust dried. Clutt's last attempt to improve conditions, 'harrowing in thousand of tons of sawdust', Beryl had to admit 'had not helped . . . after the rains, the greenness never lasts . . . sun dries it up in a week . . . so . . . underneath the turf is always doing strange things . . . cracks as large as three inches – enough for a hoof to lodge in an uneven position while galloping. There is . . . nothing more damaging to tendons and other sprains'.[14]

Here on the course at Eastleigh, Beryl earned her reputation and the admiration of her peers for her dedication as a trainer. Her Swahili name in 1922 was as complicated as it was flattering, *Mutu ambaye hawezi kwangusha na farazi* – 'one who cannot fall off a horse'.[15] Possibly an even higher accolade, in Nandi eyes, was made by one of her old *syces* who conceded, 'She was white but she had a black heart'.[16] Her singlemindedness in the eyes of a Somali – 'to see her she is like a spear' – was no less admirable but the Secretary of the Jockey Club thought less of that quality: 'she also harboured a ruthless will to win'.[17] For the cost of success in Beryl's case was often envy. She made enemies simply by winning consistently, as well as being one of the most alluring women in her profession. 'She was always a celebrity rather than a success,' the Secretary commented. 'The star quality . . . with the touch of nonconformity could exasperate as well as delight her owners and associates.'[18] Idiosyncrasies apart, that competitive streak touched whatever Beryl tackled. Once she set her mind on some achievement, generally she emerged as victor. She did not like losing. Not that she was a bad loser. In fact she was gracious, shrugging off defeat; her attitude was 'we'll do better next time'. But Beryl found it impossible to apologise. And in the African world, until apology ceases to be regarded as a sign of weakness, it remains imperative to seem implacably in command in the face of defeat.

During race week Beryl always stayed at Muthaiga Country Club; after it opened in 1914 Nairobi Club was relegated to 'trade'. Muthaiga always cultivated snobbery carefully. For years Jews were not allowed to enter its portals, yet safely inside its *mal maison* pink exterior the wild carousing by Kenya's exuberant community could not be held back. Like sailors in port, its members achieved a darkly intriguing reputation for Bacchanalian revelry and, just as at any select point where the gilded gather and bask in one anothers' glow, Muthaiga was looked upon enviously by non-members as a sort of *Moulin Rouge*. When accommodation was at a premium, Beryl would occupy one of the loose-boxes but otherwise slept under canvas; a tent was pitched for her in the grounds with her name-board staked outside. From now on, no matter where Beryl might be in the world, she could always be contacted via Muthaiga Club, staying on average once a month for the next ten years.

In 1922, Denys Finch Hatton, as a connoisseur, was voted on to the club food and wine committee. He chose the vintages for its cellars and had hired its chef in Paris.[19] So Muthaiga was also the perfect place to bump into Denys whenever both he and Beryl happened to be in town.[20] In keeping with the best London clubs, facilities were excellent and included two motor-cars complete with European chauffeurs, tennis courts, a croquet lawn, spacious garages and stabling, not to mention the *pied à terre* used by Denys and D which Beryl would pass at least four times a day on Pegasus, *en route* to and from the course. Though others would occupy it, including herself, to her dying day she referred to it as 'Denys's old cottage'.[21]

Beryl harboured no resentment that she must work while her friends played; returning from morning gallops to late breakfast, 'I would see tired happy people crawling away in cars to their beds . . . by lunch time . . . to return to start all over again'.[22] At this age Beryl denied herself the freedom of gallivanting, much as she loved to dance. She limited late nights to the final day of her racing commitments. For all that Muthaiga was her second home, her social centre for secret meetings with lovers, and synonymous with both hard work and fun, surprisingly Beryl never celebrated her victories with even mild excess. And despite the club's usefulness to Denys, Beryl had not managed to become any friendlier with him, seeming unable to penetrate his and Tania's *milieu*. Months passed. Denys came and went.

There had been mad musical evenings when Denys and Tania were present, times when Beryl felt acutely self-conscious because she was tone-deaf whereas Denys possessed a fine tenor voice; he and Tich Miles had once sung 'the whole of Carmen, as toreadors with Ben (Birkbeck) as the bull'.

On the whole Denys managed to escape those social duties expected in one of his background – as the son of an Earl – and, at thirty-four, instead took out Americans on safari or equally well heeled noblemen to shoot. But he also owned a string of *dukas* so as to trade with the Maasai, and would take off to oversee these along the border at Lemek, sometimes for weeks. All his interests took him away from Nairobi. He owned a farm in partnership with A. C. Hoey* beyond Eldoret, an estate agency, Kipliget Ltd, and was a director of the Anglo-Baltic Timber Company. When he came back from these unpredictable absences, it was to be with Tania at Mbogani sixteen or so miles from Muthaiga, within sight of the Ngong Hills. After her existence with Blix, Denys's presence gave Tania an invigorating sense of freedom and dashing impropriety.

Meanwhile for nearly a year Beryl had gone through enough lovers to create an aura of casualness that was irresistible to men, though she was selective. On these occasions members appeared on the threshold like herself, dishevelled from toil or coated in mud or dust after a long safari, only to reappear within the hour, perfectly groomed, in an ambience as genial to a hunter in khaki as to a visiting dignitary in evening clothes. Nights, as Beryl put it, when 'Everyone dined at one table . . . black tie was worn. The Governor would come down . . . from G. H. (Government House, on the Hill) . . . dances went on until daylight . . . Delamere and others kept the band going on champagne and caviar. People sang when they felt like singing no matter how loudly the band might have been playing a different tune.'[23] It must be said that evenings were particularly riotous if D was there; he had retained his public schoolboy taste for rough-house games, to which Beryl was not averse: 'We all ragged and played like . . . children, George Wood and Tich . . . called upon to perform mad antics.' Tich's standard feat was to climb all the way round the dining room for a bet without touching the floor, 'like a monkey hanging on to the picture rail'.[24] Tania deplored the English goings-on as 'uncouth', but Cockie, who was to become the second Baroness Blixen, insisted, 'We had such fun in those days', a sentiment Beryl shared. As no stranger to steeple-chasing over furniture, she once competed with Elspeth Huxley's mother over the Muthaiga dining-room chairs, 'to get a rupee note which had been put on the clock'. The race was a dead heat. Both 'grabbed the note and tore it in half'.[25] Beryl seldom paused to look back, but sometimes she would indulge herself, recollecting 'busy evenings, tables overflowed into other rooms . . . even outside . . . A Frenchman's party would be singing French songs and [sic] Englishmen's [sic] . . . bawling out the Eton boating song, or the Harrovian Forty Years (sic) on'.[26] One of her zanier escapades concerned Sir Edward Northey, the Governor, just before he was recalled to London. His wife, Evangeline, a flamboyant and beautiful South African, had impressed Beryl with her devil-may-care attitudes, known to 'dance *à pas seule* on the table'.[27] Evangeline was therefore the last person to object when Beryl, 'dragged Northey by the seat of his pants, all the way across the dance floor'.[28] Beryl was amused by the repercussions: 'News of this flashed back to England – fancy the representative of the King allowing such a thing to happen.'[29]

Shortly afterwards Beryl struck a rapport with Tania at a joint party both to say farewell to Northey and to welcome his replacement, Sir Robert Coryndon. Northey had been recalled to London because his political leanings towards African labour problems and Indian immigration were viewed as 'negative'. Coryndon, regarding the appointment with a jaundiced attitude, cabled a friend, 'Have accepted Governorship of Kenya; no more peace.'[30] How right he was! Before long, plans were afoot within D's Vigilance Committee to seize the postal and telegraphic services and the railway by surprise raids and to kidnap the pro-African Coryndon, who was to be hidden on a remote farm sixty miles from Nairobi until D's demands were met. D's fierce cry that Kenya was 'a white man's country' was to grow more insistent now as labour problems escalated. Denys and Tania, D and Beryl were among those fore-gathered to welcome Coryndon; Denys had come from up-country and left with Tania afterwards for Mbogani.[31]

In Beryl's fixation for Denys, she will have been pleased when two more of his friends consulted her about racing. Lord Frances and his wife Lady Eileen lived at Deloraine, forty miles away at Rongai. Their double-storeyed house dazzled other settlers with its proper plumbing and stood in 3,500 acres of bush. Lady Eileen found Denys 'so charming and civilized' that he often spent the night there. One afternoon the Scotts sent word from Galbraith Cole's, where they were lunching, that they would like to inspect D's bloodstock.[32] By the time they arrived, Beryl saw that they were exhausted. It was so hot that waves of heat shimmered like a mirage; the Scotts were on foot because the band of the low gear of their car had worn through, so they were forced to trudge the last mile uphill to keep their appointment. After their inspection, Beryl offered each of them a horse, to save the trek back. Lady Eileen was grateful but, not having ridden astride very long, begged not to be put on a racehorse as Beryl led forward a two-year-old. 'Oh no, not one in training, something quiet,' Beryl reassured Lady Eileen, who recorded in her diary, 'I heaved myself on with the utmost difficulty . . . no sooner in the saddle than the mare leapt like a circus horse . . . gave a huge kick . . . unfortunately caught Francis in the *derriere*'.[33] Her husband had a game leg from a war wound, and in her concern of having hurt it, Lady Eileen had fallen off. She pleaded to be allowed to walk to the car but Beryl insisted that Lady Eileen remount, and 'mercifully . . . with Beryl clinging to the bridle got safely to the car. Her 'most disagreeable day'[34] had none the less established Beryl socially with them; a week later she joined their party at a Fancy Dress Ball at the Rift Valley Sports Club in Nakuru where Lady Eileeen 'chafed Beryl Purves . . . over her quiet pony in training'.[35] Next month Beryl was up for the Nairobi races when the Scotts gathered at Muthaiga where they had 'a most amusing dinner at D's tiny house where . . . D provided superb food and *bombe* champagne . . . Denys was doing butler most efficiently.' Most of them did not go to bed at all that night, 'playing golf and squash racquets at 7.30, how they kept this up for five consecutive nights', Lady Eileen, 'could not imagine'.[36]

The timing of Beryl's affair with Denys Finch Hatton is one of the many mysterious elements in their relationship. Both led nomadic lifestyles and, as Beryl made a conscious effort to be close to him, possibilities for trysting grounds were endless. Since both were discreet, private characters, they gave away no clues themselves. In later life Beryl would give cryptic answers to questions about Tania and Denys. She would remark: 'I used to walk Tania's dogs as a child.' In fact she was twenty years old when she first met Tania and Denys. This obliqueness was symptomatic of Beryl's intrinsically private nature. But Denys's name seemed to pierce through her reticence: she would speak more of him than of anyone.

Tania at this time thought of Beryl as 'no competition' – irksome for someone whose life, like Beryl's, was devoted to winning. In Tania's letters to her mother, Ingeborg Dinesen, she alluded to Beryl as 'a child', an attitude which might have had some bearing on Beryl's subsequent references to herself as a child in anecdotes concerning Mbogani, as above.

Whether the delusion surrounding her age was deliberate or subconscious, Beryl was fooling only herself when she repeatedly implied that Denys and Tania never consummated their love. Denys was attracted to Tania not only physically but also intellectually. Tania's fantastic imagination could transform a potato into a troll and concoct amusing tales. On a more domestic level she took pride in each meal she placed before Denys on her table gleaming with crystal and silver. Twice she believed herself pregnant by him. Both were false alarms distanced by several years, casting her into the deepest of depressions.

Exceptional 'long rains' in April 1923, prompted Beryl's move into Tania's household when racing was suspended toward the end of that month. Rainfall was to double in May and Beryl had even more unforeseen time on her hands. Pathways turned into rivers of red Kikuyu soil; roofs would leak like colanders. Wet conditions prevailed, affecting everyone's activities. Beryl had marshalled her insouciance and arrived at Mbogani one afternoon in the last week of April, uninvited, to stay with Tania. No invitation was needed in the old days in the Colony; anyone could go to any house, receiving instant hospitality; African servants made unexpected guests and their entourage welcome in the absence of an employer. Spare rooms were always kept ready for this purpose.

From the beginning, Cockie and Ginger could not help but wonder why, when Beryl had suitors beating a path to her door, she had set her heart on so confirmed a bachelor as Denys, and both warned Beryl of his involvement with Tania; Beryl knew that competition was keen – others remarked that Denys was 'the beau ideal'.[37] Ginger was aware that 'about eight women . . . attempted to get him as a husband including Beryl, which is why he shied away from their scheming. Denys was a lovable person, but he was also very selfish.'[38] By all accounts, Denys Finch Hatton was an uncommonly agreeable companion with flawless manners, whether attending the ballet or tracking buffalo. The fascination of his conversation, the sympathy of his perceptions, the way in which he excelled at sport – 'a fine left-hand bowler' who played cricket for Eton[39] – imply that he was a man for all seasons. And Beryl, who devoted herself during this interlude to discovering all that she could about him, was to end up painfully aware of her own lack of formal education.

Falling in love is after all not unusual, but Beryl was new to this grand obsession. Like a general in the field, Beryl needed to know as much as possible about her adversary in order to undermine Tania's place in Denys's life. Beryl's decision to approach Denys through Tania appears to have been a cold and ruthless one, a determination to sit out what she saw as merely an interlude, and eventually gain more access to him. And she could have had no idea that she was embarking on an eight-year marathon. But patience is an African virtue, and in this case involved mounting an elaborate cover-up, and Beryl was an artist in this field.

Both women preferred the company of men, and yet Tania was to give Beryl the run of her house now, and once Denys returned, so convincingly did Beryl play the part of the *ingénue*. Yet when Tania's own brother, Thomas Dinesen, was at Mbogani from Denmark, she would get him to move out to her original dwelling on Mbagathi Ridge, some half mile away, in order to have Denys to herself. Beryl, in no hurry, stayed for three weeks. Even so she was conscious of a certain superiority in her hostess which made her uneasy: 'Tania overlooked me, perhaps I was too young – perhaps she thought me foolish: she was rather remote and set herself apart.'[40] Tania's innocence of Beryl's tactics is shown by Tania's letter dated 29 April:[41] 'Beryl Purves is staying with me at the moment . . . she is only 20, really one of the most beautiful girls I have seen, but she has had such bad luck. She is married to a man she doesn't care for, and he won't agree to a divorce, nor will he give her any allowance, so she's pretty stranded but full of life and energy so I expect she will manage.'[42] Tania was even inspired to paint Beryl's portrait while Denys was on safari visiting his partner at Hoey's Bridge. But the paints, which were on order from Paris, never materialised during Beryl's stay. Tania described her as 'really . . . unusually lovely – something like Mona Lisa or Donatello's Holy Cecilia'[43] – Beryl's smooth, golden complexion, the tilt of her head, lithe body and limbs, expression, those down-tilted almond shaped eyes, the narrow, bare feet and long-fingered hands, thick hair, falling in streaks of uneven gold to her shoulders. One of the things Denys most admired in women was beautiful hair. Although Beryl personally disliked her slightly hooked nose, it none the less lent an appealing *hauteur*; she wore no make-up and, even from across a roomful of people, retained that mystery and grace with a hint of mischieviousness.

Compared to Beryl, Tania, 'painted terribly' as Ginger Birkbeck put it, referring to Tania's mask of face powder and application of kohl; she also emphasised her eyes at night with belladonna drops, which made her pupils dilate and appear all the blacker, but this was part and parcel of her bewitching image as a teller of tales.

Tania looked upon Mbogani as an oasis of civilisation; her cuckoo clock reminded her of the passing hours, filling Denys's absence in the writing of another story, in preparation for entertaining him on his return. The ambience in Tania's home was tasteful, but more contrived than anything Beryl had known: she felt uncomfortable with superfluity such as the refinement of Limoges. Even so, although disparate attitudes toward domesticity show, yet again, how different Beryl and Tania were, Tania's diligence – probably because it was in Denys's honour, made a lasting impression. Beryl was to pride herself on 'keeping a good table' in years to come, for all that she had pooh-poohed Tania's making a necessity of it in 1923.[44] 'Denys and Tania shared their love of beautiful china, glass, food and wine. Living on the farm . . . suited Denys perfectly until she became too possessive. I didn't like her very much . . . couldn't be bothered with her . . . always fussing about this and that.'[45] Beryl found especially pernickety the way in which Tania insisted that her servants wore white gloves at meal times and worse, for luncheon or dinner parties, when each plate for every course had to be placed in an embroidered linen slipcover, to be slid off as the plate was set down.[46] Throughout her house were always 'the most lovely flowers . . . Candidum lilies . . . in vases with little red rose sprays', an unusual but 'perfect' combination.[47] Beryl's understanding of housekeeping was that it was the servants' domaine. According to more than one lover Beryl would have preferred to 'hose down' the place, like a stable, to keep it clean.

Tania's concern for Beryl's circumstances continued but she took the optimistic and accurate view that her young guest was a survivor. Tania was struck by Beryl's 'cheerfulness' in the face of difficulties such as a drunken outburst by Jock: 'I am so sorry for her, her life is in such an awful mess and she is such a child and cannot cope at all with it let alone realise what is happening.'[48]

Mrs Kirkpatrick had returned to Nairobi by 1923 bringing with her Beryl's two half-brothers, Ivonne (pronounced Ivan) and Alex, aged nine and seven respectively. No one quite understood why 'Mrs KP' came back, unless it was in the hope of making up for lost time with Beryl, or to share Dickie's life at Molo. She had rented Tania's old manager's house on Mbagathi ridge 'for about a year' and Tania assumed Beryl would have a cosy reunion with her mother: 'It would be nice to have them as neighbours, Beryl and I could always have some fun together. She has her horse here and you know how pleasant it is always to have someone to go riding with.'[49] However Beryl had never told Tania that she had not spoken to, heard from or known anything about her mother for seventeen years.

Beryl's mother emerges as a manifestly pathetic figure, although she was to go on to gain a reputation in Kenya as 'a merry widow type'.[50] Whatever happiness Clara had had with Harry Kirkpatrick was short-lived. Having divorced Clutt in November 1914, she had married the next day; Harry had left for France immediately. Like many couples during the war their lives were made up of protracted separations and brief joyous reunions which were truncated finally in March 1918 when Harry was wounded in action and died: 'Alex' – short for James Alexander, after Clara's maiden name – was born after Harry's death.[51] Mrs KP's resettling in the Colony was to be an awkward turn of fate for Beryl; her desire to distance herself from someone who had abandoned her, whom she resented and despised, remained uppermost. She was to give Mrs KP a wide berth and, though at times living only three or four miles away, rarely saw her. Nor did her mother fulfil the term of Tania's lease in 1923. The roof at Mbagathi leaked so badly that Ivonne and Alex had nowhere to sleep. Her notes of desperation to Tania as her landlady, asking for help when forced 'to keep moving beds around to find a spot where it didn't rain in on them', brought sympathy but no solution and, by 21 May, Mrs KP retreated to Molo and anchorage with Dickie for her smaller sons.

In the midst of this *shaurie*, leaving Beryl alone to care for the deerhounds, Tania had disappeared to Muthaiga to meet Denys who was *en route* for Lemek. After lunching and spending a night with him, next day Tania returned to the farm alone. On 6 May she drove Beryl to Muthaiga to dine with 'Lord Carbery' whose young wife, Maia, was just learning to fly. John Evans Freke Carberry had dropped his title, although Tania persisted in using it. Like everyone else in Kenya, Beryl addressed him by his initials, JC. Beryl's introduction to the reluctant Irish peer proved another fateful encounter; it was to be at his coffee estate, Seremai beyond Nyeri, that Beryl would train for her commercial flying licence, and he who would challenge her to fly the Atlantic in years to come. At this point, all that interested Beryl was that Denys turned up as they were finishing dinner. Inevitably he and JC, both pilots, discussed aeroplanes. By the time the group was ready to retire in the early hours, it was too wet to drive to Mbogani and everyone slept at the Club. Tania drove Beryl back in the morning to the farm; that afternoon Denys arrived in his Hudson.

Most photographs do not convey what Beryl found irresistible in Denys Finch Hatton but there is no doubt that he measured up to her ideal of 'a real man'.

Denys was 6ft 3 ins tall, as lean as Beryl, with brown eyes. His slow rakish smile was said to have a devastating effect on women, especially when he was tanned. He almost always wore a dark blue narrow-brimmed bowler, from Lock's of St James's – quaint for a land where the solar topee reigned. The number and variety of his hats hinted at his vanity. He was thirty-four, and bald, but his lack of hair had nothing to do with age. Aged nineteen, at Brasenose College, he and his brother had shaved all their hair off, the then fashionable method of improving its thickness. When regrowth was slow, they allowed a barber to apply ammonia to their pates as a remedy. Denys's hair never grew back again. However, even at Eton, his penchant for hats may have been due to the pun on his name, first made unintentionally when a master rebuked him for wearing his boater into the classroom and ordered, 'Take your hat off, Hatton', reducing the boys to fits of giggles. So hats became integral to his persona and might even have influenced Beryl's accumulation of headgear. Poignantly, while Tania remained in Africa, her symbol of reassurance was the sight of his small blue bowler. So long as it hung on her hat-peg, she knew that he would be back.[52]

Even from the age of twelve at Eton Denys had induced wild, overstated admiration which triggered his emotional retreat. Oversolicitude became so stifling that he had taken the first opportunity after leaving Oxford to put oceans between him and his family and friends. With his excuse 'England is small, much too small', he sailed to South Africa, only to find that Cape Town was too suburban. Instead, he bought land in BEA in 1910.

Denys's role of leading man in the lives of two fascinating yet utterly different women in itself shows how charismatic he was. He was fourteen years older than Beryl and a little younger than Tania. Beryl was fair, willowy and gauche. Tania was dark, petite and cosmopolitan, striving to make something of herself intellectually. Beryl reigned supreme as a woman of action. And where Tania could not get enough of his company, Beryl was to show him that she could do without him very well. Denys possessed that enchanting but most dangerous of gifts, an ability to make whoever he was with believe that no other person in the world existed.

Fundamentally he was as much of a loner as Beryl, yet their common interests were nothing compared to those which Denys shared with Tania; this was Beryl's problem. For example, where he loved music, ballet and opera, sang well and played the piano. Beryl was tone deaf. However, given his need for space, sharing less common ground was to be to Beryl's advantage in the end for they were both free spirits, neither was possessive. Denys was happiest in the bush lifting his field glasses to learn everything about Africa. His relish for life was infectious yet countered by his determination of how much of himself he was really willing to share.

Denys served as Captain in the KAR in BEA, during the war and with the Royal Flying Corps in Mesopotamia. He met Tania on one of his leaves in Nairobi. She was the first woman with whom he openly flouted moral convention. They could not have lived together outside marriage in those days without being ostracised by their families in the countries of their births.

For all Denys's congenial company or his influences in other ways, he only widened Beryl's cultural horizons with one poem, 'Song of Myself', by the American Walt Whitman. Sometime during these handful of days that Beryl spent with Tania and Denys, he produced a copy of *Leaves of Grass*, which he had purchased on his last trip to London. That Denys chose to read one particular stanza from 'Song of Myself' for Beryl says much about Denys's sensibility, his awareness that their young guest could feel excluded by his intimacy with Tania and their eclectic choice of subjects under discussion:

'I think I could turn and live with the animals, they are so
    placid and self contain'd,
I stand and look at them long and long.

They do not sweat and whine about their condition,
They do not lie awake in the dark and weep for their sins,
They do not make me sick discussing their duty to God,
Not one is dissatisfied, not one is demented with the mania of
    owning things,

Not one kneels to another, nor to his kind that lived thousands
    of years ago,
Not one is respectable and unhappy over the whole earth.
So they show their relations to me and I accept them,
They bring me tokens of myself, they evince them plainly in
    their possession.

    I wonder where they get those tokens,
Did I pass that way huge times ago and negligently drop
    them?

Myself moving forward then and now and forever,
Gathering and showing more always and with velocity,
Infinite and omnigenous, and the like of those among them,
Not too exclusive toward the reachers of my remembrancers,
Picking out here one that I love, and now go with him on
    brotherly terms.

A gigantic beauty of a stallion, fresh and responsive to my
    caresses,
Head high in the forehead, wide between the ears,
Limbs glossy and supple, tail dusting the ground,
Eyes full of sparkling wickedness, ears finely cut, flexibly
    moving.

His nostrils dilate as my heels embrace him,
His well-built limbs tremble with pleasure as we race around
    and return.
I but use you a minute, then I resign you, stallion,
Why do I need your paces when I myself, out-gallop them?
Even as I stand or sit passing faster than you.[53]

Through Whitman's pen, Denys showed a willingness to defer
to Beryl's interests, especially rewarding to her in this case since
the poem touched upon a world of stallions, in which she already
shone. At any rate *Leaves of Grass* appealed to Beryl enough for her
to memorise that part of 'Song of Myself' which Denys introduced

her to in 1923 and Whitman was the only poet she mentioned until she discovered Kipling in her fifties.[54]

Beryl's love – which bordered on obsession as opposed to reverence – for the legendary white hunter was sustained through the detours lying ahead and ultimately brought them together. More than anything else, Denys's tendency to stand back undoubtedly attracted Beryl all the more to this strong, sardonic man, who fiercely guarded his independence. Instinctively she seemed to know, as with a bloodhorse, how best to inch toward him without making him shy away.

In contrast to the praise heaped upon him customarily by others, Beryl's reaction was touchingly direct: 'Denys? He half taught me how to live . . . I was with him very often . . . I was very young . . . he was a wonderful man, tall, good-looking, a smile . . . always played about his lips.'[55] Beryl thought Denys, unequivocally, 'Marvellous . . . his voice was soft and gentle'[56] and his impartiality and ribaldry pleased her as much.

At noon at Mbogani, whenever Tania had house guests, in a ritual instigated by Berkeley Cole, Farah, her Somali major-domo, brought chilled wine and glasses to a glade of *mugumu* and cape chestnuts, where she and her friends would converse. The lawn was vast, lending grace to an otherwise ordinary dwelling of blue Nairobi stone. From one verandah, and most of the garden, the view of the Ngong Hills was unsurpassed; their five distinct peaks, Kasmis, Oljoro, Onyore, Olorien and Lamwia, resembled knuckles on a clenched hand. According to Beryl, Denys and Tania pointed out Lamwia together as 'the site of our graves'.

Unlike with Tania, Denys never took Beryl on safari. She was content to accept his invitation to accompany him into town, noting already Tania's tendency to cling: 'She hated him going off on safari'.[57] Denys was to spend more time with Tania than with anyone else in Africa yet it was not enough: 'He also went off to visit friends by himself. She didn't like that.'[58] While Tania attended to what they would be eating for dinner, Beryl sat in Denys's passenger seat while he undertook commissions in Nairobi; Abdi, the younger of Denys's two Somali servants, sat in the back. Beryl explained, 'The Somalis called him *Bedar*, meaning "balding one" . . . when driving, his hat used to fly off. Denys would say, "Get that bowler of mine Abdi" and, if he weren't quick enough, "Curse Abdi" but the Africans adored him . . . He was very fair.'[59] His Swahili name was *Mwakanyaga* ('he who can tread upon one with his tongue').[60] Billea, his older servant, had given this information to Beryl – Africans were always to confide in her those things they generally kept to themselves. She could appreciate how fitting the epithet: his was a 'cold quiet humour which cut the air. Unlike many other *mzungus* [white men] Denys had no need to raise his voice . . . Africans held him in high esteem because of this.'[61] A rebuke from him went home like the slash of a razor-blade, so sharp there was no pain when it cut. His response to a cable he received from Sir Philip Sassoon, 'Do you know Buns Cartwright's address?' typifies his dryness: 'Yes.'[62]

When they returned from town and Tania was out in the coffee *shamba*, Denys would set the gramophone going announcing his arrival. Beryl could see how, after months under canvas, Denys regarded the prospect of running water from a tap and cool linen bed-sheets as attractive as good conversation.

It was while Beryl was staying at Mbogani that she first realised how sketchy her education had been as the three lingered with the candles burning low at Tania's dining table, and she listened to their conversations. She was aware of their usage of French and Latin, to give nuance or venom. Beryl knew nothing either about Greek gods, paintings and prose. Here were large tracts of literary wilderness. But it was not all heavy going. When Berkeley came to dine, they amused themselves, building Tania's crystal wine goblets into tall shining pyramids on the dinner table. Before retiring for the night, they usually sat at the millstones, one on either side of the door leading to the garden at the rear of the house, to smoke a last cigarette.[63]

Beryl retained a fairly dismissive opinion of Tania: 'She was all right. I can't say I thought the world of her. She wasn't my cup of tea, really. First of all she was much older and Tania didn't like the things I liked though she used to ride a bit, footle along a bit, but she was always a little bit sort of unhappy. She was always waiting for him to come back. Obviously she was a bad picker after all, two men on who [sic] obviously in a way, was [sic] dependent on them.'[64] Beryl's allusion to 'Poor dumpy Tania' shows her certainty of Denys's preference for her own youth and coltish appeal. Beryl probably felt that she could have taught Tania a thing or two about men and horses. That Tania appeared superior, 'set herself apart – not like Denys, everyone loved him' irritated Beryl and provoked her 'bloody women' reaction. 'The number of times I have lain on the floor and listened to Denys telling Tania about the classics. Of course she spoke English, but not in the way Denys knew, he taught her, imparted the knowledge which made her able to write books in English. He used to read passages from the Bible from the Book of Job. He would say, "No, No, No, Tania, not like that, like this!" – or if he was near, if I was writing a letter, I was quite illiterate you see, he would say, "No, No, No, Beryl, NOT like that. Write it out like this." Denys would make me write it out again. He was highly educated and could not bear to see things done badly.'[65] While Beryl resented Tania treating her like a child, she bore no such grudge with Denys. She may well have been seized with jubilation and fury in equal parts, much like a child. It was the essential 'child' in Beryl's make up that made her endlessly appealing, earning the forgiveness of others, as well as a need to protect her; many agree that in spite of the veneer of sophistication Beryl was to cultivate so as to impress Denys, beneath she remained a straightforward child of Africa. 'As she became older, disillusion set in, but somehow she never matured. In many ways that was part of her attraction.'[66]

Physically Tania was no match for Beryl whose own charismatic effect on the opposite sex can hardly have been regarded as luke-warm. But where she managed to hold all her other lovers in the palm of her hand, she could not do this with Denys. During her sojourn, Beryl had achieved all that she had set out to do: the newfound freedom to come and go at Mbogani with Tania's blessing, which she never put in jeopardy through audacity or insensitivity.

For the next seven months she trained for the Birkbecks and D, taking on a couple of Camciscan's progeny, two-year-olds belonging to Lord Francis Scott. Denys had returned to the wilds then, in September, re-joined Tania on Mbogani for four weeks. Beryl ran into Denys with Tania twice that month at Muthaiga among friends when plans were already under discussion for Christmas. He was on his way out with a hunting client but Tania expected him back before 'leaving the country in January' and hoping he would 'perhaps stay for Christmas' in between. Dependent on the whim of his immediate client Denys could promise nothing, except that if he was delayed, they would see in the New Year together at Mbogani. He was to take out a second safari before proceeding to London and must remain flexible.[67] Cockie was leaving for Europe too, promising Beryl that since she was going via the Cape she would see Clutt, and let her have news of her father.[68] Denys's plans and subsequently Beryl's changed. Denys, *en route* but too late to reach Mbogani for Christmas itself, opted for a few days of duck shooting, staying with Galbraith and Nell Cole, taking advantage of their standing invitation and arriving at Kekopey on 24 December 'out of the blue'.[69]

On Christmas morning Denys left with 'Dempey', who recalls the day vividly: 'We were up at 4 a.m. shooting duck all day from Naivasha to Gilgil. Denys was a wonderful bird shot. On the way back, the car broke down. Luckily Denys was quite a good mechanic ... The garage at Naivasha of course was closed ... so we literally parked his Hudson in the middle of the road, where the Bell Inn is today ... proceeded to mend the springs ourselves, wrapping the leaves with rawhide, which Denys liked to carry for emergencies.'[70] By the time they reached Kekopey it was dark. Guests were gathering for Christmas dinner – Berkeley Cole from Solio, Galbraith's ex-manager Will Powys, from the Kinangop, D, Tom, Boy Long and Beryl from Soysambu among others.[71]

It was during these few days together at Kekopey that Beryl and Denys at last went to bed together, allowing Beryl to believe that she now stood a chance with him. Denys's aberration, in the light of his subsequent behaviour, seems to have been due to a combination of wine and mood – about as harmless as accepting one chocolate from a box handed around during festivities. Beryl, on the other hand, seems to have felt convinced that she had found the right partner, really 'became mad for him' according to Cockie. Ginger's impression was just as strong: 'Beryl was deeply and passionately in love ... so much more beautiful than Tania and younger.'[72] However on 28 December, while they had been enjoying the bucolic delights of the Kinangop, Jock Purves had created a ghastly scene involving D on the steps of the latter's hotel.

One version of the eruption was that 'Jock hit him (D) and broke his neck for going off with Purves's girl'. Jock was plastered, out of control, and had intended to hit Tom Cholmondeley, not his father.[73] Details of this fracas were provided by Denys to Tania upon reaching Mbogani next day, as her letter to her mother dated 29 December shows: 'her husband, who thinks he has been trated badly by Delamere's manager Long and partly by the Delamere's son Tom Cholmondeley, and thinks they have lured his wife away from him, attacked Delamere outside the Nakuru hotel the other day, knocked him down . . . injured him quite seriously . . . He will be in bed for at least six months . . . for the sake of his son and Beryl, Delamere does not want the cause of his injuries made known, but everybody knows about it. Long has gone home in a panic as Purves threatened to shoot him.' (In fact, Boy was due to marry anyway, leaving for Dorking.) Tania went on, 'They say that Delamere is very worried . . . depressed . . . it is very damaging for the whole country, most of the political meetings take place at his house now' (the Vigilance Committee). Tania's opinion was that it would be better 'if Beryl stayed away from the races now but I don't think she has the slightest idea that in some ways people are blaming her, and how indignant they feel about Purves – after all Delamere has a special position here.'[74]

For all their discretion Beryl and Denys's conspiracy had not gone unobserved. Even if either imagined that their 'little walk out' was their secret, as Beryl had slipped away into the night with him, Denys certainly provoked envy. For 'Beryl was fantastic in bed' as two other lovers had concurred at Soysambu, while a third bachelor confirmed, 'We knew about her affair with Finch Hatton', regarding her as 'a bed-hopper, flighty and flippant, who would tumble into bed with any man who took her fancy [but] she was always up at dawn to be with the horses as usual.'[75] In other words, Tania had no need to worry; they were not overly concerned. The few who knew denied 'gup', as Beryl called tittle-tattle, equally certain that the whole business would pass, be forgotten; but her attraction had been fuelled, even though chastity was not her way.

By 18 January Beryl, knowing not a soul, but assuming that Denys would be in London before long, took a cheap passage home, 'about £60 for a single fare then, for an inside cabin without ventilation'.[76] Tania's description confirms this. She and Flo Martin, whose husband Hugh was Denys's friend, saw Beryl off at Nairobi station, feeling 'so sorry for the poor child, she is so boundlessly naive and confused . . . has more or less fallen out with all her friends . . . after that *shaurie* with her former husband . . . A year ago she was the most fêted person out here, now she is travelling . . . second class . . . only £20 in her pocket . . . will have to manage for herself . . . But she is cheerful enough . . . has no idea of the difficulties she will have . . . is very beautiful — but it's not certain whether that will help her or not.'[77]

Evidently Tania never realised that Beryl, like the lonely cat, would continue to present herself at more than one back door to get what she wanted.

7

Life

(1924–7)

Beryl's voyage was a nightmare and she was seasick throughout. She had never been taught to be thrifty and with a bankrupt's nonchalance reached England in a state of insolvency. The only people she knew there were Kenya settlers in London on holiday or in connection with political *shauries* – namely D's forthcoming confrontation with the Colonial Office. For six months she was to rely on the charity of such friends. She stayed first with Boy Long, whose new wife welcomed Beryl to Anstie Grange, Genesta's family home in Dorking. The weather was bitterly cold. Beryl had no warm clothes and for one who was unusually hardy did not feel fit. Genessee, as friends called her, luckily was as tall as Beryl and lent her country attire. But transition into the twentieth century in a northern climate was a bizarre contrast to the sunlight and stone age existence to which Beryl was accustomed.

Somehow Beryl got hold of the address of the flat Cockie had rented in Belgravia and, in early March, turned up one blustery afternoon, having trailed aimlessly round London, seemingly defeated by things over which she had no control. The maid at West Halkin Street informed Beryl that Cockie was due back soon and asked her to wait but she left and returned next morning. This time Cockie was 'shopping in Harrods' but now Beryl took a seat as she was bid. Upon Cockie's arrival, 'my maid told me that a woman had been waiting all day to see me. I asked her what she was like and she told me she was very beautiful and was wearing a badly hand-knitted suit. I knew immediately it was Beryl. She had no money at all; one of my friends gave her a lovely dress and I took her shopping.'[1]

Cockie ordered tea, exchanged pleasantries, passing on to Beryl news of Clutt from South Africa, but she also had to impart some very bad news which she had received by letter from Gerry Alexander, that 'Dickie Clutterbuck had died at Molo'. Beryl received this information without a flicker of emotion. It was likely that the cause of her brother's death was 'tuberculosis or malaria'.[2] Cockie, like Ginger, was not as a rule judgemental, but she was nevertheless nonplussed by what she considered Beryl's 'callous disinterest': 'he was her own brother and . . . after all, only twenty-four'.[3] In real terms Dickie was little more to Beryl than another jockey; as brother and sister, they hardly knew one another. Beryl could not grieve hypocritically simply because this was the done thing.

Cockie detected Beryl's penury immediately, being no stranger to poverty herself; her own father's lesson for self-reliance came when she was just thirteen. Cockie's mother was left only £350 upon her father's death. Since Cockie's two brothers were beneficiaries also, she, as the only daughter, was left without a penny. Their mother had been forced to rent a bed-sitting room and to share it with their oldest maid.

Like so many with little to spare, Cockie gave in other ways. Generous, merry and as pert as her name implies, her presence became vital to Beryl as she guided and assisted her until August 1924. She introduced her to 'the right sort of people' and given her understanding of Beryl's Colonial background, there could scarcely have been a more suitable guardian angel to steer her around those invisible tripwires of London society. Cockie was not only chic, a woman of the world, but unshockable. She did not find it easy to influence Beryl's sense of style and she also found her stubborn. Apart from hats and handbags, Cockie possessed nothing in her own wardrobe that Beryl could use. Cockie was petite and well rounded. Once when they were out shopping, 'the thing she wanted more than anything else was a pair of sunglasses with tortoise-shell rims'. These were not at all fashionable at the time and she told Beryl so but 'she insisted on having them . . . opened an account and charged them to it'.[4] According to the late Hilary Hook, an old flame of Beryl's, 'Money to her was like snow on desert sand.'[5] In London, Beryl soon got herself into debt. Settlers in Kenya used the chit system. Beryl, accustomed to sign for everything, never questioned credit. But then everyone she had known and every item they had wanted – from a martingale to boxed kippers – had been charged to an account. In Nairobi *dukawallahs*, sensing that a customer was going through a lean time, in some cases would not submit bills for years.

Cockie, to whom parties were the breath of life, noticed that Beryl lacked any enthusiasm for gallivanting. At first she concluded Beryl was simply shy and less gregarious than herself when she shrugged off invitations. One day, however, Beryl looked 'unusually seedy and complained of nausea' so Cockie cross-questioned her for the symptoms, insisting Beryl consult her own GP. She practically had to drag her to the surgery. Having examined Beryl, Cockie's doctor dismissed her on the grounds that there was 'nothing wrong, just constipation'. He wrote out her prescription and Beryl left London for Dorking for about six weeks.

Beryl distrusted European doctors. Even if she had had money she would have been reluctant to go to see the GP. She and Kibii had been taught by *arap* Maina never to trust *mzungu* doctors because they put someone else's *damu* (blood) into one's body; she was never to overcome childhood qualms related to clinics or medical personnel. In April 1924, Beryl's apprehension was confirmed when she went to London again. Cockie saw that Beryl's health was unimproved and forced her to go back to the GP who now admitted that he had made a mistake in his diagnosis: Beryl was nearly five months pregnant.[6] So she had conceived at Christmas. At that time she had had several lovers, so it would have been very difficult to establish who the father was, but Beryl wanted to believe that the baby was Denys's and told Cockie so.[7]

In 1924, an unmarried pregnant woman would dare to walk the plank between opprobrium and social prestige only if sure of the man in question. Convention did not matter to Beryl but the prospect of bearing an illegitimate child was unthinkable to her anyway because she knew that a resulting confrontation with Denys would put paid to any future involvement with him. Well-to-do women, finding themselves in Beryl's predicament, would not risk prosecution or scandal in London; they would disappear to Paris, where the unwanted pregnancy could be dealt with discreetly. However time was of the essence in Beryl's case. She was already 'showing'. Neither Cockie nor Beryl had any funds. None the less, Cockie took charge, reprimanding her doctor, 'You got Beryl into this, now you can get her out of it.'[7]

The most likely candidate to have bailed Beryl out was Frank Greswolde-Williams who had lived in Kenya and whose pocket was as bottomless as his heart was sympathetic to all women, and he had known Beryl since she was little. Once Beryl obtained the money, she was dispatched by the GP to a shady character, Dr Richard Starkie, who had been struck off the list of practitioners following a case at the Old Bailey in 1921. This *cause célèbre* left a number of society women trembling for fear of exposure once Starkie admitted charges for 'using an instrument with intent to procure a miscarriage'.[8] Starkie had been out of prison for eighteen months when he agreed to oblige Beryl. Cockie accompanied her to his rooms in Brook Street and during the short taxi ride, Beryl broke down and wept abjectly that she was about to rid herself of Denys's child. While Starkie performed the operation, Cockie waited: 'I was in the next room and overheard her cries of anguish when she had the baby taken away. The sound was terrible.'[9] Since Beryl normally never shed tears nor gave vent to physical pain we may deduce that her distress was beyond herself. Whether the baby had been Denys's or not, Cockie believed Beryl.

Beryl's estrangement in England from everything with which she was familiar was now complete. After the spring of 1924, she never alluded to herself as 'a child' again.[10] Beryl recuperated in the country, staying occasionally at the Longs' but mainly with Galbraith Cole's in-laws, Alison Milne and significantly Dr Milne – Nairobi's chief medical officer – whose daughter had been Beryl's bridesmaid, in 1919.[11]

Meanwhile Cockie had run into Denys unexpectedly in May outside Harrods in an encounter that she was never to forget and which confirmed for her all that Beryl had claimed. Unbeknown to Beryl, Denys had reached London on 7 April having learned that his mother, Lady Winchilsea, was gravely ill. His brother Toby (Viscount Maidstone) had collected Denys in his new Rolls-Royce from the Conservative Club, his London base, and driven to Lincolnshire; on arrival at Halverholme Priory, they found that their mother had rallied temporarily so, with no immediate cause for alarm, Denys began a round of visiting. Cockie realised that Denys must have been aware, through mutual friends, that Beryl was in London, yet evidently did not intend to see her. His clubs – he was also a member of Whites – those mysogynist preserves and worlds of escapist fantasy peculiar to the English gentleman, would have been protective had Beryl tried to make contact with him. Then following his birthday on 24 April, he had been whisked from the Conservative Club into St George's Hospital in Knightsbridge, for an emergency appendectomy.[12] He had just been discharged when he mentioned his operation to Cockie, who told him that Beryl had been unwell too. She got no further, meeting a barrier with the impact of an insect hitting glass, so abrupt she was struck by 'the indifference Denys took no pains to conceal'. His curt 'Really, I'm so sorry', passing on to other matters brusquely, made evident that for the moment Beryl had ceased to exist for him.[13] Cockie wondered if Beryl had contacted him and faced him with her pregnancy, for Denys's reaction appeared to corroborate Beryl's beliefs. Yet just as he would not go so far as to propose to Tania, nor did he acknowledge the lust that had taken him into Beryl's bed five months earlier. Echoing Cockie's impression, Ginger also noticed, once everyone was back in Kenya, how Denys put up his guard. He was to go no further in the months to come than the occasional silent, interlocking gaze with Beryl. It would have been quite out of character for Beryl to jeopardise her affair with him by trying to use emotional or any other form of blackmail; possibly when circumstances altered in her favour, she may have told him about the abortion.

Beryl's gratitude to Cockie echoed her reverence for Lady Delamere; likewise whenever Cockie's name cropped up, she responded with her sincere accolade: 'a marvellous character'. Few realised how close, or dependent, she had been on Cockie during that first painful summer in England. On Cockie's part, her participation at this watershed in Beryl's emotional relationship with Denys only fostered more sympathy for Beryl, who continued to go to great lengths to flaunt her independence and ensure that Denys knew what she was up to whenever that was possible through Tania, an effective medium who seemed unable to resist charting Beryl's progress. Beryl sailed back to Kenya with Frank Greswolde-Williams in June.

On 29 July, by which time Beryl, Ruta and Pegasus were already ensconced in the Rift Valley, Tania wrote: 'Beryl Purves was back again, dressed like Solomon in all his glory with big pearls around her neck, and as she was in the greatest need when I saw her last and nothing in her situation has officially changed, it was quite hard to know how to behave towards her. They say Frank Greswolde-Williams is paying for it, she is living with him anyhow. I'm most inclined to think it would be better if they got married, though actually it is too ghastly to want anyone to marry Frank. He was as drunk as a lord at the races.'[14] Before Beryl had gone to London in January, Tania was already referring to Jock as Beryl's former husband', implying that the couple had divorced. We have no date for when this legal transition took place. Records in Kenya do not exist.

Beryl was living at Knightwyck, Frank's cattle ranch at the bottom of the escarpment. Frank was overweight, as degenerate as Tania implies, 'a great boozer', one of Clutt's generation whose drinking companions were Jim Elkington and Archy Cartwright, Rose's husband. He wore a black eye patch to conceal the damage done in a shooting accident, in which he had lost an eye in his early fifties. Sensibly Beryl did not dally at Knightwyck for too long. Frank dealt in hard drugs, being one of the shiftless, upper-class Happy Valley set, and may be regarded as their puppeteer, encouraging their traffic in cocaine while they covered one another's wives and husbands. Beryl and he were together one night at Muthaiga while the band continued to play, as Frank drew a bag of cocaine from his pocket, dumping it on the piano declaring, 'There you are fellows, and there's plenty more where that came from.'[15] Beryl was often thought foolhardy, imprudent, generally criticised for not taking the cautious and sensible approach, yet she displayed all those qualities now. Extricating herself without discussing the whys and wherefores she rode north to Molo on Pegasus, Ruta like her faithful shadow following on foot.

Tania was not to see Beryl until April 1926. Until February that year she had been in Denmark – while for two months Denys occupied Mbogani – which is why she seems strangely uninformed: 'I saw Beryl recently, she seemed very happy, working hard training racehorses, I think she is probably very good at it. It seems to give her only just enough to live on but she finds it a very pleasant change from marriage. She looked fine, had just driven her car down from Nairobi along the most impossible roads where nobody would get through.'[16]

Beryl had had a successful and busy year, but had moved home three times. After leaving Knightwyck she had joined Gerry Alexander (Cockie's cousin), Master of the Molo Hounds, at his highly regarded training establishment, Westerland Stables, whose partner, John Drury, was a product of Hanover Military Academy. She had been given a mud and thatch hut to live in by Mr and Mrs Cardale Luck on Inglewood Farm, training their horse Melton Pie in lieu of rent.[17] 'Old Mrs Cardale Luck' was one of those Molo wives who, being childless, had Beryl to stay, hoping to improve things for her, deploring her exposure in adolescence to tribal life.[18]

Beryl was responsible for about twelve racehorses at Westerland for a number of owners besides the Birkbecks' string – the Stanning brothers' and one jointly owned by the Campbell Black brothers, coffee farmers in the area. Tom fell heavily for Beryl; in 1925 she was 'carrying on' with a young farm manager, David Furse, and did not bother with the diminutive ex-RAF pilot who was to achieve more fame, ultimately, as her flying instructor than for his own achievements in the air. Nobody but Tania was surprised by Beryl's success on the turf; in July Wrack took second place twice, only just beaten in the Produce Stakes and winning for the Cardale Lucks several times. Where Beryl fell short was with the owners, not the horses. She took the line that owners knew nothing when a filly belonging to Mrs Cardale Luck got loose from Westerland stables and Beryl was expected to foot the resulting veterinary bills.[19] Beryl did not feel it was her responsibility as she had been absent when the filly escaped the stable. The vet concerned, Billy Poulton, and his wife Pearl took Beryl's side, causing a serious rift by providing her with a temporary roof. By Christmas, exasperated by petty back-biting, she obtained permission to live on Nakuru Showground, her home when Tania returned from Denmark.[20]

While Tania had been away, Beryl had learnt to drive so that she could visit Denys while he was staying at Mbogani. Beryl had taken a spill on a motor-bike in Langata forest hitting the *donga* in the road to Ngong. 'Her accident had entailed a walk of several miles . . . in the middle of the night, with her nose streaming blood.'[21] It is believed that the Harley-Davidson actually belonged to Tania's brother, Thomas, who kept the machine at Mbogani for use while over from Denmark. Friends say that Beryl 'borrowed' this machine when visiting Denys, and was returning it before Tania came back when the accident occurred, always blaming the spill for the 'bump' on her nose.

From 1926 to 1927 Beryl's home was one of twenty-five stables, 'very rough and badly built with wattle poles under a corrugated iron roof', between the feed and saddle-room, at Nakuru Showground.[22] Once she had 'a few spare shillings' she replaced her camp bed with 'a real bed and a mattress', and, because it had no frame, placed it directly 'on the bare boards of the Steward's Box high up in the grandstand'.[23] The capacity of the grandstand – accommodating 750 spectators – gives an inkling of how the settler community and public interest in racing had increased in the Rift Valley since Clutt's day. Two strangers, a young Englishman and a Swede, Hjalmar Frisell, sought Beryl's company one evening, and the latter, then a budding writer, recorded his impression in a book: 'Our slim girl stood in riding boots and shorts against a gate-post, looking dreamily over the lake . . . outlined against the water surface with the dark forest in the background as rose-coloured clouds of flamingoes floated high in the sky.' Once they felt they could disturb her, she made them welcome; sitting on her camp bed, her guests in the only chair and on a bale of hay, the three shared a bottle of wine before going to Nakuru Hotel to dinner to 'change her loneliness a little'.[24]

If Beryl's desire to get close to Denys again had been less reciprocated than ever when he next left Kenya, by May Tania was also suffering his humiliating rebuff after cabling in code that she was pregnant. Initially she had written in April then not posted the letter. (He was at Haverholme, this time on account of the Earl of Winchilsea's ill health.) Her cable made clear that she was not seeking assistance from Denys, only consent. Apparently his 'tone of reasonable indifference' to the possibility, caused Tania offence and outrage.[25] Beryl happened to be suffering also from two quite different blows, in quick succession. First Camciscan died, which upset her deeply. She had convinced herself that if she had not left Soysambu he would have lived. Second, the Cardale Lucks had sold Wrack and Melton Pie, the latter going to Major Cavendish-Bentinck who left him with Beryl. But Wrack on the other hand, one of Camciscan's progeny and nurtured by her since he was a yearling, was placed with a rival trainer in Nairobi by Ogilvie-Boyle, his new owner, three months before the Derby and the St Leger. Beryl was furious. Wrack was her potential winner for the classics; Ogilvie-Boyle's action left Beryl with only one hope for the 1926 St Leger, Wise Child, albeit a filly by whose bloodline she set great store. By Wise Dove, out of Ask Papa, Wise Child had been brought into the world by Beryl. Clutt had trained Wise Child's grand-dam and grandsire, Gladys and Referee. Wise Child had broken down in the 1925 Derby but her owner, Eric Gooch, from Naro Moru, was counting on Beryl's reputation for 'difficult legs' to get his filly back on form. Trials began on B. F. Webb's course at Molo. Ruta and Beryl were optimistic; she relied much on Ruta's 'mystic powers . . . as a *murani*'. Based on their knowledge of the competition Wise Child might face against Wrack, Ruta told Beryl sagely, 'I don't know *lakini* (*but* . . .) I think Wise Child will win.'[27] Paradoxically, the trouble was to be that Ruta was absolutely right.

Someone noting their optimism had taken the opportunity maliciously that August to inform Gladys Gooch that Eric was having an affair with their glamorous trainer. A huge row ensued between the Goochs. Gladys presented Eric with an ultimatum: take Wise Child away from Beryl immediately or face a divorce. Gooch complied three days before the St Leger was to be run. The corollary to this public slap in Beryl's face was that Wise Child went down to the start 'owned by Gooch, trained and ridden by Sonny Bumpus'.[28] Sonny himself found the situation unbearably poignant: 'From the time the trap went until the post, I nursed the horse the whole way . . . I was particularly out to win because Wrack had been a stone cold certainty for Beryl, a cracker jack, then the bloody fool [Ogilvie-Boyle] and Gooch took her [Wise Child] also away from Beryl . . . left her high and dry. Beryl had treated that horse as her nest egg. When we got back . . . Beryl was speechless. Couldn't say a word.'[29]

Beryl's chagrin was inestimable as Wise Child pulled away from Restless after the mile 'and came in to win at a canter'.[30] She had been choked with emotion; she regarded that St Leger* as her and Sonny's joint triumph and showed her appreciation to her former classmate, whom she used to coerce into playing cricket, by commemorating the occasion with a silver cigarette box, engraved with 'Wise Child' and the date. Everybody on the course was aware that Beryl's training had made Sonny's victory possible. He treasured this box; in his eighties he would take it into his gnarled brown hands, running his fingers over the soft metal, damaged by the teeth marks of a puppy, reflecting, 'I got the ride, she got the glory.'[31]

In 1926 Beryl showed only her good-loser side, repressing the outrage, hating Gladys Gooch's victory over herself, the reminder in the racing columns, 'WISE CHILD WINS ST LEGER'.[32] Beryl never forgave Gladys Gooch for undermining her publicly, but then Gladys never forgave Beryl.

Things soon looked up in 1926. At Eldoret by October, Beryl won the Uasin Gishu Guineas, followed at Nakuru when Melton Pie won the Christmas Handicap. Charlatan, Francis Scott's runner, and Welsh Guard, on which 'Mrs Purves holds a very strong hand' brought more glory in the East African Derby, coming second.[33] That year Beryl had been irked by her mother's growing habit of 'turning up at gymkhanas whenever Pegasus was entered' and where 'Mrs KP sat propping up the bar as she sipped a pink gin . . . not saying much, observing Beryl from a distance' which was found odd since, 'They were never seen speaking to one another'.[34]

On one such occasion, while winning a bending race at Nakuru, Beryl met the Hon. Robert Watson, heir to the Sunlight Soap fortune. For three months she and 'Bobby' Watson, a keen equestrian, went everywhere together – Muthaiga, dancing at parties – and Bobby helped Beryl put the Birkbecks' filly, Camiknickers, through trials at Bertie Webb's.[35]

That March Beryl's betrothal to Bobby was announced: 'Engagement. Watson – Clutterbuck . . . between the Hon. Robert Fraser Watson, 2nd son of the late Lord Manton and Claire, Lady Manton of Offchurch Bury, Leamington Spa, and Beryl, only daughter of Mr C. B. Clutterbuck, late of Njoro and Mrs Kirkpatrick.'[36] Yet Ginger found it odd that no sooner had this news been digested by the Colony's socialites than Beryl began to back-track. Ginger wondered if it was a simple matter of apprehension, but then the notion struck that Beryl was not intending to march up the aisle. Her participation was almost a game, the need to emphasise her own desirability as a wife to an aristocrat, for the benefit of Denys.[37] Beryl was to use identical tactics again, so successful were they to be. Sure enough Bobby soon complained about Beryl's outrageous and continuing flirtations, asking the Birkbecks whether Beryl took the betrothal seriously. Plainly she had no intention of settling down.[38] Bobby was adamant. He was 'not going to put up with this carry-on'. Ginger recognised how it suited Beryl that her admirers had not heeded developments. At parties, she 'never beat it up', always entering a room with 'that slinky, graceful walk' making for a corner where 'she would sit talking quietly to some-one'[39] or, on account of her height, find something against which to lean, making herself less prominent. 'Within minutes the men moved in, surrounding her as surely as bees to a honeycomb.'[40]

Ginger's advice to Bobby now and to Beryl at different times, was to break off the engagement 'at once'. Then Beryl fell ill. She was already suffering a high temperature while loading the horses for a race meeting. On the platform, Ginger made Beryl promise to see Dr Burkitt for 'a terrible sore throat' the minute she reached Nairobi. The long rains were overdue when dust was usually blamed for a recurrent condition known by settlers as 'Nairobi throat' In the best interests of her trainer, Ginger cabled Denys to prevent Beryl breaking her promise, asking him to take her to his eccentric Irish friend, 'Kill or Cure' Burkitt. Burkitt's remedy for anyone with a temperature was to plunge the patient in a bath of ice-cold water. Denys confirmed to Ginger by cable that Burkitt had diagnosed tonsilitis. He operated at the Escateen Nursing Home, removing not only Beryl's tonsils, but also her appendix. When the Birkbecks enquired as to why he had taken such a drastic step, Burkitt's unusual logic was, 'it had seemed a waste of anaesthetic not to remove them both' [41] Beryl's mistrust of doctors re-enforced, she was also livid to have a brief interlude with Denys ruined.

Directly she came out of hospital she gave Bobby's engagement ring back[42] but carried on seeing him as before.

Mansfield Markham entered Beryl's life conventionally, correctly introduced at a dinner party held for him and his older brother, Sir Charles Markham. Mansfield was rich, sophisticated, stimulating and *au courant* with all things Parisian.

Mansfield had been eleven years old when his father died in 1916. Sir Arthur Markham was the first holder of the Baronetcy, created in 1911, a Liberal member of Parliament who owned collieries throughout Britain's north. His uncle's fortunes were buried in the steel industry, so Beryl's next husband was accustomed to immense wealth and Gar O'Hea, his mother, was described as 'a very grand Dame'.[43] Newstead Abbey, Linby, near Nottingham, was their backdrop. Mansfield was born there in 1905. His aesthetic preoccupations grew out of sickliness as a boy. He was not at all athletic. His best friend had been the gardener and gardening Mansfield's only outdoor activity. But he knew all the Latin names of plants, being nurtured on books and history, his home stimulating pleasure in botany and architecture early on. Mansfield and his two brothers 'inherited far too much money'.[44] Each received 'about two million pounds' when their father died.[45] Their mother, Linga Markham, was also left extremely rich; the boys were attached to her deeply, regardless of their disapproval for her next husband, a likeable vagabond, Colonel James O'Hea whom they judged the proverbial scrounger. Their mother had been coerced only because he threatened to shoot himself if she declined his proposal. O'Hea was fifteen years younger than she and thereafter was given an allowance by her. The boys, through ignoring his presence in their mother's life, sought to improve relations.[46]

Mansfield attended Radley and should have gone to Oxford, but tuberculosis prevented further education. Instead, this dark, willowy young fellow, whose eyes burned with the notable zeal of this disease, went to Switzerland for treatment. He was good at languages and, at only twenty years of age, was appointed Honorary Attaché to the British Embassy in Paris.[47] He was to become Beryl's Professor Higgins.

It was Ginger who had played cupid, entertaining the Markham brothers who were visiting Rongai for two reasons: first, to find a suitable home for their mother, Mrs James O'Hea, so that she could escape Britain's winter climate; second, to go elephant hunting with Blix in the Belgian Congo.[48] Gladys Markham accompanied Sir Charles who had been married to her for 'seven years with some conspicuous unfaithfulness on both sides'.[49] Mansfield was twenty-four years of age and had been christened after their father's constituency near Nottingham. The Markham brothers selected Kampi ya Moto near Rongai for their mother's winter home on the strength of her future neighbours, 'a number of aristocratic persons . . . there, at least two Ladys and two Hons with whom Mrs O'Hea would feel at home socially'.[50]

In the event Mansfield cancelled his participation in the safari with Blix, marrying Beryl instead. Her ability to buttonhole a potential mate for life, within hours, was matched only by Mansfield Markham's impulsiveness. He was not even looking for a wife when he left London, yet his desire to groom Beryl is understandable. It was obvious to anyone of that class that she had the potential to become a great beauty and was not making the best of herself. But all she lacked was polish and guidance. To transform her, to regale her with the trappings of which she knew nothing, indulged Mansfield's own generous nature when he had inherited so much money that he hardly knew what to do with it. Mansfield was to place the rough-hewn diamond into an Asprey setting. And for ten months, in keeping with her longing to shine in Denys's eyes, Beryl's aim was to present her new, *soignée* and improved self, accepting such effort – like training – as a lesson that she knew she required.

The whirlwind romance had taken place almost under Ginger's nose. She was non-plussed by the exercise. The morning after her dinner party for the Markhams, Beryl had left Mgunga, going ahead with the horses as usual for racing. On Friday morning she was nowhere to be found; the Birkbecks' concern for the welfare of their entries took them to the Jockey Club Headquarters in Government Road where they had drawn a blank again, but they were relieved to be informed by Ali, the Club's chief steward, '*memsahib* Purves has taken the cottage with Mr Mansfield Markham.'[51] Ginger describes herself as 'open-mouthed', not so much at the fast work, of which she was already aware Beryl was capable, but at how Mansfield had secured Denys's former *pied à terre* for himself, when this was booked a year in advance. A further surprise awaited them across the golf-course; Beryl emerged through the door, with 'glee' declaring without preamble, 'We are engaged. Isn't that wonderful?'[52]

Fidelity never being a condition of love with Beryl, marriage to the suave son of a coal magnate was part of her campaign to win Denys. As Cockie observed, a husband enhanced Beryl's status; once legally pinned to Mansfield, she was no longer the threat she may have seemed since her estrangement from Jock. Ginger's opinion of Beryl's point of view was that she 'quite liked Mansfield but was not in love with him'. The Markham family described the couple as 'poles apart'. Mansfield hated horses, could not ride and in Tania's opinion, this marriage was 'more of a lottery than usual'.[53]

Supportive friends had kept from Tania what had taken place at Kekopey – not so much contradicting tittle-tattle as repressing it, not so much disapproving now of Denys as sympathising, both with Tania and with Denys. Beryl straightaway introduced Mansfield to Tania, whose absolute authority on entertaining locally was put to good use. Her response to the needs of bride and groom is clear enough: 'The wedding took place yesterday and went well in every way – the ceremony . . . lunch at Muthaiga. Delamere gave away the bride, who looked so lovely – I had provided the bouquet of lilies and white carnations. We were 65 at lunch. Delamere and the bridegroom spoke . . . the lunch was excellent.'[54] Denys had been invited; Beryl had not seen him since her tonsillectomy. He was due back to refit before proceeding to Uganda, from Tsavo.[55] Beryl's only chance of seeing him possibly for longer than half a year now was to stay on Mbogani. That opportunity, too, Tania provided: 'I have had such pleasure in lending my house to my newly-weds . . . the climate out here makes everything like that easier' – referring to its leaky roof.[56] In return, Beryl insisted that Tania receive their double bed as a thank-you present when they left. Mansfield designed it, and got an Indian *fundi* to make it since there were only single beds at Mbagathi.

Beryl was not marrying for money; had she wanted riches, Bobby Watson could have provided abundant security, but Mansfield's artistic sensibilities were on a par with those of Denys's, as were his standards. Mansfield was also quite a catch. Mansfield was a born visualiser, he loved theatre and the cinema; it was he who had persuaded Beryl to try a shingle; he who chose Beryl's 'simple bridal frock of crêpe-de-chine with tight fitting sleeves, its bodice figured in silk and over the skirt was a long silver fringe'.[57]

Yet the wedding photograph shows a joyless bride. In fact Beryl hated this picture and is the one person not smiling. It is also the only record of her mother and herself taken within spitting distance. There are a number of characters present of interest. Tania in a dark tricorn is overlooked by the Best Man, A. C. Hoey, the tall man behind Beryl's mother, who seems well-pleased. But Tania was suffering a blocked tear duct, causing tears to stream down her face 'so unceasingly that everyone must have thought I (was) in despair at not getting Mansfield myself or plunged in the most sorrowful of memories'.[58] Mrs KP's stout and comfortable figure next to her appears on the verge of resignation. She had travelled from Soy, where she was working as somebody's housekeeper to give Ivonne and Alex a home. They are flanked by Beryl's jockeys, Walters and Hamlin, seated like them on the grass; their discarded terais are in the foreground. Whenever their or Mrs Kirkpatrick's presence came under scrutiny, Beryl could not help but feel uncomfortable. To keep away was Beryl's manner of protecting herself from any reminder of her mother's treachery. On the whole Beryl remained impervious to such stigma but undeniably at such gatherings it would brand her again. These elements were not conducive to elation and perhaps are the cause of her lack-lustre. In contrast to Beryl's indifference, Mansfield appears keen, his mouth is generous under the well defined moustache; his head, neat, the hairline receding. He was 6ft 1in. tall but Beryl's height makes his seem less because she sits upright; one leg is visible, pigeon-toed, uncomfortable, in its silver kid shoe.[59]

'They went off joyfully covered in confetti poor things,' Tania wrote of their exit to Mbagathi.[60] Denys had not returned from Tsavo during the week Beryl and Mansfield spent there. Tania, with other friends, waved off the trio on the boat train. The Markhams' 'unusual gift'[61] arrived at Mbogani that day: 'a lorry came out with the bed . . . it's as big as the car in itself!'[62] As none of her sheets or blankets were large enough to fit it, Tania's time was taken up finding solutions, mostly sewing alterations: a curtain had to be adapted for its bedspread.[63] Beryl's reconnaissance in 1923 had not been wasted. Familiarity with the pattern of the days Denys and Tania spent together ensured Beryl that her honeymoon bed would continue to be a conversation piece. And every nuance guaranteed to keep Beryl, the libertine, alive in Denys's mind during her absence, at Tania's prompting.

The bed had in a way been an inspired choice for Beryl's purposes. Tania was unable to find the right place for its awkward bulk, describing her trials with it in a letter the following day to her mother: 'I have had it put with its back to the window, and you can lie on it and see the Ngong Hills through the door out to your verandah.'[64]

Like a blackamoor Ruta accompanied the Markhams throughout their honeymoon. In 1924, after Beryl's return to Knightwyck with Greswolde-Williams, she had promised Ruta that one day she would show him England. Now it was possible to keep her word.[65]

Meanwhile Mansfield was happy making Beryl an extension of his creative urge. During the European leg of their honeymoon his goal was the transformation of Beryl, preparatory to introduction to Gar O'Hea, his beautiful but formidible mother. Like the Cypriot King, the sculptor in Greek legend, who fell in love with his ivory statue and married her, Markham's devotions were unreciprocated.

8

Life as Beryl Markham

(1927–9)

Beryl's honeymoon in Mansfield's hands was to prove as effective as six months at the best finishing school in Europe – a crash course in manners imbuing something of the aristocratic polish which Beryl lacked, growing up in a Colonial backwater. By the time she met Denys again the illusion of the *soignée* Beryl Markham, an icon which was to endure, was complete. Beryl now experienced for the first time the epitome of luxury. Mansfield chose gowns for her from Lanvin, Chanel and Worth. They stayed in Rome, at the Hassler Hotel just off the Piazza di Spagna, in Paris at the Georges V, in London at Claridges.

Before Mansfield left Nairobi he had arranged with the firm of Louis Vuitton to engrave the lock of a cabin trunk with the date of their wedding and for it to be delivered to Villa Veronele, Le Trayas, near St Raphael where they stayed before driving to Paris.[1] In Paris, Mansfield filled the trunk with 'the most wonderful *trousseau*'. Cockie was a little envious of the abundance of choice: 'a fur coat – five evening dresses from Chanel and Lanvin – I don't know where she wore them.'[2] When they reached Claridges, in Mansfield's Rolls-Royce, 'the doorman and porters, all dressed in their most emaculate [sic] uniforms . . . rushed to the car. Ruta with his usual alertness . . . grabbed each bag in each hand – the porters were horrified and grabbed them from him – Ruta was equally surprised that anyone but himself should carry our luggage'.[3] Ruta confessed after a fortnight in England that he thought that white people needed no sleep, on account of endless electric light. He could not understand how in the countryside stock could be left safely in fields to graze unattended. Were cows of no value?

As for learning that white girls could not be sold off by their fathers, for any amount of cattle, that there was no bride-price high enough, this Ruta could not accept.[4]

Wherever they went – Ruta in tow – they made a handsome, intriguing trio, turning heads in each city. Ruta's sense of wonder delighted Beryl. Like a lucky talisman, his presence kept her amused and brought her pleasure. She shared his astonishment at the Western world; they exchanged asides in Swahili, laughed at European manners, derided their absurdities, by comparison with African culture and beliefs, just as they had since they were *totos*. Of the impact of the Hassler, she wrote, 'Ruta had never seen such a building in his life . . . After Ruta pressed and laid out our clothes he was instructed to go down to the servants' hall for dinner . . . dressed in his Somali robes what [sic] we thought the most suitable and comfortable attire.'[5] Ruta found himself entering the main dining-room: 'the head-waiter, confused by Ruta's fancy turban and waistcoat, took him for no less than an Indian Prince and showed him to the best table they had and served him with the best food Rome could produce.'[6] Ruta confided later that he realised something must be wrong, 'but didn't like to say anything to offend anyone'.[7] Beryl and Mansfield were kept continuously amused: 'You can imagine our surprise and joy, when we walked into the dining-room dressed in our best evening clothes, to find Ruta at the best table . . . waiters were bowing and scraping and the rest were obviously discussing and wondering which Maharajah he might be.'[8] Ruta's aquiline nose, colouring and natural arrogance showed off to good effect in Somali dress.

Sonny Bumpus observed that though Ruta addressed Beryl as *Memsahib* (or Madam) he 'seemed to be on terms of friendship rather than that of master and servant', comparing his swagger to the Scots notion of 'having a good conceit of yourself'.[9] Where in Kenya it was Ruta who 'took all the rough edges off and dealt with people for Beryl' in Europe the role was reversed. Beryl's observations on Ruta reflect many of her own attitudes. She savoured Ruta's appeal for European females: his power to command respect among white women impressed her as much as his ability to get what he wanted from them. A recurrent theme and criticism among friends and mere acquaintances was that they felt Beryl had used them, whereas she sees this ability to exploit as Ruta's strength – a cleverness to be lauded: 'Though Ruta practically spoke no English . . . his personality and charm got him what he wanted in any country.' Her own dealings with others were often to be marred by the same skill. Obviously she enjoyed Ruta's new dependence upon her: 'The housemaids had an eye for his beauty. But Ruta never did like white women he was well known amongst the Nandi for being a great ladykiller and other *Murani* [sic] were in constant fear of losing their girlfriends if Ruta was around.' Because he was admired so greatly at Claridges, 'It was all he could do to persuade them to let him do any work.' 'He would come and talk to me for protection . . . If I was out would lock himself in his room'[10] against wily females. 'Ruta was an extremely handsome boy . . . everyone, in different parts of the world, remarked on his looks'.[11] Beryl adopted the predominantly African view, one which she certainly practised, that the more lovers one had, the better: 'There was nothing Beryl liked better than to creep barefoot into the bedroom of her choice at the end of a day's work.'[12]

Beryl's recollections of this honeymoon are light-hearted. She laughed mischievously at any misunderstandings or difficulties. She was always an amusing companion and was intolerant of those who were dull.

Before Beryl's crucial introduction to Mansfield's mother, he took her to have her first beauty treatment at Elizabeth Arden, to put the finishing touches to his almost completed canvas. Their maxim happened to be 'Treat a horse like a woman and a woman like a horse',[13] instilling in Beryl lifelong allegiance; whenever in London, through the red door in Bond Street she would go regularly for professional treatment. Nevertheless for all Mansfield's effort and expense, Beryl failed to come up to the exacting standards of her mother-in-law. Mrs O'Hea lived at Swiftsden, her country manor at Hurst Green in Sussex, commanding a great deal of space and needing a great many servants to run it. While Linga O'Hea and Beryl rubbed along, Mansfield's mother was the sort who automatically regarded any woman who earned a living as 'riff raff'.[14] Beryl took refuge in Ruta's company and, unlike a number of men, Mansfield did not feel excluded by their closeness. Introducing Ruta to the wonders of cinema she chose *The Battle of the Somme*, hoping to ease his incomprehension of white patriotism, but the image of the indignity of men in trenches had him more confused than before; to her unending disappointment Ruta merely asked if his father 'died like that'. To Ruta it looked as if the army was hiding; and the last thing *arap* Maina had been was a coward.[15]

The highlight of December was when Beryl drove Ruta to Newmarket, on the lookout for a new stallion for Kenya. D had Velvet Glove but he was no replacement for Camciscan. When she saw Messenger Boy paraded, Beryl decided to bid as he had an excellent bloodline. He was out of Fifinella – a Derby winner – and by Hurry On – unbeaten, 'the sire of the greatest race horses in the world'. 'A little martinet,' called Fred Darling was selling him. Messenger Boy was knocked down to Beryl for only 240 guineas, being one of 256 stallions to be exported from Britain in 1927. He was to prove most valuable to racing and breeding in Kenya.

Christmas was spent *en famille* at Swiftsden, where it became abundantly clear that, in the opinion of her new relations, Beryl was 'a country bumpkin' from a Colonial farmyard, unlike Mansfield who 'had so many other interests, that after the first flush of honeymoon they just had not much in common'.[16] Incompatibility was the least of her worries in this marriage. As Ginger confirmed, 'It was all over by the time the Markhams returned to Nairobi'.[17] Beryl was totally in control; this was clear the very afternoon of the day they reached Muthaiga, driving out in the yellow Rolls-Royce to take tea with Denys and Tania. Beryl would have been gratified to have read over Tania's shoulder when she wrote, 'Lady Markham [D was to marry her in June after her divorce from Sir Charles,] told me the marriage is a complete fiasco but I thought that they seemed very pleased with each other. Beryl looked well and lovely and I had the impression that she is keen on behaving properly and making a success of it.'[18] Denys was about to go to Rejaf 'with clients down the Nile'.[19] For four years Beryl had never given herself away in the company of Tania. Had she been less reticent by nature, less disciplined by culture, she could easily have betrayed herself. Envy runs deep in the psyche when inspired by physical desire. Beryl had sex with many men, she continued to sleep with Mansfield now, but she was after Denys. She was drawn to see him on any pretext, and observing him with Tania incited her desperation for some response from him. Hitherto she had felt out of her depth perpetually in Tania's condescension. Now Mansfield had enabled Beryl to change all this.

The Markhams, hoping to beat the heaviest of the long rains, proceeded up-country to the Elburgon district to inspect a property below Molo that Beryl wanted Mansfield to buy, which a butcher and a keen amateur horticulturalist was selling. Quentin Grogan, brother of Ewart, of Cape-to-Cairo fame, had a reputedly interesting garden.

Indeed Mansfield settled to buy this property. Most unusually, the place had no Swahili name; nor did the Markhams bother to give it one. Of more significance to Beryl was that whenever she drove to Nakuru she could call in at Sergoita, a failed flax farm owned by a Swedish couple, Ingrid and Gilles Lindstrom. They ran the farm in a muddled, open-house way and were generous to a fault. Ingrid's husband, went by the Swahili nickname of Samaki – dependably as silent as a fish.[20] Ingrid was a particular ally of Denys's, the kind friend who sacrificed duties on her own farm when Denys summoned her before his departure for any particularly long safari, hoping that Ingrid's company would overcome Tania's loneliness. Although apparently impromptu, Ingrid's visits to Mbogani were anything but coincidental. They were the outcome of Denys's elaborate attempts to assuage Tania's growing insecurity. She was never to realise that he resorted to such lengths, accepting Ingrid's appearances as strokes of luck. Denys's insistence over his cherished freedom was taking its toll on the idyll at Mbogani. Yet, if his patience was wearing thin, his concern for Tania still predominated, necessarily so, he felt, when 'Tania liked to use suicide' as a way of having emotional leverage over him.[21] Whether Beryl was aware yet of these manoeuvres is impossible to calculate but she had noted Ingrid's link to Mbogani if not Denys's motive. Ingrid who could not fathom why Tania was so welcoming – 'Tanne did not really like women that much'[22] – was destined to feel more or less the same about Beryl.

Ginger's observations concur. Denys was evidently attempting to alleviate Tania's depression, but his own feeling 'of suffocation through Tania's needs of him' was also surfacing.[23]

Beryl had been adjudicating Denys's movements with the penetrative skill of a Maasai tracker for so long that it was a way of life. She appeared to lack any fear of her own impotence – that private terror of not having the power to enslave Denys – but this very tenacity Ginger found as admirable as Beryl's discretion. Beryl had few illusions about herself. Her self-mockery showed a steadfastness which, even if unpalatable at times, had to be wondered at. She had the courage to admit that she was 'an absolute bitch'. Her cordiality to Tania was completely disingenuous, leaving no doubt that Beryl's at times genuine helplessness had not left her bereft of shrewdness.

The Markhams left Ruta at Elburgon to deal with the recruiting of Beryl's servants, to start the fencing and the building of a loose-box for Messenger Boy whilst they headed for Nairobi,[24] where at Muthaiga everyone was talking about the Colony's first flying tragedy which had occurred while they had been in Elburgon. JC Carberry's young wife, Maia,* had been killed with her pupil, the twenty-two-year-old Dudley Cowie while his twin, Mervyn, having completed his lesson, was looking on. Beryl passed the wreckage of the machine on Nairobi's original airfield at Dagoretti, as she was driving to Mbogani on the assumption that Denys would have returned from his Nile trip.

Denys returned on 1 April and was immediately preoccupied by his next client, the Prince of Wales, who was to come out with Prince Henry on a semi-official visit. Denys was to be taken up with directives from Buckingham Palace for one reason or another for the remainder of 1928.

The demands of such an undertaking left little time for anything else until December. Plans had to be watertight yet flexible for royalty. Denys's efficiency had earned him the reputation of doyen of the African Safari. Now he was answerable for everything from tents to ammunition, cameras to vintage wines for two individual parties going in opposite directions, the larger group with the Prince of Wales, the smaller party with the Duke of Gloucester. Beryl had never more intensely focused her eye on Denys.

In the interim April to June, however, the Markhams settled in at Elburgon; Beryl, 'engrossed in the horses', Ginger recalled, left

'Mansfield condemned to read out-of-date newspapers, to listen to regurgitated gossip in the company of exiles, to play endless games of second-rate bridge to fill the yawning evenings. Beryl loathed cards and refused to play.'[25] Their wood and iron home, standing on stilts, was comfortable enough, its tin roof draped charmingly in a riot of bougainvillaea, orange flame vine, morning glory; purple and blue convolvulus and passion fruit vine,* spilled over onto its verandah. It was all a bit too rustic for Mansfield's tastes. The only time he could be sure of seeing Beryl was over breakfast. Every morning she disappeared to meet Ruta at the stables – as is customary with racing trainers – returning after morning gallops. Beryl resumed training for the Birkbecks and was now also in a position to acquire the best horses in the Colony.

Elburgon is cool at dawn at 9,000 feet above sea level. The air sparkled as Beryl's string bucked and cavorted in the chill, and mist clung to the hollows. The scene was different from her childhood – thousands of acres of fenced paddock kept zebra and antelope at bay at last, where there had been nothing but bush. Horses from other racing establishments from Elburgon to Molo were out exercising. As the sun came up it burnished the coats of strong healthy brood mares, grazing or galloping against a backdrop of emerald pasture bordered by dense cedar forest. The area itself had proved a place to breed winners. There had been only one outbreak of the killer disease horse-sickness.

After supervising morning feeds Beryl joined Mansfield at about 9.30 for a hearty breakfast but the *mpishi*, worried that Mansfield was too thin and ate so little, insisted he ate extra bacon and eggs. Unable to contain himself, one morning he asked Mansfield if Sir Charles really was his brother. When assured that this was so, the *mpishi* expressed the opinion that all their mother's milk must have been used up by Sir Charles before Mansfield came along.[26]

It is impossible to pin-point the date when Beryl became aware of the royal visit, but since Tania talked about it at D and Glady's wedding it is likely that Beryl learned about it from Tania's lips. Tania had wanted Denys to escort her to this celebration in the third week of May, and her excuse to the other guests that he had not done so was that he was in Mombasa 'in absolute despair because he has been asked to take the Prince of Wales, who is coming out here in October, out on safari. I laughed at him for taking it so hard, but he says that I do not know what English royalties are like, or the *"fuss"* that is made about them. I can well imagine it, already now people are thinking and talking of nothing but this visit.'[27] Denys's commission was to cause extreme tension between himself and Tania, primarily because divorcees were denied invitations to Government House functions, due to protocol. Tania was now free to marry, but Denys seemed to ignore the invidious position in which Tania was placed now that Blix had made Cockie his wife, making a second Baroness Blixen.

The next time that Tania met the Markhams she was struck by the difference in their mood since D's wedding party. After lunching with the couple toward the end of July she wrote that Beryl 'looks ill and I think they are rather unhappy'.[28] Tania did not realise that Beryl had conceived a child, and was suffering the same appalling morning sickness that she had done before. A child was clearly no bond in a precarious marriage. Mansfield, dismayed as to what to do about the horses, had already sent for Clutt to return to Kenya to run her yard, which he agreed to do from September; Ruta would manage meanwhile.

The greatest riddle of Beryl's life was the identity of the father of this child; she never bothered to contradict widespread speculation that the father was royal. While Beryl was incapable of fidelity to any man for long, there is no evidence to suggest that she was carrying anyone but Mansfield's baby. Toward the end of August Beryl had almost recovered from morning sickness and was socialising again. She had told no one about her pregnancy, either in keeping with current social modesty or perhaps deliberately to prevent the news from reaching Denys's ears for the time being.

Denys had been immersed in preparations for TRH (Their Royal Highness), but he and Tania snatched a brief holiday, driving up-country together in his new Hudson. The time-bomb of Tania's possessiveness was ticking away steadily, exacerbated by the unabated fuss wherever she went over the royal tour, which was to stretch latent social tensions to snapping point. Tania acknowledged her snobbery: 'I also know . . . I am God's chosen snob, and if I cannot be with the aristocracy or the intelligentsia I must go down among the proletariat, or what corresponds to that out here, the natives, because I cannot live with the middle-class.'[29] Possibly Denys and Tania had argued over the ramifications of such things and over what Denys will have regarded as interference *vis-à-vis* the Prince. While staying overnight with 'the slightly dotty niece of the Duke of Marlborough, Lady Colvile, owner of the Gilgil Hotel, Tania confided in Lady Colvile her quandary as to what to call herself, 'now that there will be another Baroness Blixen'. Lady Colvile's reassurance, 'My dear, you will be the Honourable Mrs Denys Finch Hatton' had the opposite of its intended effect on Tania. She became pale and silent.[30] At Sergoita Ingrid noticed how solicitous Denys was with Tania. The impromptu party held for them also brought Beryl and Mansfield along to Sergoita. There were tensions which Ingrid believed were because Tania and Denys argued over marriage, 'Perhaps she [Tania] confronted Denys with it', for they had some kind of quarrel there, one 'which left a reserve of bitterness in both of them, to be tapped later' according to Tania's biographer, Judith Thurman.[31]

By now it was regarded as social suicide not to be able to do the royal curtsey. Ben Birkbeck had teased Beryl, asking if, like every other Colonial housewife, she had practised hers; Beryl's lofty retort, 'I bow to no one' might have come straight from Whitman's *Leaves of Grass*.[32] Every female was concerned as to what to wear and now Beryl's *trousseau* really came into its own.

The Markhams based themselves at Muthaiga Club for six weeks – the probable duration of the royal tour – from 28 September. That day Denys dutifully met the Princes in Mombasa off the SS *Malda* and, after paying his formal respects, retreated into the bush to complete the necessarily elaborate arrangements which are always an appendix to royalty.

On 1 October the red carpet was in place; Nairobi station was adorned in bunting and banana-leaf arches, looking 'like a flower show and a circus combined'.[33] The Princes' host, known as Uncle Ned, had been Private Secretary to Edward P, as his circle called him, in 1921. The plan was that after the Princes had undertaken semi-official engagements and separate safaris – long rains permitting – they would join up again, continuing overland to South

Africa so as to spend Christmas there with the Athlones. Their entourage consisted of the one-armed Brigadier General G. Trotter, an amiable old *roué* who was looked upon as 'a right old rip', whose function was 'to facilitate the Prince's pursuit of pleasure';[34] Sir Alan Lascelles, Assistant Private Secretary, and 'the most highly principled' of Edward P's household; Lieutenant-Colonel the Hon. Piers Legh, and Mr Edward Brook of 20th Hussars, the friend who was to hunt with the Duke of Gloucester; and John Aird who would join Edward P's party later, to shoot with Denys.

Beryl was presented at the Ball on 2 October to mark the opening of Kenya's royal season. Although Beryl loved to dance, friends say that she was 'too tall for most men to be really good'. She would have towered over the diminutive Prince and partnered the Duke in a more complementary way. Edward P's stature was that of a jockey; his charisma was said to compensate for his lack of height yet, though his blue eyes were puckered as if from laughter, those lines showed endless late nights and drinking and in repose his eyes were melancholy with a haunting wistful quality. He apparently suffered insomnia which was given as a reason for his late departures. No one could leave before he excused himself from any function. That night Beryl and Mansfield reached Muthaiga at 4 a.m. Beryl was on the racecourse two hours later to watch Cambrian gallop.

Among a larger knot of interested bystanders than usual, Beryl stood with the Birkbecks and watched the Prince of Wales holding on to Sonny Bumpus's stirrup as he cantered Cambrian 'slowly round the course, because Edward P wanted to run'. Everyone in Kenya was incredulous at the ferocious battery to which he subjected his body – a regimen of endless runs, a minimum of food and sleep. His official biographer, Philip Zeigler, concluded this 'must have been in part, a mortification of the flesh to assuage his conviction of his inadequacy'.[35] Beryl, in the grip of this physical marathon, suddenly found herself confronted by the Duke. Instead of making the customary 'bob' she flung her arms above her head, palms open, in a typical African salaam of defencelessness, greeting him with, 'Hello there.' 'From that moment', in Ginger's opinion, 'the Duke became besotted with Beryl'.[36]

That afternoon the Prince came second on Cambrian, and subsequently Mansfield was never to lose the opportunity to criticise him over the Duke of York Plate, 'The only time Cambrian was ever beaten was because Edward P was such a bloody awful horse-man.'[37] Beryl led Edward P and Cambrian into the paddock, under the begrudging stares of less fortunate women. One race-goer – Derek Erskine, a new-comer to the Colony – recorded how a 'tre-mendous competition' took place for Edward P's attention and that his entourage was often kept waiting for 'several hours' while he took his pleasure with 'a certain blonde'. That blonde was Beryl.[38] Beryl's *sang froid* and her conquests were to make her an object of enduring jealousy, yet her approach was so different from the usual simpering bids for favouritism. Looking faintly bored, with that hint of irony missing in the others, she shrugged off the *mauvaises langues*, aware that she could have given them far more to wag about. Her chief competitor during the forthcoming weeks was Glady, whose behaviour was outlandish at times, and to a lesser degree Lady Grigg (née the Hon. Joan Dickson-Poynder) to whom Queen Mary had evidently issued her own royal command: no divorcée was to be received at Government House. Glady, who was 'clever and suggests Elinor Glyn and sofas strewn with tiger . . . skins' never recovered from her success with the Prince of Wales.[39] Beryl took it all in her stride, attending the informal sup-per at Government House on the evening which followed the day of the races, and certainly by 3 October Beryl had established her-self incontestably as one of the inner circle. The night before, while partnering Ben, having initially seemed pleased, Beryl grumbled, 'The Duke is being a pest. How can I get rid of him?'[40] Ben was puzzled until it became apparent that she was adopting tactics used on Bobby Watson. Muthaiga was to be dubbed 'the Royal Waiting-room'[41] and 'Tommy' Lascelles was to find it harder and harder to condone the revelry: 'night after night sandwiched between "hi-jinks" at Muthaiga Club as the month progressed'.[42] So, as the Princes were fêted in the grand Colonial manner, it was as if Beryl had entered a revolving door behind Tania and mysteriously walked out in front.

Edward P's restless womanising marred excursions abroad for his staff. He was 'continuously in the throes of one shattering and absorbing love affair after another (not to mention a number of streetcorner affairs).'[43] The Duke, by comparison, was a much less complicated character, 'Much more sober, a better horseman . . . polo player . . . and behaved much better in every way.'[44] Beryl's trysting place with him was Muthaiga Club where, as Bunny Allen observed, 'more often than not Beryl and the Prince were together having a splendid time with a crowd of friends . . . were well matched . . . made a handsome couple . . . a magnificent girl . . . very feline. He was tall, slightly arrogant . . . a fine figure of a man.'[45] And while the Colony was watching, fascinated, open-mouthed at Beryl's affair with him, she and the Prince were also meeting at a bungalow rented for the purpose whenever complicated schedules permitted. Doubtless Trotter and a minion such as Tich Miles, ADC to Grigg, rented this house along a little-used track known today as Serengeti Avenue. The path ran along to the club boundary and the dwelling was put at the disposal of the Prince, where he could meet Beryl unobserved.[46] It was next to become the bachelors' mess for Gilfillan & Company, an up and coming firm of manufacturers' agents, whose young salesmen, in their unbridled admiration for Beryl, dined out on the fact that theirs was the house where she had slept with the Prince of Wales.[47] Bunny retains an image of Beryl strolling back from it over the green lawns of Muthaiga, as if taking the air, 'more like a creature . . . such wonderful legs for slacks . . . only just coming into vogue.'[48] She wore trousers with men's shirts and audaciously 'left the top buttons undone . . . took no care to hide herself . . . to attract some man who had taken her fancy'.[49]

'Security' in the form of top-notch officers of the Kenya Police actually checked and confirmed that Beryl was 'no security risk'.[50] Jacko Heath – another who knew about her passion for Denys – was one who vouched for her:[51] Beryl never gossiped or bragged about her conquests,[52] all she really wanted was for Denys to sit up and take notice.

The Prince's journals indicate how regularly he shuttled himself from Government House to Muthaiga – some five miles apart – despite an itinerary that was already packed. Beryl clearly enjoyed the cachet such company brought, and in turn her uninhibited manner can only have been refreshing after the type of fawning to which the royal party were accustomed. Beryl's own nostalgia

1. Beryl's father, 2nd Lieutenant Charles Baldwin Clutterbuck in uniform c. 1891.

2. Clutterbuck's mistress, Emma Orchardson, with her husband c. 1904. In the years shortly following her mother Clara Clutterbuck's departure Beryl believed Emma was her mother.

3 & 4. Westfield House (above) Beryl's birthplace
nr Oakham, Leics. The contrast with her next home,
Ndimu Farm in Kenya (below) shows the transition in
lifestyle which Clara found impossible to make.

5. Neighbouring children, the Powys Cobbs (mounted) and the Hill Williams with the Nandi syce c. 1909.

6. Beryl as Alice, presiding at the Mad Hatter's Tea Party, aged 14. Jock Purves, who married her at sixteen, had already fallen in love with her at this time.

7. Denys Finch Hatton, whom Beryl would pursue for 8 years with eventual success, at Brasenose College Oxford c. 1909.

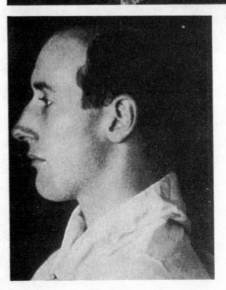

8. (from left) Emma Orchardson, Beryl, Arthur Orchardson and Charles Clutterbuck in front of the new house at Ndimu Farm shortly before Beryl's marriage to Jock Purves c. 1919.

9. Beryl's first wedding: (from left) Jock Purves, Beryl, Clutterbuck and Capt. Lavender, best man.

10 & 11. Denys Finch Hatton (right) and JC (Lord Carbery) c. 1914. Denys would inspire Beryl's love of flying. It was JC who challenged her in 1933 to fly east to west over the Atlantic.

12. (left) Mbogani –
Karen Blixen's house,
where Denys lived
between hunting safaris
and where Beryl stayed
in 1923 'to get nearer to
Denys'.

13. (right) Denys as he
was when Beryl first
knew him.

14. (below) Line
drawing of Muthaiga
Club, regarded as a sort
of Moulin Rouge by
non-members.

15. Beryl's and Mansfield's wedding reception at the Muthaiga Club, 1927. (Seated from left) Tania [Karen Blixen], Mrs Kirkpatrick, Markham, Glady stands behind him, Beryl, Lord Delamere.

16. The Nairobi Races, 1928, during the Royal Tour. Tom Campbell Black stands 2nd from left. Sonny Bumpus is left of the central Prince of Wales. The Duke of Gloucester is 4th from right.

17. Beryl consorting with the Prince of Wales
at Eldoret Races 1928.

18 & 19. Formalities pertained on safari:
above, the Duke of Gloucester, left, having breakfast.
Beryl is behind the camera, her vacated chair
in the foreground. Below, a four o'clock ritual –
the hunting party tea. From left: Jock Aird, game warden;
Denys Finch Hatton; Edward Prince of Wales, 1928.

20. The Kikuyu gathering in honour of the Prince of Wales' visit to Mbogani. Beryl attended the dinner held there for the Prince afterwards, 1928.

21. The Prince of Wales in camp with Cockie von Blixen, Bror's next wife after his divorce from Tania.

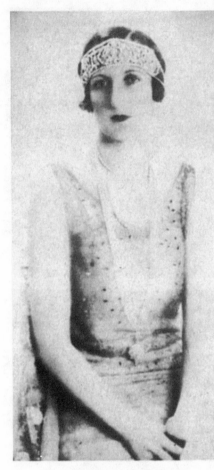

22. Beryl in court dress
for presentation to
Queen Mary, 1929.

23. At Rongai, 1929.
'Poor dumpy Tania'
claimed Beryl, who
nonetheless found in
Karen Blixen a fierce
competitor in her
affections for Denys.

24. The wreckage of Denys Finch Hatton's Gipsy Moth, May 1931, a few days after Denys was killed.

25. Enid, Lady Furness, whose friendship with Beryl endured 30 years.

26. From left: Woody, Beryl and
Chris Langlands on the steps of
Jack Schofield's cottage c. 1933.

27. The Blue Bird Flying Circus c. 1933, by which Beryl briefly
made a living. From left: Chris Langlands, Sir Ali Bin Salim,
Beryl, Sydney St Barbe and Sylvia Temple 'the Afghan Princess'.

28. The Duke of Gloucester in the year of his marriage to Lady Alice Montagu-Scott.

29. Seven-year-old Gervase with his father Mansfield Markham at Swiftsden, a month before his mother's record-breaking flight.

30. Beryl at Gravesend, early September 1936, with The Messenger, prior to flying it to Abingdon for her transatlantic take-off.

31. Beryl by the propellor of The Messenger just before take-off on 4 September 1936 – the pensive expression on her face is a rare evincing of her apprehension.

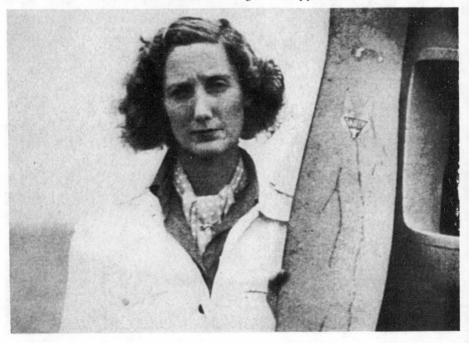

was unspecific, of frivolous evenings spent in the company of the Duke and the Prince 'dancing, dancing, dancing'.[53] Bunny Allen's interpretation of this light-hearted flirtation with power was that 'she needed to have her fancy tickled . . . by the Prince of Wales's feathers'.[54]

The day before Beryl slipped away on safari with the Duke, they all attended the races; Edward P 'somewhat uneasily' won the KAR Cup on Spencer Tryon's Merlin. That night the Princes entertained the Griggs with dinner at the New Stanley Hotel, followed by dancing and, later still, supper at Muthaiga with more dancing. 'A real hoo-ha occurred': Archie Ritchie (subsequently Kenya's Game Warden), a big strong man, 'had to pick up Frank Greswolde-Williams "tuck him under his arm and walk out of the room with him"'. When Derek Erskine asked why it had been necessary to lug Frank's bulk out of the dining room, Ritchie replied, 'Well there's a limit, even in Kenya; when someone offers cocaine to the heir of the throne, something has to be done about it.'[55] Next morning, Tommy Lascelles breathed a sigh of relief as 'a blessed calm settled' at Government House as the Duke left for safari on the Kapiti Plains with Bunny Allen. The Prince travelled to the Rift Valley where he was D's guest. Beryl joined the Duke's cavalcade at a discreet distance. Bunny was in charge. His vehicle had wooden wheels; the Rugby Durant, 'squeaked and squalled'. When it spurted water 'I put *posho* in, to seal the radiator up'.[56]

Camp awaited them on the Kapiti Plains. With towering Kilimanjaro in view, the site had family connections; the mountain had been a birthday gift from the Duke's grandmother Queen Victoria, to the Kaiser. The hazards of bush travel have not changed: it is always a relief to reach camp where the same routine is followed. The joy of hot showers, rinsing away the dust of a hundred miles, brought an unequalled sense of luxury, followed by chilled champagne at sundown around the camp fire – the prelude to dining under the stars. Although critics have described the Duke as Hanoverian – slow, stodgy with 'a whinnying laugh' – away from prying eyes he 'would rather put on breeches and an open shirt and gallop over the hills than receive the curtseys of innumerable debutantes' and clearly found Beryl relaxing.[57] Education at Eton and Trinity College had not deflected his intention to follow a military career. 'Harry' remained unspoiled by privilege and on this safari 'there was much laughter' and both he and Beryl enjoyed 'a good joke'. They 'spent a lot of time in camp . . . riding horses a lot.'⁵⁸ A photograph of the Duke pouring coffee, breakfasting with their other companion, Edward Brook, from Tidworth, shows Beryl's canvas and leather chair empty – while she is behind the camera.⁵⁹ Trophies were 'mediocre': the Duke bagged a buffalo, an eland bull and more ordinary plains game, but seemed content with his lot.

Before parting from him in camp Beryl agreed to go to London to be with the Duke. He must have asked her to cable her date of arrival, promising 'to meet her off the ship at the wharf'.⁶⁰

On 12 October, Beryl was driven back to Muthaiga to await Edward P's pleasure. Bunny was aware that 'our gutsy lady was well able to cope with two or more affairs . . . at the same time . . . and now precisely that, was going on.'⁶¹ While Beryl was camping with the Duke, the Prince, who made several safaris, summoned Denys to Soysambu to discuss schedules, the options for which had remained open, and Denys had been hanging about at Mbogani for instructions: by cable he was informed that an aeroplane was standing by to fly him to Soysambu. Tania drove him to the newly opened Wilson Airfield, 'the machine (was) ready to take off for its propellors were turning, so that Denys could jump in and start without delay. He was not allowed to take any luggage except what he could pack in a handkerchief; they said he was already too heavy himself.'⁶² Within an hour he was sorting out contingencies with Edward P in the Rift Valley; there is no doubt that this example of the benefit an aeroplane could bring to the planning of safaris impressed him. He returned 'most enthusiastic' over the flight.⁶³

Earnings from the royal safaris were to enable Denys to buy his de Havilland Gipsy Moth. Aeroplanes were to enable Beryl to share with Denys the realm of flight, bringing her rivalry with Tania almost into the open at last.

Edward P's decision to go to Uganda set off a flurry of re-organisation. By the date of Beryl's return to Muthaiga from the Kapiti Plains, Denys must have been aware of the possibility that

the Prince might announce that Beryl might be his guest in Tanganyika. Entrusted with the delicacy of strategic placing of tents, his
was the responsibility to see that neither Edward P nor any para-
mour could be intruded upon or overlooked; that they alone
shared a fire; thus the Prince was always placed at the end of the
line in camp. By the time Denys got back from Soysambu he must
have known that Beryl was the current favourite. Tania grumbled
that Denys 'would never go out' and that night he made an exception, going with her to Government House to see Martin and Osa
Johnson's film, *Simba* – Tania's first chance to meet the Prince,
who turned up from Soysambu toward the end of the screening.
Tania found him 'really absolutely charming . . . I am so in love
with him that it hurts.' By the time the Prince returned from
Uganda, his staff did not share her enthusiasm. The problem was
that Edward P would abandon any arrangement to seduce almost
any personable female who crossed his path. Tommy Lascelles was
exhausted, 'always having to be thinking twelve days ahead like a
harassed chess-player'.[64]

Though scheduled to leave at 1 p.m. on the Royal Pullman for
Uganda, setting off five hours late, Edward P kept everyone waiting, 'while he played one more game of squash.'[65] Beryl's assignation with him next was for Tuesday 30 October. Four days after
her twenty-sixth birthday, close to the Uganda border, she waited
for him at Kitale Club, on the slopes of Mount Elgon; she was then
to travel on the Pullman making its way back to Nairobi in easy
stages.[66]

The Uganda trip had been fraught for his staff. Trotter had fallen
prey to a heart attack. The load of extra duties affected Tommy
most directly; he was suffering from the recognition that 'no matter
how hard he tried, he could never make the Prince fit to be King'.
The burden of trying to keep the 'bad-mannered, selfish Prince
happy' was driving his staff to despair in continuing to uphold his
image.[67] Beryl had arranged for her horse, Gay Warrior, to be at
Eldoret for Edward P to ride. He won £14 for the five-furlong
sprint, winning on another horse besides that afternoon. Together
outside the weighing-in room Beryl and the Prince were photographed, she, wearing the outfit in which she led Cambrian in,
would hardly merit a double take. The pleated skirt of her woollen

suit adds to the heaviness of her torso; her legs show neat ankles clad in silk stockings; the shoes she hated to wear are suitable brogues. Their heads incline over the race card with a certain intimacy. Beryl was repeatedly referred to as ravishing, yet there is no hint of the siren beneath her felt cloche.[68] They dined that night with Denys's partner and his wife, Mr and Mrs A. C. Hoey, at Moiben, driving back along the rutted track to Eldoret Club for a Ball among an overtly South African gathering. Ginger remembers the disarming sincerity displayed by Edward P when he invited the wife of the leader of the Boer community to open the dance. She was monolithic, wore red and succeeded in exaggerating her height to 'about seven foot' by clamping on her head, three ostrich feathers in his honour, dwarfing him entirely.[69]

The next stop was Rongai where Lord Francis Scott and his wife were the hosts at Deloraine. Sunbirds hovered in the ornamental shrubs and Hadada ibis let forth their harsh cries above the formal brick paths. Edward P played golf all afternoon at Njoro, but a very embarrassing scene occurred that evening. 'The upper crust of Rongai' were to dine and, so as not to encroach on his leisure, it was agreed that they foregather at a house nearby to be summoned once Edward P was ready to receive them – around 8.30 p.m. The houseguests at Deloraine were still upstairs changing for dinner when Glady Delamere, seizing on Beryl's temporary absence, made a beeline for the Prince on his way in from golf, disappearing into the Scotts' garden 'for nearly two hours'.[70] Arrangements ran late. The guests did not dine until 11.30. And everyone was offended when Edward P did not bother to change for dinner.[71] Tommy Lascelles had by this time had enough, and while Edward P had taken himself off to play golf he retreated to confirm in a letter to his wife that he was resigning his post, and was literally sealing the envelope when her coded cable arrived, supporting his difficult decision.[72]

On 5 November, under cover of darkness, the Pullman began its long haul out of the Rift Valley to Nairobi. Beryl returned to Muthaiga. Denys met the Prince over breakfast at Government House, going shopping afterwards for gadgets, for which they shared a liking, intended for the Tanganyika safari. With Denys in charge, Tommy Lascelles felt that he could at last relax, 'I *fiche* myself of all anxiety . . . Denys has come on tremendously . . . was always a remarkable chap . . . I know nobody in the world who inspires me with more complete and child-like confidence than he does . . . he has organised the whole expedition down to the last sheet of Bromo . . .'[73] Even so emotional strain at Mbogani had brought about bickering over the Prince's safari and increased conflict in a deteriorating relationship. So Tania was pleased to be invited by Edward P to dine unexpectedly on the Pullman before he proceeded to Nanyuki, 'ostensibly for the local race meeting'. If Beryl attended this supper, Tania omitted mention of her, noting how well appointed the Pullman was, and how 'frightful' the meal.[74] As Denys and Tania were leaving, 'The Prince came up and said that he, Lascelles and Leigh [sic] would like to come to dinner on Friday and if possible see an *ngoma*.'[75] After midnight the Pullman, with Beryl aboard, set off for Naro Moru, below the western spurs of Mount Kenya. The first engagement was luncheon with Eric Gooch and Beryl's *bête noir*, Gladys.[76] To her chagrin Gladys was now forced to welcome Beryl into her home. Beryl's presence, her triumph socially, sealed in Gladys a lifelong enmity.

Tania's dinner party for Edward P at Mbogani was on the evening of the day Beryl got back to Nairobi. Tania's biographer, Judith Thurman, observes that 'Beryl was a sort of Circe' that Tania could not have been blind to Beryl's allure 'and it speaks highly for her dedication as a hostess – and her sense of fair play generally – that she still invited her to dinner, placing her beside Denys.' The question is, had Tania's snobbery eclipsed all else? Did the Prince suggest Beryl? Or was it Denys's idea? Or had Beryl persuaded Edward P to suggest the *ngoma* in the first place? One cannot help sensing that Tania was dazzled at the notion of entertaining the future King of England, and her own description supports this theory. 'It is such a great help that Denys pays for the drinks and cigars on these occasions; partly because it saves me a lot of money and partly because he is so knowledgeable . . . I think I can say that the dinner was a great success; the Prince of Wales said it was the best that he had had in this country, and Denys, that he had never had better, so all honour is due to Kamante. I gave them clear soup with marrow, fish from Mombasa, a kind of turbot, with sauce hollandaise, ham, that Denys had given me, with

Cumberland sauce, spinach, and glazed onions, partridges with peas, lettuce, tomatoes with macaroni salad and cream sauce with truffles, croustades with mushrooms, a kind of savarin and fruit – strawberries and grenadillas . . . I was "short" of one lady, as I had only been able to get hold of Vivienne de Watteville* . . . and Beryl, who was in Nairobi on her way to Mombasa and home, and looked absolutely ravishing that evening. I had sent a message to the Prince of Wales saying that I had left one free place in case he wished to bring a lady with him, but he did not do so, we were only seven . . .'[77]

The Prince was due to go to Arusha 'to find a lion' on 13 November and as Armstice Day fell on the Sunday before he left, the Griggs held a cocktail party at Government House on the Saturday before. The Prince disgraced himself yet again arriving hours late 'after dallying with a certain blonde of easy virtue',[78] offending the Griggs further by retiring for bed early. So as to meet Beryl privately the Prince shinned down a drainpipe from his window, leaving Government House by this less orthodox route, and was apprehended by the *askari* on duty. On account of this strange behaviour, he had not recognised 'Kingi Georgie's *toto*' and arrested him. Nor would he let the Prince go until he had convinced him that he was.[79] A wild evening ensued at Muthaiga. Tania turned up unescorted as Denys refused to go with her. Glady, as usual in a cloud of Chanel No. 5, a gardenia pinned to her gown, was equally determined not to miss a last chance of flirting with the Prince. Her dark hair was severe, pulled back in a chignon and, according to Tania, Glady behaved 'scandalously at supper . . . bombarded the Prince of Wales with big pieces of bread, and one of them hit me, sitting beside him, in the eye, so I have a black eye today, and finished up by rushing at him, overturning his chair and rolling him around on the floor. I do not find that kind of thing in the least amusing, and stupid to do at the club; as a whole, I do not find her particularly likeable and she looks so odd – exactly like a wooden doll.'*[80]

Beryl, five months pregnant, sat on the other side of the Prince; again Tania does not mention her or that it was she who left with Edward P. Beryl drove him herself back to Government House. He was to inspect the Armistice Day parade at Nairobi Cathedral and was in no fit state to attend morning service at 10.30 a.m. before-hand. Beryl parked the royal Buick in a secluded grove of eucalyptus trees above Ainsworth Bridge, in the hope that Edward P would sober up. The European milkman, just setting out on his round of Parklands at 5.15, recognised the Buick and its occupants, 'realising that the Prince was trying to sleep it off'.[81]

The Prince delayed the safari departure by twenty-four hours on the grounds that it was 'not propitious' to set off on 13 November. Next day, Edward P, Tommy Lascelles and Joey Legh disappeared toward Tanganyika with Denys, whose warning with regard to trophies was that 'Africa does not wear her heart on her sleeve – even for a King's son'.[82] But with Blix, whom Denys coerced in Arusha to help, the Prince bagged his lion, 'an oldish beast in good condition measuring 104″ from nose to tail tip' which was 'skinned by Finch Hatton's boys in about twenty minutes'.[83] Edward P invited Cockie to join the safari party, which was to have repercussions for Denys once Tania found out.

The safaris of both Princes were cut short: the King fell ill and although the first cable was sent to the wrong address and neither son was aware of the danger, doom-laden messages began to arrive. Edward P's party was halted in Dodoma station, wrote Tommy Lascelles, 'I remember sitting deciphering, with the help of dear Denys . . . the last and most urgent of several cables from Baldwin, begging him to come home at once. The Prince came in as we finished it . . . I read it to him, "I don't believe a word of it," he said. "It's just some election dodge of old Baldwin's. It doesn't mean a thing."'[84] For the first time in his long association with the Prince, Tommy lost his temper over this 'incredibly callous behaviour', ' "Sir . . . the King of England is dying; and if it means nothing to you, it means a great deal to us." He looked at me went out without a word, and spent the remainder of the evening in the successful seduction of a Mrs Barnes, wife of the local Commissioner. He told me so himself next morning.'[85] The Duke's reaction to 'Papa's illness' shows a different nature: 'I am so distressed . . . I am proceeding home as soon as possible via Cape Town.'[86] HMS *Enterprise* was standing by at Dar-es-Salaam to take the Prince of Wales to Italy. Edward P invited Denys to take advantage of the passage to Europe but, on the strength that he had promised to spend Christmas with Tania, Denys declined. The *Enterprise*, steaming at 27 knots, sailed from the Indian Ocean into the Red Sea, through the Suez Canal and into the Mediterranean, covering 4,700 miles, and reached Brindisi in eight days. Mussolini put two aeroplanes at the Prince's disposal, but Stanley Baldwin, England's Prime Minister, advised against the risk of flying at so crucial a time for the Heir Apparent. The King, on 12 December, just recognised his son before lapsing into unconsciousness and was saved only by an emergency operation to drain an abcess on his chest. The intention of Tommy Lascelles to 'have it out with HRH' dissolved in this crisis.[87]

How Beryl settled the matter of sailing for England alone at the end of November, not even Ginger is certain, but Beryl and Mansfield appear to have agreed amicably that this would be for the best. There may well also have been the pique of anger in her passion by now, a touch of 'I'll show you, Mr Finch Hatton, what you could have had,' particularly in her royal conquests. There is no doubt that her liaisons with both Princes were undertaken in the usual vein – all for the sake of Denys. Clutt stayed at Elburgon and would maintain the Markham yard until 1935. Mansfield reached London in January so as to be in the arena, as it were, when the baby was born, toward the end of February. When Beryl disembarked, 'the Duke met Beryl on the wharf'.[88]

Virtually on the doorstep of Buckingham Palace, with less discretion than was wise, the Duke continued his affair with Beryl. He arranged for a corner suite at the Grosvenor for her, where she stayed for the next five years whenever in London.[89] The Grosvenor Hotel stands next to Victoria Station. Its main entrance in splendid pink marble is columned with a central staircase over which gazed down from its cornice a dozen plaster lions. The advantage of the Grosvenor was that its foyer could be avoided by using side entrances. In the Duke's case, he reached Beryl's apartment by the staff side entrance into the basement and ascending the back stairs.[90] Ginger would never have witnessed 'the Duke making a fool of himself' had she not been in London for several months, unwell, waiting for, then recuperating from, an operation. Ben was unable to get their usual suite at Brown's in Conduit Street, taking instead the one on the opposite corner to Beryl's at the Grosvenor. Ginger was astonished to see the way in which the Duke pandered to Beryl throughout this period.

The Birbecks' involvement with Beryl's pregnancy had begun in July when she failed to keep an appointment at their stables and they had driven to the Markhams' to investigate. Beryl had been prostrate in bed, 'looking ghastly and vomiting a good deal'. Ben had not hesitated: 'We must get her to a doctor, she's pregnant.' Beryl had become 'very agitated' but was too ill to resist when they bundled her into their car, taking her straight to Dr Tennant in Nakuru, who had confirmed Ben's prognosis. It was then that Beryl 'flew into a rage and denied vehemently the possibility'.[91] Marooned in London for darkest winter, Beryl could not hide her now advanced pregnancy from anyone. As Ginger explained, 'People naturally assumed, with the Duke always dancing attendance, in and out of her suite, even going to the nursing home the day that the child was born, that it was his.'[92]

In the last week of February, Beryl reluctantly moved into a nursing home, 9 Gerald Road, off Elizabeth Street, not far from Eaton Square. Beryl later provided, for her memoir, a description of Coquette's labour as she was giving birth to Wise Child, a harrowing account which suggests a first-hand experience of a difficult birth: 'dreadful birth throes began tearing her insides from her body with sickening regularity'.[93] The notice published in *The Times*, 'On February 25, to Beryl, wife of Mansfield Gervase, a son' did not appear until 16 March in Nairobi. Gervase Markham's certificate shows that his 'birth was not registered for sixteen months, which delay (in English law) actually rendered the mother liable for prosecution. None the less an adequate explanation . . . was given to the Registrar General, who personally approved the certificate.'[94]

The reason for the delay was that Beryl's infant son was not expected to live. He suffered from 'an imperforate anus' and, as Ginger recalls, 'her baby had to have several operations to correct something amiss with his rectum'.[95] To be told that her child was imperfect must have been as offensive to Beryl as had he been born with two heads. The medical profession regard the condition as congenital. In some families malformation repeats itself down the generations in varying degrees of seriousness, but there is no history of the defect in the Markham family.[96] Therefore one can only consider the line of Clutterbucks and wonder about the foreshortened lives of so many males, who were not robust and died young. Beryl's baby required 'two operations immediately', indicating that the hymen-like blockage was too tough to perforate without anaesthetic and surgical instruments. Occasionally this condition is so drastic that colostomy is preferable to the complications arising from corrective surgery.[97] Nothing could have offended Beryl's perfectionist side more thoroughly than to have produced what in Africa would be regarded as a freak. In Kipsigis culture, midwives decided the fate of any child suffering abnormality. The infant would be placed on the ground outside the hut. If the baby was meant to live, it would survive the pounding hooves as the herdsmen drove their stock out to graze, *shaurie ya mungu* – God's will – and accordingly was nurtured. If it perished, that was that. Tania was shocked by 'quite uncaring' native women that September who almost let Juma, one of her servants, die.[98] But Africa in the grip of atavism bows its head to customs centuries old, by fear and talismen. And Beryl had come to accept such callousness. By such rules her son should not have lived.[99] When the time came for Beryl to leave the nursing-home Gervase's constitution was too frail for discharge; he was to require professional care for months.[100] In the interim, Gar O'Hea, wanting the best for her grandson, took decisions as he grew stronger. Once he was robust enough to be cared for at home, she hired a nurse to rear him at Swiftsden until he could be taken over by a nanny. Beryl was regarded as a negligent mother but, like most rumours about her, the accusations gained acceptance without being looked into. Not being maternal in itself was no sin. Gar O'Hea's was an act of clemency, the direct result of decisions taken with Mansfield to give Gervase the best possible chance. A weakling – and Gervase was never to be strong when young – had no place in Africa, and the stigma of having produced a puny son was to render it impossible for Beryl to come to terms with her own inadequacy. She was never to feel comfortable in Gervase Markham's presence.

The day after the announcement of Gervase's birth in Nairobi, Tania wrote to her mother, 'The Duke of Gloucester, who was out here, is said to be very attentive and attending on [Beryl] day and night and I think everyone in Kenya was counting on their fingers like Corfitz in *The Lying-in Room* to see if the child could be reckoned to have royal blood, but unfortunately it doesn't work out.'[101] Tania followed the scandal keenly, as it hummed now in Nairobi and London. Her novella, *Ehrengard*,* written under her pseudonym, Isak Dinesen, and published toward the end of her life, could well have been inspired by this scandal. The heroine, Ehrengard, reflects Beryl's character intrinsically; the plot concerns the birth of a child which could threaten the line of succession to the throne, depending on the date of its arrival. A ruling family in an eighteenth-century imaginary principality of Germany is disturbed when the Prince discovers that his child's arrival is two months too soon for propriety 'on which the whole matter turned'. The qualities of a 'trusty factotum' 'Herr Cazotte' mirror those of Denys. Ultimately Cazotte is Ehrengard's seducer. Tania's story seems to be a transmutation of what took place between Beryl and the Princes in 1928. It is a fable where, above all, the royal name must be protected.

In the novella where Cazotte describes Ehrengard, it could as easily be Denys discussing Beryl, in 1923 at Mbogani with Tania: 'All marble she is not . . . She has fire enough in her for an artillery charge . . . I might seduce her, for she is impulsive and unreflecting, in a particularly impulsive moment . . . And Madame, it would mean nothing.' Cazotte 'found that the girl had read little and lent her books from his exclusive library or read to her, in the shade of the big trees. Poetry, new to her, puzzled and fascinated her . . . Cazotte had a voice . . . for reciting . . . had often been asked to read by *beaux esprits*. . . would lower the book . . . with his finger in it . . . go on reciting . . . his eyes fixed on the treetops . . . he was silent for a while, the girl was silent with him . . . her face very young still. "A penny for your thoughts my Lady Ehrengard." She looked at him. "I was not", after a pause she answered gravely, "really thinking about anything at all" . . . no doubt here, as ever, she was speaking the truth.'[102] But in real life, the birth date of Beryl's alleged royal child precludes any breach of propriety regarding Gervase's paternity: he was conceived before either Prince met Beryl.

By mid-March when Beryl was at the Grosvenor once more,

'The Duke was more or less living openly with her . . . champagne flowed . . . parties were held in her suite' and Ginger noticed that, for the first time, the Duke was drinking excessively. It was well known that he 'got into hot water with his mother over Beryl' and equally well known that Edward P was 'delighted that for once, Queen Mary's blue-eyed boy, was in trouble instead of himself'.[103] The Duke was now to be moved about with pawn-like accuracy for the next three years, as a precaution against anything more permanent with Beryl. In fact she was the last courtesan to worry about. But his mother was not to realise this. Queen Mary informed her staff that the Duke would perform his first ambassadorial duty and present the order of the Garter to young Emperor Hirohito.[104] Within a month to the day of Gervase's birth the Duke was on his way to Japan. To mark their parting on 24 March, Beryl gave him a silver cigarette case, engraved in her hand, 'From Beryl. A sad day after many happy times'. Upon his death in 1974 this, and another keepsake, a pair of gold cufflinks, were delivered back into her hands by a Clutterbuck relative – a total stranger.[105] In 1942 when the Duke learned of the Japanese attack on Pearl Harbor, he commented bitterly, 'To think that they made me travel ten thousand miles to give the Garter to that damned Mikado.'[106]

Beryl stayed in London until the end of 1929, and while she saw Edward P intermittently, and observed his plans for a second safari with Denys, at Court she was described as 'the Duke of Gloucester's love'.[107] Meanwhile came the extraordinary confrontation between the Markham brothers and the Palace.[108] Mansfield had 'unearthed a bundle of letters from the Duke to Beryl' which could only have been lifted from her bureau at the Grosvenor. Beryl created a scene which developed into a huge row with him and Charles at their house in Connaught Square. Sir Charles, as titular head of the family, now threatened to blow the whole affair with the Duke wide open, citing him as co-respondent in divorce 'unless the Duke took care of Beryl'.[109] Gar O'Hea pursued this action in May, when she presented Beryl to Queen Mary.[110] There could never have been a reason for Beryl to be presented – she was a twice-married commoner – when divorced persons were unacceptable in the Royal Enclosure at Ascot. Whether the Markhams intended to exert the necessary pressure psychologically, by parading her, is open to speculation. As Ginger points out, Beryl would never have instigated the presentation.[111] Yet on 10 May, Beryl came face to face with Queen Mary clad in all the trappings.[112] Beryl is barely recognisable in her white satin gown and long gloves. She is overweight still from confinement; her face is stolid. Her eyes lack sparkle. The lids, down-tilted, seem to emphasise her nose. Her mouth is hard, outlined in lipstick. The Prince of Wales plumes, from which her veil was suspended, *de rigeur* for presentation, are just visible. Not a jot of the flirtatious creature, the inscrutable, unknowable, mysterious and eternally feminine woman who was to continue to attract men from far and wide, can be detected.

Shortly afterwards, the Markhams 'threatened to cite the Duke of Gloucester. Rollo [well-known divorce lawyer of that period] went to the Palace. Said they had two days to settle. Duke settled a large sum on Beryl. The date was 1929.'[113] In the event, no petition was lodged, possibly thanks to the advice of Cockie's brother, Sir Ulick Alexander, Keeper of the Privy Purse. Queen Mary summoned Sir Charles Markham and had it pointed out unequivocally that 'one simply could not cite a Prince of the Blood in a divorce petition'.[114] Mansfield was also summoned. Queen Mary did not even invite him to sit down. He was lectured for 'over five minutes before being curtly dismissed'. Mansfield felt that he had been 'treated like dirt by the fearsome old lady' saying so and admitting that he was 'terrified of her'.[115]

Arrangements took time and contractually the matter was resolved in December. Cockie maintained always that 'Old Queen Mary opened her purse-strings' whereas Beryl's authorised biography states that the Duke himself provided her stipend.[116] The capital sum of £15,000 was used to create a trust fund, based on bonds with a fixed-rate return, providing Beryl with an annuity of £500. This was paid regularly into her account from the end of 1929 until her death in August 1986, and was administered by London solicitors. The Duke's name did not appear on the contract, but his handwriting on the reverse of the document 'makes it clear that it was Prince Henry who had provided the necessary funds' and this 'annuity is traceable to a single source'[117] Much nonsense continued to be talked over Beryl's son. Much was speculative, false and unfair. Later on Colonel O'Hea carried the child's photograph around in his wallet, producing it as his own entrée into society, falsely perpetuating the myth.

Life with Denys

(1929–31)

Beryl played the role of courtesan unerringly all summer. True, neither Prince was married, but had her involvement with either of them been known, the complications with Freda Dudley Ward and Thelma Furness – favourites at the same time – would have been hideous. Had Beryl been the type she was branded, often with extravagant scorn by women, the upright face of the Monarchy would have been exceedingly red at a time when the Heir Apparent threatened all that his parents stood for.

While the Duke was out of London, Beryl's meeting-place with Edward P was the Royal Aero Club in Piccadilly. She admitted that 'The Royal Aero Club fixed up a lot of things for me', obliquely alluding to the secrecy required for these liaisons. Intermittently Edward P arrived by the rear entrance to the club, buying up entire cartloads of white flowers for Beryl when their meeting coincided with those three days during the week when an old man sold flowers from a trap there, drawn by a Shetland pony.[1] The ritual has been mistakenly attributed in the past to Beryl's association with the Duke. In his seventies, Wing Commander 'Jacko' Heath, his bold black eye-patch adding to his saurian, hermit image, lived with his memories on the Kenya coast, marvelling still at Beryl's audacity and the persuasive vulnerability that was her camouflage. Among Jacko Heath's treasured letters, diaries and photographs padlocked in a trunk were 'pictures of the little pug that the Prince gave to Beryl, with a little coat and collar bearing the Duke's crest and racing colours, to keep her company in the solitude of her suite at the Grosvenor'.[2] Jacko had not only acted as a sort of security guard in Nairobi, but in London as well, keeping an eye on proceedings. In 1929 he was called upon to dispose of a roll of film when a member of the Press caught Beryl with the Prince as they were either leaving or entering the Royal Aero Club. The film was promptly removed from the camera by one of the Prince's aides and Jacko was instructed to ditch it in Regent's Canal, which he duly did, but an ill-wisher threatened to dredge for this roll of celluloid.[3] It would not be the last time in Beryl's presence that film was confiscated on the spot on Edward P's instructions.

Unlike the King, Edward P, with so public a role, soon found that the camera could be an enemy; he loved danger and Beryl represented it – the more so, somehow, for coming from Africa. It was her 'delicious recklessness' that appealed to men deprived of spontaneity.

Gossip had not been entirely curbed; the inner circle at Court was select but resembled an isolated village in microcosm. The men knew enough to chit chat in their Clubs, and to drop the odd hint to their wives. Certain women were regarded as necessities at court, and referred to as 'respectable whores'.[4] Beryl, keeping her council as one of the *demi-monde*, never let others know for certain how far she was included in this bracket. The women who sneered, priding themselves on their own respectability, were jealous of her success, not daring to tread the same course yet hating her for being liked so well.

Then Royalty had decided to 'dine out' and for the first time the Princes were prey to Fleet Street. Where it had not been possible before, Edward P was seen about with Thelma, Lady Furness, wife of the owner of the Furness-Withy shipping line; this vital, dark-haired American also had a young child, but that did not stop the Prince's eye wandering in her direction, no more than it had in Beryl's and, until Wallis Simpson took Thelma's place in Edward P's life, his promiscuity continued unchallenged. On one occasion, Beryl was sneaked into Buckingham Palace – either to meet the Duke or the Prince, though the brazenness suggests the latter – possibly for a bet. While Beryl was there, the Queen made an impromptu call upon her son; Beryl hid behind a folding screen until Her Majesty departed.[5]

To the man in the street, the Prince of Wales, aged thirty-five, had enormous charm to commend him; his courage to speak out endeared him to every class of society. Two themes – an impassioned speech on the miners, the other on unemployment – upheld him in his rejection of puritanical restrictions. Alas, as the summer of 1929 wore on, no one at Court was any longer convinced that he should sit upon the throne of England.

In London at this time, the general spirit of the jazz era prevailed but to most upper-class Britons the very word 'American' evoked pejorative connotations. Women had been given the vote the year before, bobbed their hair, smoked in public and drank cocktails. The group among whom the chief protagonists moved was not approved of by Queen Mary, to whom Beryl was already very much *persona non grata*. It is hardly surprising that Buckingham Palace disapproved of such influences on the Princes when a climate of great puritanism prevailed too. In June, Ramsay Mac-Donald had replaced Stanley Baldwin as Prime Minister; Britain exchanged Conservatism for Socialism. The Church of England was attempting to gain more followers as King George, now recovered, led the country with Queen Mary in a dull, orderly routine by which their subjects felt reassured.

Meanwhile by night, the clubs patronised by royalty at this time were Quaglinos, the Kit Kat and the Ambassador, and the smartest place to be seen after the Embassy, the Prince's favourite spot, was the Café de Paris in Coventry Street – a regular haunt of Beryl's and the Duke with whom she went 'dancing, dancing, dancing.'[6] There and at the Embassy gossip columnists lurked nightly in search of new material. Beryl moved assuredly now with those hand-picked for Ascot, Henley and Sandringham and, like her royal admirers, her inclinations were for the fast-moving Anglo-American Bohemians who were mistrusted by Buckingham Palace, with their tendency to flit between continents with the ease of migrating flocks. They included the Cunard sisters, Emerald and Nancy, Thelma Furness and her identical twin, Gloria Vanderbilt, the Astors, Iris Tree (Denys's former girl friend) and her extremely handsome photographer husband, Curtis Moffat, and Belle and Kermit Roosevelt, the latter a great friend of Denys's with whom he had served in the War, and Denys's sister-in-law, Margaretta, Countess Winchilsea.[7]

And now in the second half of 1929, to Beryl's joy, Denys

unexpectedly appeared in their midst. He was in London to renew his pilot's licence, a brushing-up process at Croydon which was to last for nearly five months. The justification for so long an absence from Kenya served also as a dignified alibi for Tania. Tania's covetousness was explicit enough now for Denys to have resolved to extract himself from the *modus vivendi* at Mbogani. Continuing financial losses and *shauries* over the destiny of the coffee farm consumed Tania's waking hours, but she stubbornly refused to accept advice to cut her losses, clinging to her dream of harvesting a bumper crop, when the location of Mbogani had proven unsuited for coffee. By now Denys had decided that he could not throw good money after bad in further loans. For nearly ten years, Denys had believed that Tania was exceptional, the one woman to whom he would return – indeed his evasion of Beryl upheld this.[8] In Nairobi Tania and he were regarded as a couple. Even so, to be his legal partner was still Tania's dearest wish. Their affair had been founded upon two ideals, 'I will not let thee go, except thou bless me' and Shelly's stanza, exacting, misquoted by Tania, but perfectly understood:

> You must turn your mournful ditty
> To a merry measure.
> I will never come for pity,
> I will come for pleasure.

But after all these years, Kenya friends sensed between the pair a tension which they did not want to see. Denys was ready for change; his decision to buy his own aeroplane would point the way for Beryl.

Beryl and Denys shared an addiction for action which Tania never had to the same extent. Those rides with her on the Athi Plains in 1923 had shown Beryl how nervous Tania was of Rouge, unlike herself not quite in control. It was in Beryl's nature to despise wimpishness; she was a Valkyrie in comparison. Her opinion of Tania's equestrian abilities was that of an adversary, a retaliation provoked by Tania's exclusion of Beryl from the literary world which she and Denys shared and where she dominated. Fearlessness and dominance over the most savage of stallions was

Beryl's regime and her pride.[9] She would exchange the Turf for the air. The sky itself, an element she would dominate one day, was to provide Beryl's solution – one arena which Tania could neither enter nor compete in. Beryl's companions played their part. Edward P and the Duke, encouraged by Denys, were as engrossed as he in the rich man's latest fancy – flying. Three of the princes were already taking lessons. Edward P, Prince George and the Duke made headlines for newspapers, but when they wanted to become pilots, it caused difficulties. The King and Queen were apprehensive that if their sons used RAF machines there would be criticism. Sympathetic intervention by Lord Thomson, the new Labour Government's Secretary for Air, resolved the matter: landing strips were being made at Sunningdale and Windsor.

Denys's own days that summer were divided between flying hours at Croydon, socialising from his London base, the Conservative Club, and continuing a campaign already begun – to have the Serengeti declared a protected area for wildlife. Whether Beryl got closer to Denys privately in those months of sharing English soil is impossible to say. He certainly made no attempt to avoid her socially now. Meanwhile his crusade, lobbied daily in the national press, enlisted his most powerful ally, the Prince of Wales.

Denys's fear for the decimation of the game was something he never stopped talking about that year. He promoted the alternative of shooting with a camera rather than a gun in an urgent need to protect elephant, pressing for rhino and giraffe as well to be classed as royal game. Until now, the only animals that were photographed were dead animals, mostly with the marksman's foot placed smugly on the head of the trophy. Thanks to the Prince of Wales's support, Denys's cause would be debated in the House of Lords; the matter was to be gazetted in November and the Serengeti was subsequently proclaimed a reserve.[10]

When Beryl noticed Denys's flirtation with his glamorous sister-in-law Margaretta, Countess of Winchilsea, in London in 1929, she was encouraged by hope rather than cast down by jealousy: she could sense that Denys's fidelity to Tania was waning, an impression reinforced by news from Nairobi that Denys had fathered the child of an Indian girl living there.[11] Realising Denys's commitment to Tania was breaking down and having no scruples where the older woman was concerned, her purpose became annihilation of a rival female. The longer it took the more ruthless her attitude became, the more significant each small advance.

Ginger confirms that Tania's engulfing *shauries* had reached the stage that Denys 'no longer wanted to know', but that despite a refusal to commit himself for life, he was 'so charming that he was impossible to be angry with, but he was selfish'. It was also true to say that when he had had enough 'of what he wanted . . . with women, that was that. He used his charm to get what he wanted.'[12] Denys had clearly been brooding over the question of whether or not he should leave Mbogani, confessing as much to Rose Cartwright. Rose triggered Denys off on the subject of wedlock, seeking advice over lunch from him about her own disastrous marriage to the hard-drinking Algy. They had just been up for a 'flip' at Croydon, stopping on their way into town. Denys's views on marriage were as well known as they were dismal – he regarded bridal veils as shrouds. To anyone foolish enough to have ventured into matrimony, Denys's advice about incompatibility – whatever its causes – was the same: 'If you have done all in your power to save it, and it still does not work, you must leave as soon as possible.' In the next breath, Denys was unburdening himself about Tania's possessiveness. It had become intolerable: 'If I do not move off the farm, we will lose all that we have been to one another, even our happy memories.'[13]

Several Kenya settlers were in London and 'half of Whites' joined Beryl in her suite at the Grosvenor after the Duke returned from Japan, where parties for the Colonial influx were held 'with champagne flowing and the Duke . . . always about' and caviare circulating like pepper and salt.[14] And once the hunting season opened, Beryl was seen out with the Quorn, riding astride, startling the social climbers among the field by appearing on the Duke's horses regularly – her harmless revenge for all the ostracism she had endured a relatively short time ago. Those mounted side-saddle professed to be shocked at her display of access to the royal stable. It was not just her success that outraged them, she posed a threat to a pecking order that was strictly protected; they could not accept this Colonial *arriviste*. Just how had 'that blonde from

Kenya' managed this? She was not to be dismissed. They sensed that her talents led her into the bedrooms of men they would have loved to seduce themselves.

October was the specific month when the notion struck Beryl like the glimmer of sheet lightning that aeroplanes would bring her Denys's love, and she was swept agreeably along with the Prince, the Duke and Denys in their newest enthusiasm. Her hunch and her timing were faultless.

October was when Edward P announced to Tommy Lascelles, 'I've bought a Moth, flying is my latest craze.' This model, with a cruising speed between 85 and 95 m.p.h., cost £675. Edward P's was red and blue and mounted on its fuselage was his crest. Denys's de Havilland Gipsy Moth was yellow and its colour was to give rise in Kenya to its Swahili name for locust, *nzige*. It was to be shipped to Mombasa for delivery in 1930. They had already experienced the benefits of moving from one end of England to the other with ease; Denys and Edward P were all for spotting elephant from the air, so as to film them with Edward P's new movie camera during his forthcoming safari in Kenya in February.[15]

That October Beryl and Tania paid separate visits to Sherfield Manor, the Hampshire estate of Denys's brother. Shortly after Denys had sailed to England, Tania's mother had fallen sick and she had gone to Denmark. Once the crisis passed Tania resolved to make a detour to London to see her lover.

Tania's stay was strained; her introduction to Toby was partly to blame. The Earl of Winchilsea had not taken to his brother's mistress, calling her 'Blixen' behind her back, while their cousin recorded in her diary, 'I don't like that woman; she is trying to take possession of Denys. It won't work'.[16]

Beryl's visit to 'Buckfield House' near Basingstoke, a week later, was undertaken quite differently – as a member of a shooting party. Toby had inherited Sherfield Manor in 1927 when the Earl died, changing its name to Buckfield House. It had a two-mile-long drive, twenty-five bedrooms and was a grand Edwardian pile with excellent shoots.[17] Denys could land an aeroplane on the lawn and when Toby invited Edward P for a day's shooting, they had flown down.

Beryl's twenty-seventh birthday on 26 October also marked the

jettisoning of the racecourse in favour of the airfield, her acceptance of a fresh challenge; her gathering determination to become
a pilot routed all disbelievers. Flying became vital, special to her,
eclipsing her other profession for twenty years. Denys abruptly
changed plans too, sailing for Mombasa, two days after her birthday. They had attended the Schneider Trophy[18] with the Winchil-
seas, after which Toby tried to prolong Denys's stay by offering
him £100 to fly back. Denys opted for the voyage as if needing
time to work out changes in his personal life before tackling the
demands of organisation for the Prince's second safari.

Ginger Birkbeck remembers how, after Denys left, 'Beryl had a
few flying lessons in England ... We discussed how good her
hands were on a horse: there was a saying then, that this meant
she would make a good pilot too.'[19] Beryl's flying instructor was
to be Tom Campbell Black, whom Denys planned to commission
with an aircraft for Edward P's safari, easing transport and supplies
and to attempt for the first time to scout elephant over Tsavo.[20]
Everything was fortuitous; Tom would give Beryl lessons; she
would have easy access to camp, albeit only for a few hours at a
time, without Tania.[21]

It is worth noting that Beryl *après* Mansfield was a different
proposition, say, from the Beryl who had pitched up at Mbogani
to seek Denys's attention from a closer vantage point. Her hair was
blonder, shaped by skilled hands; the raw beauty had hardened
into drop-dead glamour; the power was more mature, virile, intelli-
gently held in. Her clothes were simple yet stylish, no longer *gauche*
but *avant garde*. Her long legs looked divine in slacks, worn with
men's shirts. Her cool detached manner provided a refreshing challenge, which Denys needed when domesticity had cornered him.

Beryl's return to Kenya in 1930 coincided with that of the royal
hunting party; Edward P reached Mombasa on 10 February, with
his entourage: the fully recovered Brigadier Trotter, Joey Legh and
a newcomer, Major J. H. Aird. Denys and Blix met them off the
SS *Modessa*.[22] They went straight into conference at Government
House to go through any rearrangements. During the briefing,
Edward P informed Denys that Thelma Furness would be joining
camp at the end of February, preceded by a week of socialising in
Nairobi so that he could meet up with her. There would be no

formalities; the Prince would be staying with the Griggs again. And the safari party was gradually to make its way to Khartoum by 13 April, in readiness for HRH's return to London on 25 April with Denys and Joey Legh.[23] The conference at an end, by nightfall they were under canvas in Tsavo.[24] It would be fascinating to know, if Denys's enlistment of Blix was deliberate or politic, so as to provoke confrontation, when it was certain such a choice would cause a row with Tania.

It was a remarkably exciting period in which to join aviation in Kenya. The enhanced promise of opening up Africa heralded change unprecedented in the world of safari and travelling. During the next eleven days, when Campbell Black flew into camp, if the passenger seat was free, Beryl went also. Tom was flying for Lord Furness's safari concurrently and could not take Beryl for lessons until his commitment was fulfilled. So while the Prince filmed and hunted around Kasigau, Beryl would arrive with replenishments of whisky, champagne and vegetables, bringing mail and, as Bunny Allen observed, she 'seemed to know what everyone wanted and doing a bit of a hostess job . . . as a friend of HRH and some of his henchmen'.[25] They all admired her boldness as much as her unabrasive company, yet they tried to warn her against flying. She laughed off the danger, 'had made up her mind', even recognised in herself perhaps that she needed daily infusions of risk to feel whole. Nothing was going to stop her from becoming a pilot, like Denys.[26] Elephant spotting was attempted, but Tom thought it was too dangerous from a pilot's point of view; everyone tried his hand, even the Prince. The knack was to catch the ears moving; elephant in Tsavo are easily confused with rocks, being coated more often than not in red dust.

Filming and photography were regarded as the new African sport but, as Denys cautioned, 'equal knowledge of the quarry's habits, equal skill in tracking and finding unawares and great patience on the final approach' was required. One elephant led them forty miles with little more than blisters for their efforts.[27]

Nursing hangovers next morning, the Prince bet Denys and Ray Hewlett, seconded from Tanganyika Game Department, that they could not 'stick a picture of my father on the backside of a rhino'.

'Sir,' replied Hewlett with respect, 'we should be delighted to prove that you are wrong. Unfortunately we have no picture of the King.'

Silently, Edward P withdrew from his wallet two ten cent stamps of East Africa, bearing King George's image in yellow and black, flanked by tusks.

Around midday the challenge was taken up. Denys was aware that noon was siesta time for rhino; sure enough, within a hundred yards of camp they found one, inert as a grey boulder, dozing under a flat-topped acacia. Insisting that their client watch from a safe distance, the hunters crept forward, licked the stamps and simultaneously stuck one on each of its buttocks. The rhino never flinched.[28]

There was little shooting; trophies were modest in comparison with Edward P's earlier safari. It was time for the Prince to meet his new favourite, Thelma, Lady Furness; she was waiting for him at the Norfolk Hotel. During a hectic week of socialising for the royal party, Beryl retreated to Elburgon to see her father after an absence of six months.

Meanwhile the Prince had blotted his copybook with the Griggs over Thelma even before reaching Government House. His train had pulled into Nairobi station, the band struck up the national anthem, but no Prince appeared. After an embarrassing lapse of time, it was discovered that Edward P was not on the Pullman. At Athi River, he had alighted to greet his old friend Henry Tarlton, and seized the opportunity of an invitation to take tea at Ndurumu, so as to escape to Thelma alone, going by road and arriving at Government House two hours late. The breach of etiquette set the tone of ill-ease between himself and the Griggs; they informed Lady Furness that she was *persona non grata*.[29] Edward P never fully forgave them, repaying them at his farewell party for them at Muthaiga, before disappearing with Thelma into the bush, by all but ignoring them.[30]

Thelma Furness was not the only one snubbed by the Governor. Tania was not invited to the ritual lion hunt, the *bonne bouche* of Edward P's picnic with Thelma, at Selengei and attended by many mutual friends. At the Griggs' request it had been laid on in the Prince's honour by Denys, with the Maasai. While Denys was double-checking that the camp was ready to receive the Prince and

Thelma, Edward P was considerate enough to drive out and see Tania informally, as she put it, 'as it is impossible for me to go to Government House'.[31]

It is easy to see why Tania felt so left out. The African safari offered unprecedented quiet for men of significance; white hunters have ever been renowned for prudence in the matter of mistresses. Denys saw to it that Thelma's tent was pitched next to Edward P's, always at the end of the line in order that the Prince 'shared a fire' with her, though for all Tommy Lascelles's admiration of Denys, he had disapproved of the arrangement.[32] For four days camp was as peaceful as any pair of lovers, surrounded by trusty aides, could wish; tents were pitched under towering yellow-barked fever thorns, overlooking a wide sand river. For guests – some forty or so – attending the Maasai lion hunt, extra tents were erected to accommodate, among others, the Delameres and D's son, Tom Cholmondeley, Jacko Heath, Cockie, Archie Ritchie, Kenya's Chief Game Warden and the Griggs. Tom flew Beryl into camp for the day. Champagne was chilled properly by a new-fangled essential, the miraculous Crichton ice-making machine.[33] Everyone intended to film the lion hunt with 'the latest Bell and Howell, lots of gadgets . . . the new 6" lens' light filters or screens and Panchromatic film had been exclusively supplied plus 'half a dozen films in colour' with which the Prince might experiment.[34] People were relying on black and white film for important pictures; as the *moran* gathered, again for Edward P the camera proved unwelcome, for its all-inhibiting, all-seeing, artificial eye.

Unlike Beryl, Glady Delamere mistook flirtation for something more significant. Spotting the Prince perching on a chop-box, *sans* Thelma for a few moments, she walked by twice and, failing to get any response from her former admirer, wandered up and sat herself down too. Edward P, in chilly but audible tones, informed her that she was not welcome. Archie Ritchie meanwhile had happened to be tinkering with his movie camera under the fly of his tent. Ritchie's lens had been focused on the sequence, from Glady's parade to Edward P's rebuff, culminating in her crestfallen exit. By then, Edward P, becoming aware of the whirring of Ritchie's camera, reacted: 'We cannot have that sort of thing recorded,' ordering that the film be destroyed at once.[35]

If the camera was the enemy of the imprudent, it was the friend of the game, upholding all the excitement. Ritchie located a rhino and elephant for Edward P to film and with Ritchie, Denys brought down an angry rhino before it flattened the future King, making 'matchwood of the camera, not six yards from the lens'. Beryl was caught unawares by the Prince's Eyemo movie lens as he filmed Denys's car being heaved out of the sand river on to firm ground. This fleeting but telling moment of intimacy captures Beryl looking straight into Denys's eyes, moving towards him as if about to kiss him; his gaze, locked to hers, is broken suddenly within touching space, when they slip past one another, as propriety demanded. Someone had taken the wheel from Denys, so that he could add his greater weight to the others, and Beryl had joined in the task. She is easily distinguishable even from behind, the tallest female besides the only one helping in the rescue.[36]

The lure of Africa for the European seems to lie in its savagery; never more was such fascination clearer than in the audience observing that Maasai lion hunt. Several courageous *moran* clad only in a *shuka*, with just shields for protection, foreclosed on the lion. The crowd of white onlookers seemed transfixed, eager for blood, as if some atavistic need, long-since buried, had surfaced; the warriors, chanting, close in, slaying the lion with spears. At the kill, its head resembled nothing so much as a giant pin-cushion. Thelma described one of her own snapshots as 'wonderful . . . though harrowing . . . of the Prince photographing a native boy at the instant he was clawed by one of the lions'.[37] Afterwards, everyone returned to civilisation. Campbell Black flew Beryl to Nairobi and she disappeared up-country to be with her father before leaving for Europe. Mindful that Denys was to fly back from Khartoum on 13 April, she was to schedule her movements to follow his.[38]

When Edward P drove Thelma alone in his Buick to Voi where she was to rejoin Furness on the boat train for Mombasa so as to sail to England, the Prince's temperature soared to 105. He was rushed by rail to Nairobi where, at Government House, malaria was diagnosed. Massive doses of quinine ensured a quick recovery, enabling him to leave on 9 March, as planned, with his entourage and Denys for Juba.

On the last day of April 1930 came the end of the masquerade in Beryl's final act under the pretext of friendship toward Tania. Never again was she to voluntarily seek her company. As if to see that Tania did not misinterpret or suspect anything about herself concerning Denys, she took the unprecedented step of summoning Tania by telegram to lunch at Muthaiga Club. Tania's correspondence shows a notable lack of reference to Beryl becoming a pilot, which surely she would have found worthy of mention. But nor was she aware that Beryl had been in Kenya since February. Tania's ignorance can only suggest that mutual friends were already treating her like Denys's betrayed wife and protecting her from the truth. Tania's reaction to the plan, when in fact it had been Beryl's intention since February, was one of surprise: an 'extraordinary plan ... Considering she only came out on 1st March [sic].' Tania was consumed by curiosity. 'When we met,' wrote Tania, 'I heard to my astonishment ... she was on her way ... to Europe ... the same day for Mombasa to catch the Italian boat.' Frustration was all the greater when they were interrupted by 'a stupid man ... who asked to join us'. Thus Tania was prevented from anything further, speculating: 'Perhaps it is the Duke ... who cannot do without her any longer' and supposed that it was better for Beryl to be 'at home ... If he is going to support her for a lifetime, the way her miserable husband has arranged things, then they can at least enjoy each other a little.'[39]

Beryl was criticised for being '*very* naughty over Prince Henry' and levelled at for breaking rules where Queen Mary was concerned. Barely three months passed before she got back to England.[40] According to Ginger and Cockie, Beryl was becoming impatient for public association with Denys. The tensions, loyalties and counter-tensions over this eternal triangle were weighed down with intrigue in 1930, particularly with Cockie's brother, Ulick, as Keeper of the Privy Purse within the Royal household, supplying occasional gossip to her.

Ginger and Cockie were more sympathetic towards Beryl, who represented all that Rose disapproved of except courage, which, for all her antipathy, Rose acknowledged. Ginger was conscious of all those difficulties Beryl had faced while growing up. Her sense of inadequacy in terms of education was only complicated by her dogged need for Denys's approval. None was more understanding

than Ginger of Beryl's struggles since Clutt's bankruptcy; his all
too public failure; Beryl's need to redress her mother's absence
and neglect; the gossip (with her mother residing in the Colony)
that Arthur was really Clutt's bastard; and on top of that, Beryl's
shame over her own infant – 'an invalid' from birth.[41]

Ginger's criticism of Denys was balanced by affection despite his
self-centred life. Unlike most people she did not believe that he
could do no wrong, having seen his effect on two women who had
pinned their hopes too high on him; in 1930 in Ginger's opinion
his detachment from Tania was 'typical'. One could say that Denys
and Beryl deserved one another in their similar heartlessness, their
ability to enchant the opposite sex. For Denys 'there was no mad-
dening involvement' while Beryl always responded better to those
who did not fawn upon her.[42] Denys's recalcitrance served only as
a greater challenge and spurred Beryl on in her desire for victory
over Tania. Yet Beryl was never certain of her triumph after Tania
had written about Denys in *Out of Africa*. This literary legacy
explains why Beryl's need to get even with Tania endured. Tania's
affirmation of Denys's presence in her own life continued to irk
Beryl until she died.

Before Denys left for Khartoum with Edward P, he had shied
away from a contretemps with Tania – though obviously with less
damage than she expected when, by Tania's own admission, before
parting 'I made a scene of the first water because he had taken on
Bror as *second white hunter* for the Prince of Wales'.[43]

Tania was at the end of her financial tether; as each month
progressed, she could see that she was going to lose her coffee farm.
As suggested by her biographer, Judith Thurman, and revealed in
Tania's letters to her brother, Thomas Dinesen, Tania's feelings of
helplessness and despair also reflected a trenchant fear of losing
Denys, with little chance of reversal. And, as we now realise, with
good reason.

Beryl had become a stalking-horse to her own needs, never
revealing anything yet covertly threatening Denys's relationship
with Tania. Cockie and Ginger sensed what was going on, observing her independently all these years, and even then could be
caught out. Beryl was so African and her thought process so alien
to their own way of thinking that they only knew that one never

knew what to expect. And the unexpected happened again. Denys's guard against Beryl was now dropped.

His undated letter to Tania written from Trent, Sir Philip Sassoon's estate, reached Mbogani in May; it is perfunctory, abruptly signed 'Denys' – distant, even for him. Avoiding intimacies, writing about the slump during the Depression in Britain, the letter's only personal news is of having attended Vivienne de Watteville's wedding and that Tommy Lascelles had been best man.[44]

Meanwhile Beryl's life with the Duke ran its usual pattern from the Grosvenor except that the hotel was fast becoming *de rigueur* for flying celebrities. Record-breaking aviators had fired the imagination of the public and Amy Johnson, who happened to be staying at the same time, caused quite a stir in the street below. The Birkbecks often witnessed Beryl and the Duke observing, like themselves, from their small balcony, fans clustered about its steps below, waiting for the flier's appearance. Sometimes the Duke ran into Amy on the back stairs, avoiding the public like himself.[45] According to Ginger, Beryl 'got all her wrong ideas watching Amy Johnson. The *Daily Mail* had laid on yellow and black cars to transport her; Amy bought clothes in department stores on credit for promotional purposes and the newspaper footed her bills.'[46]

In the interim, moves were afoot at Buckingham Palace to remove the Duke from Beryl's influence. The King, supported by his consort who frowned on Beryl's presence in London, brought pressure to bear in stipulating that the Duke represent his Majesty at the Coronation of Ras Tafari of Abyssinia, when the latter became Emperor of Ethiopia. He was to depart for Addis Ababa on 16 October. Beryl would then return to Kenya; the Duke was to impress everyone during the assignation although the strains of enforced separation from one for whom he obviously cared were great. For his part, it was 'a really big affair'.[47] Before long he suffered shingles, which notoriously afflicts persons with repressed emotional problems.

Denys reached Nairobi in September and, before Beryl's return, Tania flew often with him and was euphoric from fifty-six hours in his company: 'the loveliest days . . . It is a magical effect . . . he has upon me; never have I known such . . . happiness as . . . in his company . . . I went flying with him yesterday . . . I think it is doubtful whether greater happiness could exist for me than to fly over Ngong with him.'[48] Tania made one last plea for financial help from him while he was camped in the bush with Mr and Mrs Marshall Field, millionaires from Chicago, that November. From the bush, by runner, came Denys's unconditional refusal.

That month Beryl rented his former bungalow, across the golf course at Muthaiga. For five uninterrupted years it was to become her base with Ruta whose role was mostly to tend to her domestic needs.[49] It was modest accommodation – a living room with a stone fireplace, an alcove for dining; the sparsest of furniture: a small bookcase, a coffee table, skimpy chintz curtains to match a loose-covered sofa and armchairs; one bedroom, a bathroom and an outside *jikoni* where Ruta presided over a *kuni* stove.

During the first months of 1931 Beryl shared eight carefree weeks with Denys – at the most. Except Denys was not entirely carefree. Tania troubled him deeply at the time with the heart-rending task before her. She was surrounded by defeat: her possessions, packed in tea-chests, were being made ready for shipment to Denmark. A clear conscience was Denys's key to contentment: in *Out of Africa* Tania had recorded that he was 'absent minded as if sunk in contemplation'.[50] Meanwhile his Gipsy Moth, *nzige* – its arrival had coincided with that of a small plague of locusts – stood on a landing strip cut from the *vlei* on the flattest part of Tania's farm*. The exact date for Denys's withdrawal from Mbogani has remained hazy. However the depressed tone of Tania's letter dated 17 March indicates that it could have been around that time that Denys had taken out another American couple, the Sofer-Whitburns. The departure was triggered by 'a most shattering row'. Most friends agreed that the reason behind it was Tania's possess-iveness although Beryl admitted finally in 1974, 'I'm afraid I was probably the cause'.[51] Tania's newest biographer suggests that Beryl 'put the lie to Tanne's careful construction of Denys's death',[52] but everyone close enough to them, including the Winch-ilseas – whom Tania told the next time she saw them – and Beryl knew that their confrontation was bitter enough, passionate enough, incensing Denys enough, that he demanded back the Abyssinian gold ring which he had given to Tania in 1928. Slipping it on to his little finger during this crisis, he grabbed immediate belongings and left; he never did get around to transferring the bulk of his books and records.[53]

Tania's pride was spared. Denys was moving to town for a series of dental appointments with Jack Melhuish, anyone tactless enough to ask was told. Denys's forty-fourth birthday was approaching; his problems with his teeth were a painful reminder of the family weakness – and worse still, of his age.

'Officially' Denys was staying with Hugh Martin, a civil servant in the Department of Lands, whose failed marriage left room in his house and enough cynicism in his heart to be understanding. Hugh was Denys's alibi, helping him to look for a suitable plot to develop. But Denys was so half-hearted at the thought of suburbia: Nairobi was changing so rapidly, he talked of living in a tent in the Maasai Reserve.[54]

If Denys wanted his youth back, Beryl was one fillip to vanity; his ego had been soothed since birth by the balm of extravagant praise. Beryl's irreverence made Denys feel young again, living up to Blake's dictum 'to kiss the joy as it flies'. Denys only ever did what he wanted. His elusive, captivating yet essentially self-centred nature inevitably had thwarted definition as much as Beryl's and was as beguiling to those drawn to it.

Beryl's prodigious sex life and Denys's hitherto untouchability because of Tania caused sceptics at Muthaiga Club to dub Beryl's bungalow 'the way of all flesh' on account of their relationship.[55] In a gossip-ridden village such as Nairobi – for all its commercial growth – their involvement was not easy to conceal. They restricted their activities to Wilson Airfield, flights in *nzige* and dining *tête à tête* at Muthaiga. Beryl's *penchant* for random loving and Denys's prerequisite of freedom demanded urgent passion. She had wanted him for too long now and needed her physical desire for him to be satisfied. When Beryl was twenty-one, she had been too intellectually distanced from him. Now because Denys had moved away from the constraint of Mbogani somehow they seemed natural as a pair. They had that same fatalistic streak, the same sardonic humour, a shared interest in flying, had a hundred new ideas to explore at a time when the last thing Denys was seeking was soliloquies of undying dedication. 'The radiance of love, compensating for make-up, and wheaten gold hair' were enhanced by the masculinity of her 'slacks, worn with a pale blue shirt . . . stunning but efficient', emulating Denys's style, tying a silk scarf in the neck of her shirt, leaving the ends to fly in 'a dashing way. They were impulsive, free and full of fun'.[56] There was a lot of laughter. Beryl could be coaxed into talking about him, mentioning his 'terrific sense of humour – funnier still when he'd had one over the odds', implying that Denys was drinking more than usual.[57] Quizzed as to how things stood at Mbogani, damning with faint praise was her way of continuing to get back at Tania: 'The thing is, he did like lovely food and good things . . . Tania was *very* good at looking after everything . . . of course he was very well bred, but I don't think it really happened. I think that's what buggered up everybody.'[58] Whatever anyone thinks about such tactics towards others, Beryl nurtured no illusions about herself either. She was as fearless in self-condemnation as she was courageous physically.

In 1931 Denys's impeccability would not allow him to turn away from Tania entirely. As if to endorse her good faith in him, he wrote, 'Let me know if you would like me to run out if you have anything to arrange in your own plans . . . in which I could help' making clear her onus and signing 'Best love' – neutral as can be. His aversion to emotional scenes, Beryl pointed out, made Denys 'pretty bored . . . She was obviously . . . rather demanding.' He therefore dispatched Kamau, his chauffeur, to collect his Jaeger dressing gown 'and a box of letters'.[60]

Two personal letters indicate Denys's indecision in 1931; in January he intended 'in May . . . flying to England' in his Moth. But then in May he was 'thinking of going on safari by myself to get a few elephant pictures in June'.[61] Torrential rains made repairs to the roof of his Takaungu house a priority. Having re-organised arrangements around this trip, Denys seemed reluctant to go alone and asked Beryl to join him. Whether she would have shared a space in further immediate plans is difficult to determine; he seems to have been marking time, waiting until Tania left the Colony before making any open declaration.

While Beryl expected the relationship to continue *pro tem* she clearly had no illusions about permanency. Marriage? Beryl knew 'he didn't really believe in it.'[62] So as far as she was concerned his rootlessness and stubborn commitment to liberty were no worry.

They mulled over the idea of her going to Takaungu, forgetting that she had a flying lesson in the afternoon on Friday 8 May. Weeks earlier she would have leapt at any chance but now that he had left Tania, Beryl's sense of competition had evaporated.

Two days beforehand, Denys had retrieved from Mbogani Iris Tree's slim volume, *The Traveller and Other Poems*, when Tania had asked to go with him to Takaungu. After absent-mindedly agreeing, Denys reneged, pointing out the hazards of elephant spotting in Tsavo. She reminded him that he had brought his Moth out to fly *her* over Africa. His argument was that he might have to sleep in the bush, and, besides, air turbulence at Voi was notorious. Before driving off, opening the book, Denys quoted to her the poem Iris had written for him, 'I saw grey geese flying over the flatlands . . .'.[63] In keeping with his style, it was to prove an elegant exit. He also agreed in a conciliatory arrangement to meet her at Lady McMillan's for lunch, to which they had jointly been invited on 14 May.

Beryl spent that evening of 6 May with him quietly at Muthaiga; nothing had been settled either way about her flying to the coast with him – they would let the weather decide. The next night Denys was the guest of Jack Melhuish, his dentist and whose dark-room he shared. Beryl's relationship with him was too covert still for her to be accepted by certain friends of Tania's; and Melhuish's mistress, Joan Waddington, was one who had 'glared at Beryl' in disapproval. She was 'the cipher queen' at Government House; so partisan, that years after Melhuish's death, in coming across 'hundreds of Denys's photographic plates', she smashed 'every single one' as if her act of vandalism against 'that tramp', as she called Beryl for stealing Denys, could ever have assuaged Tania's loss.[64]

In the face of Joan Waddington's antipathy, Denys had driven to Melhuish's without Beryl. And, Nairobi being chilliest in May, he flung his camel dressing-gown over his dinner jacket for extra warmth in the Hudson. During conversation, Joan asked him about Takaungu; Denys half-jokingly told her to fly down and see it for herself. Her reaction had been shrill, 'Good God Denys! Do you want me to commit suicide?'[65]

Next morning, Beryl drove in her car, and Kamau chauffered

Denys, from Muthaiga to Wilson airfield. Beryl's recollection is
that as 'it was a flier's day'. Denys took Kamau instead, promising
to dine with Beryl on the night of his return. Campbell Black had
tipped the balance, ' "What do you want to go with Denys for?
You've got a lesson." He felt strongly about my not going . . . so
Denys took off without me.'[66] Afterwards she drove back to
Muthaiga to study aviation in preparation for her flying lesson in
the afternoon.

Beryl disliked dining by herself and therefore had suggested that
Tom join her at Muthaiga on 13 May. At 8 p.m. when he had not
turned up, her sixth sense told her something was amiss, compel-
ling her to drive to Wilson airfield. She had been right. He was still
in the process of attempting to land with improvised illumination,
headlights of cars. Over a belated meal he explained events that
had caused his arrival after dark.

He had been in the bush with an American crew all day, to film
lion on the kill. One cameramen, enthusiastic for a close-up, had
rushed toward the animal, whereupon it sprang and the shot
intended for the lion missed its heart, so the man was mauled to
death. Before a second bullet could be put into the maddened
creature, it injured someone else. Worse, the widow of the mauled
man watched on the side, as the mechanical camera recorded the
grisly episode to the end. Tom had insisted on cremating the body.
When he clambered from the plane, his first order was for an
ambulance for the widow, who was in shock. Tom was clutching
a Huntley and Palmers tin at the time which someone attempted
to relieve him of, dropping and spilling not biscuits but ashes. But
with Beryl at Muthaiga, he nearly became hysterical with laughter
recounting the day's events.[67]

On 14 May, Beryl had breakfast served to her as usual by Ruta,
dismissing him to immerse herself in her flying manual. Usually
Ruta was off duty until 5 p.m. once he had cleared away after
Beryl's light lunch. Thus Beryl was unprepared for his knock on
her door and his question, 'Have you heard from Mwakanyaga?'
His use of Denys's epithet may have alerted her to disaster. Obviously Ruta could not bring himself to utter what he already knew
of the plane crash at Voi.

News of Denys's death had been relayed up-country tapped out in morse-code by *babus*, Indian or Goan station masters, along the Uganda Railway line and by 11 a.m. the whole of Nairobi was talking about the accident. Nor did Ruta say that Kamau was dead too. Had Beryl gone instead, she would have been killed. Knowing Beryl so intimately, knowing of her love for Denys, waiting on them each day in the last few weeks, Ruta suggested, in the oblique way in which Africans react to ill fate, '*Bwana* Black might have some news . . . ?'[68]

The shock was agonising to Beryl, Ginger recollects. Beryl had worshipped him, longed for his love since she was twenty-one. And, 'while Denys's death was devastating for Tania, for Beryl it was terrible. Terrible . . . In a way, worse, much worse.'[69] Beryl's control over her repressed emotion was now extraordinary.

Tania was a guest at Lady Mac's where Ginger was also at the time of the accident; no one in Nairobi had been brave enough to tell Tania anything. Thus at Chiromo Lady McMillan arranged that everyone behave over luncheon as if nothing was wrong; afterwards, Lady Mac would take Tania into her little drawing room and somehow break the news.

As information percolated through to Nairobi both Beryl and Tania were in the same boat, having to rely on others for details of what had transpired during Denys's last hours. He had been staying with Vernon Cole, the DC, and his wife, Hilda; the tiny community who had attended a party for him the night before went to the airfield at Voi so as to wave him off just before 8 a.m. In his usual way, he had offered to take one woman friend, 'up for a flip' before leaving, but one of her daughters became hysterical at the idea, so she had declined. At this, Denys loaded the *kikapu* filled with oranges, freshly picked from Hilda Cole's *shamba*, clambered into the cockpit and ordered Kamau, who joined him as soon as the engine started up, to swing the propeller. The Kikuyu and Denys taxied, took off and circled once, heading low over the Mwakangale Hills for Nairobi. Then the Gipsy Moth seemed to stutter and plummeted out of sight into dense bush.

Denys's hunting colleague, J. A. Hunter, happened at that moment to be setting out with Lee Hudson, an American client, on safari. They were astonished to see 'clouds of black smoke' darkening the sky. Racing to the source, they were confronted by an inferno, from which a few blackened oranges rolled.[70] Hunter was too stunned to do anything less than abandon his plans so as to take Denys's remains to Tania.

What those were is fearful to contemplate. The photograph of the wreckage shows how little was left. The bystanders were dumbfounded. Hilda Cole, who was three months pregnant, miscarried as a result. John Cole, their son, explained, 'Denys's death affected my life . . . I am an only child.' Vernon Cole had had his camera with him to photograph the Gipsy Moth in the morning; his shot of Denys in the cockpit immediately before take-off is eerie, it is so spectral. Vernon and Hilda Cole told their son that a few minutes before, 'they found a 10-inch crack in the wooden propeller'.[71]

Strange *lacunae* surround that crash; no one was able to draw any satisfactory conclusion. Even Beryl, who was not reflective, remained puzzled. What struck her later was how odd it was that Tom had never mentioned, after telling her about the biscuit-tin and ashes episode, that Denys had wired him as soon as he had reached the coast, requesting a new propeller as *nzige's* was chipped by a coral outcrop in landing at Vipingo. The replacement was to be sent to Mombasa by train.

Tom's omission nagged at Beryl until the end of her life. How had he forgotten to tell her about Denys's message? He was fully aware that Denys was now Beryl's lover. Apart from any personal aspect, more baffling in Tom's oversight was that surely there was some lesson, somewhere in the accident, for any pupil learning to fly.[72] One wonders if Tom dispatched a replacement after all; or whether this one was damaged in transit. Tom was conspicuously absent in the investigating commission which flew down next day. Vernon Cole photographed what was left of the fragile fins and wings of *nzige*. Most irregular of all was that Denys's crash was never registered with the Civil Aviation Authority as it should have been, particularly since it was fatal.[73]

Denys's death brought the two women who loved him in Africa face to face in the Ngong Hills. Beryl grieved entirely alone; her worst ordeal was his funeral, a ritual as alien to her in concept as the prayers, catafalque, entombment and coffin. Beryl recalled how, 'The grave-diggers were unable to get to where Denys had wanted to be buried.' Though she trudged up the steep incline with the other mourners behind his coffin draped in the Union Jack, the procedure was repugnant to her. She vowed NEVER to attend another funeral, so distraught was she over the exercise.[74] Beryl's dread of European burial was to reach the point of paranoia eventually.

That Tania was accorded all the sympathy of a widow, Beryl found unbearable. Expressionless, she stood opposite her rival above the hole, at the end of the masquerade, as the armature of their relationship was lowered into the red earth.

Cockie and Ginger understood Beryl's grief-stricken bitterness as she was forced to accept the hollowness of victory; nothing could bring back her trophy. Of Denys, Beryl said, 'I thought the world of him.'[75] Because she and he had been discreet, for Tania's sake, and to please Denys, worse by far was that 'He was *Hers* for always. When he crashed, no one else could have him.'[76] However, she managed to be eloquent in defeat, cheated though she felt: 'Death marked a turning point in Tania's life; she was able to claim him as her own.'[77]

Tania contemplated suicide; Ingrid Lindstrom, who so often comforted her, tipped off by Denys upon his departures, did so now. Ingrid had no idea why Denys had left Tania, until Ginger told her. Her comment was resigned: 'Oh, it *was* Beryl was it?'

Until she died, Beryl would use each small opportunity to get even. She was certainly resentful of *Out of Africa*, the book in which Tania had claimed Denys – '*She* would not have been able to, had they both remained alive, and in Africa.' With one crumb only did Beryl continue to console herself: 'I knew, afterwards, when Denys said, "Please come" on that flight when he was killed, I knew he liked me.'[78] Beryl maintained her opinion that, 'Tania owed everything to Denys. His part in shaping her literary career has never been acknowledged fairly.'[79]

From Denys's Obituary in *The Times* one sentence was plucked from the copy Beryl kept, for her memoir: 'something more must come from one so strong and gifted; and, in a way, it did . . .'[80]

10

Life as a Pilot

(1931–2)

In Africa people believe that everything must be paid for. Now, almost with a vengeance, as if accepting that the price of Denys's love had been to forfeit him, Beryl devoted herself to flying. She gave up horses for machines and within four weeks of his funeral made her first solo flight. Indeed, flying would dominate her life for five years. For seven years previously, Beryl had contrived to share any of Denys' preoccupations in the hope of shining for him, yet had ended up with nothing and had narrowly missed dying with him. In all her bitterness toward Tania, Beryl somehow found compensation in embracing the pain of loss and devoting herself to the one activity that had finally brought her and Denys together. At least Tania no longer had him either.

From May to June, Beryl's need to escape became even more urgent. There is something infinitely touching in her discovery of herself as she soared above Africa, helmeted and goggled. In the sky, even loneliness could not touch her, it seemed. In reaching for the stars, she was gripped by what the poet-aviator Saint-Exupéry called 'the witchery of flying'. She discovered, aged twenty-nine, the space to stretch mentally and physically. Where she had hated lessons, now these became her release, providing all the zeal of man's ancient urge to become 'fully fledged'. By all accounts she was 'a born flier'.[1]

Finding a good instructor had been more a case of good luck than judgement. Friends say that Tom Campbell Black, Managing Director of Wilson Airways, could not believe his luck when Beryl had applied to the Aero Club of East Africa for tuition in the Gipsy

Moth donated for this purpose by Lord Wakefield. Tom had volunteered his services; she had been merely happy to learn in a machine identical to Denys's *nzige*.

Even Cockie, besides those up-country, the Birkbecks and George Alexander, were aware of how heavily Tom had fallen for Beryl when they met in Molo after she had defected from the drug scene at Knightwyck to work for George. Tom and his brother, Frank Campbell Black, soldier settlers like Purves, had a horse in training at Westerland Stables. Beryl had barely acknowledged that the Campbell Black brothers existed.

In 1931, Tom's chances through teaching Beryl were only improved in mid-May by the unexpected if shocking absence of Denys in her life; his ill fate had altered everything in Tom's favour. After all it was Tom who had prevented Beryl from going with Denys to Takaungu; by reminding her that she would miss a lesson if she went he might even be seen as her saviour. Now that Beryl needed comfort in her grief, Tom was on hand, providing more than that; he had the opportunity to be physically close, guiding her, passing on his knowledge, and this gave him extra confidence to press his suit. One can understand how in this sudden reversal of fortune, Tom relished the role of instructor, allowing Beryl to get into difficulties, rescuing her and showing her how to redress near disaster only at that moment of panic in the cockpit. Beryl claimed that the benefit was that she never got out of a machine without knowing what might have happened had she taken another course of action. Especially because she could never forget how she might have perished at Voi. Besides Ruta, 'Tom . . . was the only living person who knew . . . my various emotions.' Beryl ever valued that 'patience . . . beyond human understanding . . . of a singular and wayward character' – herself.[2]

Tom was an ambitious man, attractive in a Puckish way, nudging forty. He had blue twinkling eyes and dark receding hair and was currently working for a widow, Florrie Wilson,* of Wilson Airways, with prospects of a partnership in her firm. In 1929, he was hired by Florrie Wilson to fly her in J. C. Carberry's Fokker Universal to London, and brought back for her a new aircraft in which Wilson Airways was to carry the mail. The upshot was that she offered Tom a job. Denys had commissioned him for the Prince of Wales's safari; Beryl was having her first high-altitude lessons while Tom was also alternating pilot duties for Lord Furness.

Tom recognised Beryl's potential as a record-breaker early on; and he imposed upon her the kind of strictness he had experienced in the Royal Flying Corps.[3] It was like being trained by her father all over again.

Tom was a short man and compensated for his lack of height by outshining those around him with dare-devilry – less for kicks, than to gain attention. He spoke well, which Beryl always found appealing in a man, not recognising that his manner was entirely cultivated; his father, as Mayor of Brighton, was *nouveau riche*, which enabled him to give his sons decent schooling. It was while attending the Royal Naval College at Greenwich that Tom had taken on the manners and accent of the English public school. As a Flight-Lieutenant, Tom was given a taste of glory at the end of the war when he was part of the first British Squadron into Cologne.[4] It was evident to Tom after a decade of indifferent progress just how wise he had been to renounce Brighton – possibilities thereafter seemed limitless. On top of it all, there was Beryl suddenly at Tom's side, his only pupil, a much more seductive assignment than running a fleet of seven machines.

Beryl was in her late twenties. Whenever she asserted herself professionally, she was quickly respected by her peers and Tom fell into this category as well as being in love with her. For Beryl, the assumption that she was his girlfriend suited the hooded side of her nature. Once he was seen emerging by early morning golfers from 'the way of all flesh' at Muthaiga.[5] Gossips alerted Mansfield, who grabbed the first opportunity to sue her for divorce. To cite Tom was tricky as she was not 'living with him' and, as usual, was seeing numerous men besides. Mansfield's lawyer, Theodore Goddard, found it was difficult to get sufficient evidence to 'satisfy a stuffy English judge' and dropped the matter for now.[6] Those closest to Beryl and Tom were sceptical, with good reason. Tom was not even a substitute for Denys, her pursuit of whom had been an obsessive reaction to his laid-back attitude to her. Lovers in between, even Mansfield, had meant little. She had given them, including Tom, only the shell of herself. At night she hated going to bed alone, as Ginger elaborated, 'Tom was in love with her but as far as Beryl was concerned Tom was a means to an end . . . it was Denys whom Beryl loved. She was mad about him.'[7]

There had been nothing to prepare Beryl for flight in the Gipsy Moth, so fragile, more vulnerable than a human would expect a machine to be. As a pioneer pilot, Beryl took enormous risks. Owing to the height of many landing grounds in Africa, she could not expect the same cruising performance discussed in English manuals, on account of the rarity of the air at such altitudes. The few maps that were available for such areas showed little detail, with a scale of 32 miles to 1 inch, covering country which had, as often as not, never been surveyed. In Europe pilots used 4 miles to one inch on the map.[8]* In Kenya, the only sign of life might be a wisp of smoke, a tell-tale spiral of human life.

Beryl's greatest apprehension when tackling anything new was that she might bungle it. Disgrace for not coming up to scratch had been so drummed into her by her father, as well as the fear of ridicule in defeat from Kibii's age-group, that the idea of failure caused in her an angst almost painful to assimilate: 'She had the courage of a lion' yet could not face criticism, or worse still, jeers. 'What disgrace would I be in, should I make the same mistake twice . . . made to feel I was wasting my own and someone else's valuable time – and that dreaded word, FAILURE would then loom up in large block letters'.[9] Her standards were to become more exacting as she aged. She was conscious of Tom's feelings for her and understood that he was, naturally, 'desperately ancious [sic] . . . fearful . . . something might go wrong . . . would feel akin to a murderer if anything should happen to me in the air'.[10]

Beryl's private battle with .her own pride continued each time she went up, Tom sitting in front of her, shouting back instructions, conveying the next manoeuvre over the drone of the Moth's engine. Trickiest of all to master was landing; over and over she practised approaching the runway, beginning her descent, landing, rolling, pushing forward the joy-stick, ascending once more until 'having gone through shattering dissappointments [sic] . . . one is beginning to feel . . . one can fly'.[11] Slowly she discovered the effects of down-draught, of turbulence, absorbing how lack of attention or observance and laziness could lead to fatality. But she was nevertheless impatient, '"Why can't I go solo?" she persisted. "You will go solo when I think you are ready to go solo".' Eight hours logged 'had seemed like a lifetime' when, on 11 June, her chance arrived unheralded, jolting her after a fourth landing when Tom got out of the Moth, taking all his cushions, and, seeing her hesitate, ordered, '"Off you go", walking off'.[12]

Having undertaken 'circuits and bumps' with Sisyphean dedication, self-doubt racked her. 'I could not honestly say I was afraid but a great sense of the loneliness of it came over me – mingled with . . . intense desire . . . of getting up . . . and not being able to get down again.'[13] Unaccountably she found herself singing: she was acutely self-conscious about being tone-deaf – doubtless, being musical himself, Denys had teased her for it. His fine tenor voice, accompanying the strum of his guitar, had enthralled each woman he had loved. Beryl, up in the sky, was freed of constraint: 'I began singing to myself (a thing I never do when there's a chance of anyone hearing me, so badly do I sing).'[14] Soaring higher still above Nairobi dam, finding it 'impossible to explain what my feelings were really like, it was an emotion one only experiences once in a lifetime . . . mingled with a kind of independence . . . I have never been able to find in any other walk of life . . . suddenly . . . had the greatest desire to fly . . . into space . . . keep on . . . I was at one with the aeroplane, all feelings of doubt, left me . . . I was the happiest girl in the world.'[15]

Next came fear: 'a latent fear came creeping over me . . . I must shamefully admit, how often I would pray for some little thing to go wrong . . . that I would not have to go up alone.'[16] Slight as Tom's weight was, Beryl had not been prepared for the difference his absence made to her handling of the Moth at '5,600 feet above sea-level' and where now the 'slightest misjudgement' meant that she was done for; she watched the aerodrome, 'as one possessed by fear . . .' lest she loose sight of it.[17]

And yet there was one occasion when Tom told Beryl to do one spin, but allowed her to spiral into nine, to 'hurtle to earth unchecked . . .'. It was only when Wilson Airfield 'looked dangerously near to us' that Tom straightened up and landed. Her 'complete inactivity' alarmed him; yet such muscle-numbing impotence confirms Beryl's fatalistic nature, her acceptance of danger, defined by challenge from the time she had sat close to a lioness, in a hide with Kibii, watching its face, bloody from the kill.

Once in the air she felt safe, and tried to 'figure out why I was always so scared before solo flights', continuing her battle with cowardice until she logged fifty hours. Then, as naturally as a butterfly emerging from a chrysalis, she slipped the caul of fear, and solo flying became a joy. On 13 July 1931 she obtained her A licence.[18]

No span of time is so carefully documented as the working hours and minutes of a professional pilot. Having decided upon that course, she recorded her flying hours in a fine-lined log-book, needing three hundred to get her B licence. 'How zealously did I enter up my hours . . . more precious than any diary.'[19] Indeed, things aeronautical took on special significance for her, became precious even where other possessions were strewn across the world, every chart and log-book was kept safely, stored in one of Mansfield's wedding gifts from Paris, her Louis Vuitton trunk.[20] This relic of their honeymoon was to assume for Beryl in her dotage the importance of Pandora's box. Years later during the filming of the documentary *World Without Walls*, there was an extended shot of her poring over creased charts, unfolded on a table on her verandah. Reading with nostalgia she lists each destination: 'Naivasha to Naiwobi: Naiwobi to Kilimanjawo: Kilimanjawo to Naiwobi', and, had these been old love letters, they could not have been studied with more affection.

In 1931 Tania departed from Kenya. Beryl made no attempt to say goodbye; the minute she no longer needed to feign friendship, she had ceased the pretence. Because of Denys's *modus vivendi* in May, his possessions had been divided between three places. Those books and records remaining at Mbogani went to Denmark, and today are at Rungstedlund. His bits and pieces at Hugh Martin's home were dispatched to Denys's sister, Topsy, in England. Typically, anything left at Beryl's cottage, including his monogrammed guns, a Mauser Magnum by Gibbs and a Mannlicher 256, a 'pretty ivory handled sheath knife', she sent to Sherfield; she also returned his silver-backed hair brushes. In her disregard for material things, it had not occurred to her to withold anything as a keepsake.[21]

For all that Tania appeared broken upon leaving Nairobi, Beryl's most serious rival was to find recovery from all hardships through her pen. In Denmark, Tania became a literary figure as Karen Blixen, and under the pseudonym Isak Dinesen, the renown of which could not have been foreseen before she died. Meanwhile her African squatters bestowed the eponym Karen upon that part of Ngong which had been her coffee farm.

Beryl was always ill at ease in accepting or showing gratitude but none the less took every opportunity to credit Tom as her initial instructor, 'no words of mine can express how much I owe to the man who gave me two years . . . conferring on me, *all* his knowledge and skill.'[22] Though she slept with Tom, they actually only stayed under one roof with Clutterbuck at weekends, on those jaunts to Elburgon which were primarily intended to log Beryl's flying hours and also provide night-flying experience.

Beryl contrived to leave Nairobi with Tom on Fridays at sundown, getting friends to provide illumination by the headlights of cars, and landing in the dark on flattish property up-country, *en route* for her father's when 'With one or two oil hurricane lamps placed at intervals,' Beryl wrote, 'such primitive conditions is [sic] invaluable, when one finds oneself in a tight corner.'[23] Even old Delamere obliged. Impromptu or no, the flare-path none the less had strict rules by which amateurs assembled it. She had to land into the wind, so D had to lay the longest run, clear of obstacles in an L shape. Red obstruction lights marking the limits for landing were substituted with a white sheet. If goose-necked flares were used, dry grass was cut against bush-fire and natives warned not to wander on to the flare-path to replenish paraffin, half an hour before Beryl was expected to land.[24] Beryl fought faint-heartedness each time she took off in the dark, begging Tom, ' "You take over and land". He was adamant, "No, either you land the machine . . . or we fly back to Nairobi."' Beryl admitted that had she 'thrown in the towel . . . Tom would never have saved my face by landing for me' so did as she was told.[25]

Clutterbuck never adjusted to the way Beryl could charge across Africa in a matter of hours as 'the advent of airplanes [sic] seemed to open a new life to us'. They would depart on Sundays, attempting to reach Muthaiga for dinner but so as to incorporate more night-hours for Beryl. Clutterbuck protested, 'What difference can it make? If you get to Nairobi in fifty minutes or four hours ... to England in seven days or three weeks ... ? You people are always in such a damned hurry ... fly if you like, but don't ask me to go up there.'[26]

But Clutterbuck was naturally not the only one to be wary of aeroplanes; the Swahili for aeroplane, *ndege*, meaning 'bird' entered the vernacular in 1926 when the RAF, *en route* for Cape Town, took off from Dagoretti in four Fairey IIIF's. The sight of them so startled one Kikuyu labourer that he asked his *neapara* if the strange birds were God. The headman, whose smattering of written knowledge was confined to the New Testament, explained that they were not God but 'Matthewi, Marki, Luki, and Johnnie.'[27] Ruta, his high-boned face expressing superiority, doubted the wisdom of flying, his suspicions only confirmed by Denys's death. Resignedly he swung the propeller for Beryl, Ruta's duties besides major-domo extending, on the airfield, to removing the chocks before take-off. 'If you must fly, you must fly' was his attitude; in due course, according to Beryl, 'he no longer regarded the machine like a bird as other natives did'.[28] Gradually the sound and sight of *ndeges* became ubiquitous in Kenya skies; even Clutterbuck was by degrees 'becoming quite air minded' about the 'crazy unbalanced ideas ... from young people'.[29]

It was at this time that Mansfield chose to act on Beryl's philanderings, finding that she was as slippery to catch as some of her paramours.[30] He attempted to cite Tom but could not obtain enough evidence as Beryl was not living with him. One gentlemen was Josslyn Hay, 22nd Earl of Erroll, whose second wife, Molly, owned Oserian, a lake-shore home at Naivasha, more notoriously known as the Djinn (Gin) Palace. One weekend, Beryl gave a lift in the Avian, to a friend staying elsewhere round the lake, putting up at Oserian herself. Joss Erroll's motto, 'to hell with husbands', was preceded only by his reputation as 'a pouncer' and his gaze quickened the heartbeat of many women. He found Beryl irresistible; with his old Etonian manner, the impudence of his 'oblique blue glance under half-closed lids' nor was Beryl impervious.[31] That weekend, when Beryl and he slipped into the back of his

Buick, they found that another house guest and her lover had beaten them to it. The woman turned out to be Beryl's *bête noir*, Gladys Gooch, who allegedly bit Beryl's finger to the bone. Such was Beryl's *sang froid*, however, that she did not utter a sound, depriving Gladys of even that satisfaction. It took Beryl some twenty years to redress the injury, when as trainers in the 1950s, they lived next door to each other. Beryl paid Gladys back by loading her own runners into the boxes ordered for Gladys's entries – a ploy so adroitly handled that Gladys hardly realised that she was being set up.[32]

This brief episode, the harmonious accord that Beryl established with Joss Erroll and the majority of her lovers, formed the basis for deepening affection which, though disrupted by months and in some cases years of separation, she managed to maintain. Beryl discovered quite early that even a short time as lovers can be one of the strongest supports to enduring friendship. Where others might find such links fragile, hers were surprisingly hardy.

Shortly after Beryl's *contretemps* with Gladys Gooch, Lord Delamere died in mid-November; his body was taken from his Nairobi home, Loresho, back to Soysambu, where Beryl had worked for him years before, for burial. Although D had been like a father to her, and many distinguished Europeans gathered to pay their last respects, Beryl stuck to her resolution never to go to another funeral after Denys's. But Kenya Colony had lost the man at the political helm, whose place was to be taken in due course by one of his mourners, Lord Francis Scott. The Maasai flocked in too, 'carrying spears . . . shining from head to toe with red mud.'[33]

Early in 1932, Tom's attentiveness to Beryl's needs, Florrie Wilson* noticed, was to the detriment of Wilson Airways. Furthermore Tom seemed drawn to Lord Furness for whom he was flying over Christmas and in January. 'Duke' was to prove useful as a touchstone in Tom's quest for style – something which Tom had hankered after since the Prince of Wales's safari in 1930. Furness, an extremely wealthy man, was accompanied by a widow, the great beauty, Enid Cavendish, whose looks were compared to those of Diana Cooper and Violet Trefusis. Enid was to become a close friend of Beryl's not long after making Furness her third husband. She was said to have 'fantastic posture' and wore cabochon emeralds or rubies, dressing for evening in diaphanous gowns. When presented to King George and Queen Mary, she was regarded as the most beautiful Australian ever seen at court. She and Beryl were to be compared often for their 'drop-dead' glamour over the next five decades.

On safari, Enid looked stunning in khaki and a solar topee, drinking 'Coca-Cola morning noon and night'.[34] Furness transported her about in a Rolls-Royce, specially fitted with zinc-lined trunks for ice and champagne – a ploy to keep her from the silky attractions of European society at Cap Ferrat, and smoothing her way into the bush.[35] Tom had never seen anything like it; his eyes were opened even further when he flew them up to Clouds, Alice de Janze's home in the Wanjohe Valley, one evening, coming into the house to find 'the drawing room, one moonlit night, full of writhing naked bodies'. Happy Valley was a far cry from Brighton.[36]

Immediately after Furness had returned to England, Tom, who had mentioned nothing to Florrie or Beryl about having been offered a job with Furness in England, entered the Wilson Airways de Havilland Puss Moth in a competition to fly the five capitals of East Africa in March. Covering 1,600 miles in one day, stopping only for refuelling, his speed of 17 hours and 15 minutes won him the Mansfield Robinson Golden Trophy, awarded by the Aero Club of East Africa.

With the benefit of hindsight, Beryl wrote that Tom's 'ambitions grew as machine ranges got bigger'.[37] Even so this had not prepared her for his unscheduled departure for England nor for Furness's suggestion that Tom take the place of his former pilot, Winifred Spooner, permanently. Tom, knowing how Beryl depended on him and found it difficult to function alone, rather than face her cold anger chose to say nothing, when she was still answerable to him during flying exercises for her for analysis of height and speed, proving that she had used each to her advantage. Sensing finality, Beryl still relied on Tom for tuition. Archie Watkins, the Wilson Airways mechanic, had drilled into her the importance of certain rules as he demonstrated how to tighten all accessible nuts, screws and bolts. Three weeks after Tom's defection, she had effectively ended her apprenticeship with him. Beryl, leaving no time for Archie to service the plane she had leased in October, the Kan as her Avro Avian (reg. VA-KAN) was known, and, with only 127 hours logged, on 24 April made her maiden flight to England.

She paid for her rashness in the resulting treacheries of that journey; they instilled in her a healthy respect for the role of ground engineers that she never forgot.[38] Refuelling at Kisumu, crossing Lake Victoria's sprinkling of papyrus islands, over Uganda's lush banana plantations and forests, then over the Nile shining like a smooth ribbon below, heading for Juba, her hasty departure led now to a hasty descent. Before her second refuelling she was forced down with engine trouble, 'just clearing a swamp' south of the airfield. Having to spend the night there, next morning she flew to Malakal; yet again repairs delayed her.[39]

En route to Khartoum, she was forced down at Kosti, where 'my aeroplane was . . . surrounded by . . . grinning natives' until she got the engine going again. Heading toward the bleached shores of North Africa, to Beryl Omdurman and Khartoum were less distant places than landing grounds, waiting among the interlocking patterns of the sky, in her faith to reach them. Close to the Nile lay the immense railway line stretching back across the desert to Wadi Halfa. On the west bank nestled Omdurman, a town of oriental Africanised Dervish faith; while on the east, Khartoum itself, of Western Christian faith; two places, like religions, staring back at each other with tolerant regard. Landing between the golf course and the town, Beryl found the dust whistling across the aerodrome, pattering on the tiny windows like hail, stinging her when she emerged.

Only here did she discover that the Avian's piston ring was cracked; she was told her only hope for a replacement was at Atbara. Luckily her informant was right; while it was being installed, she met Sir Philip Richardson *en route* for Nairobi, sending back messages with him to Archie that she was proceeding 'home' when the repairs were complete.[40]

Her troubles were not over yet. Running into a sand-storm at Cairo, forced again to land, she was rescued by the RAF, who flew a mechanic from Heliopolis to retune The Kan's engine. Luckily there were no more hitches; she progressed to Alexandria, following the southern Mediterranean coast via Tobruk, Benghazi and Tripoli, crossing Malta into Sicily. After Africa, the European night landings were incomparable. Beryl wrote, 'how easy it was . . . on an airport floodlit from end to end . . . boundaries so clearly lit.' She then flew on from Naples, via Rome to Pisa, Marseilles, Lyons and Paris, reaching London on 16 May 1932 – just two days after the first anniversary of Denys's death. Reuters covered her arrival: 'Mrs Markham startled Heston Aerodrome yesterday . . . stepping out of an aeroplane . . . from Kenya in seven flying days.'[41] It was no mean accomplishment.

The casual way she informed the Press that she was taking a holiday because she hadn't seen England for eighteen months, for all that it was low-key also heralded years of interest and mis-reportage internationally. All the flattery in the world did not beguile her as the reporters heaped praise upon her for crossing the Sudd alone. (Sudd means barrier and that floating vegetation from which the area gets its name alters according to rainfall and is regarded as one of the most impenetrable parts of the world.) She told them how she had worn an inflated inner tube at Tripoli and had 'not been at all chirpy at crossing the Mediterranean'.[42] Realising what she had risked and how foolish she was for not allowing time for Archie's engine checks, she elaborated only later how 'far too little (glory) . . . is bestowed on . . . mechanics'. She admitted too that 'we would all be in a sorry plight without these men . . . the backbone of aviation.'[43]

For braving all these perils Beryl's contemporaries recognised her as a pilot to be reckoned with and conceded that her 'navigational instincts were uncanny . . . not inconsiderable . . . with only stan-dard Avian sports instruments, compass rev counter, altimeter and lateral bubble indicator'.[44]

The Grosvenor was her next stop; her suite there was to be her haven for nearly five months. The luxury of not having to pay for it herself was a very welcome buffer for her, culturally adrift in the alien English way of life.[45] Dishevelled, tired, wearing the clothes in which she had landed – grey flannels, blue sweater and white oil-stained mackintosh – she checked in. The first people she tele-phoned were the Duke of Gloucester and Tom. The Royal Aero Club informed her that Tom could be contacted at Burrough Court, Melton Mowbray. During their conversation he announced that he was now private pilot to Furness and had been given the chance to fly Furness's de Havilland Puss Moth the following year in the King's Cup Air Race, a privilege conditional to the deal.

Beryl was deeply affected by what she saw as Tom's defection. Just as her mother had abandoned her and Denys had died, Tom's tardy admission of his plans effectively led her to feel forsaken again by one in whom she had placed faith. Tom tried to make it up to Beryl by arranging for her to borrow another Avian until July while The Kan was overhauled, promising too that when the opportunity presented itself, he would invite her to stay at Burrough Court.

Friends describe Beryl's relationship with Mansfield at the time as 'reasonably amicable' but, rather than Beryl going to Swiftsden, they met in town occasionally for lunch.[46] His latest interests revolved around Soho, as a director of Rex Ingram Films, that master of the silent cinema.

The question of Gervase's paternity continued to spice chit-chat in Belgravia. The fact that Beryl was never seen with her son lent weight to speculation that he 'must be' royal. In an almost exhibitionist silence, Beryl refused to satisfy the gossips. Her ego took an impish delight in letting them run up the wrong garden path.

Meanwhile her protracted affair with the Duke of Gloucester continued much as before except that, as he was in charge of an armoured car division at Tidworth with the 11th Hussars, his time was limited. His desire to keep racing fit kept him working regularly on his favourite horses, Birkhall and Ocean III, as well as sneaking up to London to be with Beryl, taking Winks and Dougall, his Scotties, on a rug in the back of his Sunbeam saloon.[47] On several occasions Beryl flew the Duke; once visiting his trainer, Henry Cottrill, at Seven Barrows, Lambourn. Humphrey, Cottrill's son, recalls the stir Beryl's appearance created when the Duke arrived 'by air ... piloted by a very attractive female ... Beryl quickly caught the eye of all the stable lads and others ... After the gallops, the Duke, his two Scotties, Beryl and all came into the house for drinks and lunch to meet my mother, a formidible lady ... certainly outspoken. The dogs, as was their habit ... proceeded toward the drawing-room curtains against which to "spend pennies" much to the annoyance of my mother.'[48] Once they had gone, Cottrill's wife tackled him (he, in passing, had taken more than a keen interest in Beryl) with words to the effect that she could put up with the dogs making use of her curtains as a loo, but most strongly objected to HRH bringing what she described, in anything but friendly language, as his 'Lady Friend'. Would he please advise the Duke that though the dogs were always welcome, the lady certainly was not. 'I fear that was the end of Beryl's visits.'[49]

Over the course of that summer Beryl established her friendship with the Furness family at Melton Mowbray after Tom 'fetched Beryl to Burrough Court'.[50] Her visit was to found two important female relationships for Beryl; one with Enid Furness herself, the other with Enid's eight-year-old twin daughter, Patricia, with whom Beryl remained friends into old age in Africa.

Patricia's first sight of Beryl was as enchanting as it was unforgettable, 'wearing an all-white flying suit. Whether I heard my mother saying she was a great beauty, I do not know . . . to my childish eyes Beryl had stepped straight out of my fairy tales.'[51] Comfort was the keynote at Burrough Court with its furnishings of mahogany and chintz and where Beryl found herself among an already expanding menage. Besides Tom, there were Patricia and her twin brother Carryll,* soon to become Furness's step-children, and his own daughter, Averill – a tomboyish girl in her early teens, plain except for a mop of curly auburn hair, as well as Andrew Rattray, Furness's white hunter. Averill's growing crush on Rattray had already begun during Beryl's stay.

Enid was to marry Duke the following year, each the other's third spouse. Like Beryl, her lovers were legion; like Beryl, she would carry the same ineradicable burden of scandal. Like Beryl, she could not enter a London drawing room without whispers; she too was misjudged, though for quite different reasons, and both loved to take risks in the company of men. She rode well, hunted, shot and fished. Enid's talents were creative – painting, needlework, a marvellous cook – altogether she was a most accomplished woman. Diligently unpunctual, she was known for making spectacular entrances in floating chiffon and jewels. Enid's reputation was for marrying for money, and her fabulous wealth, it was reported, came from deceased husbands, Although in fact Enid and her four siblings were wealthy in their own right. Their father Charles Lindeman introduced vines to New South Wales, thereby pioneering the Australian wine industry.

In 1932, Emerald Cunard took to referring to Enid as 'the stucco Venus' for her involvement with Furness was slightly surprising. He was not good looking nor tall and his title was but one generation old. In 1912 he had become Viscount Grantley, inheriting a shipping empire, a country seat in Yorkshire, Burrough Court in the most fashionable hunting county, as well as Sunderland House in London. Besides these he owned a private railroad and two yachts as well as the aeroplane Tom was flying. In Kenya the Africans called him 'Champagney Lordy'. Beryl let him pay out for things beyond her reach that summer, when usually Furness sought confidence in titled women. Forty million pounds in the bank ought to have helped him cope with his sense of his own shortcomings, including the fact that his father had begun life as a stevedore in Hartlepool Docks.

That Furness scuttled along a passage at Burrough Court at night slipping into Beryl's room seems likely. Certainly Rose Cartwright, who took Rattray's place as Furness's white hunter, believed that Duke succumbed, because he 'found beautiful ladies difficult to resist . . . and paid for Beryl's plastic surgery.'[52] Furness guarded Enid jealously while his own dalliances continued but it was she, when Beryl complained of not liking 'the bump on her nose', who encouraged her to alter its shape. While Beryl had no means with which to pay for such an operation, the ambience at Burrough Court spelled for Beryl such wealth that the cost for the alteration to her nose – two hundred pounds – seemed insignificant. She had blamed her profile on that spill from the motor-bike in Langata Forest when trying to reach Denys at Mbogani. Given her hatred of human medicine, even of the suggestion of illness, she evidently felt strongly enough about her looks to obtain a consultation with the brilliant plastic surgeon, Archibald McIndoe, on Enid's advice. Currently the 'McIndoe bob' was not just fashionable but considered 'highly desirable'.[53]

When the bills came to be settled, they were sent to Burrough

Court, 'the accounts, all the doctors' hospital bills' were submitted. Beryl 'also bought herself an entire new wardrobe'.[54] It was plain that Furness was paying for everything. Enid was not amused; Beryl's reaction was of slight surprise, since Enid had encouraged the notion and so, she had assumed, the *carte blanche*. Among the wealth of comment deploring the results of the plastic surgery lay an iota of truth, 'It spoiled her aristocratic looks . . . a natural hauteur . . . Her face was far more beautiful before . . . its hooked nose . . . more character than the retroussé effort'.[55] No matter what their opinion, men converged. Men would always defend Beryl when women criticised her.

Proof enough that Beryl intended to make a fresh start was that her plans excluded Tom, although each attended the King's Cup Air Races with the Burrough Court party. During this event, Beryl encountered John Carberry from Kenya again; Tania had introduced Beryl to Lord Carbery, the Irish peer who had renounced his title, in 1923, all those years before when she had first stayed at Mbogani. He was born John Evans Freke, inheriting the title 10th Baron and 3rd Baronet Carbery at the age of six, yet preferred to be known as plain John Carberry and in Kenya was called JC. He had been the first person in Ireland to learn to fly but was a disappointed pilot himself; he longed to set a record over land and water in the air, was obsessed with speed and breaking records, never having recovered from his humiliating withdrawal from the third Schneider Trophy seaplane contest in Monaco in 1914. JC was now to become Beryl's greatest benefactor.[56] At the King's Cup Air Race in 1932 JC was casting about for someone suitable to replace his resident pilot at Seremai, his coffee estate just outside Nyeri. Among possibilities in attendance was the celebrated sky-writer Sydney St Barbe. He had just lost his job with Beecham's Pills for scrawling in huge letters across the sky, BEECHAM'S BALLS. JC and Beryl, whose humour was as irreverent, got talking to this 'amusing . . . attractive personality' whose other role was as part-time flying instructor with the prestigious London Aeroplane Flying Club.[57] It was Beryl who urged St Barbe to take the job as JC's private pilot, suggesting that she fly him herself to Africa in The Kan on 22 October. On the brink of her thirtieth birthday,

Beryl left with him, taking ten days to reach Nairobi with two off for relaxation at Mersa Matruh.[58] By the time they reached Kenya, Sydney St Barbe was 'desperately in love' with his pilot;[59] and within six weeks Beryl was invited by JC and his wife, June, to spend Christmas at Seremai as Sydney St Barbe's girlfriend, a move which was to lead directly to her making aviation history.

11

An Ocean Flier in Embryo

(1932–5)

By the time Beryl joined Sydney St Barbe for Christmas, his appeal was waning; his wit had given way to a craving for attention that Beryl found boring and was unable to respond to. Displays of self-pity at her growing indifference to him only exacerbated his insecurity and Beryl's impatience.[1] Even so she accepted the Carberrys' invitation, determined to continue as if nothing had changed, which was her instinctive response when any crisis loomed.

She flew up on Christmas Eve, and as she soared above the green hills of Kikuyuland she looked out for Nyeri Hill. This dark cone of forest is easily identified by pilots *en route* for Nanyuki. It marked the border of rank-grassed cattle plains of the Maasai beyond. The Carberrys' long, low-lying house faced Mount Kenya, and sat in the broad valley between the Aberdares and Kirinyaga as the Kikuyu call their sacred mountain. Seremai – 'place of death' in Maasai – took its name from their old battleground with the Kikuyu, now JC's landing field. Seremai had established itself as *the* social centre of flying in the Colony. Beryl had intended to leave after New Year festivities. Having the aeroplane gave her enormous flexibility and she could fly off anywhere at a moment's notice.

Among the cavalcade of men who pursued her during the seasonal parties held at and around Seremai, Beryl was diverted by a comparative newcomer, an Englishman, Christopher Langlands, whose private income came from the famed Langlands racing stables in Britain and enabled him to do as he pleased, and who unequivocally wanted Beryl for his wife.[2] And since his proposal placed her at a crossroads, her decision to remain at Mweiga, especially with JC's blessing, would make common sense.[3]

Since Maia's death in the flying accident in 1928 at Dagoretti JC had re-married. June née Weir Mosley was his third wife and was South African. The first time that JC took her stunt flying, to prove she was not intimidated June undid her safety harness.[4] Despite JC's reputation for 'monstrous behaviour', perpetrated by those who feared him, Beryl liked him and he was well regarded by neighbours. One who played bridge with the Carberrys defended him: 'he was not so much wicked . . . as naughty . . . *agin* the Government . . . always taking the "micky" taking a macabre delight in pretending to be more of an ogre than he was.'[5] With his long, lanky frame, his grey eyes set in a somewhat cadaverous face, in his flying gear JC's dashing quality is undeniable.

In keeping with Irish sentiment, JC hated England. His feelings were further soured by teaching at Harrow and Trinity College; this well educated Irishman's preference was for Switzerland and Leipzig as places of learning. His defeat in the 1914 Schneider Trophy contest at Monaco brought out his obsessive nature in that he nevertheless maintained his interest in amphibians, upon the outbreak of war, as a temporary flight Sub-Lieutenant in the Royal Naval Air Service at Calshot Seaplane Base, Southampton. It was odd, given the forced-growth conditions of war that, after transfer to Eastchurch in Kent, he was never promoted. Resentment toward 'Johnny Bull', as JC called Great Britain, increased. Immoderate as ever, he emigrated to California, developing a passion for all things American, changing his name by deed-poll to plain John Carberry. JC's attempt to become a citizen of the United States failed on account of his 'bootlegging' activities during Prohibition; his naturalisation papers were withdrawn[6] and, doubtless, lack of restrictions on alcohol in Kenya decided his future there. By 1932 he and his partner from Jamaica, Maxwell Le Poer Trench, were producing eau-de-Cologne, cheap gin, crème de Menthe and Jamaica rum from the Seremai still.[7]

If June had won JC's heart by standing up to him, Beryl equally won his respect that Christmas. He was watching her put his daughter's grey Somali mare through her paces, betting that Beryl could not retrieve at a gallop a handkerchief that he had dropped on the ground. Beryl trotted off, urged Lele into full gallop and, in a style worthy of any cossack, scooped up the white silk square, presenting it to JC with a bashful grin.[8] It was at this moment that they both recognised that they had each met their match. She had called his bluff so effortlessly, and was amused by his eccentricities, his fake American accent, and the way he called her 'Burrrll'. Certainly JC was never dull. If alone at mealtimes, he entertained himself by taking pot-shots from his fifty-foot dining-table at portraits of his Irish ancestors.[9]

JC's circle tended to dismiss June as 'common', but recognised her kindness, for all her peroxided hair and chorus-girl make-up – mascara framed her large eyes, excessive scarlet lipstick matched her bass voice and drinking habits. She and JC were generous hosts; when an aeroplane landed neighbours could expect a party. Pilots would 'buzz' the house as a signal to foregather. To those living out in the back of beyond, news from Nairobi was welcome; alcohol flowed; Seremai was a convenient stopping-off place for the rich and idle Happy Valley coterie. These personalities (who gained even more notoriety by James Fox's account of murder and licentiousness in *White Mischief*) were *en route* for Nanyuki to stay with Rhoda Prudhomme whose home, Mawingo, is better known today as the Mount Kenya Safari Club. Beryl's friendship with Rhoda began here. And this wealthy American socialite was to prove staunch years later in Santa Barbara. She was currently married to a French pilot, a playboy and daredevil by the name of Gabriel Prudhomme from Alsace-Lorraine. His reputation as a womaniser was based upon his flying other men's wives to Nairobi on shopping sprees, returning them to their husbands the same day, having seduced them first.[10]

Beryl developed a remarkable knack in the coming year of mixing freely, yet at the same time disassociating herself from the flow of aristocratic rotters and prodigal sons who passed through Seremai. She achieved this because for all that she provoked scandal, her life was characterised primarily by extremely hard work. Though this feat went unnoticed by most of the world, it is a fact that, in the next three years, her freelance piloting totalled a quarter of a million miles over dangerous country.[11]

Once Beryl knew her objective, saneness of vision was aided by her usual indulgence – the leavening joy of encouragement, help from those who understood her needs: in this instance, JC and 'a great athelete but a poor flier', the blonde and languid Christopher Langlands. 'Chris', therefore, on the brink of 1933, found himself competing for Beryl's favours as her new suitor. He stood tall and debonair and was well connected; his cousins, Cecil and Charles and their uncle, Walter, were Clerks of the Course at Epsom for a thirty-year span. When he fell in love, he was aware that Beryl was involved in a prolonged, somewhat desultory affair with St Barbe, yet he determined none the less to win her; he was used to getting what he wanted.[12] For all his wealth he was no lay-about and was currently running a milk delivery service from Mutunguru ranch next to Seremai for his hosts, Commander Grenville Temple and a childhood friend, Sylvia, his beautiful wife.

Chris's friendship with Sylvia Temple had strong Anglo-Indian underpinnings; their parents had lived in India. Sylvia was a Durani, daughter of the ruling Afghan family – hence her nickname 'the Afghan Princess'. She and Chris were expected to marry into the aristocracy, had become engaged, but remained friends when Chris was eclipsed by an older man. Chris had even gone along with the 'Afghan Princess and the Cowpuncher', as Grenville Temple was known locally, on their honeymoon. Locals had it that Mutunguru was a *ménage à trois*, calling him 'Baby Langlands', a nickname attributable either to this arrangement or on account of his fair hair, golden skin and the divinely innocent expression in his blue eyes.[13] When he confided to the Afghan Princess that he had proposed to Beryl, while Sylvia was fond of her, she was also privately taken aback. To caution Chris would bring out his stubborn streak, so, keeping her counsel, her solution 'to cure Chris', was to get Beryl to stay. Her reasoning was that on a daily basis Chris would discover for himself why she could never make him happy as a wife and 'complications were great enough already with Sydney St Barbe mooning over Beryl'.[14]

Everyone became fed up with St Barbe, not least JC who eventually, out of sympathy for Beryl, got him on to drugs to help him to forget her. Meanwhile 'night after night' he prevailed upon the Afghan Princess 'until the early hours, complaining in his cups, of Beryl's cruel treatment of him'.[15] Far from being put off by Beryl's interest elsewhere, he appeared more enamoured of her than ever.[16] During the three months that Beryl stayed, the Afghan Princess observed 'it was the men who suffered, Beryl took everything in her stride'.[17]

Few environments could have offered Beryl the means that Seremai provided so that she could advance toward her B licence – so as to fly 'for hire and reward' – with every facility at her disposal: a well maintained runway, hangar and workshop manned by JC's full-time French mechanic G. F. Baudet, who also serviced The˙Kan. St Barbe gave Beryl advanced instruction and, when flying was over, on the ground, Beryl applied herself to the practical – cleaning jets under Baudet's expert eye, changing plugs, stripping an engine and adjusting magneto points.[18] She became 'brilliant' with engines. In the atmosphere that earned JC his reputation as 'a solid booster of aviation in Kenya', Beryl had fallen on her feet among all things aeronautical.[19] Beryl's presence at Mweiga contributed to a distinctive emergence of a group, recognised today, of pioneer fliers in Kenya. The security of a small nucleus of pilots within the larger uninterested world encouraged her natural boldness and originality. She was in her element.

Beryl welcomed the ease she found in the company of men at Seremai (usually only interested in her sexually), which encouraged her liberation in the sky. She was not merely someone to bed, she was admired for her potential skill and increasing proficiency, and dressed like themselves in overalls and goggles was treated as one of a brotherhood. Such respect had happy consequences for her work. Each had some aspect of flying to contribute to the other. Owing to the short time in which pilots must gather experience, talking shop was encouraged. With so many possible errors of judgement, learning from others was vital, not least through conversation. The merits of the latest records were discussed. Where such talk went over the heads of most women, Beryl joined in, arguing the variables of wind, altitude, temperature; the weight of each machine. With speed changing at any moment as one element affected another, flying would remain inherently chaotic. That was its appeal for Beryl, keeping her on the edge. Respected by her peers, steeped in admiration, as if this were not enough, she had no need even to forego her cottage at Muthaiga.

Beryl was entering one of the most fulfilling phases of her life. All was set fair for 1933.[20]

Just one snag remained. Paperwork of any nature was an ordeal for her and she had to produce written as well as oral evidence to support the practice and theory of air-law and navigation for her B examination. Like words, figures were anathema to Beryl and she feared equally having to deal with either, never overcoming what was ultimately to amount to a phobia. To surmount this formidable hurdle for the test in 1933, Beryl took 'special instruction' from a young army officer in temporary residence at Muthaiga who 'tutored her in the evenings . . . in order to get her B licence'; aged ninety-seven, now a retired Brigadier, he prefers not to have his name linked to hers today, nor could he recall if she was 'an apt pupil', but the important thing is that she passed. Her Certificate of Competency allowed her to carry, 'Passengers, Mail and Goods in flying machines (Public Transport) Grade B No. II for the following types of aircraft: Avro Avian, D-H Gipsy Moth; D-H Dragon.' In qualifying, on 18 September, she felt an enormous sense of relief, greater than others realised since she had never let on how big the milestone was: 'I told myself, "My girl, you are really getting somewhere, at last."'[21] Yet here was a woman with the courage of lion, and the first female commercial pilot in Kenya.[22]

Meanwhile, Chris Langlands had offered Beryl and St Barbe partnership in his air-charter company, the Blue Bird Flying Circus, founded with Beryl in mind as second pilot. In Mombasa, on the same basis, Captain George Wood with his own Klemm had agreed to become Chief Pilot. Readers of *West with the Night* will remember him as 'Woody'. It was he who arranged Beryl's first commission, flying passengers over the Old Town for 'five shillings a flip' as promotion of Osa and Martin Johnson's new film, *Congorilla*.[23] Woody had reached Kenya as Louis Rothschild's pilot for his 1927–8 safaris and had decided to stay on.[24] Woody's smooth good looks, evoking a 1930s Brylcreem poster, and his utter dependability endeared him to Beryl, for whom he arranged everything.

Beryl's romance with Chris ended one night when he was attempting to impress her by landing his Puss Moth at full moon, crashing it instead. The Afghan Princess heaved a sigh of relief and

Beryl moved out to live with Woody.²⁵ At the end of September, Beryl performed at one of Nairobi's earliest displays at Wilson Airfield. Chris's photograph of this event shows six biplanes, awaiting their turn, dwarfed by the immensity of sky and Athi Plain – unrecognisable as the same spot today as one of the world's busiest charter airports. In the snapshot, a line of bulky vehicles is drawn up to watch Kenya's fliers of whom Beryl was to become the most famous.²⁶

From the moment she had appeared at Mweiga, Beryl's private life was steeped in a number of bewildering, triangular liaisons. Bystanders were entertained, exasperated, frustrated in their inability to get to grips with Chris's significance for Beryl when already confused over St Barbe's role, as JC flirted with her and as new escorts were seen in her company.²⁷ And as Dan Trench, Maxwell's son observed at seventy, having seen Beryl first through young enquiring eyes, 'She was at it to a ripe old age.'²⁸ Chris maintained that his sexual relationship with Beryl had been 'the most startling and erotic' he had known. She appears to have walked a tightrope of masculine emotion. How she contrived to keep her balance, let alone confront the practical vicissitudes of bedding each one individually, is mystifying, even given her skill for concealment. Yet she was able to make each feel that he was the one who interested her. Just to list her known lovers during these few months leaves no doubt about her talent to arouse, again and again, the same men; Sydney St Barbe; M. C. P. Mostert; Jack Soames; Guy Repton; 'Joss' Hay, Earl of Erroll; 'Boy' Long; 'Jacko' Heath; Gabriel Prudhomme; Woody; Roy Garten; Captain the Hon. Roddy Ward. Each was hopping into bed with Beryl whenever it suited *her*.

There can be no doubt that her affairs with royalty marked and defined Beryl as an object to be prized – so indelibly that she might have been tattooed. She was still more so after her Atlantic feat, when to be seen in her company imbued any man with glory. In this light Beryl was to become both the hunter and the quarry. Meanwhile her code of reasonableness on the face of things outlawed the irrational passions of men – their jealousies, angers and hurts – except for St Barbe whose maudlin sentiment left him drowning in that strange disbanded intimacy of people who have once briefly been lovers and from which, at Mweiga, there seemed no escape.[29]

One might imagine that a woman with such a reputation for sexual encounter would not have been shy yet Beryl was, always preferring *tête-à-têtes* to parties, cringing from contact with large groups, even gatherings of people whom she knew well.[30]

Where romantic love is short-lived, in Beryl's case predominantly, it is a mistake to dismiss it as insignificant on the grounds of its transience. Love, after all, is not a commodity for storage. Where others glorified fidelity as proof of true love, possession bespoke all that Beryl was against. For this unusual liberation she paid a high price. Women hardly had a good word for her; so it was just as well that she did not heed their opinion. In Africa she failed to live up to the exacting standards of the truculent *memsahibs* of how European females should react toward men. And in England her refusal to join the caryatids, supporting masculine dominance handed down by the chauvinists of state and society, outraged them, as did her lack of manners. Beryl, meanwhile, devoid of 'polite' training from babyhood, was an initiator with no notion of submission unless she chose. Possession never ceded to experience. Chris Langlands recognised that criticism by females was induced by envy and fear. They were baffled by her ability to enslave 'and run parallel with any man', making her, in her thirties, a formidable opponent.[31] In his spiritual inclinations, Chris reluctantly concluded that for his needs, Beryl 'had a cylinder missing somewhere. She was tough and detached over each of us at Mweiga . . . If a man caught her fancy, she was a real go-getter . . . not approved of, in those days.'[32]

Beryl's lack of a mother, teachers, church and conventional society had left her unsullied by erotic inhibition. Adept as any *moran* at choosing a partner for the night, as Chris Langlands verified, her primitive side was thrust into view, in her contradictory needs for privacy, guidance and independence.[33] Indeed Beryl's independence appeared torn by a desire for intimacy, in conflict with public proof that she did not require the security of fidelity.[34] Throughout her life, her most powerful weapon in her arsenal of charm was not just that easy grace with which she captivated, but how she made every man feel that if *he* let her down, 'it would be terrible . . . as the one person she had been counting upon'.³⁵

Beryl was thirty-one when she got her commercial licence. She had never looked more svelte or glamorous in the pale blue shirt, teamed with navy blue slacks for flying. Her long legs looked longer and her eyes seem bluer in a face devoid of make-up.

Soon Beryl and Woody were freelancing for others as it became clear that air-charter was too *avant garde* for Mombasa. Flying took them more often up-country, journeys undertaken without notice, Beryl in The Kan, Woody in his Klemm.³⁶ Beryl found its 90h.p. Pobjoy engine sensitive and reliable but preferred her Avian to his low-winged monoplane as it was less adaptable for bush landing.³⁷ Acting as ambulances for people and animals, rescuing the injured from motor accidents, taking a vet or doctor to the scene of an emergency, rushing business people about, in a hurry to get to their destination to make a deal – they both enjoyed such demands. Beryl would fly off on some commission which Woody had fixed up for her, promising to be back that night. If she went to Nairobi she was often prevented from keeping her word. By the time she returned, he was so relieved to see her and the Avian in one piece that he found nothing to forgive.³⁸

She would eventually find his passion and solicitude for her intrusive and demanding, but when their affair was at its height, if either was in the Mweiga district on a Friday, separately or together they joined the flying crowd from Seremai in Nyeri at the White Rhino, a small hotel built by Denys's friend, Berkeley Cole, Fridays being significant throughout the Colony as 'farmers' day'. In each town, settlers descended in hordes. Every week, the Carberrys, in JC's huge American drop-head coupé 'a lovely Auburn Straight, which did twelve miles to the gallon' raced along the narrow track at a ferocious pace to Nyeri, round the series of steep hair-pin bends 'knocking anyone to smithereens who obstructed his way'.³⁹ Anyone heading for Nanyuki 'in the opposite direction on Fridays, drove hand-on-horn in deadly fear of meeting JC on the road'.⁴⁰

Some time in 1934, in the bar of the White Rhino, JC dared Beryl to fly the Atlantic against the wind, during one of these lunch-time sessions in its crowded, small, dark, cedar-panelled room. As Beryl's own laid-back recollection indicates, 'We were all having drinks and laughing, joking when JC came up with the idea.'[41]

Jim Mollison's failed attempt at crossing from Portmarnock in Ireland non-stop to New York two years earlier had been under fierce discussion. JC had never forgotten the 'popping and banging' of his machine as it expired over the sea at Monaco in 1914. Nor had eighteen years obliterated his chagrin at having to scratch from the Schneider. He was bent on redressing that failure, arguing the difficulties of Mollison's attempt, pointing out the effects of head-winds on engine performance.[42] Somehow, some day, JC intended to break a record over land and water himself. At random, he suddenly taunted Beryl, 'Think of all that black water. Think how cold it is Burrrl.'[43]

JC knew Beryl would have to pick up the gauntlet, could hardly refuse before that crowd of madcaps, especially the show-off Prud-homme, whose antics had included 'flying under a bridge of the Nile to amuse himself'.[44] JC himself refused to wear goggles or a helmet while flying, defiantly smoking his pipe in the cockpit.

Beryl could not ignore the challenge – 'So I ended up flying the Atlantic, which wasn't very clever ... rather stupid,' conceding, aged eighty, 'Lucky to be alive.'[45] Mrs Weir-Mosely, June's mother, had urged Beryl on, promising to welcome her in New York if she would try. Now JC's ambition crystallised too as he sought the best and latest design capable of long haul over water. The Vega Gull which Beryl was to fly was not even on the drawing board yet at de Havillands.[46]

Whether Beryl was already dead set on the attempt is less significant, perhaps, than a turn of events which resulted in the desire for revenge. On one of her trips to Muthaiga Club, she discovered that Tom Campbell Black had been in Kenya for six weeks for the the 1934 safari season, with the Furness family on Duke's annual shooting expedition, yet had made no attempt to contact her. His negligence cut her to the quick, demeaning her in the eyes of mutual friends; especially awkward was a rumour about Tom's intention to break sóme record with a flying ace.[47] In addition, though less hurtful to Beryl, was gossip over a *contretemps* between Duke, his daughter, Averill, and Andrew Rattray his white hunter;

the whole Colony seemed to know about their elopement except Beryl. The drama had unfolded in camp. Tom, little better than an errand boy, was dispatched to find them – too late, for they had married – then to place an announcement in the *East African Standard*, to the effect that Rattray had 'ceased to be' Duke's white hunter.[48] Duke was 'in such a stew . . . he wanted to shoot Rattray' and had ended up 'by cutting Averill off without a penny'. The Colony was obsessed by the matter,[49] and assumed that Beryl could enlighten them. The degree to which Beryl felt obscured and insulted may be measured by the letter she sent Tom demanding an explanation. His sheepish reply in April from the Royal Aero Club in London, filled with lame excuses, begged Beryl to ignore 'never-mattering-people . . . in the little tin-pot land of Kenya' because the Colony suffered 'deadly undercurrents of jealousy'. Pre-empting her reaction did nothing to appease her. Tom confirmed that C. W. A. Scott was to co-pilot *The Comet* in the Mac-Robertson Air Race from Mildenhall to Melbourne in October which was more than she had bargained for. Given their involvement, she had not expected to be the last to know.[50] To dampen adverse reaction, and wrest her sympathy, Tom emphasised his sense of oppression in working for a man so powerful as Furness, 'I long to become a personality again . . . freed from the monotony of a well-paid job' and that a victory in the air offered one solution.[51] His mistake was to whinge; Beryl despised grumbling, regarding it as a weakness much as she did Tom's inability to realise his desire for betterment. In the role of employee it was considered bad enough that Tom's reputation was tarnished in Kenya since abandoning Florrie for Furness. Tom was accused of 'leaving his partners in the shit, with a plane they could not fly which Tom was no longer interested in flying.' Meanwhile Florrie's biplane, the Waco, lay idle for six months until Tom's replacement was found. 'Mossie' Mostert, the new head of Wilson Airways, took his place in more ways than one as another of Beryl's conquests.[52]

Whatever spurred Beryl on, she was to notch up 2,000 flying hours by September 1936.[53] Certainly interviews indicate that she had been mulling over her assault on the Atlantic for over a year. Now, like a horse impatient to be off at the starting gate, her practical response within a fortnight of receiving Tom's news was to enter the Aerial Derby, flying over childhood territory, competing against Woody, 'Silver' Jane Stanton, Chris Langlands, St Barbe and Gabriel Prudhomme to inaugurate Njoro Airfield by winning. Victory came almost too easily. Part of her first prize was a joy ride in an RAF Vickers V1. The Captain was Malin Sorsbie who asked about her future plans. She told him she was leaving for London forthwith in connection with a 'solo' attempt on the Atlantic.[54]

Because of exceptional rains, Woody and JC were against her going. Beryl hated to be stymied. Arguing that she was committed to giving a lift to a nephew of Blix in return for the cost of her fuel, she made ready. JC's landing field was waterlogged; her passenger's luggage had overloaded The Kan. St Barbe, seeing she would not be deflected, offered to fly the Avian to Nyeri for her, where, with a chance for better take-off, she could re-load; to this compromise she agreed. However, poor visibility, due either to weather or drugs, impaired St Barbe's judgement causing him to hit a furrow on JC's runway, overturning The Kan, damaging its propeller. Spares took six weeks to come from England.

A further delay ensued when Beryl came down with malaria, a disease notorious for emerging when its victim is below par. Her fever increased as Woody flew her to Nairobi to hospital. She refused to be admitted, so he took it in turns with Ruta to nurse her at Muthaiga. Woody's capacity for unselfish love and prodigious energy were qualities that had earned him Rothschild's praise and later the Duke of Windsor's.

Once Beryl recovered, 'to cheer her up' Woody flew her in the Klemm to Europe.[55] They got no further than Paris. In the Hotel Meurice they 'had a tremendous row over money' in a quarrel so serious that it culminated in returning to Nairobi the way they had come.[56] On top form once more, Beryl shared the flying but on that homeward journey Woody announced that he was resigning from the business.

Beryl ensconced herself at Muthaiga again, working instead from Nairobi. St Barbe had repaired The Kan. Woody joined the burgeoning East African Airways. They forgot their differences, staying friends. Beryl was getting less and less work from the Flying Circus; that November Blix hired her for her first elephant-scouting commission. Experimental flying is perhaps the most inspiring yet fateful of all. In the next six months, she was to evolve her own means of getting vital information in the bush to hunter and client below. In this highly dangerous and exacting task, Beryl would scrawl information on a pad attached to her knee; these notes were stuffed into weighted canvas and leather pouches, with yellow and blue ribbons attached; the Markham racing colours stood out among dense wait-a-bit thorn.[57]

Blix had failed for three weeks to find prize ivory for a Member of Parliament, Colonel Leonard Ropner. On Ropner's last day out, thanks to Beryl, he bagged an elephant and was indebted enough to record this in an article for the London *Evening Standard* when he got home.[58] Blix was so impressed that he booked her immediately for two American clients, Alfred Vanderbilt and, no less important, Winston Guest, whose father, Captain Freddie Guest, was first Air Minister for England and owned land at Nanyuki. It was through Vanderbilt and Guest that Beryl encountered (albeit briefly) Ernest Hemingway.

Hemingway was out with Tanganyika Guides run by his hunter, Philip Percival (Percival had become *doyen* of African safari guides since Denys's death) who was in loose partnership with Blix. Beryl was instructed to go to their office in town near the Norfolk Hotel, collect any mail or supplies for Alfred Vanderbilt, and fly these to Percival's ranch, Potha, before Blix left for the bush with him.

Percival's house stood on a pimple-like hill. Its shady verandah was reached by a steep flight of steps and offered a panoramic view of the Kapiti Plains where Beryl had made her first solo bush landing. It was the ideal spot for recounting yarns. Potha spelled adventure; its outer walls were hung with trophies of every sort from python skins to impala horns. Hemingway was to immortalise Percival as 'Pop' in *The Green Hills of Africa* and it was among the house-party that Beryl met Hemingway. Percival's most illustrious client was recovering from a bout of dysentry but well enough to go out for a ride, accompanied by his wife, Pauline Pfeiffer, Blix and Vanderbilt, besides Percival and herself. While hacking over the plains the Americans teased Hemingway for the way in which he sat a horse – solely as a means of locomotion. Hemingway's riposte was that he took after Tod Sloan (an American jockey, who used notoriously short stirrups), dismissing the jibes. However the teasing was to prompt Hemingway later to paraphrase in a letter one of Blix's oft-repeated quotes, 'riding is riding, and fun is fun and as old Blicky used to say "It's always so quiet when the goldfish die".'[59]

Whenever Hemingway heard a good line, like many writers, he hoarded it to use later. Once Beryl flew out of Potha, Blix's run-down on her love-life intrigued him. Shortly after his own forth-coming safari with Beryl, Blix was to recount to Hemingway what happened during self-exile in Tsavo with her. Blix was notorious for boasting openly about women with whom he'd slept[60] and, in this instance, the repercussions of his bragging resulted in Heming-way's now famous quote, 'I knew her fairly well in Africa'.[61]

While Blix and Vanderbilt headed by car for camp, Beryl flew to Denys's favourite area near Voi, scouting elephant. Vanderbilt's bag was dismal yet Beryl's success for Ropner had convinced Blix that they could improve upon Vanderbilt's bad luck for Winston Guest. Blix asked Beryl to accompany him on a two-month reconnaissance, again into Tsavo. Her contribution was The Kan and her skill; Blix supplied fuel, a mechanic, the camp and running costs. Above all Blix wanted the exercise kept secret, writing to Cockie in London that she tell no one – possibly to avert gossip over Beryl: 'We intend to make a lot of money for us both.'[62] Blix pitched three camps, one at Makindu, the others at Voi and Tsavo. Beryl flew between each for two and a half hours every morning, and again over the same territory in the afternoon, carefully moni-toring the creatures. One herd at Makindu were so accustomed to her manouevres that they became 'as familiar as domestic pets'.[63] If she made twice as much money on such assignments the risk was double. Bush landing is ever hazardous; wild pigs dig holes overnight, termites create hills where none were the day before; she had to be constantly alert to meandering game, scanning a crude landing strip several times before coming down.

Some were puzzled by Beryl's fling with Tania's former husband. Beryl herself claimed to know Blix 'too well' to have an affair. Even so she may have been compelled to prove again to herself that, as different as she was from Tania, she could seduce the two men whom Tania had elected partners for life. Beryl made the point more than once how possessiveness was Tania's undoing with both; indeed Beryl's conviction was that, of all the men in the world whom Tania had chosen to pinion, Blix and Denys were the worst candidates.[64] While Denys had loved, discreetly, several equally fascinating and ardent women, Blix, in a word, was incorrigible. Blix was less selective and, aged fifty, 'of undiminished appetite, stamina and extravagance'. Gin was Blix's elixir and he blamed his needs on the mythical Dr Turvey. Bunny Allen remains baffled that both these women could have been attracted to two men, who, beyond legendary physical stamina, were so different. Bror 'wrought from crude pottery . . . rough . . . ready, [was] more at home in a low-class beer garden'. Denys had been 'the copy-book gentleman . . . delicate as Royal Doulton'. [65] Beryl's explanation is uncomplicated. She slept with Blix; she was in love with Denys, enthralled that he had responded to her, even for a while. He would remain special because he had offered the challenge, missing so often in her other relationships. Beryl made no bones about the chance element with Blix: 'We were alone . . . in elephant country . . . drinking champagne. He said to me, "Darling (he called everybody darling), do you realise, we get paid by the hour for this?" '[66]

Upon their return to civilisation, each confronted trouble. Chris Langlands had decided to close the Blue Bird Flying Circus – 'not just because there was not enough work, Beryl was very awkward about money. We did not see eye to eye.'[67] Chris expected her to pool all earnings whereas Beryl, as the only pilot specialising in elephant scouting, assumed that she could keep such money for herself.[68] Brushing aside his displeasure, she left to meet Blix for the Guest safari. As for Blix, Cockie not only found on her return from Europe that he was more broke but that his affections had wandered towards another blonde pilot, Eva Dixon. Divorce was instigated.

At least the Guest safari looked as if it would meet expectations; though Winston disapproved of aerial scouting, his brother Raymond could not have cared less if it was unsporting.[69] 'Wolfie', as Hemingway called Winston, stood over six foot. Both brothers had the wide shoulders of American football players, their handicap at polo was 10. Beryl got to know the entire family now, flying each at different times into camp, including their exquisite sister, Diana, aged twenty-three, for whom Blix fell heavily.

The Guests' relationship with Beryl was one of mutual admiration, as Diana recalled. They willingly cleared the bush of anthills, and filled ditches to make it safe 'for Beryl to descend upon unknown fields . . . putting out sheets to show her its limits for a splendid pilot with a great sense of navigation . . . we all loved her'.[70] Thanks to her efficiency, Blix was in his seventh heaven, with Diana around and not a care in the world.

The highlight of the safari was the day when Beryl attempted to photograph elephant using Chris's Leica. At the click of its shutter, a bull advanced; when its trunk went up Beryl fled and, after it gave two ear-splitting blasts, exclaimed, 'By Jove, I've never been so frightened in my life.' As they were exhausted from trekking, the notion of a swim was irresistible. Beryl flew Wolfie down to the Indian Ocean for a dip, skimming over the Balanites thorn to bathe in the rough surf of Malindi Bay. They flew back along the strip of white sandy coves with shallows patterned like jade turtle-shell, for sundowners in camp before dark. That night, replete around the fire, they marvelled at the scope of their day's adventures. The safari at an end, Beryl returned to Muthaiga. Blix struck camp, going by train from Voi to Mombasa, meeting up once more with Vanderbilt and Hemingway's party who were also bound for Marseilles with Blix, on the liner SS *Gripsholm*. As they steamed towards the Mediterranean, hour after hour was spent in the Ritz Bar in the stern, drinking gin and swapping hunting yarns.

Dissolution of the Blue Bird Flying Circus raised awkwardness over earnings which Beryl had failed to submit. She was to remain uneasy over depositing cheques, maintaining that 'banks were robbers with licences,' never grasping that the system, the accountant or bank manager were there to help her.[71] Beryl's proof of solvency was what was in her pocket; her image of wealth was embodied in those stacks of coins that her father had amassed on pay-day, to be buried by the Kipsigis labourers after collecting it. She had no confidence in any system of deferred payment. The time would come when her attitudes were detrimental. Cheques for considerable sums were to be left unbanked; once these resurfaced the bank clerk informed her not only were they invalid, but years out of date.[72] It dawned upon Chris that Beryl was neither a snob about commerce, nor had she tried to chisel the company; she was adrift in a sea of European standards which were beyond her comprehension. She had seemed incapable of understanding that she was expected to live on her basic salary until the end of the year when bonuses were paid out.[73] Chris continued nevertheless to carry a torch for Beryl, for it came as a surprise to him, as it did to others in her thrall, that Beryl was desperate for evidence of her worth, reassurance of her desirability, even where there was already ample proof.

Her overlapping affairs with Boy Long and Roddy Ward ought to have given her confidence. Her trysting place with Boy was now Torr's Hotel, opposite the New Stanley in the heart of Nairobi. Rose Cartwright likened Boy's aura to that of Denys, 'a Lothario whose looks belied a good, solid farmer'.[74] Boy would book a table regularly on the balcony overlooking Torr's ballroom and the musicians would strike up, 'Miss Otis Regrets', as Beryl took the floor with him for the first dance of the evening. Afterwards 'a couple of bottles of champagne were sent over for the band.'[75] Boy's wife came to loathe what the Torr's drummer called 'Beryl's signature tune' because he tended to hum 'Miss Otis' absent-mindedly after returning to Naivasha, signifying his latest assignation with Beryl.[76]

The day after her thirty-second birthday, Beryl's vanity was wounded by Tom Campbell Black, when she found herself in the ignominious position, in October 1934, of having the local rag thrust at her, beseiged at Muthaiga for a reaction to his 'superhuman' win. Tom and Charles Scott had taken a few minutes under three days to reach Australia. Less easy to assimilate, impossible to parry was the headine 'AIR RACE ROMANCE' datelined London, 23 October, syndicated from the British tabloids. Tom's passion for an actress, Florence Desmond, had prompted an exchange of keepsakes beforehand with the probability of marriage, dependent on his victory.[77] For the third time, Tom had pulled the rug psychologically from beneath Beryl. Loss of face was paramount, but she cabled sweetly: 'DARLING IS IT TRUE THAT YOU ARE TO MARRY FLORENCE DESMOND? STOP. PLEASE ANSWER. STOP. HEARTBROKEN.'[78] Tom ignored it.

At Burrough Court, when Enid Furness saw the publicity on

Tom's romance, she predicted, 'If Beryl finds out about this, there will be hell to pay.' Enid had watched the relationship develop between their pilot and the comedienne; Duke had introduced the couple at Le Touquet.[79] Enid was right. Beryl's intuition usually dictated that she did the leaving. Tom knew well enough that if Beryl's pride suffered a blow, it was time to watch out. Retribution was on the cards. Curiously, while he did not reply, Tom put Beryl's cable in a trunk where his log-books and charts were stored at the Royal Aero Club.

It was agreed in some circles that the reason Beryl never opted out of flying the Atlantic was that too many of her peers had witnessed JC's taunt. The authorised biography suggests that the intention behind the flight was to show Tom that Beryl was no nonentity 'after he'd dumped her, for Florence Desmond'.[80] This is undoubtedly true, although Beryl was hardly 'dumped'. Tom had been living in England for almost two years. Beryl had never heard of Florence Desmond. The world of music-hall and theatre until now had been closed to her. What Beryl did understand was Tom's escape from the bourgeoisie via marriage to 'a name'.

JC now ordered the Percival Vega Gull in which Beryl was to meet his challenge, with one caveat: she must bring his machine back in good order so that he could race it for himself.[81] By any standards, it was a tall order.

Beryl had taken delivery of a blue and silver Leopard Moth that September. Still preferring The Kan for bush landing, the advantage of the new machine was that it could carry two passengers side by side behind her. This high-winged monoplane had a cruising speed of 120 m.p.h.[82] and now she pushed herself with a stamina that was daunting, mainly flying to the Kakamega goldfields. Beryl was also commissioned to carry the mail 'for about three weeks', deputising for the Chief Pilot of East African Airways, 'Flip' Fleming, who was indisposed from malaria.[83] Beryl's first assignment in the Leopard Moth had been to search for Woody who had gone missing in the Serengeti. For two days she flew over and over the same terrain in the hope of detecting a wisp of smoke, signalling that he was alive still.[84] Beryl found him suffering from nervous exhaustion.[85]

The minute Beryl heard that the Vega Gull was advanced enough for JC to meet her in London, she sold The Kan, bade Ruta and her father farewell, and made arrangements to fly to England in her Leopard Moth. Blix, who was desperate for money and to reach Diana Guest in Paris, begged Beryl to take him with her, needing also to escape his creditors. Wolfie and Freddie Guest loaned him the money towards her fuel. Clutt warned Beryl that he was giving up the responsibility of her yard. If she needed him, she would find him in Durban. For the first time in his life, Ruta was thrown on his own resources by Beryl's departure.

In the equivalent of a six-thousand-mile moonlight flit for Blix, Beryl left Africa with him while the Abyssinian War was in progress and at a time when North Africa was controlled by Mussolini's troops.[86] Beryl knew the route but it was still dangerous; airfields resembled in places the surface of the moon. It was lucky that she had Blix for company when no woman was allowed to fly between Juba and Wadi Halfa alone during the war without permission from the RAF headquarters at Khartoum, because of the risk of forced landing in the forbidding swamps of the Sudd. Dust storms alternated as the country below turned from green to gold and back again.

At Luxor, the hotel booking-clerk tried to get them into a double room. Only after Blix protested, 'I snore,' could they get separate accommodation.[87] At Cairo neither wished to be beholden to the other for entertainment. Beryl's friends were at Heliopolis at the RAF and Imperial Airways bases.

Back at Shepheards Hotel at midnight, one Imperial Airways Captain, hearing a tap on his door, opened it to find Beryl standing there, smiling the smile of the Sphinx, having decided to spend the night with him. Next morning, his junior officer, 'Jimmy' Algar, was dispatched to waken him when he failed to report for duty. Algar was embarrassed to find the pair still in bed, nervous that he would be in trouble for disturbing a senior officer in delicate circumstances. 'Not a bit of it,' Algar later gloated, 'I was taken care of by Beryl myself, for the rest of her stay in Cairo.'

At Benghazi, Blix and Beryl stayed in a brothel. The military had commandeered everything else. They took off next morning in a formidable dust-storm, typical of the area; the headwind assisted take-off, her machine becoming airborne within twenty-five yards, veering over bent date palms. As they flew towards the sun, below was a carpet of dust. 'Beryl smiled and took out her bearing on Tripoli'.[88] Here soldiers suspended their documents; while these were cleared, they dined in solitary confinement, 'on spaghetti and chianti, in our rooms in bad humour'. They were glad to leave, hurricane conditions or no. Beryl's absolute calm reassured Blix to a degree but even he wondered whether they should re-route to Cagliari; but with too much risk of running into the mountains, Beryl took the machine up to 6,000 ft instead, where they saw the sun again. After two hours, spotting a hole in cloud, down through it she came, to plane the surface of the sea. Sighting land not twenty miles from her target, her bird-sense had brought her almost to St Raphael, near Cannes. Nerve-racking as the trip had been, Blix thought it, 'much more fascinating than a voyage with deck chairs and stylish bars'.[89] In Paris, Diana Guest was waiting for him so Beryl took herself to bed. At 4 a.m. she was awakened: 'Get up and open the door, we must have champagne darling!'

'That was OK for him,' Beryl pointed out afterwards, 'but I had to fly to London later that morning.'

'Get the hell out, Blix,' she ordered, 'I'm fast asleep.'[90]

That brisk dismissal was farewell to Africa until her fifties, and to Blix forever.

12

The Waterjump

(1936)

Beryl blazed through her thirty-fourth year like a comet. The thrill of record-breaking flights was momentous; indeed the world was waiting to be astonished by the woman-across-the-water race and Beryl would not disappoint it. Transatlantic crossing had become a matter of national pride among pilots worthy of the name. The British would try 13 times; the French would make 12 attempts; the Germans 10; the Canadians and Poles, 4 each. The 'Waterjump' was the term fliers used for this route among themselves.[1] Out of 15 attempts by women, 1 ditched, 1 returned because of bad weather, 3 crashed unable to continue and 5 simply disappeared.[2]

Her attempt on the Waterjump preoccupied Beryl's waking hours from the time she reached London: she went straight to JC's flat in Park Lane for a meeting about it. JC had reserved and paid for a suite for Beryl at the Mayfair Hotel into which she moved. She felt uncomfortable about this arrangement, especially as since 1928 she had always stayed in the suite regarded as hers at the Grosvenor. She feared the condescension of friends who might sympathise with her over the loss of this former luxury. Beryl was always happy in the most spartan of humble of dwellings, except while in London. Staying at the Mayfair demeaned her. It also emphasised that the Duke had moved on, after so many years. None the less, the moment she got the chance, she moved to Claridge's, staying there afterwards when needing a hotel in London.[3]

Beryl could not ignore royal protocol in 1936. The fact that Queen Mary 'never wanted to hear the name Kenya uttered again' was well known at Court after Beryl's settlement. Equally, though no formal conditions were imposed upon Beryl, the Queen did not want her in England: visits were supposed to be limited to three weeks per annum. Nor was she supposed to contact the newly married Duke, residing with his wife at York House.[4] The Duchess of Gloucester, née Lady Alice Montagu-Douglas-Scott, was the niece of Lord Francis Scott of Rongai. The couple had married in a quiet ceremony in Buckingham Palace Chapel on 6 November 1935.

Such developments effectively cut Beryl off from the life to which she had become accustomed in London. Besides, the mood had altered in England itself with King George's death in January when the Duke's brother, Edward VIII, ascended the throne. His reign was greeted with the hope that his boyish charm and pledge of reform would herald a new era for his subjects. But already the monarch's life was worrying his statesmen. Understandably enough, he had sought relief from the strain of his exalted and lonely position; there were fewer chances than ever for him to indulge in casual affairs such as he had conducted with Beryl and other women. Freda Dudley Ward and Thelma Furness had been one thing. A twice-married American, Mrs Simpson, was hardly what the King's advisors had in mind for a consort. As Wallis Simpson's company became more vital to the King, anxiety mounted when the scandal they created made clear that he could not relinquish his relationship with her in favour of his Crown.[5]

Down the years Beryl's friends in Kenya, especially Ginger, were convinced that, owing to her tenuous connections with the royal brothers, 'the establishment ensured that coverage of Beryl's flight was minimal.'[6] Cockie's brother, Ulick, implied that this would have been preferred at Court but Beryl was news anyway once it leaked out that she would attempt the Waterjump. The Press had marked her out earlier as a headline personality and now would beseige her.[7]

Meanwhile she was to be a working woman; JC arranged for her to meet François Dupré, owner of the George V and Plaza Hotels in Paris. Dupré took her on to replace Amy Johnson in their firm, Air Cruises, which provided pleasure trips 'for fastidious clientele', flying between European capitals and putting them up at the smartest hotels, including Dupré's own.[8] Beryl's role at Air

Cruises involved ferrying the Frenchman between Hatfield and Le Bourget in his new twin-engined de Havilland Dragon, and as Dupré had many business interests in America and Canada, there was ample time for her to visit Gravesend regularly, as the Vega Gull took shape.

Beryl had just started work at Air Cruises when Tom Campbell Black decided that it was time to introduce his actress wife to Beryl. Coming face to face over afternoon tea, with the woman Tom had eulogised, Florence Desmond was non-plussed. 'Certainly the ·attractive woman . . . with wavy hair . . . and long, thin nervous hands' did not fit his description.[9] Her impression had been of 'a dreamy personality' and it never ceased to amaze her, as she got to know Beryl better, that this most feminine of creatures 'could drive, let alone fly an aeroplane'.[10] Each person meeting Beryl for the first time was struck by her unique qualities. Dupré had been impressed by her briskness and punctuality; for Tom, it was her 'magnificence as a horsewoman' – something Florence could never emulate, as she was nervous of horses and rode badly. Whether Beryl deliberately disguised herself or whether her camouflage was unconscious, it is clear that it worked. She had quickly shown Florence Desmond that 'knowing' her was impossible. Part of her was inscrutable; a trick learned at her father's knee.

Beryl's forthcoming flight provided the explanation for what Florence assumed was her preoccupation. But there was undoubtedly a strong antipathy in ·Beryl towards the woman who had caused her to lose face. Beryl's talent to arrest was possibly threatening even to Florence Desmond, who used her own charisma on stage to earn a living. Beryl's presence alone provided an aura. Florence Desmond's inability to understand Beryl's sexual attraction was possibly a wilful denial; perhaps Beryl's inscrutability stood in the way. Wherever Beryl was, she had that dimension which, in any walk of life lends to the legend – distinction. She would continue to baffle, continue to break rules, remain her own woman, do everything her own way, yet she was more practical, had more of a grasp on reality than she has ever been given credit for, concealing these qualities with that free and easy manner, that light-heartedness, so appealing to men. Tom had not given his wife a clue as to the nature of his earlier relationship with

Beryl. He had played up her outdoor-girl style, so that Florence was also surprised, when she saw that on Beryl's dressing table in the hotel bedroom stood a large assortment of face creams, lotions and perfumes. These were actually a gift-sample from Amy Johnson, whose beauty case design for Air Cruises was to attract the female tourist.

Like most high-definition performers, Beryl found no hardship in applying her energy to a goal. Kipsigis games had taught her the patience to inch toward improvement. In 1936, as spring gave way to summer, with efficient detachment Beryl divided her free time, plying between Heston, twelve miles west of London, and Gravesend, home of the de Havilland flying school, eight miles north, where, under Edgar Percival's eye, the Vega Gull was taking shape.[11]

Heston was a socially smart club and run on oiled wheels by Airwork Limited. Its well heeled members took to Beryl at once, because in spite of not being gregarious, she 'was never heard to shoot a line' and, for someone as beautiful, her modesty and unobtrusive personality made all the more impact. These qualities won her the unequivocal respect of her peers. No one realised where she was planning to fly, though she was noticed continually 'poring over maps'. But once she had etched her name in aviation history, all who had met her earlier at Heston wanted to make it into a turning point.

Beryl, who as usual never embellished the depth of any relationship, 'seemed to be JC's girlfriend' and was one of only three or four female pilots to frequent the club house. Usually she was accompanied by 'the bold, lecherous, brave and dissipated JC', Jim Mollison or Tom Campbell Black, and just occasionally by all three. Beryl was never seen in the bar, only in the restaurant or on the tarmac.[12]

Tom had left Furness. His own small air-charter company at Heston Park kept him busy delivering British Gaumont newsreels all over England. He too had an entry for the Schlesinger, a Percival Mew Gull, *Miss Liverpool,* which the city of that name was sponsoring. Tom's antipathy toward Mollison was no secret. Mollison was currently escorting Beryl in the evenings, usually to the Hungaria in Lower Regent Street, favoured also by the King and Mrs

Simpson. What puzzled members at Heston was Beryl's attachment to the 'aloof, unpleasant' JC. Had they known that his was the flying machine in which she would make her record-breaking attempt, rumour might have been quashed.

Beryl commanded a great deal of respect at Gravesend among the team of engineers working on the Vega Gull, where her knowledge of engines was obvious. Ninety Vega Gulls were built there, their works numbers ranging from K20-K109. The pale yellow model that Beryl would blood bore the serial number K34, indicating that production had been under way for almost a year. The P10 Vega Gull was developed out of the Gull designed by A. A. Bage, using the same form of wooden construction, and the prototype had been flown the November before by Percival himself. Since then its fuselage had been lengthened by 9 inches, and widened by 44, to allow side-by-side seating for two passengers. Dual controls were fitted, split edge trailing flaps incorporated in its folding wings. The engine was a standard 200 h.p. de Havilland Gipsy-Six – cruising speed 163 m.p.h. – to drive a newly introduced French Ratier, electrically operated variable-pitch propeller, enabling the aircraft to fly higher and faster; but there was no wireless. Equipped with full 'blind' flying instruments, in all major respects, JC's machine was standard apart from the extra tankage to provide a total of 255 gallons, permitting a range of the order of 3,800 miles with an airspeed of 150 m.p.h.. This model, with its Kenya registration VP-KCC, was christened *The Messenger*. Timing was becoming crucial; Percival was running late on delivery by the end of July. The longer he needed, the less chance Beryl had of good weather, and she was mindful of JC's entry in the Schlesinger Air Race marking the Golden Jubilee of Johannesburg where the victor hoped to mark the start of celebrations in October.[13]

The Press learned that Beryl had been at the controls of *The Messenger* on 15 August preparing for a record-breaking solo flight, and needed little encouragement from then on to write up scandalous titbits so as to boost circulation of their newspapers. The banner headlines, 'SOCIETY WOMAN PLANS TO FLY ATLANTIC ALONE' initiated twenty days when journalists shadowed her continually.[14] The image of Beryl captured for posterity in the international newspapers and flickering newsreels is a lingering one; the shy hesitant smile breaking into the full grin of a far younger person; the tacit grace; the tall glamourous woman in male attire who captured the heart of flying enthusiasts everywhere. She was quoted, photographed and every possible angle of her life was exploited in daily reports. She pleaded over and over to be left alone; privacy was always important to her; her requests were ignored.

With her past royal attachments she made even more delectable copy. The cruellest aspect for one so genuinely shy is that her life could never be private again. She had learned to let the gossip flow, shrugged it off in her philosophy of 'let-them-say'. Now the attitude of the Press disquieted her. She found herself always on the defence. She fought belittlement on account of her sex. With no preparation for such a barrage of publicity, in a manner as understated as it was charming she handled the hordes eager for a scoop with dignity, never allowing herself to be phased by outrageous insinuation, which even by today's standards was insulting. The Express Group, through the machinations of Harry Bruno, Beryl's publicity manager, realised that she had no newspaper backer (unlike Amy Johnson who had been sponsored by the *Daily Mail*) and signed Beryl up for an exclusive story. The *Daily Express* now began to build readership of the event and published Beryl's views on the daunting prospect. Her modest approach is as apparent as her serious intent: 'Two weeks from now I am going to set out to fly the Atlantic to New York. Not as a society girl. Not as a woman even. And certainly not as a stunt aviator. But as a . . . graduate of one of the hardest schools known, with 2,000 flying hours to my credit. And I have a definite object. It is true that I am known as a society woman. But what of it? The only thing that really counts . . . is whether one can fly . . . I can take an engine apart and put it back. I can navigate. I am fit . . . given ordinary luck I am sure I can fly to New York. This is to be no stunt flight. No woman's superiority-over-man affair. I don't want to be superior to men. I have a son. If I can be a good mother to him, and a good pilot, I'll be the happiest creature alive.'[15]

Mention of motherhood was just the hook that the journalists needed. As they descended upon Swiftsden, the Markhams refused to answer prying questions. A photograph of Gervase was published; in the caption he was called Gerald. Someone had confused his name with that of the road of the nursing home where Beryl gave birth to him. Beryl went once to Swiftsden, at Hurst Green in Sussex, to see Gervase, now seven years old. Mansfield's mother, Linga O'Hea, called by her grandchildren 'Gar', ran her home – like all country manors then – with a fleet of servants. These were mainly women and doted on Gervase who, on account of his puny constitution, always needed pampering. A retinue of nannies, maids, cooks and Gar saw to his comforts, while a French governess ensured that he was bilingual. Nor did he want for company of his own age; his cousins, Sir Charles's three, often stayed. But already, perhaps redressing his lack of physical strength, Gervase asserted himself with 'a frightful temper, virtually uncontrolled at times, screaming with rage, getting himself in a frenzy for no reason at all', an impulsiveness that was inherited from Beryl and Mansfield.[16]

It was unfortunate, given Beryl's repulsion for the weak, that Gervase happened to be recovering from meningitis that summer, the only record being a snapshot showing him pallid and sickly, sitting in an old papier-maché bath from nursery days, cooling off on the lawn at Swiftsden with Mansfield posing as protective father. The illusion was deceptive; their relationship was never a happy one. When irritated by him, Mansfield was apt to let fly snide remarks giving Gervase 'a complex about his paternity'.[17] Neighbours recall 'a strange, shy boy'.[18] If family resemblance is anything to go by, his looks show that he was indisputably a Markham, and male cousins in the next generation photographed in prep-school uniform, are so alike, that Gervase may be mistaken for them.[19]

Every so often Beryl would allude to that summer, mentioning that if she was 'out on the town' Gervase would not sleep until she came home. This is a disingenuous comment, given that she only made half a dozen visits to her son and only initiated a visit to Swiftsden once.[20]

Beryl and Mollison's assault on the Waterjump had drawn them together. By now he had admitted 'numerous infidelities from the first month of marriage' to Amy Johnson. The title of his auto-biography *Playboy of the Air* sums up his philandering nature.

Until 1929, aviation had been a male preserve; then the decade of the female pilot began and Beryl became integral to it. Flying was the very symbol of female emancipation. Fashion featured 'quick-change' flying suits for women as a result of the newly developed zip-fastener, even though air shows still tended to resemble garden parties at Brooklands. According to *Vogue*, Amy Johnson insisted on dressing for record-breaking 'as if on a lunch date.[21] Beryl, as usual, opted for the male prerogative; sensible shirts and pullovers, grey flannels worn under white overalls, with no concession to gender, in which she looked fetching none the less. As August drew to a close, the *Daily Express* declared 'ATLANTIC HOLDS NO TERRORS FOR FLYING WOMAN'. Low cloud and squalls of rain increased Beryl's anxiety. She was pictured and captioned, 'a lens-shy beauty . . . fleeing the camera'.

Whether attending the races or relaxing *tête à tête* over a meal, she was never allowed to forget how many had failed the Waterjump before her. Because she was detached and appeared cool and unemotional, people underestimated her knowledge of the significant risk she was taking, assuming that she did not know fear. Yet Beryl was nobody's fool. From the time she had met with JC in his Park Lane flat, she had been waiting to fulfil a goal that she realised was bound to be dramatic whether she succeeded or failed. Time and again, whenever there was a crisis involving others and herself, they would observe, 'to look at her you would not think anything was going on, yet all around her was pandemonium'.[22]

One can trace almost to its seed Beryl's measure of will and nerve, and her willingness to take risks. As a child, having faced the unforgiving nature of the African bush, she had learned that only grim determination will enable a traveller to reach his destination (such as the traversing of those precipitous hills in the dark to reach Denys). Her secret was not to allow the perverse benediction of Africa to dominate her; she made fear and anger work for her, drawing upon some secret cache, a fundamental reserve. Just as she had trained herself to jump higher than Kibii, she had to keep proving herself. She had learned to push back the threshold of fear when faced with danger, just as she had pushed back the threshold of pain. That power of concentration peculiar to her physical activity was learned with Kibii to the point where she became capable of eclipsing fear itself.

This period of waiting was almost more of a strain than the flight. A good weather report meant that she could take off within hours; if rain and cloud persisted, delay could run into weeks. Beryl danced away the nights occasionally at the Kitkat, Café de Paris or the Embassy, but mostly with Mollison at the Hungaria, where one evening a familiar voice from the band took her by surprise, 'Hello Beryl!' She found herself greeting Mickey Migdoll, the ex-Torr's Hotel drummer, whom she had last seen while dancing with Boy Long to 'Miss Otis Regrets' and, treating Mickey to her ultimate gesture of friendship, she flung her arms up in an African salaam – hands above her head, palms open, defenceless; a gesture which, within days, was to become Beryl's trademark internationally, for victory.[23]

She moved herself from Claridge's to Elstree. Lord Aldenham had kindly put at Beryl's disposal his home and the run of his stable of racehorses. Another friend loaned her his aeroplane so that she could make the half-hour flight daily to Gravesend, where final engine checks were being done on *The Messenger*. Each morning Beryl wakened to the plaster rosettes of the ceiling in her bedroom at Aldenham House, to the same thought: maybe today ... if not ... when, when?

Each day, Edgar Percival briefed her, overlooking no detail. She watched him install the petrol tanks in the cabin, and, in case she became confused by fatigue towards the end of her journey, he chalked on each, 'this tank is good for four hours'. The undercarriage was built to carry the extra weight of fuel. He impressed upon her how to avoid airlocks; she must allow the tank to run dry *before* opening the next petcock. This would take nerve he assured her: the engine might go dead, but it would start again – reminding her that de Havilland 'Gipsies never stop'.

On 1 September JC, June and Mrs Weir-Mosely sailed on the *Queen Mary* for New York, in anticipation of Beryl's arrival. The time had come to get *The Messenger* to Abingdon, the RAF base near Oxford. Inching up toward departure, Beryl piloted the machine herself. Visitors were barred from the grounds. Percival had discovered during a test flight that, even with only half the load of fuel Beryl would carry, becoming airborne had taken longer than he envisaged. Abingdon's long military runway was therefore better suited for take-off.

Young RAF officers watched Beryl over the next forty-two hours in disbelief, thought her 'quite mad to attempt the flight'.[24] The Air Ministry was equally against her going. It was too late in the year, the elements too unpredictable, headwinds were likely to be stronger than ever.

The newspapers delivered before breakfast at Aldenham House continued to goad: 'DAREDEVIL SOCIETY WOMAN LEAVES TODAY'; 'BEAUTY TO FLY TODAY'; 'YOUNG MOTHER PLANS FLIGHT TODAY'. Just as relentlessly tomorrow followed. On 2 September she was pictured looking pensive astride one of Lord Aldenham's thoroughbreds, captioned 'disappointed . . . telling her dumb friend all about it'.[25] Next morning, when fog veiled the greater part of England, the *News Chronicle* in its editorial implied Beryl's selfishness, predicting that any achievement would result in 'little but the foundation of a regular mail service' and accusing her of risking unnecessary anxiety and expense, 'to all the ships who would have to search for her'.[26]

To be told in print 'NEVER TAKE OFF', under such duress, was terrible. She would have been inhuman had she not been seized by moments of panic; the only way to parry self-doubt was to act. Mollison and Tom failed to dissuade her from going. On 4 September Mollison flew her to Abingdon but a bomber had overturned on the runway, which must be cleared before she could take off. Yet she remained unruffled.

Solo flight is a unique experience. Once she took off, Beryl's fate was entirely in her own hands. There were no options; no one to discuss or debate decisions with; no one whose advice she could ignore. She alone was obliged to honour JC's faith in her own pride, her desire for excellence, the application of efficiency and skill that Denys would have lauded, had he been alive. Beryl's highly developed peripheral vision gave her an acute sense for 'judging' height; her technical know-how enabled her to handle coolly potentially fatal crises, such as stalling, and she had acquired the intuition that pilots refer to as 'flying by the seat of your pants'.

The evening light waned, the runway had been cleared and *The*

Messenger was pushed out of its hangar and refuelled. Beryl's victuals – five flasks of coffee, a hip-flask of brandy, a cold chicken, some dried fruit, nuts and meat jellies – had been stowed. Mollison handed her the watch he had used for his flight in 1932, reminding her that he expected her to return his good luck talisman. Jock Cameron the engineer gave her a sprig of Scottish heather; she refused a life jacket, it was too bulky to take. The weather was bad. The Gull was heavy. Now, clad in her white flying suit and helmet, she asked the *Daily Express* reporter to identify himself and handed him an envelope. Its content, published next morning, was an open letter making plain how repelled she had been by the dismissive tags with which the editors had assessed her. In what could have been her last opportunity to defend herself to the world, her message is assertive: 'As I am now on the eve of what I believe to be a hazardous flight, I . . . ask the courtesy extended to the condemned, to state my . . . views. "Society-mother", "Flying-mother", "Bird-woman" et cetera, are repugnant to me, I have no pretensions . . . fail to see what an accident of birth has to do with flying the ocean. I may be "just another blonde" but as a professional, accustomed to working for my living . . . this flight could not, even in my wildest dreams, be described as pleasure, I look upon it purely as another job.' She teased Mollison, 'my very real friend' that the outcome would give him 'cause to celebrate or the reverse' and begged for credit as any ordinary human being 'without too many of the conventional virtues'. She could love, laugh, hate and share a drink at the pub with friends, she reminded her readers, 'but I am neither an innocent girl from the country nor a city slicker but an ocean flyer in embryo. If I can dispense with the last two words, I am more than satisfied.'[27]

With a few more asides to bystanders, Beryl eased herself into the cockpit. Edgar Percival swung the air-screw. She buckled her helmet, grinning at Mollison. Sound coverage from the microphone of the crew covering her departure provides another clue to her tension, her voice in a slightly higher register. Looking directly at Winifred Paul* Beryl muttered, *'Twende tu'* ('I'm going'). In all the brevity of that Swahili statement was her defiance over a chorus of disapproval in fear for her safety.[28] 'Goodbye! Good Luck!' she called, more conventionally, and with a wave, taxied down the mile-long runway, expecting that, with her 1,900lb fuel load, she would need most of the runway, but *The Messenger* was airborne in 600 yards. The hearts of onlookers 'missed a beat as its wheels dipped for a second' then rose, cleared the fence and trees beyond. 'Soon it was a minute spot glistening in the sky. At 6.50pm it was gone.'[29]

Since Beryl had no wireless, there was nothing to do but wait for news that *The Messenger* had been sighted by ship or had reached land. Edgar Percival phoned Tom in Liverpool, repeating Mollison's remarks, as the Vega Gull vanished from view: 'Well, that's the last we shall see of Beryl.'[30]

Due to poor visibility, she flew on instruments throughout that night and most of the following day, continually having to face the unrelenting concentration required for her to succeed. She had to fight the extreme tediousness, the fatigue when fuel reserves were running low, which caused her increasing concern as weariness mounted, in the knowledge that failure of a single engine would mean ditching. She could not even radio her approximate position if in trouble. If she fell out of the sky, rescuers would not know where to begin to search for her. In the vast northern Atlantic, the wreckage of a small plane was unlikely to have been spotted by ship. In 1936 few aircraft were available for search, fewer still equipped with any form of dinghy which could have been dropped. Ditching would have involved serious injury or death on impact. If she survived the impact, she would have faced drowning instead; with no life jacket if the plane sank, thirst and exhaustion would have made her chances very slim.[31]

Beryl flew against powerful headwinds, found herself flying upside-down, suffered the feeling of excruciating isolation and longed to give in, but she stood the endurance test. 'Eventually land did show up,' as she put it, in a captivating understatement, disarming everyone and masking her deep-seated dread of any suggestion of inadequacy becoming public.

Beryl had selected, as Alcock had seventeen years before her, what she imagined was a reasonable field upon which to land. *The Messenger* nose-dived into what turned out to be bog. She was near Sydney, Nova Scotia, not New York as had been her ambition. But she had done the Waterjump, the hard way, the only woman *ever* to do it westbound.[32] And she had proved that not only could female pilots triumph east–west, west–east, but on their own. She would learn several hours later that she was at Baleine Cove, some ten miles from Louisburg, Cape Breton Island (45° 55N 60° 00W). *The Messenger* was barely three hundred feet from the water's edge; fuel, as far as Beryl knew, had run out. Fog surrounded her. It was 21 hours 35 minutes after take-off (British Summer Time), a gruelling 2,212 miles from where she started.[33] It was 1.05 New York time, 5 September.

The Gull's propeller was torn off, the landing gear too damaged to make further flying possible. Miraculously Beryl was unhurt but for bruising, shock and a gash on her forehead, streaming blood. After extricating herself from the cockpit, she trudged three miles 'through engulfing mire' for a couple of hours, luckily meeting two fishermen. They guided her to the farmhouse of Alex Burke, through whom New York received the news that Beryl was safe. He also informed Louisburg Airport of her plight, which brought Captain George Lewis to her side who transferred Beryl to his own home. His brother-in-law, Dr Freeman O'Neill, happened to be visiting. He stitched Beryl's brow, treated her for shock, prescribing a mild sedative. As she sipped cups of tea in a stranger's home, the unreality of what she had achieved began to gel as details of her conquest came in.

One aspect in the report that she 'was thrown against the instrument board' inflicting that cut on her forehead had puzzled the pilot 'Flip' Fleming, whom Beryl had replaced to fly the mail in Kenya. The first rule in any forced landing is to tighten one's safety harness. Knowing Beryl's meticulousness, he believed that fatigue had confused her and, having undone her harness to reach a petcock, she had forgotten to refasten it. This never came out in the reports because Beryl would have been loathe to admit that she had failed to adhere to a basic rule. Years after, she admitted to a panic-making moment when she switched petrol tanks and, as Percival had predicted, the Gipsy engine cut and her altimeter spun backwards. Reaching for the remaining fuel tank, 'wasn't too difficult. I just went pinker, pinker, pinker', waving her hands at imaginary petcocks at her feet. She never let on that her harness was undone.[34]

She made it seem so unserious, so easy, that gruelling haul which Reuters and BUP had monitored, though when newspapers carried the headline 'MRS MARKHAM DOES IT' they had not known where she was. She had been sighted by the captain of the SS *Paarndam* off Newfoundland, who had reported to RCA that 'at 7 a.m. Eastern Standard Time, she was in the position 47.54° north latitude and 48.22° west longtitude on course, about 220 miles off St John's Newfoundland'. His telegram also warned, 'Rain, fog, strong winds reported in that area may render her flight hazard-ous'.[35] A Swedish liner, *Kung Kungsholm*, reported also having seen *The Messenger* in the same area.

Flying buffs everywhere argue today that Beryl's feat was greater than that of Charles Lindbergh; if points had to be given to both, she would come out ahead because of the unfavourable headwind; if her speed was slower, the weather was worse, the flight under-taken 90 per cent in the dark.[36] Beryl's 'exclusive' to the Express Group, cabled by Harry Bruno, reveals how near to tears she had come, giving some clue as to how close to her limits of weariness 'battling against the icy gale' had brought her. 'I was just about ready to give up.'[37]

Beryl was ordered twenty-four hours' rest by the doctor to allow her to recover from lack of sleep and nourishment, jangled nerves and eye-strain.[38] The elation of everyone around her, mingled with her own disbelief, made sleep impossible. She insisted on telling JC herself, by phone, that *The Messenger* was crippled and could not be flown in the Schlesinger. When Harry Bruno phoned from the office of New York's Mayor, Fiorella La Guardia, JC and June were with Bruno and all three spoke to her, applauded her, told her to 'leave the wreck . . . forget about it'.[39] As her own harshest critic she could not overlook the fact that she had fallen short of her goal nor the feeling that she had wasted JC's machine and other people's time. That 'dread word failure' loomed.[40] To the world at large, she masked chagrin with flippancy: 'After all it's nice to have landed right side up on my first trip to America.'[41] Thousands of fans, already gathering in anticipation of her arrival in New York, would not compensate for that private sense of failure, made the more burdensome by displays of public adulation.

There had been little in Beryl's experience to prepare her for the tumultuous warmth of the reception the Americans gave her. She was flown from Louisberg to Halifax on Sunday morning where congratulations from the Canadian Government were conveyed by the Premier of Nova Scotia. Thousands of well-wishers had come to greet 'the beautiful lady in blue' as she was dubbed, strolling among them in the sunshine. Beryl signed autographs on improvised materials, varying from cigarette packets to the prayer books of those on their way to church. The sticking plaster on her wound looked almost fetching, as she told fans of her ordeal, 'I never felt so close to death.' Similar scenes were re-enacted at Portland, Boston, North Beach and Queens as she climbed from the Beechcraft 17, *The Staggerwing*, bringing her to Floyd Bennett Field.

At 3.16 p.m., amid frenzied tooting of motor klaxons, a roar went up from 5,000 New Yorkers; the crowd surged toward Beryl as she stepped on to the tarmac. JC, June and Mrs Weir-Mosely embraced her whilst 150 policemen struggled to keep a path for them through the exuberant hordes. People stood up on cars to get a better look at her. Though journalists loved her, confrontations with groups always made her nervous and she would come to regard such scenes as 'trial by Press'. A voice yelled, 'Hi blondie!' and others took up the cry. New Yorkers christened her 'the yellow sparrow'. 'Hello! Hello!' Beryl, responding, threw her hands up over her head in that captivating defenceless gesture with which she had greeted the Duke and now enslaved the throng.

A brief Press conference was held, where she borrowed a lipstick from a female reporter, apologising for her dishevelment. There was something irresistible about the shy Englishwoman who pronounced her Rs as Ws. 'I haven't a stitch ... except what I am wearing, nor a toothbrush, comb nor a pair of stockings.'[42] Since Monday was Labor Day and Americans realised that all shops would be closed, people were overwhelming in their generosity, sending her what amounted to several trunkloads of gowns.

Following a twenty-minute Press conference, Beryl, JC, June and Mrs Weir-Mosely were driven in a limousine, draped with the Union Jack and the Stars and Stripes, to the the Ritz Carlton Hotel. In the lobby where she was offered an orange juice, Beryl teased 'a champagne cocktail' would be more appropriate. For days, the same questions would proliferate: where was she going? What were her flying plans? Who would she see? Mostly she ducked the answers, indicating that the Carberrys would take care of her. Harry Bruno brought a doctor to her suite, to dress her wound and a scratch on one hand which had escaped earlier notice. Apart from a slight headache, Beryl seemed fit, ready to enjoy the accolades pouring in.

That evening, still wearing the same clothes, Beryl appeared on stage at the Avon Theater on W45th Street for a radio interview, a feature of a sponsored programme hosted by the comedian, Milton Berle. It was she who raised the laugh, though, when one of the audience enquired if she had had anything to drink to keep her cheerful during the flight,

'Yes, I did . . . a peg of brandy.'

'Just one?'

'Two, I'm afraid,' she replied, with a bashful giggle.[43]

Her schedule was packed. With fame as her load, Beryl became a workhorse, led out by Bruno in the vast publicity treadmill. Suppliers of parts for *The Messenger* now took their bow with full-page advertisements in such publications as *Flight*, most quoting her. Beryl's triumph became that of KLG Spark Plugs, Wakefield Castrol, Stanvano Aviation Fuel for Esso. 'If it was not for your turn and bank indicator, you wouldn't be getting this acknowledgement', Beryl's Western Union Cable to Reid Sigrist, was blown up across two pages.

On 7 September the New York shops were open again. Beryl went in search of outfits appropriate to the events arranged for her. At the civic reception where she was filmed and photographed with Mayor La Guardia, she appears bemused at the unlikely situation in which she finds herself, dwarfing her host and wearing a nifty, sprigged two-piece costume, her waist accentuated by its peplum.

Beryl found herself trapped between public and private life, which had been very private indeed. Professional recognition was one thing; personal probing never acceptable. In America, threaded through more serious coverage, were references to Beryl's awkward married status which had ricocheted from the gutter press in England so that the backlash of interest embarrassed her in New York. Her personal life was never soft-pedalled. The

Daily Express questioned if she would kiss and make-up with Mansfield. The *New York Times* sought her, but her refusal to comment did not help. Reporters merely chased Mansfield at Swiftsden for what they were after. The *New York Times* hazarded, 'Markham Union Doubted . . . broken romance will not be mended by triumph'. Mansfield and Gervase had 'gone away to escape the crowds'. When reporters would not leave Mansfield alone, he did his best to patch the rift, calling her 'grand', admitting anxiety, a 'trying time . . . a happy ending', expressing relief that Beryl was uninjured. When the *Sunday Dispatch* attempted to winkle more information out of him, he remained gentlemanly but firm, 'The whole world knows that my wife and I are separated . . . we are still good friends.'[44]

When Clutt was located he confessed that he had never been so anxious over his daughter. He too fell into the trap of qualifying her achievement by gender: 'It's the devil of a thing for a woman to have done, all on her own' echoing Mansfield's opinion, 'She's a grand girl.'[45] Few were as proud as the settlers in Kenya to whom 'the Clutterbuck girl' had become a trail-blazer of international standing, astonishing for one who had grown up at Njoro. Even Rose Cartwright cabled her congratulations. In Nairobi, by 9 September, Beryl's mother had emerged from the Aberdares, losing no time in identifying herself at the *East African Standard*, apologetically announcing that 'one of the last people to hear definite news of Mrs Markham's flight . . . was Mrs Kirkpatrick' with the excuse that she was 'far removed from stations and a telegraph line' and now 'eager for details'. Mrs Kirkpatrick declared it 'a marvellous effort . . . although I never had any doubt she would do it. My daughter has always been extremely self-confident . . . full of pluck from the time she was a tiny tot.'[46]

At the height of her triumph, when Beryl might have drowned in all the acclaim, came a numbing shock. She had news that Tom was dead. That he had been killed in an accident was told in all innocence by a reporter who telephoned asking Beryl for her reaction. She somehow managed, 'England has lost a wonderful pilot and I have lost the instructor who taught me all I know about flying.'[47] As if a trap-door were opening beneath her, she now faced a void. Again the death of someone who had been close superceded the pleasure of victory. Beryl cut all her engagements. The *New York Times* noted after her departure that the guest of honour failed to turn up for the banquet Bruno had organised to say farewell.[48]

She boarded the *Queen Mary*, one of 1,500 passengers, at Pier 54, a sad VIP singled out with John Masefield, the poet laureate, to dine at the Captain's table. During the voyage, every day she was drawn to the rail and stared at the sea as if mesmerised by self-doubt. 'If I had known the Atlantic was as big as it seems, would I have had the courage to fly across?' The question gnawed at her and was to be voiced repeatedly to friends; the goal that had once shimmered like a mirage was as insubstantial once achieved.

In dock at Southampton, Beryl, smiling but hollow-eyed, posed for photographs and for the 'talkie camera'. Wearing the latest fashion, she addressed the throng of reporters, her hair made unruly by the breeze. Afterwards Edgar Percival drove Beryl to the civic luncheon to honour her. She heard that Tom had died, 'in little more than the air equivalent to a push-bike crash', while taxiing out on the runway at Speke when a Hawker bomber came taxiing in. Its pilot failed to notice Tom's tiny Mew Gull, and the Hawker's huge propeller 'slashed through the bubble canopy' of *Miss Liverpool* 'carving through his left shoulder and lung also'.[49]

Beryl abandoned her plans. Percival motored to Portsmouth but she boarded the train carrying the reporters back to Fleet Street. One seized this chance to interview Beryl, next day making headlines in the *Daily Mail*. 'I'LL DO IT AGAIN!' Beryl had mentioned that she might fly from New York to Paris, after speaking of her reaction to New Yorkers: 'I do not care for being a celebrity but they were so sincerely kind' that she could not help liking their back-slapping, 'even those who gate-crashed my hotel to kiss the flying-girl'.[50]

Beryl's reputation, cauterised by rumour to which had been added this gigantic achievement, set telephone lines abuzz with misinformation, jealousy and outrage. Now what they did not know, they could easily invent. The *Daily Sketch* scooped her return to London with the truth. 'MRS MARKHAM COMES HOME FORGOTTEN', next to a tryptich, of Beryl in mourning, with three strands of pearls at her neck. She never wore black and since Denys's death disliked intensely the funereal connotation. The caption read, 'For this woman, who risked her life . . . made history . . . not a cheer was raised . . . at Waterloo.'[51]

When Beryl had stepped on to the platform, only Mrs Weir-Mosely was waiting to greet her. Travellers wondered who might warrant photographers descending on the train. As the two women walked towards an open car, 'The intrepid flier was received in silence'. No one recognised Beryl. When one of the journalists at Claridge's tried to edge his way into Beryl's suite, Mrs Weir-Mosely took charge. The homecoming was, 'terribly disappointing . . . the non-flying public are quite incapable of realising what a marvellous performance she has put up. She deserved a magnificent reception.'[52]

13

Life without Direction

(1936–8)

If Beryl's return to London poignantly lacked the joy any heroine of her status would have expected, her reaction was a private matter. To the world, her flight was truly spectacular; the name Beryl Markham became, for a short time, familiar to the public. Hers was a glorious triumph; she was news socially, a coup on any invitation list. Few recognised, least of all herself, that the sky had literally been the limit, that this adventure would prove an impossible act to follow. The effects of not being able to top her own achievement would declare themselves steadily over the next three years.

She had become accustomed to risk, needing action whatever such action cost. Now that she dazzled with public success for her 'derring-do', people understood even less how desperate she was for help. The key to her dilemma was an inability to think in advance, 'cause and effect were beyond her ken'.[1] On the face of it, multiple possibilities were open to her. It was inevitable that she should feel empty-handed, cheated in some way, when nothing materialised.

All Beryl's achievements so far had been inspired by others rather than through her own incentive. She kept secret, perhaps did not recognise it herself, that she had come to the point where, without a man whom she could totally trust to steer her toward her needs, she found it impossible to function. It had been her father's goal that she excel in the pair classes with Arthur. From top rider in gymkhana she graduated to leading trainer in the Colony. *Arap* Maina's approval – 'to see her she is like a spear' – transformed a slip of a girl into a warrior. Mansfield envisaged a society beauty. Barefoot or shod, Beryl had fulfilled his dream too. Denys encouraged her to fly; she had become a pilot so as to share the stars and skies with him. Tom's vision of her potential turned her into a professional pilot. JC's regard for this most daring of women brought out the international flying ace.

On the evening of her return to Claridge's, Beryl, far more of a celebrity than Tom's widow, had no further commitment beyond offering her condolences on the telephone in their first exchange since Tom's death.

By the age of thirty-four, Beryl had not so much developed as reiterated a pattern of relationships with women. Florence Desmond would join the ranks of Beryl's mother, Emma and Tania. In so far as she could ever be on affectionate terms with another female, Beryl gave the impression of friendliness to Tom's widow now. Their fate was twinned; newspapers next morning carried pictures of Beryl's disembarkation sandwiched between the inquest on Tom's accidental death and Florence Desmond's 'Great Ovation'. She was receiving acclaim for show-must-go-on courage in *Let's Raise the Curtain* at the Victoria Palace. The review had been postponed for four days on account of her tragedy. Indeed the circumstances of Beryl's bereavement echoed her position in 1931 when Tania had stolen all the public sympathy after Denys was killed. Tom's widow was repeating the exercise. That night the show had opened when Florence Desmond took numerous curtain calls; among the audience who warmed to her were Noël Coward, Sophie Tucker, Jack Hylton and Marlene Dietrich.[2]

It was at this time that Florence invited Beryl to stay at Norfolk Road, the newly furnished home she had created for Tom in St John's Wood. She had been sympathetic when Beryl 'had nowhere to go', assuming that her company would sustain her in her own grief that autumn. Beryl had talked to her with self-deprecation of 'all that black ocean. To think I did it in my tiny plane.'[3] 'It was rather a sweet story in a way, if you can say anything about Beryl that was sweet.'[4] There is no question that the kudos of having Beryl as a house-guest was also a significant feather in any theatrical cap; acting was still very much *déclassé* and, without Tom, she needed more than ever to keep her name in the public eye. Any possibility of reflected glory was not to be overlooked.

As for Beryl, JC would not continue to pay for her suite and she saw no reason to look elsewhere when offered a rent-free roof. Unlike most adults of her age, Beryl had never sought a dwelling on her own unless forced by circumstance. Even if her three-month stay at Norfolk Road is taken on face value as one of simple convenience, the women were as unsuited as friends as Tania and Beryl had been. The petite Florence Desmond, with 'eyes as dark as any odalisque', had a small-featured face so mobile that it might have been made of putty; Beryl's could have been constructed in marble in comparison. Florence worried about doing the wrong thing, was a stickler about etiquette, and was punctilious over formalities that went unrecognised by Beryl in London's hierarchical society to which the actress's talent had brought her. Florence was not grand enough or rich enough to disregard social etiquette which was utterly unsuited to Beryl's nonchalance. Florence's bourgeois values were offended when Beryl did not share them. There is nothing in African culture, even today, where being on time for social engagements, repaying loans or obeying European manners are seen as fixed virtues. Florence was quite capable of writing Beryl off for her lack of diplomacy. Of the tactful way that certain things were handled socially, Beryl had no practical knowledge at all.

She would never have any idea of how to preserve her position on the slippery social ladder. Opinions like Florence Desmond's, based on strictly European manners, would always confirm the worst in Beryl; that she was manipulative, self-centred and sexually treacherous. The value placed on creature comforts that had irritated Beryl at Mbogani was just as abrasive here: Beryl found Tom's white music room at Norfolk Road, with peach and eau-de-nil furnishings, as unmoving as its purpose.

Florence, who had been grateful for Beryl's company, 'because it made me go out and meet people', had no idea about Tom's affair with her; he had never made the facts clear. She had not suspected any infatuation in their roles of teacher and pupil. Though in Nairobi their liaison was well known, where the euphemism 'living together' referred to sharing a bed, not a roof.

But beyond Mansfield's brief attempt to cite Tom, because he could be singled out for the purposes of divorce, not a word about that relationship had reached London.[5]

Only when the Royal Aero Club sent Tom's flying paraphernalia to Norfolk Road did Florence stumble across Beryl's cable in the trunk, realising the truth that Tom had been in love with Beryl. Had she recognised this earlier, she might have spotted also the private face of vengeance. Contained in all the publicity Beryl was receiving, and the sympathy, lay the kernel of revenge, sweet revenge for the indignity she felt that she had suffered at Muthaiga, for which Tom's widow was to blame. But none of this could be detected – like the Gladys Gooch situation – in true African fashion. Like Tania, Florence was unaware of Beryl's inclination to make new enemies of female friends or that to feel sorry for Beryl, from a woman's point of view, was ultimately to court disaster. Beryl presented only her debonair self; first to laugh, last to weep, not a trace of resentment surfaced. Yet Florence Desmond felt uncomfortable with that laughter, defining it as 'silly rather than funny'.[6]

It is true that Beryl's laughter was idiosyncratic, not unlike a rebellious child mocking the grown-ups. Men found 'her delicious sense of humour . . . irresistible'[7] but women found it undermining. Beryl's humour was anything but noisy or abrasive; not brilliant or even high-spirited, it played on dry common sense. What to Beryl was an obvious, ordinary comment – 'a cow of a horse' – was bizarre enough to bystanders to reduce them to helpless laughter.[8] Driven by a sense of her own inadequacies she used her humour to get back at people. Though this too went unrecognised. When she named her cross-bred mongrel after Tania, 'because she's a little bitch with short legs' such waspish reasoning naturally provoked slightly guilt-ridden mirth.[9] Beryl's habitual self-expression was ironic; she could make any man wilt by her oblique swipes. She told one of her jockeys that he was a good fisherman because he understood fish – 'Your brain is about the same size.'[10] Often her meaning was too subtle to be appreciated unless a flicker of a smile gave the game away. Occasionally her right eyebrow would give animation where, seconds before, her face appeared deadpan. When she was happy 'her eyes lit up in an otherwise expressionless face, as usual, she explained nothing.'[11] Beryl never let on: her goal was to prevent the detection of her true feelings, a habit which had been so deeply engrained in her with Kibii that she was scarcely aware of how successful she had become. Her laughter, like her smile, was private, elusive and beguiling only to men.

Whatever misgivings Florence Desmond harboured during that autumn in London, they were often together. Indeed Beryl could be said to have more than repaid Florence by introducing her to the man she would next marry. Beryl was under constant scrutiny by the Press, especially those covering the society magazines, where she was captured for their pages as a bewitching celebrity, eating a meal, champagne on tap, rather than as a pilot, even when predominantly in the company of fliers – 'Brandy' Mollison, Hubert Broad, Charles Hughesdon and Edgar Percival. Late one night, Beryl suggested to Hughesdon that he telephone Florence at the Victoria Palace on her behalf, inviting her to make up a four. When Florence arrived at the Hungaria, Beryl was *à deux* with Hughesdon who, though smitten on sight with Florence, refrained from taking her on to the floor to dance until Percival re-joined the table. Ignoring further courtesy, he danced with Florence 'for longer than politeness demanded'.[12] So taken was Hughesdon with Florence that he had threatened to gate-crash a dinner party at the Savoy next evening. Florence spent an uncomfortable time there, glancing over her shoulder, lest the infatuated pilot appear. By the weekend, they were deeply in love and were together at Norfolk Road when, around tea-time, Beryl walked in. Having chatted to them at length, strolling over to a writing-table, she scribbled an invitation to Hughesdon to join her that evening 'if he could get away somehow', slipping the note to him unobtrusively on her way out.

'Nice friend you've got,' Hughesdon remarked, cleverly deflecting any part in his own affair with Beryl and succeeding in driving the wedge firmly between the women when he handed Beryl's message to his future wife.[13] Tension between Beryl and Florence now became stretched to breaking point.

When Beryl was guest of honour at the British Sportsmen's Club luncheon, at the Savoy, the Chairman of Anglo-American Oil dedicated his speech to her, saying that she had given 'entirely new meaning to the term, "the flighty sex"', predicting '"Beryl Markham" would be handed down among the great names of women in history'.[14] At the Prix de l'Arc de Triomphe in the company of Amy Johnson, Beryl was accorded the heroine status of 'Sister Fliers' relaxing in one another's company, as if Amy had reconciled herself to the inevitable. Later, after Beryl's romance with Mollison fizzled in 1937, Amy filed for divorce.

The hubbub of the scene that Beryl had dominated in September a month earlier subsided. The effect on Beryl was insidious. She had the trappings of international success without the wealth others assumed underpinned it. Each time she was photographed, she was asked for her plans. If she must be pictured, she wanted to wear something new. Her financial position, always precarious, was deteriorating again. Ginger, concerned that she was buying expensive outfits from department stores, tried to dissuade Beryl from running up bills. Giving the impression that she was on the brink of taking such well-intentioned advice, she ignored it. Having cautioned Beryl again, Ginger was dismissed airily, 'They let Amy Johnson do it, so why not me?'[15]

On 17 October *The Messenger* was due for off-loading at West India Docks. Before this bitter-sweet reunion, Beryl telephoned Gar O'Hea explaining that she had no means to get to Limehouse in the East End and 'could not afford a taxi'. Gar, upset that one of Beryl's standing should find herself in such a position, redressed the indignity, putting her chauffeur and Bentley at Beryl's disposal.[16] In rather grander style, Beryl witnessed the Vega Gull's contact with *terra firma* 'UNHONOURED AND UNSUNG'. *The Messenger* presented a wilfully mutilated image; the greater part of its wings had been removed for transportation. Looking pathetic, suspended by a rope as half a dozen flat-capped stevedores steadied the fuselage, it was brought ashore. 'NO ONE RAISED A CHEER' ran the *Daily Express* headline next day.[17] Only a week earlier, 750 enthusiasts watched the Vega Gull arrive by sea at St Louisburg; policemen on duty had been unable to control souvenir hunters.[18] Mechanics had also discovered that its engine had suffered carburettor icing; it was more than a miracle that Beryl had not come down in the sea.[19] *The Messenger* was returned to Gravesend for repairs.

Beryl admitted that JC 'was so mad with me' for crashing the plane.* Revealing the extent of his bitterness, he deprived her of touring and raising funds with the machine. Despite her penniless state, JC, in his 'fun-spoiling way', had decided that if he was unable to race his own Vega Gull, no one else was going to capitalise on it.[20] He shipped it back to Kenya – 'a terrible disappointment for Beryl'. The wealthy Indian gambler who bought it abandoned it to the sea air; its engine rusted, the paint peeled off. Years later Beryl would see it again.[21]

The shortness and darkness of the days did nothing to ease Beryl's sense of isolation that winter, and to compensate she went on shopping sprees, as she had seen Ginger and Cockie do when they became bored. Once Florence realised how she was taking advantage of her generosity – her astonishment turned to outrage when she received accounts for bills, run up in her name, as Beryl ordered hats and clothes for herself – her decision that Beryl must go was irrevocable.[22]

Beryl may well already have been on the lookout for 'her tiny flat' elsewhere in St John's Wood when she rang Kensington Palace. That she telephoned the Duke of Gloucester suggesting that she might come and stay is certain. The prospect threw the Duchess into a dilemma. What was Princess Alice to do? How could Beryl have breached protocol so thoughtlessly? Beryl knew no better. Over the years, Lady Alice Montagu-Douglas-Scott had ridden morning exercise from Deloraine with Clutt, while staying with her uncle Lord Francis for whom Beryl had trained. It simply would not have made sense to Beryl that someone who had breakfasted with her father while he was running the Markham yard could not befriend her now.[23]

The Duchess became calmer once she was assured that whatever happened, she must not allow Beryl to set foot in Kensington Palace, 'It would cause a scandal and an outrage' when speculation involving the King and Mrs Simpson had gathered momentum and was prominent news, overseas and at home.[24] The unreliability of fame could never have been clearer. Beryl's renown had not

been dependent on wealth or breeding but on personal performance. But the scourge of gossip over her 'mad little gallop with
Prince Henry' proved weightier.

Now that she was famous for being famous – 'not *the* Beryl
Markham' was how others reacted to her name – she was affected
at many levels. If whoever was on duty at Elizabeth Arden's salon
did not know *who* Beryl was without asking, she fled. She constantly needed reassurance, but could not express her need. Yet
her trump card was her refusal to be drawn on private matters. On
the other hand, as the crisis at Buckingham Palace unfolded,
Thelma Furness, who felt that she had been given the thin end of
the wedge by her friend Wallis Simpson and the King, discussed
intimate moments they had once shared. Beryl, however, showed
her lofty disdain by allowing scandal-mongers to believe what they
liked. Whatever the peccadilloes of any man who had loved her,
his secrets died with her; unending loyalty from lovers was her
reward.

By 25 November, Mrs Simpson's presence in the monarch's life
brought him into deadlock with Stanley Baldwin; when the Prime
Minister rejected the idea of morganatic marriage, she was whisked
out of England so that she could be spared from harrowing
exposure. In winter gloom, headlines grew blacker – 'GRAVE CON-
STITUTIONAL CRISIS' – paving the way for the King's Abdication.

As events lurched toward the King's historic speech on 7
December, the shock was none the less great for the royal staff for
whom 1936 had become a nightmare. In January 'Tommy'
Lascelles had rejoined them, as Assistant Private Secretary to King
George V, only to be thrown by his death into the service of his
former master. Lascelles reacted to the Abdication speech by walk-
ing round St James's Park in the dark for more than an hour.
Stanley Baldwin was shattered enough to go straight to bed.[25]

Everyone found it hard to stomach 'the former King's gross dere-
liction of duty', and none more so than old Queen Mary. Yet few
knew as much about the character of the former ruler's boundless
energies as Lascelles, who regarded the change as for the best, and
'inclined to think that as the years went on, the Hyde side would
have predominated . . . over the Jekyll – the pity of it all, is heart-
rending' he wrote in anguish to a friend.[26]

Seen in that light, Mrs Simpson appears to have served England better than she has ever been given credit for. The Duke of York, having had the crown thrust upon his head upon the departure of his brother, provided a far stronger reign in the ascendancy of Queen Elizabeth II. Her uncle, who gave up his kingdom, went into exile and the following summer, as the newly created Duke of Windsor, married Wallis Simpson at Château de Cande in the Valley of the Loire.

Florence meanwhile was looking for an opportunity to ask Beryl to leave her flat. Mollison, whom Florence could not abide, provided her cue by finally breaking the bounds of her tolerance. She had returned from the theatre one night to find him and Beryl together, Mollison so drunk he could hardly stand. Beryl responded to the awkward situation by asking Mollison to leave. Despite herself, Florence objected: 'You can't let him go in that condition – he can't even speak properly.' Beryl shrugged – always her signal to others to act – so Florence made up a bed for him in her spare room, the last gesture she would make on Beryl's behalf. She then broke the news to Beryl that she had bought an apartment in Stockleigh Hall, overlooking Regent's Park, into which she was moving alone, thus ending an uneasy alliance.[27] When confronted by Florence over payment of bills, Beryl explained that she had no money to pay with and, if pressed to do so, would declare herself bankrupt. It was Ginger who noted that the only lesson Beryl had absorbed over Clutt's financial collapse was that no one could force her to settle.[28]

During the first half of 1937 Beryl appeared to be searching in her retinue for some integrating spark that would light a new perspective. Her tiny flat in St John's Wood – on loan or rented – was the scene of party after party for 'the bohemian crowd'. Unable to get to grips with anything beyond their evening's entertainment, she was on her uppers. Reality was basic: hunger, shelter, love. Her time otherwise could be said to be used in trying to increase her significance: the erosive doubt of failure never left her. None the less, solemnity was not her way.

For six months she drifted, a sexual being whose loyalties lay in herself. The formal preliminary to one passionate liaison came about when Mollison took her to a party thrown by Jack Doyle, the heavy-weight boxer, at his smart Carlton Court flat in Hertford Street, Mayfair.[29] While a boxer seems an unlikely candidate for Beryl's affection, champions in any field interested her. To win was as glorious as those hours spent training for victory. The arrogance of the supreme athlete was always acceptable to her.

Doyle was eleven years younger than Beryl, haughty, and could walk into any cinema 'in the dark and be recognised'.[30] Though they made a handsome couple, theirs was an improbable relationship even so.

Doyle was the son of an Irish merchant seaman, and bore the remnant of a star-shaped tattoo between the base of his thumb and index finger on his left hand. He was supposed to be in strict training for his fight with the Dutch champion, Harry Staal, and meanwhile was hoping to woo back his estranged wife, Judith Allen, from Hollywood.

According to his biographer, Doyle had 'a basic egotistical urge to sleep with the woman who had had a long running affair with Prince Henry, in much the same way that he had been unable to resist Thelma Furness'.[31] Doyle's brother blamed the former Prince of Wales and Thelma for turning Jack into 'a pleasure-seeker', ruining him at eighteen, who, 'only four months earlier had been humping coal'. Realising suddenly his own magnetism, Doyle 'joined the superleague as a fortune-hunting Lothario' among London's elite and sexually decadent faction in the 1930s. For a man trying to heal a marital rift, the last thing he needed was Beryl. But Doyle was unable to resist the status that he treasured.

Evidently her desperation for sponsorship convinced her that Doyle might provide the answer; Beryl 'had no elaborate plan to entice him, apart from making clear that she had chosen him to fly with her half way across the world',[32] announcing to the Press her hopes of teaming up with Doyle 'for a record-breaking flight that would startle the world',[33] adding that after his big fight with Staal, she was to give Doyle flying lessons.

Doyle extricated himself, resuming training at Windsor, where a regimen of running and sparring 'brought him down from the clouds'. When Beryl lent credence by telling journalists they were to fly to a 'secret destination', implying Australia or South Africa,

he refuted it; he had no wish to pursue tuition, concluding afterwards that really this charade had been a flight of Beryl's 'fancy'.[34]
Interestingly Beryl and Doyle, being creatures of action, shared the
dread of becoming the laughing stock of their colleagues: Doyle
'feared the spectre of humiliation, like most . . . fear death.'[35]

In Beryl's quandary – 'wondering what to do next'[36] – any enterprise undertaken with Doyle would pull in the crowds: three years
earlier, Doyle had drawn 90,000 fans to White City, not merely for
boxing. His wonderful, light tenor voice was as popular, at the
time, earning him £600 a week on stage for such lilting Irish songs
as, 'How Do You Buy Killarney?'

The Press never hinted at any romance, although this was a
question of luck rather than good management: 'In pugilistic
circles, among members of the National Sporting Club, betwixt
Covent Garden and Berkeley Square' it was well known.[37] Bunny
Allen, whose fascination with Beryl's adventures continued, used
to see her with Doyle at the Café de Paris in Coventry Street and
Doyle seemed to be 'madly in love . . . bewitched by Beryl', but in
comparison to most romances, 'where the woman was the ani-
mated partner, with Beryl, the men did all the flirting . . . she was
cool, almost mannish in a subtle . . . way.' Doyle, who was 6ft 5in.,
was said to be a gentle and romantic lover, with his angel face and
dark, wavy hair, offset by a brutish quality. He was envied by men
of less stature, being regarded by women as 'an amazing specimen
of a man, with a prick like a pony'.[38] Bunny's mischievous *double
entendre*, 'I hope for Beryl's sake, Doyle was a better jockey than
boxer' referred to Doyle's reputation for wanting to get fights over
in two rounds, so as to keep his good looks.[39] Doyle's image of
the photogenic champion blowing kisses to crowds, his idolised
arrogance and talents, brought a Hollywood contract.

Beryl's offer from Jack Cohen, aboard the *Queen Mary*, to make
a film of the Waterjump, was dependent upon a successful screen
test and Doyle may well have encouraged her to take this up while
attending the forthcoming Bendix Air Race in California. There
was more chance of a backer in America where Beryl's celebrity
status was higher. At any rate Beryl decided to explore the home
of the cinema, Valhalla of dreams and shattered illusion, and seems
to have sought reassurance beforehand – to discover for herself

whether her looks might stand a Hollywood screen test – by arranging for a studio portrait by Lenare.

Beryl had come a long way since the time when she and Kibii had looked upon the camera as a weapon, believing, as Africans do, that it stole the spirit. Overcoming her distaste of having her photograph taken casually and spontaneously (she would later dismiss it as 'corny'), on the advice of Enid Furness Beryl sat for this leading society photographer off Hanover Square in Mayfair, so as to have something suitable to autograph for her fans.[40] She was pleased with the results and was to hand out copies to men friends, re-ordering new batches for herself over the years when supplies ran low.[41]

Lenare was 'a vulgar little man who wore a ghastly blue velvet tie with two nicks in it', with a talent for producing wistful studies. His portraits of Beryl and Enid speak eloquently, bearing his inimitable stamp. In Beryl's case (she was difficult to photograph, as Hollywood would prove), his talent is inspired. Her magnetism, which Cohen hoped to harness, was seldom transposed on to celluloid. Somehow Beryl's flesh did not sit on her bones in the right way, as if the planes and angles of her face were at variance with the lens. Yet in the Lenare study she is glamour personified, outshining even Enid's legendary looks, whose coronation robes impose a formality that detracts from her loveliness. Whereas Beryl – in her white flying helmet, unbuckled at the chin, and her face three-quarters away from the camera, in keeping with Lenare's style yet retaining her own – is a magical summation of opposites: her stillness yet the woman of action; her defencelessness yet the bold adventuress; all her best qualities are here.[42]

Most of Beryl's friends in 1937 had connections with America. That summer she sailed to New York on the SS *Île de France*, disembarking on 16 June. Here the Press had not forgotten her. Photographed waving, one hand gripping the gangplank rail as she descends the ship, Beryl announced that she was on 'a combined business and pleasure trip', on the lookout for a new machine but 'would not reveal her flight plans'.[43] Hatless, her hair neatly coiffed and wearing a print dress and small jacket, the contrast to her workmanlike appearance in 1936 is marked. Her half-open smile reveals the slight gaps in her teeth. Journalists were convinced, in all her uncertainty, that she had a record-breaking project up her sleeve. The ruse worked perfectly; she had no aeronautical plans. Where she stayed the first month, with whom and for how long, remains a mystery.

She resurfaced in mid-July in California, 'resting' at a Los Angeles hotel. At the time concern was growing for the missing Amelia Earhart. Reporters sought Beryl's opinion; Earhart had set off with Fred Noonan to outdo their earlier feat, this time over the Pacific, due to arrive on 4 July, but on 30 June they had lost contact with the world. All hope was gone when the *Los Angeles Times* consulted Beryl. Theories over the fate of these fliers have since filled over thirty books. Then, in January 1991, a metal box from a Lockheed 10-E was found on a deserted Pacific island. The Federal Bureau of Investigation has proved that it came from Earhart and Noonan's plane.[44]

Beryl's response has proved, forty-five years later, to be significantly close to what apparently happened. Had she run out of fuel, she told reporters, 'I would probably . . . tried to land in the water, the wheels fold under the wings,' because the plane would stand more chance like that on a jagged reef. 'Then I would have taken to my emergency lifeboat.'[45] Earhart and Noonan had not needed a lifeboat: the International Group for Historic Recovery (TIGHAR) believes that in 1937 the fliers lost their way, ran out of fuel and made an emergency landing on the reef surrounding the coral atoll where the metal box was found. This coral reef, dry at low tide, is covered by up to four feet of water when the tide comes in.[46] At the time of writing, all evidence indicates that the pair died from thirst, there being only sea water to drink.

Beryl remained in California for four months. During that time she met Raoul Schumacher, the ghost writer who was to become her third husband. When she left Los Angeles it was for Melbourne, on her way to visit her father in Cape Town. When she returned to California in 1939, it would be to live. After failing her screen test at Columbia and 'hanging about the studios' in the backwash of this disappointment, Beryl came across the writer, Scott O'Dell. It was he who introduced Beryl to his friend Raoul Schumacher.

At the time Scott was still living off the proceeds of *Woman of Spain*, his first book, published four years earlier, in which MGM had acquired the rights for 'twenty-four thousand dollars . . . a lot of money during the Depression when the average wage was less than two thousand per annum'.[47] Scott was attracted to Beryl but, being engaged to be married at the time, considered himself 'out of the running'.[48] And in Hollywood, a place not known for lack of competition, Beryl was able to hold her own. Scott saw her as 'spectacular . . . slender . . . quiet . . . stony faced', a beauty whom, for the life of him, he never could imagine having flown the Atlantic. 'She looked so delicate, so fragile that she could scarcely hold a tea-cup.'[49] Beryl may have been drawn to Scott because of his influential position in the cinema, though he was appealing physically too – fair, taller than she and with mesmerising eyes of the same clear blue. Scott had worked on the original *Ben Hur* for John Barrymore, having graduated from Stanford University as a cameraman and technician. Their friendship developed while he carried the first Technicolor camera around the Rome countryside for Barrymore, who gave Scott an entrée to the film industry at the highest level.

Among other notables at the party where he met Beryl in 1937 was their hostess, Bess Meredyth, at whose weekly gatherings over the years Scott had made friends with Noël Coward's understudy in Hollywood, Alan Vincent, and, through Alan originally, Raoul Schumacher. Beryl now became a link in this glittering chain – one which had included Rudolph Valentino, Dolores del Rio the stunning Mexican actress, Gloria Swanson, and Movita who would marry Jack Doyle and then have Marlon Brando's child in 1960.[50]

Beryl seemed upset enough over the screen test to provoke concern. So Scott and Alan Vincent decided to hold a party for her, expressly inviting Schumacher, because they thought 'they would make a good match'.[51] It was to be a double event at Strawberry Creek, in the San Jacinto mountains behind Palm Springs. Guests were invited to lunch at Scott's, going on to dine at Alan Vincent's two miles away.[52] As it happened Scott's sister, Lucile, who was 'quite smitten with Raoul', was present that day. Raoul was 'a knock out' whom she had been seeing clandestinely, as she was married. William Batey, her first husband, was handling the props and set-dressing on location in Arizona, where *North-West Passage* was to be directed by King Vidor. Batey's absence provided

Raoul and Lucile with the chance to meet, but Lucile's father disapproved of 'the spark between Raoul and herself'. 'Seeing what
was going on, he rode shot-gun and worked at keeping us apart.'
Lucile and Raoul nevertheless defied him 'until Beryl came along
and I was thrown to the wind'.[53] Lucile was nonplussed at the
ease with which Beryl usurped her place with Raoul.

But all who knew the Schumachers as a married couple agreed
that they had been so powerfully attracted, they had 'disappeared'
for months within hours of meeting. Scott's recollection is of each
arriving separately for lunch, never reaching the dinner party;
Beryl sat without talking, poised and almost bored. Guests milled
around her. Then suddenly she had vanished and Raoul had gone
too.[54] Raoul knew of Beryl's celebrity, could imagine the stories
she could provide, and Scott's interpretation is that, for all his mild
character, Raoul had not been able to wait 'to grab her, take her
away, like a starving bird . . . fly away with her'. Their attachment
was to prove 'so complex . . . so deep'.[55]

When Beryl and Raoul vanished, there was speculation that they
could have sailed off together on the SS *Mariposa* which arrived in
Melbourne in the New Year of 1938. It would account for the fact
that friends did not see them for months.

14

West with the Night

(1938–42)

Raoul Cottereau Schumacher was born on 28 February 1907 in Minneapolis, the youngest child of Henri Schumacher. A half-brother, Oscar, from his father's first marriage, was followed by Virginia and Elizabeth and finally Raoul, born to Emilie Cottereau Schumacher, the second wife.

All four children spoke French fluently. Henry Schumacher's influence was historical and political, dinning into his offspring pride in their grandparents who had been 'among the most valuable wave of immigrants to the United States in 1848, following Germany's flat-foot rebellion'. They had settled and farmed in St Louis, Missouri.[1] Their legacy to Raoul at the age of twenty presumably enabled him to buy his first ranch in New Mexico, where he profited from his sound knowledge of horses, and he sold this property with the specific intention of taking a year off to tour the capitals of Europe.

It is as a couple, toward the end of the 1930s, 'living together but not married', that Beryl Markham and Raoul Schumacher mixed with the millionaires around Orange Grove. They were not a pair one overlooked. Naturally prudes remembered disapprovingly that they were 'living in sin'.[2] But Beryl and Raoul made a striking couple. Both were tall and slender; both wore faded jeans – long before denim was in vogue; both appeared blondish (Raoul's dark wavy hair was prematurely grey) and both had bright blue eyes. The impression is that they were blissfully happy and already dependent upon one another – and would be for the next five years. The set among which they moved were influential; many were or would become famous – among them Joan Fontaine, Ronald Colman, Joseph Cotten and John Barrymore.

Raoul clearly projected control for Beryl, that steadying element for which she had searched but found lacking in all but Denys. Raoul's broad face, receding hair and patient expression appealed to her need for security, though his was a brooding sexual intensity. Friends noted that, initially, Beryl and Raoul's happiness shone when they were together. She was introduced to his coterie, as 'the first woman to have flown the Atlantic and he was writing a book about her flight'.[3] But with the benefit of hindsight, Scott was to compare their devouring passion to the conflagration in Lowry's novel, *Under the Volcano*, where sexual love is capable equally of creative or destructive fire. And in due course their relationship would produce both.

With the exception of Denys, Raoul Schumacher was the most literary of all Beryl's lovers. He also listened well and read voraciously, with a penchant for Shakespeare and Oscar Wilde. Companions were drawn to Raoul's gentleness, his sensitivity, intelligence and jovial nature, yet cheerfully acknowledged his street-wise tendencies, for theirs were enduring friendships. That he was never well-off, unlike themselves, never worried them. One friend, Teddy Baring-Gould, an investment banker, described Raoul's mind as 'like an encyclopaedia. He was an exceptional listener, keen on theatre and knowledgeable on many subjects and ... witty'.[4]

He was five years younger than Beryl, stood 6ft 2in., being slim, with long thin legs accentuating a slight paunch which he blamed on the number of flapjacks he had consumed for breakfast as a cow-puncher in New Mexico. He was always a *bon viveur* and cooked well, interests no doubt fostered by his French mother. By the time he met Beryl, he had indulged for years in a lifestyle that put on weight – cocktails prepared expertly by himself, to sip while he cooked *gourmet* meals for his peers, keeping them amused. A typical remark from this intellectually astute liberal – 'Work is the curse of the drinking classes'[5], paraphrased from Wilde – guaranteed his reputation. He was considered 'articulate and entertaining', redressing any inclination to 'sponge'. Indeed there was nothing to forgive. He played tennis with and was appreciated by a rich and idle coterie, most of whom, unlike himself and Teddy, had no need to work. His favourite way to relax when he was writing was to break for games of ping-pong; tennis was the limit of his physical exertion out of doors, but he was extremely nimble and light on his feet. As one adoring female explained, 'Somehow Raoul was nothing on his own and therefore sought those who either had money or notoriety and in return was very good company.'[6] His ability to quote from anything he had read, or overheard was notorious.

For all that, at times, Raoul's record seems as ephemeral as a ghost. Though he was capable of 'facile and poetic English',[7] where he was educated none can say – yet the assumption was that he went to university. One can only conclude that his photographic memory was responsible for this impression; every attempt to discover which schools he attended has drawn a blank. His childhood was similar to Beryl's, their passion for horses on a par. Raoul rode as soon as he could walk, growing up on a farm run by pioneering stock; unlike Beryl, his had been a large and loving family.

How and when Raoul entered journalism is the next mystery. After his European tour, in the early 1930s he went to live and freelance in New York, and to work as a ghost writer. He always had 'something in his typewriter but drink made him lazy – sleepy' so that it required a certain effort to get back to his machine. However, there were long periods also when his drinking was confined to night-time.[8] In New York, he mixed with writers, several of whom contributed to the *New Yorker*. Significantly, at that time Lillian Hellman reflected that excessive drinking among literary circles had become 'romantic, even chic'. For many, that one drank was a sure sign of writing talent – look at Hemingway and Scott Fitzgerald, went the argument – and Raoul liked to do both. However, Raoul discovered that he was not cut out for 'apartment dwelling', sticking it out only until he had saved enough money to buy another ranch. Once more he 'raised horses, played sand-lot polo for relaxation, wrote more short stories and doctored other people's books'.[9] Hollywood offered better prospects to ill-paid newspaper men and magazine writers than New York. 'Script-fixers' such as Raoul occupied 'a ramshackle warren of tan stucco' with some forty others, sitting in various stages of creating scripts for a multitude of different projects at Paramount.

Since the end of the silent movies, it has suited Hollywood direc-tors to denigrate the contributions of their writers; they can lay claim to all the best ideas, enhancing their own status and repu-tation with impunity, especially with ghost writers. Yet, as Ian Hamilton observes in his comprehensive study, *Writers in Holly-wood*, with 'pro-director prejudice, any serious consideration of an individual writer's contribution to the language of the cinema may be sought for in vain in the credits or books covering individual film projects.' By the mid-1930s – when Raoul and Scott were involved at Paramount – there were over 1,000 writers in Holly-wood, 'greedy hacks and incompetent thickheads' working from hand to mouth in this capacity.[10]

As Raoul always used a pseudonym it is virtually impossible to track down his published stories except those by Ivan Kell – one of Raoul's known pseudonyms. This choice of name is intriguing because Ivan Kell was on the passenger list of the SS *Mariposa* sailing from Melbourne back to Los Angeles when Beryl went on to Cape Town in 1938.[11]

From Cape Town, where she visited her father, Beryl went to London, stopping off in Kenya *en route* on the Imperial Airways Service. The previous autumn, Beryl had given up her lease on the St John's Wood flat so that her address for this period in London is unknown, but she deliberately kept a low profile. She regarded herself as in 'semi-retirement', confessed to loneliness and depression – to having 'buried herself away' – between now and when she returned to New York.[12] The mood was not exactly optimistic in England generally and, by the following spring, the whole of Europe seemed to be operating on borrowed time since the Munich Conference. In the summer there was respite from German aggression yet the feeling was that the shadow of war was looming.

Two more personal events had robbed Beryl of her sense of well-being that year. In March, her fame brought unwelcome pub-licity in Mansfield's attempt to obtain a divorce from her. He wanted to marry Mary Ellen Adley, who was ultimately to become his next wife, and named Captain Hubert Broad, Edgar Percival's friend, as co-respondent. Mrs Broad took Mansfield's lead, citing Beryl also.[13] In the event both cases were defended and dropped, but Beryl was very cast down by the rumours this caused.

The second disturbing event was Kiki Preston's suicide. Beryl happened to be chatting to her at Claridge's when she injected herself with heroin for the last time: 'I saw her dying . . . I ran like a rabbit. I saw her die. I thought the police might come and I'd [sic] have something to do with it.'[14] Her consternation lest there were headlines; fear because she was known; terror that fame would work against her – this was understandable, but she was ashamed of being frightened that the police might pry. Her growing confusion over tribal attitudes versus European death rituals had gained ground. She confided years afterwards that she was haunted still by her apparent cowardice yet, as a mutual friend of Kiki's rationalised, had Beryl not been panicked by African omens against dying indoors, she would have recognised that Kiki Preston had been destined for tragedy for years, distressing as the experience would have been for anyone to witness.[15]

The following month Beryl sailed to New York on the SS *Manhattan*, disembarking on 21 June with a lot of luggage. She habitually travelled light, but, the *New York Times* reported that she had 'ten daytime outfits and several billowing evening gowns in her trunk'.[16] Journalists gathered that her plans were to find the right machine, the right backer, to become an American citizen, and to divorce Mansfield.[17]

Since Beryl and Raoul were madly attracted on sight, he surely would have been there to receive her in New York. Scott believed that Raoul met her off the ship. He did all his research in the New York Public Library, and while this could merely have been convenient, there are other signs that he had prepared himself for Beryl's return. Raoul had been in Santa Fe just beforehand, vacationing 'with some high fliers, the Vanderlips and that ilk and managed to get this elaborate house near Pacific Palisades'.[18] He rented what was certainly more stylish than anything he would have occupied as a batchelor. Not that there was any shortage of women in his life – quite the contrary – but Beryl was different. Like every other man who wanted to marry her, Raoul had spotted her potential. His sort of work meant that he could exploit her in a new dimension, immortalise her on the printed page. She was alluring, famous, successful and yet still remained undiscovered country. And, unlike England, in America enthusiasm for her and her achievement radiated out through every aspect of her life there. When Raoul and she moved into Vanderlip's gate-house in what became Orange Grove Boulevard, Los Angeles was still a country town surrounded by citrus groves – 'a great place to live if you were an orange', went one quip. And it was to be from this house 'one day in 1940 or 41' that Raoul would telephone Scott 'to say that Beryl had written a memoir, asking what to do with it'.[19]

The true authorship of *West with the Night* has always been problematic. Beryl's own friends could not believe that she had written the memoir unaided. Nothing in the first forty years of her life had indicated that she was either inclined or able to write – she was not even interested in reading – nor did anything afterwards support such a theory. It cannot have been coincidental that the memoir appeared after she had been involved with a man who was an experienced ghost writer.

Although Raoul was naturally indolent he was capable of periods of intense concentration and of working and thinking very fast. When Beryl came along, nobody needed convincing that 'she gave Raoul the best story he ever handled'. In 1940, the ghosting of the memoir had been 'more or less an open secret' in California where Beryl and Raoul worked together in the daytime, stopping for games of ping-pong which Raoul taught Beryl to play, socialising mostly in the evenings. They were the stylish couple whom everyone wanted to entertain – the celebrated flier and her lover, who was writing her memoir. At parties when they were among the last to leave, Beryl's insistence, 'We *have* to leave because I have to write my book' was regarded as 'a ridiculous bluff' since Raoul was often enough introduced as 'her ghost writer' and would continue to be so, even in Santa Barbara after two years of marriage.[20] Lacunae may remain over when Raoul began work on Beryl's memoir, but various sources suggest that, while Beryl was working as a consultant on *Safari* a B-movie shooting just east of Hollywood, Raoul had already begun to draft an outline for *West with the Night*.

Despite Beryl's normal reticence, she surrendered to Raoul pages of facts – evidently typed up by her for Raoul between 1939 and 1942 – pages which fortunately she hoarded, for reasons best known to herself, in her Louis Vuitton trunk, where they remained for forty years. There were also pages bearing handwriting – identified as Raoul's by John Potter before he died in 1991. These corroborate Scott O'Dell's observations of how Beryl and Raoul were working one day in their basement, as a married couple, living in Juan Capistrano, when he dropped in on the Schumachers unexpectedly. They were urgently trying to get a short story completed for an editor who was sitting on their doorstep: 'Beryl was sitting in a chair, telling Raoul things . . . dictating. Raoul was copying . . . at the typewriter what Beryl was saying. You could see what was going on. He would ask a question. Then he typed.'[21] Scott did not linger, for they were obviously under pressure, but was there long enough to feel envious of their closeness.

Writers habitually work alone, preferring to occupy their own space as they juggle words like circus performers, unlike the double act witnessed by Scott for the short story. No doubt this method was used in a protracted way to create the manuscript for *West with the Night*. The ramifications do not stop there. Certain lists uncovered in 1983 provide the key to Raoul's fundamental sources – *Out of Africa* by Karen Blixen and *White Man's Country* by Elspeth Huxley. James Fox came across these discarded folios during a series of interviews with Beryl for *Vanity Fair*.

Proof of Raoul's skill lies in his source lists. His subtle, many-layered approach, conveying Beryl's vision of Africa, made *West with the Night* his masterpiece. How had he captured so valid an atmosphere, so African a story? Beryl's factual accounts of railing horses, payday on the farm, even Denys's death, were not enough. In Beryl's account his crash was just a date, a reference to the fact that she would have been killed had she gone with him. It is from *Out of Africa* that Raoul culled the feeling that Denys 'was a keystone in an arch whose other stones were lives. If a keystone trembles, the arch will carry the warning along its entire curve, then, if the keystone is crushed, the arch will fall, leaving its lesser stones heaped closed together, though for a while without a design. Denys's death left some lives without design, but they were rebuilt again, as lives and stones are, into other patterns.'[22]

When Scott O'Dell's open letter to *Vanity Fair* in 1987 questioned the authenticity of Beryl's authorship, her authorised biographer claimed in her defence that Saint-Exupéry, 'who was an old friend of Beryl's', had been involved. Whether or not these two fellow pilots actually knew one another is impossible to establish, but not unlikely given the small world of flying at the time. However, as Beryl spoke no French and he hardly understood English, they would have found it difficult to converse, let alone construct a three-hundred-page manuscript in the five weeks that Saint-Exupéry was also in New York in 1939. What is more, even in 1942 he was extremely reluctant to learn English, lest a second language might impinge on his native tongue – hardly the ideal coach for Beryl in writing *West with the Night*. When critics noticed the influence of Saint-Exupéry in the flying sequences of the memoir, it was evidence of Raoul's admiration and consequent emulation of Saint-Exupéry, not of the latter's collaboration.[23]

Why then, when Beryl had no use for paperwork, had she kept the drafts? It looks almost as though she had expected an opportunity to present itself to show how Raoul had written the book. And, when the memoir sank without a trace, she had forgotten the material. Otherwise there would have been no sense in keeping evidence which proved that she could not possibly have written the memoir. The answer seems to lie in republication and Beryl's attitude to overwhelming recognition. Once *West with the Night* was acclaimed by new generations, her old bogeyman, loss of face, made it impossible for her to credit Raoul with authorship. Knowing Beryl, it is understandable. It was not pleasant to be seen to be living a lie when suddenly she was foisted with the stature of Hemingway and, of all people, Karen Blixen. It is understandable that she could not bring herself to redress the past. So she handled it just as she was to continue to handle the question of Gervase's paternity, letting people believe what they liked. She was to be challenged continuously over authorship after re-issue, particularly in Kenya where few people believed she had written the book anyway.

Beryl must have known the risk of hanging on to such evidence: ultimately someone would unlock her trunk to recognise what those pages represented. They are not even extracts. Among piles of flying maps, discarded jewellery, cuttings of racing results and about her Atlantic achievement, were typed-up, un-numbered un-related descriptions which were clearly preparation for Raoul. James Fox deduced at once that some showed 'fundamental edit-ing, indeed whole paragraphs that subsequently appeared in the book, in a hand not her own'.[24] From the unpublished material Raoul selected the best stories for the book. What Beryl provided has been incorporated into this biography so that she has given voice to her own childhood.[25]

Raoul managed his task, even faced with a subject as phlegmatic as Beryl, which emphasises his achievement. Raoul's ear for a good story, his eye for detail, his love of words and knowledge of Shakespeare – all is to be found in *West with the Night*. His ability as a journalist is demonstrated in the skilful way he transformed the facts into lucid, enjoyable prose. Raoul was never one to pass up a good yarn over a drink even after Beryl returned to Kenya. Indeed in the 1950s, he took a job as bar-tender in Mazatlan, so as to ghost short stories at speed.[26] Raoul, like Dr Faustus, laid claim to a soul to gain its riches and satisfaction for himself. Once Beryl was his wife, he could live off her experiences instead of his own. Like all those earlier men with any significance in her life, Raoul was drawn to Beryl physically, adored the glamour and the guts which had put her at the top.

In May 1941, Scott O'Dell's first inkling of the memoir's exist-ence was when Raoul, having prepared enough to seek a publisher, telephoned asking for advice. Scott recommended that Raoul send the manuscript to Paul Brooks, Managing Editor at Houghton Mif-flin, adding that while he would be 'glad to have them send it to his own literary agent. McIntosh and Otis' (Ann Watkins dealt with his work there), with Raoul's experience of handling pub-lishers direct, he thought that an agent was unnecessary.[27]

Raoul followed Scott's advice. The publishers did not take the memoir for another twelve months. The next batch prompted the reaction, 'This manuscript is going to need some editorial work, but parts of it are surprisingly well written, and the material – combining the romance of flying and the romance of Africa – seems to be definitely saleable.' Brooks was 'all for publishing', scrawling across this memo, 'new chapter received and better than the first'.[28] By June 1941, an editor, Robert N. Linscott, was assigned to the project. While sharing Brooks's enthusiasm, he cautioned, 'Nevertheless revision will . . . be necessary as the style is much better than the architecture.' Bob Linscott (who had lately been William Faulkner's editor) wanted to juggle the sequences, but suggested meanwhile that they 'warmly . . . encourage the author to finish . . . if necessary . . . make a contract at this point, preferably without an advance or with a nominal one of $250.'[29]

Wartime currency restrictions meant that Beryl had to receive her annuity in a sterling area, and at the suggestion of her solicitors she could have these monies paid to Canada or the Bahamas.[30] In March 1941 Beryl elected for the latter, given her connections there: the Governor, the Duke of Windsor, and George Wood – Beryl's lover 'Woody' – who was one of his aides. George had married and lived with his wife Rosa on Nassau. The third friend, Nina Drury, was the wife of one of the Duke's equerries, Vyvyan Drury. Beryl had trained in Kenya for Jack Soames, Nina's first husband. There were plenty of options for accommodation and socialising.

Nassau faces north, braced against the sea by the low thin shell of Hog Island, housing the vulgar mansions of the *nouveau riche* used by the glamorous by day for sunning and by night for dancing. While the negro women clipped and baled sponges under the wooden awnings of the wharves, the cries of market vendors mingled with the clamour of birds and it was easy to forget the war altogether. Only broadcasts from Miami and on short-wave radio reminded those in Nassau of the nightmare Europe was undergoing.

In April Beryl appeared at The Retreat, Nina Drury's home. Nina grumbled, 'Beryl just flew in one day on an aeroplane . . . she had not been invited. She just barged in.'[31] In spite of Nina's displeasure at her lack of courtesy, Beryl stayed for two and a half months. The Drurys were further affronted when she 'more or less invited herself to Government House', oblivious to the sensitivity of Vyvyan's position: 'along she came presuming that she would be received by the Duchess, who had no clue who Beryl was, only "of her".'[32]

On 29 June, Beryl regaled Lee Barker with the 'difficulties of having to move from place to place – I only came here because of the Sterling Area – and can get no part of my very meagre income (. . . horribly reduced by war taxes) into the States.'[33] Nina, exasperated by Beryl's behaviour, had asked her to move out, and it is not clear whether she remained or went to Rosa and George Woods', but her mail continued to be sent to The Retreat.

In the interim, Lee Barker had forwarded to Brooks, Beryl's letter from The Retreat, dated 29 June, which made clear that she needed money: 'it made me very happy to know that you like what you have seen of my book. The fourth, not the second batch went to Ann Watkins some time ago – the whole totalling 110 pages. Have you read this last bit? As to where I expect to finish it, my preference would be in New York State or Connecticut', and after explaining the financial necessity of being in the Bahamas, she goes on 'I must therefore make the best deal I can on the book (the sooner the better) but naturally I would let you have first crack at it without even asking! You have been so very helpful and believe me I appreciate it. I certainly promise you that I will accept no other offer without getting in touch with you first. The weather is due to be unbearable in about two weeks and all my friends are leaving, and so I can't help hoping that some kind soul will give me a contract before the heat wave falls! Luckily I have my re-entry permit and am still on the quota. In the mean time work goes on day by day and will be shipped to New York as long as the postage holds out! Kindest regards, Beryl.' She had overstayed her welcome on Nassau, and in California, the Vanderlip lease was up. Beryl and Raoul did not know where they were going to live.

Luckily a contract was forthcoming from Houghton Mifflin and Beryl returned to the United States at the end of July. *West with the Night* was finally published in June 1942 when it sold for $3 per copy, reaching thirteen best-seller lists, including a slot on the *New York Times*. Beryl was paid $612 on publication, by which time 2,800 copies were already advanced: Houghton Mifflin only needed to sell ninety-three more copies to cover costs.[34] The reviews of *West with the Night* in 1942 were excellent, and today the memoir represents a publishing phenomenon. By 1990 even the republished paperback edition had sold over a million copies.

Reviews were so good that by August Hemingway sat up and took notice, urging his editor Maxwell Perkins to read it because 'it really is a bloody wonderful book'[35] Beryl's writing took him completely aback after his one encounter with her when she flew down for Blix to Potha, at which time no literary ability on her part had been apparent. He wrote the following ambivalent letter to Maxwell Perkins: 'I knew her fairly well in Africa and never would have suspected that she could and would put pen to paper except to write in her flyer's logbook. As it is she has written well, and so marvellously well, that I was simply ashamed of myself as a writer. I felt that I was simply a carpenter with words . . . But this girl who is to my knowledge very unpleasant and we might even say a high-grade bitch can write rings around all of us who consider ourselves as writers.'[36]

Scott O'Dell was no less confounded: 'I marveled. How in the name of Turgenev, could a woman of little schooling, who had trained wild horses, worked as a guide for big-game hunters, flew African mail and leapt the Atlantic in a single-engined Pervical Gull monoplane, spring a full-blown writer from the forehead of Zeus?'[37] Once he had seen Beryl's notes, which 'much resembled the tone . . . you would put in a log book', he was to conclude that 'Beryl couldn't write her way out of a paper bag'.[38] Elspeth Huxley had not recognised her own influence in the book, but was dubious: 'I don't believe that she wrote the book unaided, judging by its style; it is very American, derivative of Hemingway. Perhaps that is why he admired it.'[39]

Certain Americanisms are inseparable from Raoul's prose. Not unsurprisingly, these escaped the notice of critics in the United States who had not been struck by the false notes, for an English woman in 1942, of such words as penitentiary, automobile, trash, computing, motel and 'staying over'. The 'Saint Leger' should have been St Leger, an error Beryl would never have made herself. Nor would she have made slips in the flying sequences – 'ship' for machine and the aeronautical 'Turn and Bank' indicator was transposed and should have read 'Bank and Turn'. Beryl's old colleague, whose place she had taken to fly the mails, Flip Fleming, was convinced that Beryl had neither written nor checked the manuscript 'or galleys or page proofs . . . even her commercial flying licence is called "a ticket".'[40] Flip was suspicious of 'the poetical flowery prose where Beryl would have stuck to facts. She lacked . . . such words, her vocabulary was limited. What she had was true grit' but 'the most damning mistakes are in the aeronautical terms'.[41]

Evidence that Raoul wrote *West with the Night* is overwhelming. Shakespearean metaphor abounds in the narrative. Allusion to Hesperides, Ptolemy, Homer and other mythology comes directly from works with which Raoul was conversant.

Be that as it may, neither could have produced the memoir without the other and now the book has a unique place in literature for its description of a childhood. Most memoirs idealise. Any author will select details to distil a story and build a credible case. The Markham family always believed, from what she told them herself, that the memoir was ghosted for Beryl. Her nephew, Sir Charles Markham, concluded that 'it was a very valuable account of growing up in Kenya, so what did it matter?'[42] A valid point indeed. And, according to Scott O'Dell, 'Raoul would have been interested in Hemingway's tribute, interested and amused, but not overwhelmed.'[43] Raoul had never expected acknowledgement. Neither, presumably, had he expected to marry his subject.

Beryl had indicated three years earlier that she would divorce Mansfield. Whether prompted by the success of the memoir or because of America's sudden call to arms, Beryl may well have wanted to secure her position with immigration by becoming Raoul's wife and an American citizen.[44] Her intention to divorce Mansfield was published in June and that she would marry Raoul in ten days' time.[45] In the event Beryl first had to establish 'a ten day residency so as to enable her to obtain fast severance of existing matrimonial ties'[46] and to qualify she took a house at Jackson's Hole, Wyoming.[47] On 5 October Beryl filed her plaint with charges that Mansfield had subjected her to 'intolerable indignities'. Once her divorce was granted, she married Raoul next day – 15 October – eleven days before her fortieth birthday. They honeymooned in Virginia.[48]

Once the marriage was licenced, the consequence of legality took its toll. With the book published, the world that Beryl and Raoul had shared since 1939 was no longer theirs – the memoir had a life of its own. They were left facing one another like two bookends, propping it up, remaining silent about it, having little more to say. The relationship hit a minefield.

15

Life as Beryl Schumacher

(1942–9)

Beryl and Raoul would remain enthralled for a while, yet the balance of their hitherto symbiotic roles had tipped with the success of *West with the Night* making Beryl more vulnerable. For a start the memoir earned her a place in the 1942 edition of *Current Biography* as a writer. While this accolade was flattering, recognition as an author seems to have unnerved her, perhaps because all Beryl's other distinctions had been achieved by her own gifts and professional skill – the last thing she was, was a fraud.

Like many intensely private people, she must now surely have felt as exposed as a sea-creature suddenly deprived of its shell. For Raoul knew more about her than any living soul; in a sense her ghost writer had literally recreated her. Her brazen indifference to his feat was self-protective. The power of his knowledge of her was difficult for her to address.

During their honeymoon in Virginia, the Schumachers stayed for a while with Lady Northey's grand-daughter Evangeline Cloete. Beryl wrote to Mansfield informing him that she had divorced him under American law and had married Raoul, and that was thought to be that. Mansfield was delighted at the news, but application to the divorce court was rejected, despite Beryl's new Marriage Certificate, on the grounds that the law in England did not recognise American divorce. Only after Beryl had sworn an affidavit saying that she had slept with her new husband did the court reluctantly award Mansfield a *decree nisi*, and six months later he was able to marry Mary Ellen Adley.[1]

In November 1942, when the Schumachers reached New York, Beryl went through the farce of attending literary luncheons.

Joining eminent authors for cosy chats was not something she had bargained for, as undeserving reverence was bestowed upon her, with the husband who had actually been responsible for her memoir looking on.

Two short stories had been published since the memoir: 'Was There a Horse with Wings?', a condensation of Chapter 10, about Pegasus; and, for a forthcoming issue of *Ladies Home Journal*, 'Wise Child' which focused on Eric Gooch's mare running the fictitious race against Wrack; the account may be seen as having been inspired by Beryl's desire for retribution against Gladys Gooch. The equally fictitious account is in the memoir.

Meanwhile Raoul, feeling his antipathy toward city-dwelling, decided to look for a ranch for them to buy. He rang Scott and told him to keep an eye out for a suitable property, disappearing himself to New Mexico to see what he could find.[2] Beryl joined him at Christmas in California at the ranch he purchased.

Scott described their ranch, Elsinore, as 'an ill favoured resort – near San Juan Capistrano, on a hillside, a dreary place surrounded by springs' in the hills.[5] The minute Beryl left 'the Dorp', as Stuart Cloete a South African writer friend called Manhattan, he complained in a note to Dale Warren, 'I have no favourite blonde now that Beryl has gone west with the wind and the shoemaker into the snowy night' pointing a finger at the impracticality of burying themselves in the country under war-time conditions – lack of servants, supplies and neighbours making their move 'the silliest thing I ever heard of'.[3] 'Food rationing is going to give everyone something to think about.'[4] Prospects were worse for peace; Pearl Harbor's carnage left two thousand dead and air attacks in the Pacific had propelled America into the war, making Coast Guard duty essential for men who were not serving in the forces. Fighting had swayed back and forth between the fanatical Japanese defenders and the American Marines since December.

'I found them in a small house, in the basement. Beryl dictating Raoul copying, writing a short story, stewing in the torrid heat.' This was when Scott saw the New York editor who 'sat on the doorstep'. He was waiting for Raoul's copy. 'More [stories] were on the way ... The basement just dirt ... dug ... not really furnished. The walls were stark.'[6] The timing indicates that the editor was from *Ladies' Home Journal*; Raoul was trying to make the August edition with 'The Captain and His Horse'. Beryl's outline was 'I learn to shoot a revolver from a horse'.[7] The main character is Captain Dennis (no doubt inspired by Denys) and the story is based on the regular invasion of buffalo on Ndimu and of how Jock taught Beryl and Arthur to use a real gun. Scott felt intrusive when the Schumachers were under pressure, so when they had a break, he followed Beryl, leaving Raoul to chat to the editor. Scott found himself alone with her in the corral: 'They were both deliriously happy. They went about hand in hand, dressed in Levi's and concha belts and matching calico shirts – modern lovers out of ancient times. Beryl had a horse, a cat, two Nubian goats to remind her of African days. How I envied them their Arcadian lives.'[8] As Beryl kneeled down by the little black nanny goat to milk her, Scott enquired, 'Does this take you back to Kenya?' She barely responded. Scott's inability to summon any real response had to do with the way he dared to touch upon Africa. Beryl had cut him off with 'Just one or two words.'[9] Reflecting on what had seemed like an idyllic scene, Scott realised later that what he had witnessed was 'really an end to a phase' which he had not seen the beginning of. The hand-holding had been superficial. Beryl 'had not been . . . a happy woman . . . on that sun-baked hill.'[10] He left and would not see them again until they moved back to Pasadena.

Sales of both the American and English edition of *West with the Night*, published by Harrap in London, had been adversely affected by the war. In 1943, reading was regarded as an antidote to service life for soldiers. A special forces edition was printed but the paper shortage which affected all books, and restricted advertising, saw to it that Beryl's memoir was poorly distributed and printed on inferior quality paper, conforming to War Economy Standards. Beryl always explained that the reason the book was hardly known in England was that it had been 'a limited edition for the troops'.[11] In any event, though a few intrigued colonials managed to get a copy or two back to Kenya, in England the memoir disappeared. So the Schumachers were not earning as much money from royalties as they would have liked.

Whatever their income, the Lake Elsinore ranch was sold and, while friends were aware of their difficulties, they were also aware of their 'lordly' style as they dined out on other people.[12] Scott had heard nothing for about a year but was to witness another shift in the couple's relationship when he accepted Raoul's invitation to 'a farewell party' back in the Orange Grove area. Scott was sitting with Beryl on the sofa, Raoul was out in the pantry and again Scott's attempts to engage Beryl in conversation were discouraged: 'There was silence. I was not doing well. Then Raoul emerged with a tray of dry martinis, spilling one. Beryl whispered, "Raoul is always doing that."' Scott was surprised by the glint in her eyes. 'A small bell tolled in my mind, and I went out to the butler's pantry, where Raoul was mixing another round of drinks.' Scott had been upset by Beryl's expression, had stood up and left her without excusing himself, 'knowing something was amiss. I asked what they were writing (Having read and admired some of his short stories in *Collier's*. I was curious because he always used a pen name).' Raoul told Scott that he was doing a novel about Africa, and that Beryl had had an advance from Houghton Mifflin to do a book on Tod Sloan, the celebrated jockey.[13] Scott saw that something was really wrong. Raoul's face had clouded over when Scott asked what was going on. Raoul was reticent. He was always quiet, which is why so little was known about him, but as writers they shared an understanding and respect of one another's work. Scott was dubious about the subject Raoul had chosen, 'Why Africa? You've never been there?' pressing for an answer, 'Is Beryl going to support you in this?' Raoul's reaction was unusually strong. Scott spotted in him a resentment that he had never seen before. 'Suddenly out of nowhere he said, "You are my best friend. I want to make a confession. I want you to know that Beryl did not write *West with the Night* or any of the short stories. Not one damned word of anything!'[14]

Since Raoul never 'bad-mouthed' anyone and had spoken quietly, determinedly but without gesticulation or emotion, the revelation in itself was as disturbing as it was out of character. But something was preying on Raoul's mind, as 'if it had been lying there, he must have been fretting for some reason'.[15] Scott delivered 'a sharp, paternal lecture . . . "You are too fine a writer to be doing what you're doing."' His words 'definitely' had an effect. Scott, after all, had brought the couple together. He had been happy he had done so but this sinister element had entered their relationship for reasons Scott was unable to pinpoint. It struck him also that Beryl was 'not ignorant, nor illiterate but she damned well wasn't a writer either'.

Beryl recognised that the truth had dawned on Scott, and feared that he had seen through her, 'the way she would nod, smile, say yes or no, turn away was part of the cover-up.'

During their exchange in the pantry, Raoul admitted to Scott that they needed the money for that African novel, hence the 'farewell' party. They were moving elsewhere to write it.

'"You're not going to stay in Pasadena?"'

'"No,"' Raoul elaborated, '"We're going to move up to Montecito to a beautiful house, high on a hill."' Scott's reaction was to caution Raoul against moving to a socially hectic scene: '"I wouldn't go to Montecito if I were you, if you're seriously going to write. With Beryl's reputation, you'll be quickly thrown into turmoil."'[16]

In America Beryl was to remain, 'very much of VIP status' – everyone always wanted to meet her. This was not Scott's worry, nor was Beryl's promiscuity; extraordinarily enough, with the advent of Raoul her eye had ceased to rove. But Scott had rarely come across such ascendancy established by one partner over another in marriage: 'Raoul was absolutely besotted by her, it was clear that she was the task master.'[17]

The delving that Raoul had had to do not only heightened Beryl's sense of isolation and vulnerability, but a mistrust had arisen between them because of what he knew and had captured so cleverly. Adoring, and dependent on Beryl for his happiness, he had achieved success through her story, as if she had breathed life into him. Without her, he could no longer function. Feeling undermined, he ignored all but one aspect of Scott's well-intentioned advice, taking the fatal step – for his relationship with Beryl – of declaration. Raoul put his name on his work for the first time. Between publication in January of 'Something I Remember' under Beryl's name and publication of 'The Whiphand' by Raoul Schumacher, in *Collier's* in June, everything altered. Bitter recrimination and competition replaced happiness. Profiles of each of them appearing in relevant issues may have sparked resentment. *Colliers*, edited by Charles Colebaugh at this time, carried a monthly column, 'The Week's Work'. A member of staff, Amy Porter, covered briefly the lives of contributors. Beryl featured first. 'Something I Remember' was the tale of a fight between Beryl's pony stallion, Wee MacGregor, against Collarcelle, one of her father's horses at stud but given the fictitious name of Chaldean for publication. In 'The Week's Work' Beryl is quoted as saying, 'the old truth-is-stranger-than-fiction gag, is so correct with me to the extent that any inventive power I may have is stifled.' When Amy Porter profiled Raoul six months later for the June edition, this was his debut as a writer under his own name. His existence was confirmed. This seems to have posed some sort of threat to Beryl's status. Raoul Schumacher was merely Beryl Markham's husband up to this point. Nobody knew what names he wrote under. But now he had an identity. And as a writer, the next (most obvious) conclusion was that surely it was he who wrote *West with the Night*. By June they were living in Montecito, and according to 'The Week's Work' Raoul and Beryl were 'collaborating on a novel'.[18] In 'Houghton Mifflin's contracts file is a copy of an agreement for "An African novel by Beryl Markham and Raoul Schumacher" for which an advance of $2,500 dollars was paid.'[19] The joint contract suggests that as time went on, the Schumachers would have revealed Raoul's authorship of *West with the Night* if as a team they had been able to top its success – if for no other reason than to ease an uncomfortable situation for Beryl.

As Beryl could not be bothered to give Raoul the sort of co-operation he needed in order to create the African novel, his only hold over her was to refuse to write the Tod Sloan biography. Developments in the coming months were to lead to what can only be described as a shattering conclusion. For in Montecito the couple turned their Arcadian bliss into a battle for revenge. Threat of mutual psychological destruction loomed, at a property known as The Monastery, owned by the conductor, Leopold Stokowski.

Beryl and Raoul had moved in around the time that Paris was liberated in 1944. Friends believe that Rhoda Prudhomme alerted Beryl to the possibility of renting the house. The conductor had

32. Taking a stroll with R.S. Mountstephan,
a backer, shortly before taking off.

33. The Messenger bound for New York – 'the hard way', east to west.

34. A triumphant Beryl arriving in New York from Halifax greets the awaiting crowds with an African salaam.

35 & 36. Wherever Beryl went in New York she was feted
by her fans, here about to join the comedian Milton Berle
for her first broadcast from New York City (below).

MRS. MARKHAM COMES HOME—FORGOTTEN

No Crowds, No Cheers: 'Terribly

BAN ON NO
COWARD PLAY

37 & 38. By sharp contrast Beryl found irony and tragedy
when she returned to England: no victorious welcome
from her countrymen in London, and coming to terms
with the death of Tom Campbell Black (below),
her only flying instructor, killed in England just
after Beryl had completed her flight across the Atlantic.

39. 'Sister Fliers' at Longchamp:
Beryl with Amy Johnson
at the Prix de l'Arc
de Triomphe, October 1936.

40. Beryl in London
with her lover, the
'singing boxer' and
darling of the upper
classes, Jack Doyle.
Doyle's family claimed
he had been corrupted
by the Prince of Wales
and Lady Furness.
c. 1937.

41. Raoul Schumacher,
Beryl's third husband,
at a costume party in
Santa Barbara.

42. Beryl in Los Angeles, 1937, being interviewed
about Amelia Earhart's disappearance over the Pacific.

43 & 44. John Potter (above) and Scott O'Dell, two friends of Raoul Schumacher's, who both observed him collaborating with Beryl on *West With the Night*.

45. The Monastery, the villa lent to Beryl and Raoul
by Stokowski – as it is today.

46. A lunch party at the Monastery c. 1945
shows Raoul still looking thin after his illness.

47 & 48. Above, one of Millie Kelleher's costume parties
(Raoul is in the 3rd row, far left) and, below, Labor Day 1949.
Raoul in white tuxedo with buttonhole is leaning towards
David Niven's wife, with David Niven next to her.

49 & 50. Mansfield
Markham in his fifties
and Gervase Markham
at 22. The rumour that
the Duke of Gloucester
was Gervase's father,
though never
contradicted by Beryl, is
not borne out by the
distinct family likeness
between these two
men.

51. Jorgen Thrane, who
helped manage Forest
Farm and whom Beryl
loved deeply for over
ten years in Kenya.

52. Beryl's lifelong
friend, arap Ruta, who
accompanied her and
Mansfield on their
honeymoon in 1927,
with Caesar.

53. Tana receiving
attention from her
mistress Pat Cavendish.

54. Enid, Lady Kenmare,
in coronation robes,
whom Beryl persuaded in
1963 to buy the
dilapidated Broadlands
estate in South Africa.

55. Broadlands as it is today,
one of South Africa's top racing establishments.

56. Beryl at the Duke of Manchester's wedding
at Nairobi racecourse, her love of eccentric headwear
still evident in her seventies.

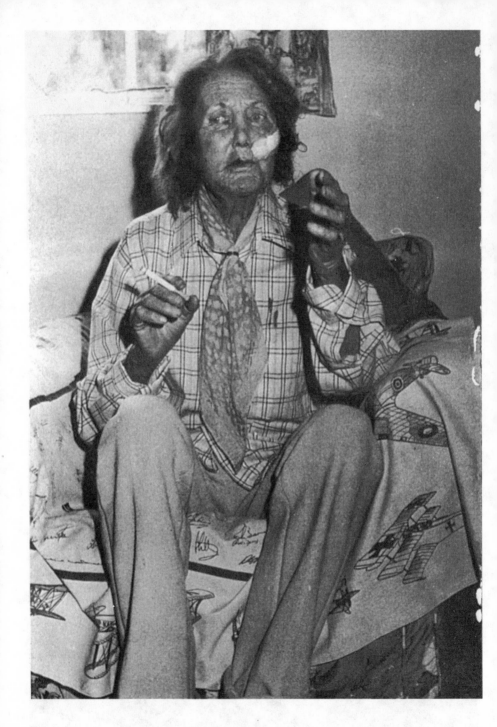

57. Beryl aged 79 recuperating in her bungalow
after thieves had broken in and brutally beaten her up.

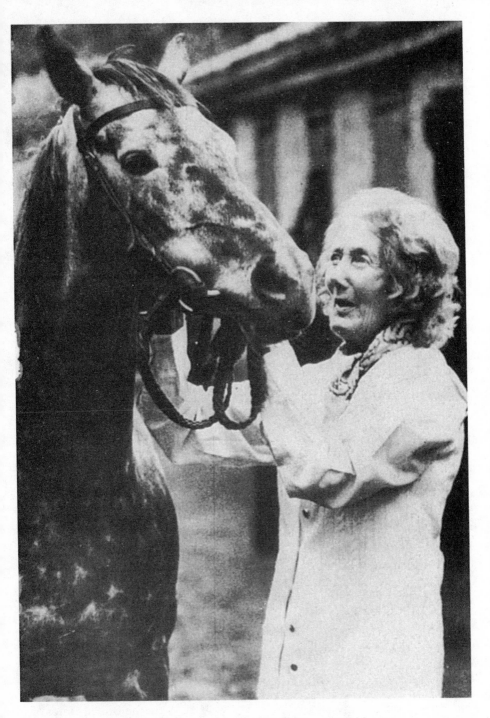

58. Back on form at 80, the trainer Beryl Markham
examines one of her horses at Ngong races.

59. Beryl with her blue Mercedes, after she and the car were shot at by an askari during the August 1982 coup in Kenya. William K. Purdy, who restored the car, ensured that the bullet holes in her bodywork were preserved.

60. Portrait of Beryl by the Associated Press to mark the republication in the United States of *West With the Night*, May 1983.

built it as a retreat from the world for himself and his wife, Evangeline Johnson, during his affair with Garbo. However, an extract from Gloria Vanderbilt's memoir, *Black Knight, White Knight* suggests that Stokowski knew Beryl already. Young Gloria Vanderbilt was enraptured and about to marry the forty-two-year-old musician who was 'even older than mummy' and Garbo terrified Gloria. She refused to get out of the bath to meet the legend, who had pitched up at Stokowski's home in 1944, hoping to rent The Monastery from him herself. Stokowski had refused, 'because Beryl Markham's rented it for a year . . . we're going there next weekend. Beryl's expecting us.' Gloria was dreading the visit to The Monastery, she was so nervous of the ghosts of the brilliant Stokowski's former wives and lovers.[20] What Beryl made of that weekend at The Monastery was recorded by neither party; Beryl had identified with Garbo's preference for solitude. Garbo's shyness was genuine when they met on the set of *Conquest*.[21]

Beryl loved The Monastery and was to spend nearly four years in this unusual furnished ranch house which 'looked out over the world' and over the spindly palms, flanking each main thoroughfare, high above the pastel-coloured houses of Santa Barbara. Here homes grew grander with the heights, beyond the limits of the town, and set in gardens of great splendour.

Beryl and Raoul became part of 'the upper upper crust' in a town described as 'a lot of dough holding the upper-crust together' – well-to-do Catholic and Protestant Easterners of Montecito.[22] The moneyed barons from across America had 'discovered' pastoral Montecito, then regarded as a fashionable health resort, in the 1900s. The Duponts, Swifts, Rockefellers and their friends built magnificent homes here, surrounding them with opulent gardens – names such as Lotusland, Piranhurst, Wildwood, Solano and Val Verde evoking the glamour of their occupants. Garden architects had recreated elaborate themes from Europe, using French, Mediterranean, English or even Persian influences. These stately homes in the foothills, among dazzling gardens through which Beryl and Raoul would also roam, made The Monastery austere in comparison. Yet if Stokowski's collection of rare plants was a simpler contribution it was no less exotic in its way.

'The Schumachers lived where the swells lived', slipping easily into the community of millionaires. In their casual clothes they conjured the image of celebrities whose luck had run out, temporarily. Compared to the circle who made them welcome they were impecunious, but if cultural snobbishness prevailed in Santa Barbara, in Montecito social stratification was fiercer still. If one hailed from the mid-west, one had better come from a meat-packing fortune or forget it. Beryl's credentials were excellent. Not only was she English, but decorative *and* a writer. Recent critical acclaim set her apart – everyone who owned a copy of the memoir sought her out. *West with the Night* became Beryl's passport.[23]

The grandeur of Toro Canyon matched that of Africa; it was so wild in 1944 that tarantula spiders and coyote abounded. Its hills were reminiscent of Soysambu, blue skies above ochre rocks, the same warmth and colouring, throwing violet shadows as the day lengthened. The clustered eucalyptuses about the house sighed in the wind at night, just as they had at Ndimu Farm. The driveway up Toro Canyon to the house was steep and winding; guests announced themselves by striking an enormous, bowl-shaped gong with a leather-covered baton. Visitors to the Schumachers remember the ritual of arrival. The resonance of the 'Kin' or resting bell, seemed to last 'for about seven minutes'. It had been used as set dressing in the original 1937 film of *Lost Horizon*. The magnificent object had been hammered from a flat disc of bronze and traditionally was used in intervals between chants, during Buddhist services.[24] The presence of Stokowski invaded every curve of the house. During its construction, he and his wife Evangeline were practising yoga. Their books on Sanskrit and Hindu philosophy were still on the shelves when Beryl and Raoul moved in.[25]

The ranch house is single-storeyed board and batten perched on a ledge, like an eagle's eyrie, eight hundred feet up Toro Canyon. Stokowski used itinerant labour to build, who 'never finished it . . . It has that camping-out look . . . walls were not joined entirely in places . . . the wind whistled through these gaps'.[26] It was shaped like a horse-shoe, situated parallel to the Pacific Ocean below, terracing the two long parts of its 'U' shape at different levels and giving each bedroom, bathroom and verandah the same spectacular view across California's only south-facing coast. The Channel

Islands, often shrouded in mist as fine as mosquito netting, could be seen once the opaqueness cleared, in a superb panorama of ocean and sky. Stokowski had chosen the site because the land could never be developed, establishing a garden, but by the time Beryl and Raoul lived here, fruit ranches covered the foothills too. The majestic San Ynez mountains stood behind The Monastery, with its view to infinity across lemon orchards, persimmon trees and avocados.

Behind the kitchen was the inner, empty part of the horseshoe; intended for a swimming pool, this contained only a patio in Beryl's day. Stokowski created a small sun-trap in the fragrance garden where Garbo could tan herself in the nude in private, at the rear of The Monastery. The sound of the Kin gave ample warning if visitors turned up, allowing Beryl, just as Garbo had done, to join them or remain undisturbed, as she wished. The arrangement suited Beryl perfectly. She liked to wander about wearing nothing if possible – quite feasible here – running barefoot up and down the steps linking the upper bedroom wing, delighting in its informality. The Schumachers used Stokowski's own bedroom, the only one facing directly east across Toro Canyon so that the sun rose into it. At full moonrise light also flooded the room, the large windows, located on three sides, letting perfume from the fragrance garden waft in. Evangeline had planted night-scented flowers and shrubs on the adjacent rear patio, and Stokowski developed it further, bringing back flora and fauna from all over the world.[27]

Summer was the time when the rich families swelled the select resident community, among whom was Rhoda Prudhomme, who knew Beryl at Seremai. Rhoda had divorced Gabriel at the beginning of the war, 'glad to get rid of that real little squirt, gadabout and show-off', but that was not to be the end of the story. She had left Mawingo, on Mount Kenya, unoccupied and, when Gabriel was killed in action, his French family tried to lay claim to it and half of Rhoda's fortune, which would involve legal wrangling. Rhoda was now an influential hostess and an accomplished golfer 'with a penchant for pursuing liaisons against a gently rolling landscape' and who, every summer, occupied her beach house on Fernald Point.[28] This vivacious, dark-haired socialite got along famously with Raoul particularly; he would partner her in mixed-doubles tennis and at weekends Rhoda joined Beryl and Raoul for their favourite way to entertain – picnics in the hills. Raoul caught fresh-water crayfish, peeled and prepared these for salads. In turn, they attended Rhoda's elaborate parties presided over by her butler, Pedro, bringing Beryl and Raoul in contact with 'the upper upper crust'. Photographs of parties at Fernald Point or entertaining in the garden of The Monastery indicate a relaxed but stylish atmosphere.

The alternative was the Coral Casino, a snobbish club – Montecito's answer to Muthaiga – considered *the* place to frolic with the Knapps and Armours although the Montecito Tennis Club was a stiff contender.[29] Just down the hill from The Monastery, the Coral Casino was the jewel in the Biltmore Hotel crown, sharing the ocean vista along Channel Drive. Like Muthaiga, its plain façade maintained its secrets when tanned bodies met on poolside decks for festive luncheons or dinner dances.[30] In Santa Barbara itself the lunchtime watering holes were El Paseo or Pete's Casa de Seville and the Harbour Restaurant owned by Al Weingan, a venue made popular by Scott Fitzgerald. David Niven and the producer Milton Spurling were often seen at the Harbour. Weingan and Ronald Colman owned San Ysidro Ranch.[31] The social line was 'very tight but underneath it all, promiscuous'.[32] A lot of drinking went on and only the most determined of writers would find the peace required for work. Night-time parties were 'black tie' affairs at which the Schumachers mixed, besides Colman, and Niven and his wife, with Evie and Van Johnson, Joseph Cotten and his first wife, Lenore La Mont, the concert pianist who was to die of leukaemia.

Tennis was part of daily life; the children growing up that summer remember Beryl and Raoul with their parents and friends, always dressed in white, like gods, always golden from the sun, always drifting from one party to the next. Their lives appeared to be forged by light and joy, full of laughter. Rhoda Prudhomme's granddaughter, Audrey, hankered, as a dark-haired child, to 'look like the great, blonde Beryl', realising even then that it would be impossible to become like 'this tall, beautiful creature so gentle with children and animals, followed by Blondie* her labrador cross

Rhodesian Ridgeback and her two little dachsunds. They went everywhere with Raoul and Beryl.'[33]

If Rhoda's granddaughter was intrigued by Beryl, Peter, the son of Chris Rand the writer and Maddie, was mesmerised by Raoul after his mother had told him that he was 'Beryl's ghost'. The role had to be explained one day before the Schumachers arrived for lunch.[34] A copy of the memoir had been brought out to show him the product of Raoul's toil. But 'what is a ghost writer?' Peter persisted. To the innocent and enquiring mind of a young boy, the notion was so odd: 'She told me how Beryl had grown up in Africa but that "this fabulous, glamorous woman, able to fly east to west over the Atlantic was unable to write about it herself" whereas Raoul possessed this gift. A different strength; the power to describe such a feat'.[35]

Peter was already familiar with the world of writers. His father was an author, working in New York. Today Peter Rand is a novelist himself and still feels compassion for Raoul's unsung role, emphasising the lack of fulfilment which Raoul must have experienced in performing this invisible feat. He concedes that Raoul 'may have been a sponge' but argues also that he 'was a wonderful person, a cut above the pulps and *West with the Night* was his masterpiece'.[36]

The last stories to appear for some time were 'Appointment in Khartoum' – a flying story which appeared in the April issue of *Collier's*. Then in September, the *Saturday Evening Post* published 'The Splendid Outcast', a story based on Beryl's acquisition of Messenger Boy with Ruta at Newmarket in 1927, but the fictitious stallion is given the name Rigel,* perhaps to differentiate from the version in the memoir. This was the sixth short story to be published since *West with the Night*. Writing about horses was never any problem for Raoul; he knew the equestrian world as well as Beryl.

But to undertake 'an African novel' Raoul needed greater cooperation from Beryl than for the memoir, where he had merely needed details on African aspects of raising horses, for example. Maybe Beryl was uninterested in the topic because it did not focus directly on herself; maybe her lack of imagination prevented her from understanding what Raoul was driving at. Maybe nothing could compensate for his own unreciprocated longings for Beryl once he became aware of her new relationships, unable to accept her physical defection as she began to flirt outrageously with men, having two affairs concurrently as so often in the past. There were those occasions when she was casual to the point of being careless, reaching for the next man having hardly finished with the last. Usually when such behaviour was detected, Beryl intended it to be so.

Obviously Beryl had never considered that Raoul might rebel by refusing to write the Tod Sloan biography. Beryl had accepted an advance from Houghton Mifflin, signing the contract in good faith, confident at the time that there was no possibility that Raoul would renege – if she thought about it at all. Possibly she fought with Raoul because he drank (she was still abstemious herself), instead of getting down to work and fulfilling his role. Maybe she flung at him the accusation that he was useless in bed when he drank; who will ever know precisely what the contention was? When they rowed over writing, however, Raoul's argument was unequivocal: 'You have posed as a writer for years. I am going to write my book on Africa . . . you can write on Tod Sloan or do any damn thing you like. But I'm not going to write another damn word for you.'[37]

The first time Beryl had heard about Tod Sloan was during the ride at Potha when everyone had teased Ernest Hemingway about the way he sat a horse. Tod Sloan was the name for James Forman, who had died in 1933, an American jockey who in adopting a crouching seat – almost on the horse's neck – had revolutionised racing in England in 1897. His reputation was only tainted by betting, for which he was banned from riding, but Sloan was none the less recognised as a brilliant jockey, having won a third of his races on the British Turf. It is a tribute to Beryl's determination not to be beaten or outwitted that she even attempted what for her was an impossible exercise.

The Monastery was ideal for leading separate lives. Each room was self-contained with its own entrance. There was no need even to pass through any other room to reach the kitchen. Total independence would be feasible for several occupants, never mind a couple in conflict, bent upon avoiding one another. She tried furiously to produce something; she shut the door and typed day after day, not speaking to Raoul except when social gatherings made communication necessary. Even so, whatever Beryl submitted to Houghton Mifflin 'bounced off the walls'. Their letter of rejection, which ultimately Raoul showed to Scott, was 'very curt, very short and absolutely insulting: "The person who wrote *West with the Night* did not write this."'[38] No correspondence survives the ill-fated manuscript because the project was abortive. Beryl hated others to know that she had been beaten; outright dismissal cast aspersions on a reputation from which she was unable to escape. She asked Scott to read the manuscript but never sent it to him.[39]

What became of the manuscript is anybody's guess. What is known is that Beryl 'quietly sought revenge, locking herself away at night' – witholding sex from Raoul – beginning an exercise of mutual self-destruction. On the surface, cannily, they remained little changed, but the lazy element in Raoul's nature which had always allowed him to accept hospitality from others seemed to take over. 'He seemed more or less in a world of his own.' Others attributed his solace in the bottle to 'not being a great success as a writer'.[40] Then they noticed that the Schumachers were behaving differently: Beryl introduced Raoul with condescension: 'Raoul is a beginning writer – for the pulps – the funny magazines – he's quite successful you know.' Raoul told Scott later, '"In every way subtle and unsubtle, she worked on me until you picked me up from the street."'[41]

Eight weeks after Beryl's call to him about the Tod Sloan manuscript, Scott had another call from her:

'"Raoul is dying. Come and get him."

'Those words exactly.

'"Where is he?"

'"Here."

'"Why isn't he in hospital?"

'A short steely silence. Then the command again: "Come and get him." To save time – I was living three hours from Montecito – I said, "Meet me halfway. At the Beverly Wilshire Hotel at noon tomorrow."

'Beryl was there. Without a word she opened the back door of her car, and out fell what was left of Raoul Schumacher. Without a word, she drove off.

'I took him to the Huntington Memorial Hospital in Pasadena.'

The Huntington Memorial Hospital was made famous in the film *Citizen Kane*. Scott had taken Raoul to the Emergency Room there. He described Raoul's condition, it was 'like picking up a child . . . he must have lost a couple of stone. He was dishevelled and in extreme pain.'

'His hands were just blisters . . . every follicle . . . of every hair on his body, were little blisters, all over his face, everywhere.

'The doctors said that his condition was terminal. On a hunch I called Joseph Griggs, a doctor who was very successful with exotic disease, especially Malta fever. He drove fifty miles in a hurry, puzzled over Schumacher for an hour, and finally decided to drain his blood. He drained it three times and replaced it three times. Raoul recovered. I got him into a nursing home in Claremont.'[42]

The Huntington Memorial Hospital confirms Raoul Schumacher's admission (and two later occasions besides); strict confidentiality about the release of patient information, particularly when related to nervous diseases, means that details of his illnesses cannot be made public.[43] What transpired when Raoul was admitted with Scott in attendance, we do know. Raoul was in the care of resident physicians and Dr Griggs was called in on a consulting basis; Griggs was 'a modest, veritable genius',[44] and Scott maintained that had he not acted immediately, Raoul would have died. After five crucial days he responded to the blood transfusions, but was not well enough to go home. Scott arranged for his transfer to a nursing home in Claremont where he and Dr Griggs lived. Gradually, in close contact with two people whom Raoul felt cared for him, he told Scott how he had reached the nadir in his emotional life with Beryl. But he had not admitted to the way in which she had 'worked on him' to Dr Griggs. As Raoul recuperated, Scott was emphatic: 'For Christ's sake, don't go back there. Stay away.' He would not listen. Scott became so alarmed that he risked the rebuke he now received from Dr Griggs: 'It would have helped if you'd told me earlier . . . it was psychosomatic obviously . . . I would have treated him differently had I known this was forced upon him by his wife.' Scott's only defence was innocence: 'What the hell. I didn't know it. How could I tell you?' The doctor concluded their encounter by expressing the hope that Raoul would not return to Montecito after what he refered to as 'a complete nervous breakdown'.[45]

Scott's conclusion was that Raoul had literally 'been sickened to death' over Beryl's infidelities, the way in which these were conducted openly: they were 'blatant so as to embarrass Raoul'. Beryl's bullying tactics, which were known to manifest themselves once she had the upper hand, were a tendency recognised by Kenya friends. But Californians were baffled because Raoul was so quiet and as if 'he was under the influence of some Swami . . . something not of this world . . . even after this terrible traumatic acquaintance with death he was still oriented and absolutely besotted by her.'[46]

And the hermetic seal around this shocking information, was to hold tight for forty years. Not until republication of the memoir in paperback and Beryl's death in 1986 ('and presumably beyond embarrassment') did the seal begin to break once *West with the Night* soared in the best-seller list of the *New York Times*.

Whether Raoul mentioned his almighty binge, whether the word 'alcohol' was uttered during treatment, is a moot point. Yet none disguised that he was a heavy drinker, consuming greater quantities under stress. Scott himself wrote that Raoul 'died from drinking, a fine writer, a quiet gentle man, always more concerned with your problems than his own'.[47] That affable and considerate disposition had been his undoing; mockery had 'hurt the hell out of Raoul as he swallowed his pride, he was that self-effacing'. Scott could see that it would have taken guts to confront Beryl. Raoul's flexible nature had allowed him to bend unnecessarily to her needs. But what Scott would never forget was 'her chilled steel voice . . . as if she was dumping garbage . . . could have a corpse on her hands . . . relieved that her obligations were over. She'd got rid of a dying man.'[48] Scott, knowing nothing of ethnic lore where the dying must be removed from the dwelling, never realised his accuracy in daring to allow himself to recognise Beryl's revulsion for the dying. Yet Beryl's action must remain indefensible.

Scott did realise how deeply the creation of the memoir had affected them both psychologically. Before 'The Whiphand', Raoul had only used pen-names. Beryl's name had freed him in one sense, given him his literary wings, yet in another, 'somehow made him fasten on to her, become comfortable with her, be absorbed by her so that he was loath to relinquish her and really felt part of her.'[49] Whereas Beryl was so accustomed to success when she set out to excel, she had 'befuddled herself . . . imagined that she could do anything . . . had so promoted herself . . . it was part of her psyche, implanted firmly in her mind'. So much so that when Raoul surrendered anonymity, it came 'almost as a surprise that she hadn't written the book', but the rejection letter from Houghton Mifflin had reminded her.[50]

However it is doubtful, even after the Waterjump, that Beryl had become so thrilled by her own potency that she would have decided alone to commit it to immortality. Her tangled network of self-perception did not tell her that it was Raoul, not she, who had recognised the value of her story. It was he who provided the method of perpetuating it; what may well have shocked Beryl was how overwhelmed she felt privately in her genuine need to find her own feet again. In fact in 1945 raising her self-esteem would not have been an easy task; she was right out of her depth, but could not admit it. She was right back where she began, sitting at Tania's table because of Denys, with her confidence wavering and all the old fears of ignorance and lack of education confronting her. The Atlantic flight she was proud of. But the book summoned questions. A memoir was a lasting monument. To what? The fact that she had cheated readers all over the world into believing she was something she was not. The best thing that could happen was to forget its existence. This is why she had provoked Raoul, providing the motive – in hand with African ruthlessness of survival – behind the scene of cold passion outside the Beverly Wilshire.

However, the Schumachers somehow became reconciled. The interlude away from one another seemed to have relieved Raoul of the pressure of Beryl's vengeance as well as of the effects of his excessive drinking. Raoul 'had found part of himself, must have confronted Beryl.' The marriage was sutured up to leave new scars. Certainly snapshots taken of them as a couple after this episode indicate intimate friendship, the camaraderie of any reasonably happy couple entertaining, and that those scars had healed over.

Certain proof was publication of another short story, in the February issue of *Colliers* in 1945, based on the incident involving Beryl's tussle and triumph over a *layoni*. Once more there are indications that this had been dropped from the memoir. Notes about *En-gai* [sic] as God appear in Raoul's hand as well as jottings about tribal culture. This was the last short story published under Beryl's name before the end of the war.[51]

Out of three marriages, Beryl's association with Raoul had far outstripped the other husbands, and any single relationship, in terms of conventional fidelity. But now Beryl's need for fresh conquest was surfacing at a time when they were more short of money than ever. Royalties from *West with the Night* had dried up completely; Stokowski had waived the rent. By October they were 'baby sitting' The Monastery and 'two or three times a week' ate with friends so as to save money. Any income from the last two short stories was no match for their lifestyle, but Beryl would not be beaten. She overcame her penury and disdain for housework. She wore white, implying glamour and total disregard for economy. She had no horse, but took to wearing jodhpurs and boots like a Hollywood director, in which, even without make-up, Beryl looked 'marvellous'. For years she had cross-dressed with innovative flair with such success that others not only copied her, they had long since stopped implying that she dressed like a man. It was to this outrageously glamorous image that the young doctor Warren Austin was drawn, when he reached Montecito in late 1945.

Fortunes of war and a chance remark by the Duke of Windsor to Captain Warren Austin, his physician, during a farewell luncheon at Government House on Nassau, prompted his call to Beryl. Raoul answered the telephone when he rang from the Montecito Inn* which was a few hundred yards from the Coral Casino. The minute Beryl heard that the Duke of Windsor was Warren Austin's contact, she invited him to come straight round for dinner, then pressed him to stay the night. Reluctantly he agreed. The Schumachers both insisted he come and stay. Raoul was to become one of his 'best friends'. As for Beryl, since Warren was prepared to meet someone special, that she was striking came as no surprise. What took him aback, being ten years younger than she, was that he was attracted to her so strongly, and 'In the end I moved in.'[52]

Circumstances had changed from those euphoric days Scott had once envied. In 1939 they had been penniless and happy; now they were penniless and desperate. In Beryl's desire for quality, everything had to be the best. She had not asked Warren to contribute to the household expenses yet 'thought nothing of charging things . . . merchants were just a bother, because they wanted to be paid.'[53] Raoul's answer was to dismiss the responsibility in an amusing way: 'If we can't be in debt to the tradesmen, what on earth is the use of them?'[54] Since none of them had any money, the three dined at home. The shortage of money was never mentioned; other people talked about it 'but not Beryl and Raoul'. Warren noticed how patently they ignored the bills.

The Schumacher marriage was 'difficult' and Warren found the snappiness and tension of living *à trois* was at times embarrassing. Raoul's quietness added to Warren's unease. 'They were so hard up that time itself became expensive. They were always at other people's houses. It was a desperate situation.'[55] In Warren's opinion, 'Beryl should have been born rich' needing 'a lot of money in civilisation', in other words, so as not to lose face in the eyes of her 'big men. She wanted to be in the most royal company present – not necessarily the richest. The best was none too good for her.'[56]

Warren's words make patently clear the one reason Warren was welcomed when they could hardly afford to feed themselves was because of the Duke of Windsor. Warren regarded himself as 'just a little boy from the sticks' yet had successfully redressed his humble beginnings in 1941. After expecting a posting to the North Atlantic Division of the US Engineers, as a newly qualified doctor he found himself posted instead to Nassau Army Hospital – actually a converted Colonial hotel.[57] His rise as Court physician to the Windsors was meteoric. There had been no local doctor so that, if the Duke or Duchess required medical attention, they flew to the United States or a doctor was brought in. When the Duke needed a blood test, he expressed difficulty in pronouncing the word Lieutenant in the American fashion. Dr Austin had joked, 'There's a very easy way to solve that Sir. Just have me made a Captain.' His promotion and the appropriate rise in salary followed next day.[58] The Duke's comptroller, Captain Gray Phillips of the Black Watch, in whom the Duke had utter faith, befriended Warren; soon he was making up a fourth at bridge with the Windsors, often partnering the Duchess. He became a frequent guest at Government House. When the war ended, Warren Austin was due to go to Japan. The day before he left Nassau, heading instead for Santa Barbara, the Duke and Duchess invited him alone for lunch to say good bye. It turned out for Warren to be a disastrous main course – steak and kidney pie, turning Warren 'green at the thought' – but when the Duke heard that he was to set up medical practice in Santa Barbara, he insisted, 'You must get in touch with my dear friend, Beryl Markham,' urging Warren twice, 'Be sure to contact Beryl. She is Beryl Schumacher now.'[59] Since the Duchess obviously did not know Beryl herself, 'only of her' Warren quizzed Gray Phillips for information. George Wood and Nina Drury had clearly discussed her thoroughly after she left Nassau in 1941. She sounded notorious. Warren made no bones about acting on the Duke's recommendation: 'Everyone likes celebrities. Beryl's connections with Europe . . . her affair with the Duke of Gloucester' had become 'all part of Beryl's meal ticket.' Warren was not disappointed in their six-month relationship. 'She had this marvellous English sounding voice too' and she entranced him when she could not sound the 'r', pronouncing his name 'Juan'.

Warren was not easy to forget himself. He was sensationally tall and good-looking; his voice was not unlike that of Cary Grant, with that same debonair quality. 'A non-venal Svengali' with dark brown eyes and hair, and a cleft in his chin.[60]

While he was preoccupied with setting up and equipping his rooms in Montecito, he could see that Beryl's irritation, as an early riser herself, was ill concealed when Raoul 'lay abed'. 'He was always going to write . . . and did . . . beautifully, when he did. The problem was getting round to it.'[61] Raoul did manage to get two stories written and accepted in 1946 – 'The Transformation', for *Ladies' Home Journal* published in January, and 'The Quitter' for the June edition of *Cosmopolitan*. They were the last two to appear under Beryl's name. He had been offered a series of five radio plays by Joseph Cotten in the spring of 1946 and worked away from home in Los Angeles a good deal.

The post-war economy notwithstanding, work was not easy to come by during the campaign of McCarthy against communism that created a web of suspicion and fear among friends in Hollywood, so Raoul was grateful not to say flattered to be offered this work. During his absences, Beryl would ring Warren, complaining how lonely she was; he would drive up to The Monastery for dinner, spend the night with her, and in the morning 'extricate myself . . . driving down to Santa Barbara Cottage Hospital in my big Lincoln . . . wondering if anyone had spotted me'.[62]

Though the last photographs of the Schumachers entertaining Rhoda Prudhomme at The Monastery belie tension yet again, it was seldom absent during 1946 when they were together. Then one afternoon Raoul returned from Hollywood unexpectedly, catching Beryl *in flagrante delicto* with a mutual friend, ending the marriage abruptly. There was no scene. He packed his bags 'without more ado and moved out'.[63] The end had come in Raoul's acceptance of his own repressed nervous intensity. His hospitalisation had shown him how easily he fell victim to the agonies of woe recognising finally that Beryl had the capacity to inflict more unhappiness than he could reasonably bear. Despite the rupture, Beryl and he kept in touch while she remained in Santa Barbara.

That July, Gervase Markham, on holiday from Eton, came to California on a one-way ticket. Presumably at his request, possibly out of sheer curiosity, Mansfield paid for him to fly out. Whatever prompted the visit it was not exactly a success from anybody's point of view.[64] Gervase was regarded already by his grandmother, 'Gar', as 'a lost soul' whose fiendish temper had seriously jeopardised entry to Eton. Gar's husband, James O'Hea, had not helped her grandson's sense of insecurity. On the grounds of 'adoring Gervase', he carried a snapshot around and would pluck it from his wallet on any pretext, crowing that here was the boy fathered by the Duke of Gloucester, giving fresh life to the rumour and, as one witness explained, 'hardly surprising when everyone in England thought the same'.[65] Gervase's tantrums had become alarming as he approached adolescence; public school curbed his emotional rebellion but the Markham family had 'questioned whether he would be able to survive Eton, with his continual outbursts'.[66] At seventeen, Beryl's son looked startlingly like her; years later a snapshot of Beryl in a flying helmet led Gervase's widow to mistake mother for son.[67] Gervase, accustomed to war-time austerity and having had a difficult up-bringing, was critical of 'self-seeking people' and his 'spiritual, over-religious tendencies' sprang from an earnest search for the meaning of life when his own had consisted of upheaval. Gar's home had been requisitioned by the Canadian Army when Swiftsden had become Brigade Headquarters. She had been deprived of her servants; they moved to a tiny cottage at Sandhurst in 'deepest Kent' where neighbours thought him 'a strange shy boy'.[68] Then they lived at Hawkhurst where Mary Ellen Adley, who would become Mansfield's second wife, 'took Gervase on in the school holidays . . . receiving a small pittance for her pains'.[69] Mary Ellen's excellent taste enabled her and Mansfield to do up houses, selling them at a profit, but this meant moving every six months.[70] Gervase's sense of rootlessness brought out all his uncertainties. According to his cousins, 'he was never a strong boy' and contemporaries at Eton recall that he was 'introspective, solitary and unhappy', though his stubbornness was akin to Beryl's determination.[71] Even his closeness to Gar had been terminated abruptly the year before. Swiftsden, 'wrecked by army officers as well as looted', had been handed back, but with no servants to run it, Gar had moved into 'a horrible little flat in Bayswater'.[72]

Gervase's existence came as something of a shock since nobody in Santa Barbara was aware that Beryl had a son. Her reaction was not to be seen with him or to allow anybody to meet him, persuading Warren to take him over. Warren interpreted Beryl's rejection as vanity: 'She had not wanted anyone to know that she had a boy of six-foot something. He stayed with me in my tiny house.'[73] Warren was shrewd enough to divine one thing '. . . the poor boy seemed to have one cold after another . . . I think Beryl saw this as a sort of weakness of character.'[74] Obviously she could not bring herself to confide in Warren her son's dangerous condition at birth; he might have judged her less harshly had he known. Beryl would not allow anyone to be lenient with her son. 'Poor thing . . . was miserable. Had no clothes. I think he'd lost his luggage. I gave him a camera.'[75] Warren was kindness itself to Beryl's son, buying suitable clothes for the Californian climate on her behalf.

Evidently Gervase valued such memories because he took views of Santa Barbara, and stuck these in an album without dating or captioning them. Lacking a mother herself, one would have imagined that Beryl might have made some attempt to redress a similar situation. But as if the hurt inflicted on herself must never be forgotten, here we discover malevolent echoes. Beryl had never heard her father speak of her mother. And once Gervase was married with daughters of his own, he never spoke of Beryl to them. Nor until the very end of her life, did Beryl mention *her* mother.

After 'only a week or so', uneasy in his presence, Beryl dispatched Gervase to Sir Charles and Lady Mendl* in Hollywood; Sir Charles and Mansfield had worked together years before at the American Embassy in Paris. John Potter remembers how Raoul, himself and other cronies 'clubbed together for his return fare' to England.[76]

It is easy to see how Beryl fell into the brazen villainess slot, as the image of the negligent mother was bandied about. Beryl gave her detractors the very image they preferred to see, taking no trouble to explain or defend her stance.

Warren remained puzzled but his affection was unsullied and Beryl continued to be 'the most marvellous woman'. She was strikingly handsome, young enough still to make a young army doctor feel a gay dog, but there is no doubt that Beryl was conscious of her age and that the discrepancy between herself and Warren accentuated a growing need for undivided attention.

Throughout the day, while Warren attended patients Beryl lazed by the swimming pools of friends, borrowing a horse occasionally to ride, keeping her figure in trim by climbing the hill behind the house. She took no interest in domesticity: 'Had she had her way she would have had a place she could have cleaned with a hose.'[77]

For all her achievement, fame and notoriety, she was never intimidating to men. In many ways she was quite boyish, with her masculine clothes and buddyish reactions – a type of independence that Warren, who was nervous of aggressive females, found particularly unthreatening although, 'She did not pussy-foot around. She was never "girlie-girlie" . . . she was not the type who walked

up and put her arms around you. The idea [sex] was born, happened, was over right away – without fuss. She never conveyed a
sense of trying to trap me, never used tricks.' One primary factor
in Beryl's success with men seems to have been her sense of
immediacy in sex.

She played soft Glen Miller music, 'her shy way of saying one
was of a high enough quality to accept' and was charming and
practical and 'repeatedly appealing'.[78] When the two of them were
alone she would walk about naked, 'Proud of her body, just like
any boy would be, she was lean, small-hipped with cute little
breasts and certainly no droopy behind . . . with that untouchable
arrogance achieved by the physical mobility of walking tall. She
was as thin as a rail, so that clothes hung well on her, even
borrowed clothes'.[79]

Poor as Beryl was, she could not accept that Warren had to go
off every day to earn a living. The Duchess of Windsor's recommendation had everybody queuing up to consult him – the scarcity of
doctors helped. Warren had borrowed to the hilt to equip his surgery. Beryl could not understand that his debt must be repaid. First
she had mocked him over his patients – 'What do you care about
these stupid people for?' – trying to get him to charge more money.
He almost envied her freedom from convention, her contempt for
the bourgeois. She was 'ruthless and disdainful of petty things'
with that ability to spot weakness in others which enabled her to
pick on them – never hurtfully, more like teasing. None the less,
such mockery had proved effective before and because she had
been unusually good company, was now more so than ever. Her
relationship with Warren became strained. Warren extricated himself when he could see that the effects would damage his career,
especially since his conscience nagged continually about the moral
aspect of his relationship: 'one didn't drink and carry on' as a
doctor.[80]

Warren played bridge, Beryl hated the game. He would socialise;
Beryl refused to 'kowtow' on account of a meal. One evening,
invited by affluent patients of Warren's to dine, Beryl arranged to
arrive late for dinner and leave early. Their hosts' wealth came
from the manufacture of farm machinery; their taste made her
shudder. On the hottest night that summer, dinner was laid on in

a tiny folly, oval-ceilinged, brightly lit and dominated by an oval table. The door was shut, the windows closed; the heavy scent of cut flowers added to the sense of stagnation, death and claustrophobia. After the meal, the host announced, 'I want to show you something special.' He touched a button. The fountain lit up, ascending and revolving toward the ceiling with the floral display. Beryl's face registered horror as he announced proudly, 'I made it from an old barber's chair.' 'Oh my God!' she cried, fleeing into the night.[81]

Despite his better judgement, it was not easy to walk away. Warren began to accept invitations without her. She cooled toward him, resenting his independence, but every so often would seize him by his shoulders to mutter, 'This is disasterous!' And off they would go again. She became watchful of Warren. Passions and jealousies over younger women raged within her. She suddenly felt the physical wear and tear of age, sought solace in fresh conquests without relinquishing her hold over Warren either. Small indignities grew; rifts widened. Warren found himself filled with self-doubt. He had not allowed himself to be dominated but even in something small such as table manners, Beryl jeered at his eating the American way.

Their conflicts were not yet over. At a beach party one night, Warren's car was broken into. His Lincoln bore the MD plate, allowing doctors to park illegally and to break speed restrictions – and to be frequently vandalised for drugs. To get back at Warren that night for paying attention to someone else, Beryl had used the situation, let the tyres down, smashed the windscreen, so that Warren could not move. This trick was so advantageous that it became a favourite way to immobilise men whose attentions were wandering; if her escort was caught flirting or dancing too long, she made certain that that man was not going anywhere with anyone else.[82]

Yet, as Warren explained, for all the seemingly selfish, single-minded behaviour Beryl was 'really an enchanting partner and an absolutely loyal friend'. In their mature years his one regret was that he wished 'to have told her so again'.[83]

Beryl's remaining years in California were frittered away in parties and affairs, putting off the day when she must come to terms with the possibility that if Raoul divorced her, she would not have her United States visa renewed.

Raoul was still working on the Cotten radio plays in 'the-drive-through-and-under-house' belonging to a close friend, Varick Foster. In between writing, seduction, and drinking Raoul cooked up hare-brained schemes to make money such as the marketing of frogs' legs which he and Varick caught at Lake Zach; they could never get enough of the creatures to make the scheme viable. He also tried to recreate Al Capp's L'il Abner cartoon characters in candy, which could be sold from vending machines. John Potter and Raoul both wanted Beryl to leave The Monastery so that they could move into it themselves. When she disappeared to Holly-wood for a quick fling with Sir Charles Mendl in Beverly Hills, who, as Warren saw, 'only wanted Beryl as another little jewel in the Mendl crown' (his estranged wife Elsie de Wolfe was the Duchess of Windsor's decorator), she suddenly reappeared at The Monastery again, to their disappointment.

Attending a New Year's Eve party in 1947 Beryl was drawn to her next interesting conquest, the talented red-headed sculptor, Renzo Fenci,* whose recollection of her is of a 'reserved, direct and attrac-tive woman' ten years older than himself. 'Beryl invited me after the party to the Stokowski house. At breakfast I was still wearing my evening clothes . . . she made a point of leaving the house to meet John Potter who, as usual, was taking his morning walk up the hill, to show me off possibly. I was slightly embarrassed later when I heard Beryl talking on the telephone, saying what a fast worker she was.'[84]

The year 1948 had started well – and she was not going to allow Raoul to believe otherwise; tales of rejection slips for stories she had submitted were doing the rounds and she was not going to allow anyone to believe that she was holed up in The Monastery licking her wounds. Behind what might seem a breach of discretion was not even conceit, Beryl was just making sure that Raoul realised that her latest conquest looked like Van Johnson, and that she was courted, feted and staying right where she was.[85]

Beryl drifted from lover to lover. She thought she was preg-nant and, seeking confirmation from the Santa Barbara Cottage

Hospital, was relieved to discover that the result was negative. However, the laboratory technician whose friend, he wrongly imagined, Beryl might try to implicate, broke the code of medical practice, tipping off the young man concerned, warning lest, 'Beryl came up with the cock and bull story that she was expecting his child, to ignore it.'

Beryl was very worried about her US Immigration status, especially now that Raoul's relationship with Mary Lou Culley, a widow, had developed into 'a really big thing'.[86] She was so concerned that she tried to coerce the excessively rich owner of Val Verde,* Wright Ludington, into marrying her. This, everyone thought, was a bit ludicrous, 'some kind of love-game – a *folie à deux* – between an ardent homosexual and a divorcee.' Beryl moved from The Monastery to 9 Tumrel Road, Santa Barbara for a while.[87] The neglect of The Monastery when Raoul returned to it, as described by John Potter, is indicative of Beryl's overwhelming sense of defeat: 'There was a typewriter in the room that Raoul and Beryl had once shared but . . . no paper in it, which, when Raoul was there, there habitually was . . . obviously the machine had not been used for months. Crossing the dusty floor was a track made by Beryl's feet from the bed to the adjoining bathroom.'[88]

Beryl continued to feel that she needed to spite Raoul, and put about the rumour that Raoul was more interested in men sexually than women. Everyone knew that men loved oral sex and couldn't get enough of it. John Potter laughed his head off, having witnessed Raoul's affairs with beautiful women, dismissing the rumour as 'distasteful and malicious gossip'. Others thought this competition to outrage, funny and ludicrous, especially as once Raoul and he moved back into The Monastery, 'We lived like bachelors . . . the *chasse-cruise* of females which took place . . . the pursuit and attempted seduction of passing and resident females, was incessant and probably our chief occupation.'[89]

Gradually Beryl gave up looking for a fourth husband in Santa Barbara. According to her authorised biography, she beachcombed the remaining days away in America, having 'a romance with a well-known folk singer . . . in one of the villages . . . dotted along the Californian Coast'.[90] When she left the United States in 1949 to head back to Africa, she took to Kenya all the gramophone records Burl Ives had made to date. He is still considered one of the most talented folk singers of the twentieth century.

16

Life in Kenya Colony Once More

(1950–64)

From the heights of fame in the United States, Beryl returned to Kenya empty-handed in 1950. The only thing in her favour was true grit. With no money, no home and no supporter, she was also in poor health. Most of her friends there had not laid eyes on her since 1935, yet if someone of repute is expected to arrive with a flourish, Beryl did not disappoint her fans or her enemies.

At Muthaiga where she first stayed, the stir was considerable when Beryl (who was strictly *persona non grata*) entered the ballroom, strolled up to the Duke of Gloucester and, bussing him on the cheek, said, 'Hello Sweetie.' Somebody in authority hissed, 'For God's sake! Get Beryl out of here.' and, like a parent escorting an errant child, hustled her out through the back entrance to be driven away before there could be any redressal.[1]

The Duke of Gloucester was in Nairobi to confer on it official city status in the name of the Crown. Newspapers worldwide made much of the presentation of a Royal Charter on 31 March. It was the first town in the Colonial Empire to be thus honoured.[2] If nothing else, reactions among the gathered assembly left no doubt that the free-spirited Beryl was back and continuing to live in unswerving devotion to risk.

Half a century of hazard, unconventionality and notoriety had left its mark. If anything fame had harvested her lack of confidence, and her talent for adventure had superseded that of joy. Her return to the Colony had to be seen as triumphant, to *kushinda* (overcome all) was almost a reflex reaction. She was the sex goddess that men must have, one whom no man would abandon. Yet beneath the drop-dead glamour of celebrity, truth be known, she needed more support than ever – like a mega-star with no new role to play. At an age when most women would begin to wind down, when she spelled success in others' eyes, Beryl was beginning, from scratch, a ten-year struggle toward glory. But for two years, ill-health undermined her.

When she had presented herself at Santa Barbara Cottage Hospital, it had not necessarily been to frame one of her lovers. Irregular periods indicated that she could have conceived. Warren Austin's theory – that Beryl had never ovulated properly and had been told early on in life that her chances of pregnancy were remote – was linked to the fact that she never used any form of contraception. In years of promiscuity Beryl became pregnant only twice (1923 and 1929) and was now approaching menopause. By all accounts she was irrational, bad-tempered and suicidal by turn yet she was not usually a candidate for depression. It is hardly surprising that her swings of mood would prove the result of hormonal imbalance.[3] An operation would do the trick and she would recover her carefree nature. Meanwhile her hormones played havoc with her confidence and all relationships.

Beryl never wanted anyone to realise that she was sick. As usual she would not consult a doctor, therefore she had no idea that she was suffering anaemia from ovarian cysts. She viewed illness like a curse, *iliminiweza*, something that has been caused, as if she had been victimised by evil spirits. To acknowledge symptoms would be to succumb. Instead she must show how ready she was to tackle any eventuality.

In fact Beryl had already prepared the groundwork well, as if knowing, whatever the cost, she must get back to her grass roots. From California she had made her way to Nairobi in easy stages. First she visited the Delameres at Six Mile Bottom near Newmarket. Tom (now 4th Baron Delamere) and his first wife, Mary,* were appalled at her poverty but, with faith in her training abilities, Tom hinted that if she re-established her yard, he would bring his horses to her. Tom offered Beryl, should she need it, the use of his Kikambala house outside Mombasa, usually reserved exclusively for Delamere staff, and paid her air fare to South Africa for a refresher course in training with Clutt.[4]

Her relations with others were not as felicitous. Conflict with

Clutt's wife caused her to look for alternative accommodation with a South African writer Cloete and his wife, with whom 'a very awkward situation' arose. Having offered to do some 'nocturnal typing' for Cloete, according to her authorised biography, Beryl sent copies of his stories to Mackintosh and Otis as hers. The agents, realising that they could not be her work, alerted Cloete. Beryl moved out. The Cloetes discovered that, 'hand-made silk shirts and scarves had also left' concluding Beryl had 'charm . . . no warmth and was completely amoral'.[5] Her parting with her father after these unsavoury revelations was no less acrimonious. Clutt warned her that she would get nothing when he died as his wife would inherit everything. He promised to leave Beryl his best horse in his Will. And giving her 'enough funds to buy a second-hand car and fuel', they parted. She drove 'this huge blue Plymouth' overland via Rhodesia to Kenya, alone.[6]

Nairobi's growth since the Second World War was remarkable. No less remarkable was that Kenya's entire settler history was more or less contained in the span of Beryl's lifetime. From a railway station and a small river where the Maasai watered their cattle it had become a commercial centre of three territories, the hub of rail, road and air communications as the seat of the High Commission of Kenya, Uganda and Tanganyika. Its population numbered 130,000 (60,000 Africans; 50,000 Indians; 12,000 Europeans and 7000 of mixed race). Bus routes catered for pedestrians; trousers and shoes had replaced the *shuka* and bare feet. Plate-glass-fronted department stores had taken over from *dukas*; parked wing-to-wing were cars lining Delamere Avenue and Government Road. Nairobi was ugly, unrecognisable but, in Africa, a modern miracle.

On the surface, Beryl's earliest encounter with old friends at Muthaiga was as balmy as the temperature of the Indian Ocean, and underneath as full of cold currents. For pure enchanting malice the reunion in the dining room, witnessed by the Afghan Princess, Sylvia, and her second husband, Derek Richardson, takes a lot of beating. During lunch 'in walked Beryl, looking *wonderful* in slacks. We all greeted her with acclaim and asked her to join us. Then, the naughty, asp-tongued Gypsy got up as if to embrace her, but remarked, "Darling Beryl, how lovely to see you. I've just been reading your wonderful book. Do tell me darling, *who* wrote it?"

Beryl, like a hawser in a high wind, turned away, livid and walked out.'[7]

Bush telegraph brought Ruta to Beryl's side in a reunion of unchanged friendship, but a web of suspicion now dominated Kenya racially. The dark eyes of the Africans, their smiling welcome and the deference of attentive servants was underpinned by a fear, where before Beryl had known only fearlessness.

Politically the Colony was threatened by Kikuyu subversion leading to a State of Emergency on account of the Mau Mau Rebellion. Affecting Nairobi, Nyeri, Nanyuki, the Aberdares and the Kinangop, Mau Mau spilled into the Rift Valley. Kikuyu who refused to take the oath were terrorised. A massacre at Lari devastated the Kenya Police when the tribe turned upon itself; an entire village attacked, a hundred and thirty 'loyalists' were killed and mutilated obscenely as a bizarre object lesson. Overall the number of Europeans to be murdered was negligible compared to Africans, but the manner in which Mau Mau took life was so shocking that this made world headlines. It took the united effort of the KAR, the British Army, the Kenya Police and the loyal Home Guard until the end of the 1950s to bring this secret society under control. The *mise en scène* at the Norfolk and New Stanley Hotels was more reminiscent of the Wild West than Africa; everyone carried guns. Barbed wire enclaves sprang up around Nairobi. Beryl was advised not to live alone. As it was she was based among a hotbed of Mau Mau activity around Naro Moru, where life under Emergency conditions governed all routines with its dusk to dawn curfew.

Beryl, as a woman on her own, was especially vulnerable. Love affairs took her to various homes in the Nanyuki area at this juncture; one husband was so smitten with Beryl that his wife, rather than lose him, invited her to stay, taking the same initiative as the Afghan Princess all those years ago at Mutunguru to 'cure' Chris Langlands. Beryl moved on – she never had been a home wrecker. There were a couple of pilots, Mossie Mostert and Mongoose Soden, who paid court to her with whom she established a drinking pattern – not heavy so much as regular – at Nanyuki Sports Club for a pre-lunch 'pinkie', gin and angostura bitters. The illuminated Roll of Honour in the bar bore the name of another lover commemorated in gold, 'Gabriel Prudhomme (1939—1945) Commandant of the French Free Forces'.[8] Rhoda had won her case against his family to claim their old home, Mawingo, now an exclusive hotel which was to soon change hands in a card game. Beryl loved Mawingo,* her outstanding success in training was to be for Tubby, the second son of its newest owner, Abraham Block.

Beryl's fiftieth birthday occurred while she was temporarily residing on Warassa with Brigadier Forster and his wife, Helena. Four days later, a State of Emergency was decared. The active wing of Mau Mau was forced into the Aberdare and Mt Kenya forests where they conducted their campaign from impenetrable lairs until the end of the 1950s. As with all political revolt, aspects of truth (and not the whole truth on either side) justified the struggle. Jomo Kenyatta was arrested and exiled for his involvement with Mau Mau. Though the Forsters were 'very kind to Beryl' she moved on again, having met a new couple, the Hon. Charles Bathurst Norman and his wife Doreen, whose guest house was standing empty. They offered it to Beryl on compassionate grounds; she would live on Forest Farm until the end of the decade. People spoke of it as 'the top farm' because the Normans' lonely, white homestead could be picked out against the dark forest belt of Mt Kenya — a typical target for terrorists provided easy escape for a gang in search of meat: they could melt into the night with looted cattle long before any alarm could be raised. Guarding wives and children, white farmers set up their own patrols in each area by rota, until Mau Mau was quashed.

Beryl was 'difficult', as the Normans discovered, but their son, George, and his sister, Victoria, clearly adored her. Victoria Norman, aged about ten at the time, was aware that Beryl's moodiness was connected to ill health 'of a female nature' but as 'she never spoke about herself, it was difficult to know how her mind worked, when she was alone'.[9] Depressions were not purely the result of gynaecological problems. There was a scandal surrounding the alleged suicide of her half-brother Sir James (Alec) Kirkpatrick. Alec, living at Limuru, near Lari, had been showing his wife how to use a gun. It went off, wounding him, and the police just got to Alec for his statement before he died.[10] Rumour of suicide persisted and focused unwanted attention on Beryl. Robert Ruark's ambiguous reference in his novel, *Something of Value*, refuelled the theory that Alec had taken his own life: 'James Kirkpatrick . . . who shot himself . . . a kind friend in what I believe to be the best and most dedicated public service I know.' The death of Beryl's half-brother occurred when, as a member of Nairobi's Game Department, he failed to take a stand over ivory poaching where others had protested. Suicide, it was imagined, was perpetrated out of guilt as a beneficiary of illicit ivory trading. Word of mouth, newspaper reports, questions – all drummed up discussion on Beryl's relatives. She wanted no part of this. It also accelerated her mother's drinking problems. Beryl was embarrassed by her mother, and Mrs KP became increasingly resentful of Beryl.

Some instinct in Beryl's fifties told her that if she was to survive the myth she had created with Raoul, she must overcome the inertia of Africa. She must find her own pulse again through industry, the sort of industry she had known as a child. And, in a series of brilliant manipulations, she was literally to reach back into her legend as portrayed in the memoir, summoning the realities which had been omitted in the book: she forged a new beginning with Ruta, with Arthur, with a father figure, with a new lover, with two children of the age she was herself when devastated by the truth that Emma was not her mother. With one horse, in pioneering style, Beryl began to redress all that she had lost and lost touch with. Forest Farm and its incumbents were Beryl's foundation – with Doreen Norman as the female in authority, George and Victoria Norman like Arthur and herself. Victoria actually sensed that Beryl was reliving her own youth: 'mad about horses, mad about the African countryside, playing with Africans in huts . . . running wild as possible.'[11] Whether by design or coincidence it was as if Beryl nurtured a deep-seated need to banish the images conjured in America, having caught a reflection of herself in a distorting mirror. She never minded the struggle, what she wanted was a true picture again. She had always needed to have her hand held metaphorically. Here, the Normans held her hand. On their broad acres, this family brought Beryl's life full circle. Buoyed up by the hard work, she could not run away. The restrictions of the Emergency in a curious sense brought Beryl a blessed security, a happiness she had never known in her family, exposed to that comforting mixture of give and take, compromise and emotional daily support which had eluded her from the age of four.

Most surprising of all, Beryl squeezed herself into the maternal role, allowing Victoria to penetrate the inner sanctum of her bedroom. She became Victoria's heroine. Her gentleness was her most striking quality and with her 'slightly American cult' Beryl was all the more seductive because she extended latitudes that Doreen would not have contemplated. Victoria suspected that they were 'divided by one catastrophic difference . . . Beryl was brave and fearless. I was brave and terrified.'[12] What Victoria feared most was Beryl's displeasure; in her quiet voice she would expose false values which Beryl's 'bullshit detector' would unearth in seconds. Weaknesses and cover-ups could not be hidden from her and Victoria thought that her cowardice might elicit Beryl's scorn. To her amazement she was wrong. Beryl had decided that Victoria should ride George's horse, Diamond, in the Naro Moru Hunter Trials, rather than her own steady grey Somali mare, Cigarette. Victoria lost her nerve: 'I fell off at every fence . . . finishing the course in great disarray, reputation for courage intact. Beryl at the same age, would have been able to control Diamond.' Badly as Victoria had fared, Beryl was kindness itself, making her realise that what she could not stand, above all, was hypocrisy: 'her perspicacity brought a tirade of ridicule . . . upon the offender of any "bull".'[13] On the other hand, the minute Beryl intuitively analysed any problem for anyone, she also grew bored.

Doreen Norman was well known for her volatile nature and, once she and Beryl clashed, Beryl recognised soon enough that she was jeopardising her future unless she sorted out her health, as the latter was affecting her temperament quite noticeably. Coming to her senses, consulting a doctor locally, Beryl found herself in the hands of Mr Tommy Adamson, Nairobi's newest gynaecologist. He diagnosed ovarian cysts but only when Beryl was on the operating table of the Princess Elizabeth Hospital for Women did he decide to perform a total hysterectomy. Major surgery did not impede Beryl's sense of priority. Instead of remaining in hospital for ten days, she insisted that she return with the Normans to Naro Moru the day following, convincing them that she would not pose a hazard, and they could not leave her behind. Next morning she proved to them how much she scorned physical pain. Her boxer puppy, Caesar, had a scrap with two other dogs in the yard. Doreen was about to put an end to 'the fearful racket' when Beryl, in pyjamas, stormed through the door, took each dog by the scruff and hurled them apart and, not saying a word, strode back to bed.

Gradually her sunny nature and equilibrium returned. In return for her keep, she went with Charles Bathurst Norman 'to his grotty little office in Nanyuki, for tuppence a week', as Victoria put it, 'to type my father's letters'.[14] Primarily Charles Norman was a barrister, an old Harrovian whose style Beryl appreciated.[15]

As Mau Mau problems intensified Victoria's father refused to allow her to remain on the farm (George was at Harrow) and Doreen took her back to school in England. In her absence Beryl was responsible for bringing a new character into the lives of this family, a change for the better in every way. His name was Jorgen Thrane, a young Danish farm manager, in his late twenties. When guard dogs were at a premium, word had reached Forest Farm that he had trained his Doberman to go 'for the jugular on command'. One afternoon, on the pretext of buying a rooster, Beryl drove Charles over to 'look at the Dane and the dog' on Irima, a neighbouring farm where Jorgen worked for Eric Rundgren. When Beryl's blue Plymouth appeared, Jorgen was not in the mood for strangers. King, his Doberman, was sleeping in his kennel. After a lot of banalities, the visitors were forced to bring up the subject of his dog. Begrudgingly he offered Beryl and Charles tea, until 4.30, when King was released. Caesar was playing round Beryl's feet. 'King would have killed the puppy' had he not been called off. To Jorgen's irritation not only had his privacy been breached, he now found himself apologising.[16] They parted amicably enough but Jorgen had no plan's to take up Charles's invitation to drop in for lunch.[17] Nevertheless, just as Warren was drawn back to The Monastery, Jorgen found himself 'drawn to the top farm'.

From the moment they left Irima Beryl had pestered Charles to offer Jorgen the job of developing Forest Farm. Her argument was that 'Rungren would never have hired that sort of man, unless he knew his stuff. Don't let this one go.'[18] Doreen had built up a dairy herd of Jersey cattle but little of the Normans' 1,400 acres was cultivated. They were not farmers. George's health took them upcountry, away from the malaria ridden coast where Charles had been DC in 1949. Doctors had advised them to move where there were no mosquitoes.

Weeks later, Jorgen turned up on Forest Farm for lunch and never forgot it. Beryl was 'a presence ... hovering about ... making encouraging noises'. Charles quizzed him about double-cropping cereals; the local climate made it possible around Naro Moru to harvest wheat twice annually. Charles offered him a job: 'I already have a job with Rundgren; good managers don't grow on trees.'

'I'm not interested in a manager. If you'd like to work the land for me, the land is yours and mine. *If* you will grow wheat for me.'

To someone starting out in a new country, the notion was irresistible and Norman and Thrane Limited was founded.[19]

It would be all too easy to dismiss Beryl Markham as an arch manipulator and leave it at that. She had fallen for the handsome young prematurely balding Dane. But Jorgen claims it is entirely due to her perception that his future took an upturn. Examples of the way Beryl was a reflection of other people's dreams and clearly helped in fulfilling them, provide yet another clue to the loyalty she commanded and continues to command posthumously. Mansfield never resented her – nor the time and money spent in grooming her. Arthur continued to ride for her. With the exception of his wife and mother, there was no one he loved more. Ruta worked for her as long as she would have him. Raoul found his literary skills through her. She was responsible for a move that gave Jorgen unimagined opportunities. In each case, Beryl provided the breakthrough. The alliance of this knot of friendship in her fifties was to offer Beryl a coherent family life, a vacuum which had accounted for her own debilitating and destructive anxieties hitherto.

Jorgen was the antidote to Beryl's doldrums when, like any woman, no matter how beautiful, she recognised that her days as a *femme fatale* were numbered. There was a distinct quality of Denys about him, although Jorgen's eyes are blue. Jorgen's physique had been enhanced by rowing in Inter-Scandinavian championships, and he rode well and had hunted his own horse. Bold and sensitive,

taking everything in at a glance, Jorgen had energy, expertise
and demands for excellence – things that Beryl had also admired
in Denys. Nor would Jorgen give in to her; their arguments would
be fierce. 'She was a perfectionist. One is going to be difficult as a
perfectionist.'[20]

Jorgen was the youngest of six children whose father had
farmed; and Jorgen believed (just as Denys had when young) that
Africa offered more adventure than his country of birth. In 1952
he had worked in Kitale on a mixed farm until Rundgren offered
him a managerial post. Jorgen's discovery of Naro Moru – a railway
station, KFA depot and post office – came when he climbed down
from a bus, clutching his half-grown Doberman, King, and a suitcase, and realised he was in the middle of nowhere. There was no
one to meet him, so he walked 'the length and breadth of the
river' from which Naro Moru takes its name, with its huge black
pebbles, smoothed by icy waters from Mt Kenya. Hearing shooting,
he took out his revolver in self-defence; the volleys were from
Rundgren. His new employer was taking his turn at Emergency
patrol. Until Charles Norman offered partnership this is where
Jorgen had worked.[21]

When a small farm of 104 acres, half a mile down the Forest
Farm track, came up for sale, Beryl bought it. Though she was
mortgaged to the hilt, 'her royal stipend kept the wolf from the
door'. By now a pattern of Mau Mau attacks on European settlers
was discernible so it was felt best that Jorgen move to Beryl's
cottage for security – a set-up which suited everyone. Norman and
Thrane developed pigs, cattle, potatoes, wheat, barley and oats.
The *gemütlich* Jorgen was down to earth, responsible and prudent.
It was easy for Beryl to lean on his qualities as she began her haul
back to top trainer. And with the acquisition (a gift) of a horse that
had been ruined for racing by overdosing for worms and 'looked
like a coathanger' her life became subservient to horses once more.

Jorgen planted pyrethrum from which Beryl earned a modest
income, a fashionable crop which was to be used as an ingredient
for insect repellent, and covered her *shamba* with clouds of small
white flowers.[22] On one occasion when Jorgen's driver failed to
turn up to work the combine harvester, without hesitation (or
experience) Beryl volunteered, emerging from the bedroom in her

white flying suit, demonstrating 'how wonderful she was with engines . . . you could go to sleep as a passenger when Beryl was at the wheel . . . If the slightest thing was wrong with an engine, she knew exactly where to find the fault.'[23] Their arsenal of machinery included a bulldozer with which Jorgen made for Beryl a dry-weather gallop on the farm, and 'the top gallop' on the slopes of the mountain, hidden among cedar draped with lichen and fern, where she would encounter elephant and rhino during early-morning exercise. Out of doors each night the dark mythology of Africa was waiting.

During the school holidays, the high point of the Norman children's lives was to 'scuttle down to Beryl's tiny gabled cottage whenever we could manage it.' Everything was 'orderly yet Beryl created a feeling of luxury . . . warmth . . . amazing . . . comfort, marvellous evenings with second toasties – snacks served with drinks'. A copy of *West with the Night* propped up against Kipling's *Puck of Pook's Hill* – from Victoria's father – sat in a bookcase containing a few Reprint Society novels. Equally incongruous, among a collection of Beatrix Potter figurines on top, stood a replica of *The Messenger*, inspiring Victoria to 'become a pilot like Beryl' – but she had abandoned the dream faced with uncontrollable air-sickness on every flight to and from school. On Beryl's coffee table were racing journals, *Horse and Hound* piled up with much-thumbed issues of the *New Yorker*. Beryl enjoyed the cartoons, 'pouncing on copies each month, subscribing all the time she lived at Naro Moru'.[24] Here Beryl taught Victoria and George to play poker and back-gammon, gambling for matchsticks. Victoria remembered playing, 'Burl Ives records. In my innocence, when we listened to *Foggy Foggy Dew*, I asked about that line in the song, "How can you be a bachelor and live with your son?"' The laughter of conspiracy stung Victoria to the quick 'not because it was malicious but they knew something that I didn't'. Harmless collusion was intrinsic to Beryl's discourse with men. Even so Victoria did get close to Beryl, liking nothing better than to 'curl up on Beryl's bed' while she bathed and changed into her 'slinky blue satin dressing gown' for dinner and 'natter, natter, natter'.[25]

Where the separate adult households ended each evening

depended largely on musical taste. For the classics and Mozart, they sat about Doreen's hearth. Beryl's offerings – Doris Day or Glen Miller – were the alternative recordings: sounds of *The Dead-wood Stage* and *The Black Hills of Dakota* would belt out over Cole's Plains. Beryl would also arrange table-tennis competitions on her verandah when neighbours invited for dinner stayed the night on account of the curfew. But the mellow days of Beryl's fifties were marred by one tangled skein, that of Gervase.

It was Gar O'Hea who informed Beryl that Gervase was bringing his pregnant wife, Viviane, to Naro Moru. Gar, hating her Bays-water flat, was now more or less permanently occupying a bunga-low near Muthaiga Club,* [26] As it happened, when she heard the news, Beryl was staying with Pat Cavendish, the daughter of Enid, Countess of Kenmare (formerly Lady Furness). Enid had bought Pat land near Ngong. Pat never forgot Beryl's reaction when Gar telephoned to say that the young Markhams were coming to her 'for a long weekend'. Beryl complained that she had not seen Gervase for over twenty years. What a bore it was. 'Beryl would have done anything to wriggle out of seeing him' but Gar was adamant. On the Friday, Gervase and Viviane created an unwel-come hiatus at Beryl's cottage. Viviane was bolshie by nature, now seven months pregnant, 'harboured no good will for Kenya or Beryl'[27] and was acutely sensitive in sympathy with the self-protective cocoon that Gervase had woven round himself. Beryl's daughter-in-law hated the nudges, the quick run-down of 'idle and malicious gossip', particularly at Muthaiga, on the unsettled question of her husband's paternity.[28] The latest opinion was that Gervase 'didn't look the least bit like the Duke of Gloucester'. Redressing his lack of parental love, Gervase was 'an altruistic and devoted husband'. Both families had opposed the marriage – Mansfield thought them too young. Viviane Bruiltet was three years Gervase's junior. He was still at Oxford where, on Bastille Day in 1952, in defiance, they married. A second ceremony in Paris held four weeks later was begrudgingly attended by Mansfield and Mary Markham, who gave no present. Viviane felt so rebel-lious that she refused photographs.[29]

Viviane's preconception of Gervase's mother was based solely upon 'rumour and legend: I succeeded in maintaining indifference to an agreeable, pleasant enough but hedonistic woman'. Observing mother and son together, it struck Viviane that Gervase's weakness lay in wanting to please his friends whereas Beryl's strength lay in not caring whether she was popular or not. The young people had nothing in common with Beryl; they spoke three foreign languages apiece and their interests were the arts, but all Beryl could talk about was horses. Feelings were mutual. A day after their arrival, Beryl got herself to a telephone, begging Pat Cavendish, 'Come and collect Gervase, he is such a bore; I can't stand another minute of him.'[30] But Pat confronted her: 'No Beryl. There are a lot of things I will do for you, but this is *not* on. You *must* see this through.'

On Monday, Jorgen drove Gervase and Viviane to Muthaiga. None concerned referred to that 'strange and strained weekend' until Christmas 1962 when, 'unaccountably', a card inscribed by Beryl arrived, 'with love and blessings to my little ones' (her two grand-daughters). It was to be their only and final communication.[31]

In 1957, Beryl's parents died. Clutt's death inflicted 'a terrible blow' on Beryl, and although she inherited his best horse, she had no means to take delivery of her inheritance. Mrs KP died 'alone and unmourned' in a Limuru nursing home.[32] When 'she hadn't two brass farthings to rub together' talk of death and Wills occasioned Beryl's promise to young George Norman, 'When I die I will leave you everything in my Will,' a chance remark that was to culminate in a surprising landslide of royalties for the Honourable Judge George Bathurst Norman twenty-five years later.[33]

Towards the end of the 1950s the shadows of Mau Mau lifted, and normality returned to the Colony.

Very few men had the natural propensity to excel in the air and on the Turf but Beryl's uniqueness earned her extravagant praise from her peers in both areas. In Africa, persistence is all. Just when everyone was saying that Beryl could never win again, she was to excel.

Fixtures were not confined to Nairobi as they were originally and are today. Beryl travelled to courses at Eldoret, Nakuru, Thomson's

Falls, Kericho, Limuru and Nanyuki. Once it was mooted that she might train for Tom Delamere, the new Lady Delamere refused, 'I would never let that woman near my horses.'[34] An amicable divorce had been arranged between Mary and Tom so that he could marry Diana Colvile, former widow of Jack Delves Broughton, and beauty at the core of the much-vaunted Erroll murder in 1941. Diana had been married to a rich but eccentric cattle rancher, Gilbert Colvile, owner of Oserian (the Djinn/Gin Palace) after the suicide of Delves Broughton. When Tom and Diana fell for one another, Colvile amiably moved back into one of his mud huts 'with joy'. Tom and Diana's marriage was to be enduring and happy. But reluctance to have Beryl as a trainer came out of her own ambition on the Turf and a knowledge of Beryl's remarkable achievements. She also harboured a lingering jealousy over the fact that Joss Erroll and Tom, both of whom Diana loved, had adored Beryl. To keep Tom away from her, Diana insisted on importing a trainer from Britain.[35]

There were always rumblings against Beryl's handling of two-year-olds, but her capacity to bring in winners overruled. Her bay horse Title-Deed's first success was in the Two-Year-Old Plate in September in 1958. Everyone wanted to know her secret. Beryl was always selective: a few good horses hand-picked, which had that indefinable 'X-factor' she alone could discern. Her classics winners were all bright, intelligent horses – the latter being the most elusive of genetic qualities.

Beryl's intention to train again in 1956 had made news among the racing fraternity. Mrs Kay Spiers, a newcomer from India, and owner of Lolchorai Stud at Njoro, 'welcomed' her into their midst by leasing to Beryl a horse called Ulysses on easy terms. On the 'never-never' also she next acquired Little Dancer (Thistle Brig – Geisha) and Title Deed (The Plough – Copyright). She had lost none of her ability – 'little short of genius' – to spot champions.[36] Title Deed went on to triumph in the Derby, the St Leger and the Delamare Gold Vase in the three-year-old season, when classics are run, bringing victory to Beryl no less than forty times in six seasons.

On 28 September 1958, Beryl took her first hat-trick with her runners unfancied – Title Deed 40–1, Little Dancer 16–1 and

Ulysses 18–1. Jorgen recalled, 'It was fantastic. She brought all three in. Ulysses came in, in the six-furlong sprint and Beryl broke the red tape . . . She was accepted once more.'[37] In each case the stake money had been a record and as the racing correspondent for the *Sunday Post*, Raleigh Gilbert, predicted, 'It is unlikely that punters will ever get again such a generous price about a Markham trained runner.' Beryl's second career began when Little Dancer won the St Leger thirty-three years after Wise Child had won for Sonny and Eric Gooch. Next came Niagara, 'a phenomenal flier, sporting silk as a two-year-old, coming third first time out, with two seconds winning both subsequent engagements.'[38]

There were no black owners yet, but Beryl would be the first to train for them in the 1970s. Meanwhile the Africans being inveterate gamblers, turnout for racing was keen. Beryl had lately taken on a Kipsigis called Ndungu Kigole, who had worked in Doreen's *shamba*, training him up to become her Head Lad. Indeed, Ndungu would see out Beryl's days with horses, undertaking complete responsibility for her entries and, in a total of fifteen years, he developed an affectionate tolerance for his *kali* female employer. His name for her was *nykanga*, or 'perfectionist'. With Beryl's intolerance of mediocrity, Ndungu would see owners, jockeys, *syces* come and go. If a hoof was left uncleaned, or anyone was unpunctual, the misdemeanor went into the punishments book, a warning was given and instant dismissal followed. Even Ruta proved no exception. He had recently been slinking off to a nearby farm where there was a Kipisgis Reserve with a brewery – 'like a lot of Kips, he drank'. One afternoon, emboldened by alcohol, Ruta tried to take liberties with Beryl, 'She would not have that any more and got rid of him.' To retain his respect, she had had to display her greatest power as a woman, which had been to sack him. Ruta bore no grudge, seeing Beryl sporadically, though Ndungu met him only once. What impressed him was her manner of introduction, 'This is Ruta, my dear friend' (*Rafiki yangu saana*) at a time when fraternisation was strictly confined to the role of servant and master.[39]

Had Beryl not enjoyed so unique a position with the Africans, her *syces* would never have given her the tip-off that rival *syces* from Gladys Graham's yard intended 'to fix Niagara' before the Derby. Gladys Graham (formerly Gooch) was now Beryl's neighbour; and, until Beryl's second debut, was 'Queen Bee' of Kenya's Turf. Not only did Gladys bad-mouth her, she was as obstructive as possible, refusing permission to take a short cut cross her land, entailing for Beryl, in this niggardly behaviour, a six-mile diversion to get her runners to Naro Moru siding. Beryl showed no concern (women who expected a reaction, comfort or compassion from Beryl were doomed for disappointment) and, deliberately not ordering bogies for herself, simply set off earlier so as to load her horses into those reserved for Gladys. When Gladys turned up, Beryl would sweetly apologise as mayhem ensued, calmly looking on while extra wagons were shunted on and Gladys worked herself up into a real state. This exercise Beryl repeated many times to infuriate her enemy: collusion with her *syces* only made revenge sweeter. Beryl avenged herself further by means of the memoir. Whether Gladys read *West with the Night* or not, Wise Child goes down for posterity in the book as being trained by Beryl. Given Gladys's insistence – on pain of divorce – in 1926 that her husband take Wise Child away from Beryl to deprive her of the glory, she must have been nettled when Beryl found the perfect, durable device to reinstate her status as his trainer.

In all the years Jorgen spent with Beryl he had never been able to put his finger on the special relationship Beryl had with Arthur.* It was not until after Beryl's death that he understood at last why they seemed 'more like brother and sister than jockey and trainer'.[40] One reason Arthur never fell out with Beryl is that, gentle as he was, he was never subservient to her. As for *West with the Night*, Arthur was 'rather hurt' to have been omitted from it, when Kibii was as much his playmate as the *syces* and *totos* had been Beryl's, 'tracking game together'. Arthur never let on to her that he knew about the memoir, never mind that he had read it.[41] He never believed for a moment that she was its author, only confiding how he really felt to his wife. Arthur saw no point in causing Beryl unnecessary hurt by questioning who wrote the book for her, when others had been taken in. And she trusted him completely.[42] It was Arthur whom she called upon when she received warning that Niagara might be 'got at'. Niagara was tipped to win £875 – the highest prize money in Kenya to date. Beryl's solution was to get Arthur to travel armed, with Niagara, from Naro

Moru to Kibera. Once safely on the course, Beryl insisted that jockey Thomas spend the night with Niagara, locking him in her loosebox with her.[43] Niagara won by eight lengths. She made the rest of the field 'look as if they were still standing, as she drew away, was never challenged' in a record of two minutes and thirty-eight seconds.[44]

Beryl's victories were to daunt her rivals as the racing columns shimmered with Markham triumphs; Little Dancer, Title Deed, Niagara, Cutlass, Rio Grande, Mountie, Blue Streak, Fair Realm, Lone Eagle, Spike and Athi; winning, winning, winning. Over the coming six years she notched up 384 individual victories, winning every classic, and except for the 1960–61 season, when she had no runner for the Derby, achieved virtual monopoly every year. On two occasions she won with her second string.*

Despite Beryl's success, some of her methods were rather unorthodox. Her feeding routine and stabling arrangements, racing correspondents noted, were quirky, but paid off. Many members of the Kenya racing fraternity were convinced that Beryl fed her horses 'something' because 'she could always make them win, always ran them hard, gave them lots of work'.[45] Ndungu confirms that she could confidently predict which horses would run, two weeks in advance, putting something special in their feeds, certain they would win: '*Kabisa:* She was never wrong. You could not stop the horse. It just went.'[46] Maximum attention to detail saw every horse treated as an individual. Her stabling reflected her belief that horses become bored: she housed them opposite one another so that stablemates held interest; there was never any weaving or crib-biting in Beryl's yard. The only deviation in her feeding was that she provided one additional meal, the last being given at 9.30 p.m. 'just oats five times a day'.[47] Beryl mixed the feeds herself, insisting that half-doors must be closed so that her horses were not disturbed. Both factors gave rise to those mysteries 'dispensed from her small bottle, calcium and salts'.

In speculation about Beryl, there was seldom smoke without fire. The possibility that *seketet* an ingredient known to Beryl from childhood, was added to mash in increasing quantities daily a fortnight before a potential winner ran, cannot be overlooked. Beryl had experienced its properties with Kibii: *arap* Maina's wife boiled *seketet* in the tea they drank before they went hunting. Young warriors consumed it daily in broths during that seven-month prelude to circumcision. The mature tree from which the bark comes is sacred to the Maasai. It is pulverised and taken for resistance to pain and to increase energy, to alert a sleeper to the merest alien sound. The Maasai have faith in its staying power; it increases adrenalin flow. Many tribes use it for witchcraft. Beryl wrote for Raoul about the way in which Ruta's weight and the size of his calves had greatly increased – *seketet* was responsible. It is known in Swahili as *kaita** but each tribe gives it a different name.[48]

Further clues may lie in the way Beryl's horses were to suffer in 1964 from 'something that she fed her horses and which backfired'. The condition was dubbed 'the Beryl Bloom', affecting her old horses first. These 'looked magnificent but could not gallop'. Lethargy was put down to drinking water and Beryl blamed their condition on excess fluoride. Water was brought in from elsewhere. Nothing improved. Muscle paralysis was suspected after Spike manifested similar symptoms.[49] Moreover, those horses acquired by Kenya trainers once Beryl left for South Africa were 'very muscular', a condition which other trainers were unable to maintain. Veronica Scott-Mason inherited Cutlass, Athi and Alouette, 'their quarters were like apples, they were huge and muscular and within two weeks of my regime, had lost it'.[50] Such conformation would usually be attributable in a racehorse to anabolic steroids; these produce 'muscle and weight gain too fast, make for adrenalin, so that a horse can stretch itself to win, but for a limited time only, a sort of short false burst.'[51]

One vet suspected that Beryl fed 'hash or dope' the night before a race, having witnessed the quietest of entries 'hotted up in the paddock ... sometimes unrecogniseable from the night before'. He was convinced that where Beryl got 'good results initially, these fell off with equal regularity, given time ... with every individual.'[52] Although there was speculation that a native herb was responsible for the 'Beryl Bloom', a natural stimulant had never shown up under any amount of testing. The question of 'other minerals' affecting the teeth of Beryl's horses was considered, because of the sickness biliary, once ridges began to appear in their hooves.[53] All theories met with a blank. However, it was revealed in a post mortem that Rio Grande, whose ultimate owner was forced to destroy him as a six-year-old, 'had been ruined in his racing career by massive doses of arsenic'.[54] Rio Grande bore the 'Beryl Bloom' like his stable mates. According to The Hon. George Lambton, who writes on the effects of doping before it was made illegal, arsenic imparted a certain sheen. Coincidentally, it is highly likely that the bloom on Beryl's horses was caused by the stimulant *seketet* – both effects which were cumulative. Beryl fully understood the ill consequences of arsenic used in excess, making all the more baffling the results of Rio Grande's post mortem.[55]

When Beryl's winning streak was accelerating, she needed the services of a chartered accountant, where earlier a Miss Ayres had coped. Roland Sharpe and Maurice Payne from Nakuru became Beryl's book-keepers 'for about four years travelling each month to Naro Moru to see her'. Accounting for a trainer is complex: Beryl received 10 per cent of all earnings, a jockey 20 per cent and the owner 70 per cent so there were always bills and cash flow to be sorted out, and a summary to be submitted to the Jockey Club, from where it was split among individual owners. Sharpe and Payne found Beryl 'difficult'.[56] Owners received statements monthly, starting with a hefty credit – 'their winnings'. Then, 'off came the cost of racing plates, veterinary bills etc.' from which the accountants could see that owning a racehorse was 'not very lucrative and an expensive risk'.[57] To make Beryl's initiation into proper accounting easier for her and themselves, she was instructed to 'ram invoices, cash sale chits and daily expenses onto a spike' so that when Sharpe and Payne came to tackle these, they would be in order.[58] In all the time they worked for Beryl, not once did she co-operate. Work 'involved locking ourselves in her office, going through bits of paper, ending up crawling in a sea of papers covering the carpet, so as to establish some sort of chronology.'[59] She 'never replied to queries, answered letters nor could we get dated orders out of her.' Frustration ended the association when, patience at an end, they put 'all her papers in a suitcase and dumped them, literally, on her doorstep . . . There was no acrimony; it was a question of this we can do without.'[60]

Her accountants had wanted to admire Beryl the legend, but instead they found a 'nervous but forceful' woman, whose brilliance seemed 'immaculate' only for the inadequate side to emerge. She became tearful, giving the impression that 'nobody-loves-me', if reproached. It had been more than difficult not to fall for her way of enlisting sympathy.[61] Projecting wealth, choosing the best without ostentation – or the means to pay – had always hampered Beryl's success. It seemed that she lacked the stature to free herself from the myth she had created.

Beryl's greatest successes on the Turf were achieved in association with a jockey chosen for her by Jorgen while in Denmark: Ryan 'Buster' Parnell, a character of Irish descent hailing from Fulham. Parnell had been champion jockey in Scandinavia the year before and Jorgen asked whether he would be 'interested in riding some good horses in Kenya?'[62] As Parnell was on the brink of marriage, he accepted on condition that his bride, Anna, could follow him to Africa. Thus Parnell reached Nairobi alone in August 1960, prepared to ride in the Bank Holiday Meeting. The sparring which was to continue until the last day Parnell rode for Beryl began on day one. They met at Nairobi's newest rendezvous, the Thorn Tree, the open-air café of the New Stanley Hotel. Beryl sensed at once that she would need to show Parnell who was in control. While they sipped coffee, she informed him that he would ride four of her eight runners. Parnell, who had not left behind a bride of two days for this, replied, 'Either I ride them all, or I go back to Denmark immediately.'[63] Beryl capitulated. Parnell brought in two winners and a second.[64]

On arrival at Forest Farm, Beryl's first test for Parnell was to put him through the 'We change for dinner' routine, disappearing to bathe at sundown. Everybody reappeared in housecoats, pyjamas or dressing gowns; Parnell felt ridiculously overdressed in a lounge suit. Beryl sympathised, handing him a suitable change of clothes. Over the years there were to be noisy rows; Buster would threaten to leave; Beryl would weep, beg him not to abandon her. On they went. Pat Cavendish thought of Beryl's bond with Parnell as a running competition: 'Both were capable of achieving pre-eminence, with a tendency to seek new goals when they had scaled the heights in the current scene'.[65] In the October meeting, following Parnell's initial success, he brought in four winners on both days. While Beryl and Jorgen were in the mood for celebration,

she had somehow to bring Parnell down a peg or two, again deciding this time to invite the cocksure jockey to Muthaiga when professional sportsmen were inadmissable. She was reprimanded by
the Secretary, when Beryl's defence was to enquire why a rowdy
party of polo players at the next table (where someone had been
trying to shove ice cubes down Diana Delamere's *décolleté*) had not
been rebuked for the noise. But Buster got the message, telling
Beryl *never* to expose him to such indignity again.[66]

After his first season Parnell was offered a position in Ireland.
Beryl agreed to his departure, but he had brought in twenty winners out of seventy rides, and they both knew he would return.
Parnell was to become champion jockey in Kenya five times. His
love/hate relationship with Beryl became so exasperating on
occasions, that he hated her guts, yet ultimately admitted, 'My God
I respected her. I've ridden for the best trainers in the world . . .
like Prendergast and other greats. But . . . she was the best. She
could have taken on the world and won.'[67] He had quickly adapted
to Beryl's manor-house style, taking to the isolation of Naro Moru
surprisingly well, for all his doubts initially. Anna Parnell, a jockey
herself, was less comfortable: Beryl treated her much as she might
brush off a fly – 'Run along sweetie, Buster and I want to discuss
tomorrow's work.' If Anna Parnell imagined this was personal, she
was mistaken. Girl grooms were given equally short shrift: 'Tell
little whatshername to fetch the bran.' Beryl's way to press home
their insignificance was never to address her female helpers by
name.[68] Parnell, Tony Thomas, George Price, Alec McAleer and
Derek Stansfield all contributed, as jockeys, to Beryl's legend over
the years. Like her lovers they left her only to return and nurtured
no illusions, as Parnell's view shows. 'At times she was a first-class
superbitch who never gave a damn about anyone but herself . . .
had a fantastic ego, unbelievable talent . . . a capacity to work that
you wouldn't credit.'[69] And, as Pat Cavendish explains, as owner
of a top-ranking stud today, 'The time I spent at Beryl's side . . .
were some of the most fascinating in my life'.[70] Parnell worked in
Denmark for a season, then came back to Naro Moru, but by 1961
'Uhuru' – freedom – was the persistent political cry as the Africans
clamoured for Independence.

The prospect of African self-government heralded another

unsettling period, and Kenya's days as a Colony were numbered. Every white farmer reassessed his future; many left as estates were doled out in resettlement to indigenous small-holders and co-operatives. Norman and Thrane and Beryl must look elsewhere for the future. Beryl flew down to Rhodesia to see if she could move there, deciding against it. She had set standards for the Kenya Turf which might be said to have changed the face of racing in the Colony. In the 1963–64 season she would win forty-six times in twenty-six days' racing, and over the years won the East Africa Derby five times.

Meanwhile, Beryl's performance as a trainer had been under the scrutiny of an important newcomer to the Turf, Tubby Block, whose Italian racing partner was a coffee baron, Aldo Soprani. Tubby and his brother, Jack, were the Conrad Hiltons of the Colony, the sons of the pioneer Abraham Block, who had founded the dynasty – the Norfolk, Mawingo and New Stanley Hotels. Block had arrived almost empty-handed in Nairobi the year before Clutt. The policy of the Blocks was to hire the best personnel to maintain top standards. Beryl was chosen by them because she fitted that category. It produced an illustrious phase for Beryl too. Once Parnell began to ride Block and Soprani horses, the collaboration seemed invincible. With their money, Beryl showed what she could really do with the best horses. Tubby allowed her to choose what he should buy, his accountant took care of the financial side of the business, and between 1962 and 1964 they had 'about sixty-five horses' with her.

The Lancaster House conference had paved the way for African control but also a time of more uncertainty than ever in Kenya's chequered annals; four ministerial positions were reserved for Africans in a sixty-five member Parliament. In a laudable personal struggle, Jomo Kenyatta, free but not participating in the 1961 election, returned to his home, Gatundu, on 14 August, proclaiming, 'I am not bitter about my imprisonment . . . my cause was just' continuing his creed, 'suffering without bitterness'.[71]

Because of the Forest Farm take-over by re-settlement schemes, Beryl needed a new yard. It was to Tubby Block she turned. After mentioning *en passant* that she had nowhere to go, Tubby told her about land going for £3,000, adjoining his father's lakeside property, Longonot Farm. If Beryl bought this, Tubby suggested, she could make gallops on Longonot Farm. Tubby, who was Beryl's most bourgeois owner, was put out on his return after a trip to London to find Beryl ensconced. She had rejected the next-door acreage; under the auspices of Block Estates General Manager, a cottage had been built for her; her stables were nearing completion. Since the racing correspondent had seen fit to note 'not for many years can an owner partnership have done so well as E. R. Block and A. Soprani' Tubby bowed his head to fate and continued to win.[72]

Beryl's shift to Naivasha due to re-settlement happened at a time when she and Jorgen were disenchanted with one another and arguing constantly. 'Beryl was actually still desperately in love with Jorgen' but, in her fear of losing him to someone younger, displayed tactics she had used with Warren; the letting-down of tyres; the insecurity over other women. She stirred up trouble for him for the sake of it: for example, discrediting his position with the Forest Department. Interestingly the man concerned took this escapade for what it was. Beryl reported that Jorgen was 'cutting timber illegally' knowing he had overlooked the formality of paying a royalty on cedar fence posts for the farm. Permission from the Forestry Commission was obtained by some, but only from time to time, *and* easily forgotten by others. But Beryl 'seemed only too keen on my reporting the matter to the police.' The man merely deduced 'perhaps . . . she had just had a tiff with Jorgen and was jealous over another woman . . . women were always jealous of Beryl because of her fatal attraction to most warm-blooded men.' At this time Beryl suspected a Swedish socialite of homing in on Jorgen, taking the trouble to tell her straight to her face, 'If Jorgen ever left me for another, I would shoot that woman.'[73] Beryl, who seldom took herself seriously, meant exactly what she said. Just as Warren had discovered, Jorgen could leave 'utterly furious . . . but you'd come back again, having bumped into her. She'd say, "Come and see me sweetie." Everything was forgotten.' Beryl did not sulk, she was never sullen. 'She either flew at you or was entertaining . . . company. She was never boring.'[74] Which is why, although Jorgen had found land to buy beyond Nanyuki suitable for ranching he continued to visit Beryl at Naivasha at weekends. The Normans moved to Thomson's Falls where Charles was the local magistrate.

Beryl was to spend a little over two years at Lake Naivasha, where Charles Norman and Pat Cavendish were also frequent house-guests. Pat's image of Beryl here still conjures pleasure, 'To see Beryl coming along the lakeside on horseback, she was Africa and Africa was her.'[75] On the grassy sward sloping to the water stood Beryl's cottage. Afternoon light over the lake is often dramatic as storms blow up, darkening sky and water. Birdlife teems. As dawn forces back the night, flurries of duck rise, trailing webbed feet across the glassy surface, only broken by floating papyrus islands. Cormorant keep watch and colonies of wild fowl plop and scamper among the reeds. Here and there stark white dead branches protrude where pelican preen themselves. Rock hyrax scuttle among the volcanic boulders of the shore. Brilliant yellow-barked fever thorns provide shade here and the plaintive cry of the fish eagle haunts the air above the mutter of duck and hippo.

Preparation of the gallops was difficult – sodom apple grew among the volcanic dust and thorn where 'a multitude of mole rats, not to mention hippos, plus the possibility of flooding made the whole operation great fun'.[76]

The worm in the apple of Block and Soprani's success, was that Beryl continually ran hotly tipped stablemates against one another. The rot set in once they began to notice that if she told them Title Deed would win, Spike would romp home. In the Derby (1961–62) their entry Rio Grande, ridden by the yard jockey, was tipped to win; and Beryl got Arthur to ride stablemate Speed Trial. Arthur, delighted to ride another classic for Beryl, won the Derby by eight lengths. Experienced as Arthur was, Clutt's grounding had never been abandoned; he always walked the course before a classic, analysing his chances by the going, familiarising himself. Ngong with its undulations and the fairly long pull uphill from bed to winning post represented a stiff test for any throroughbred. Victory was less sweet than it should have been behind the scenes where Block and Soprani confronted Beryl for running Speed Trial against Rio Grande. Ultimately her fundamental disregard for their feelings on the practice ruined the alliance.[77]

During the 1962–63 season Mountie and Lone Eagle (Toronto –
Xylene) were Beryl's exceptional two-year-olds. Since it was Enid's
dream to 'lead in a Derby winner', she and Jorgen bought Lone
Eagle in partnership. In so competitive a world Beryl accepted wins
and defeats graciously and could not be faulted on either count –
always modest in victory, she was also philosophical in defeat:
'We'll try again.' She could afford to be relaxed, with enough
confidence in herself and her horses, analysing calmly why one
had not come up to scratch.[78] Jorgen corroborates Beryl's reaction
from a more personal angle, 'she was gracious but determined, she
could be a bit grim-lipped but she never swore or used bad language;
she would call someone an idiot or a bloody fool, but that doesn't
mean much in English does it? When she won, and she won a good
deal, she would shrug, "Aren't I lucky." '[79] Beryl was a barometer at
the yearling sales; if she stood near someone who was bidding, the
price soared for any horse under the hammer.[80] 'Her very presence
created interest,' Jorgen explained. She herself rarely missed an
opportunity to pick up a good horse. Mountie was acquired while
Beryl was under the hairdryer; she had watched him from afar and
overhearing in the salon that he was for sale, announced that she
would take him for £1000, adding, 'Tubby can afford it.' Mountie
won eleven races for Block and Soprani and was never beaten. Spike
(KareTepe – Harpoon) was taken on without Beryl even watching
his paces; she had spotted a champion. 'We'll have him,' Beryl told
Spike's owner, who retorted, 'You don't even know how much he
costs yet.' Beryl explained, 'I said we're buying him, not paying for
him . . . discuss the price with Tubby.'[81]

Beryl celebrated her sixty-first birthday on Longonot Farm, with
the Parnells and Block's poultry manager, Pip Thorpe and his wife
Barbara who described it as 'a hilarious party, Beryl provided
plenty to drink . . . it wasn't orgiastic but there was plenty of
badinage and rolling in the aisles.'[82] It was at this point, that Beryl's
growing drinking habit began to manifest itself with her increasing
need for privacy. She was ready for 'a pinkie' at 11.30 a.m. And if
casual callers turned up, the slamming of car doors had her
retreating to the stables, as she had done as a child. She would not
face strangers, dictating to anyone who happened to be around,
'You cope.'[83]

Quite why the journalist Martha Gellhorn was persuaded to go for drinks at Beryl's home at Longonot has never been discovered. The former wife of Ernest Hemingway was renting a Block property nearby at Hell's Gate and was to regret not having taken more notice of Beryl when in 1983, she was asked to write the Foreword to Virago's paperback reissue of *West with the Night*.[84] Primarily a war correspondent, Gellhorn found herself referring back to that visit; how she had found it an effort to drive sixteen miles to meet a trainer when she had no interest in horses, reflecting, 'leaving as ignorant as when I came'. What had struck her, however, in the typical settler furnishings, was that there were, 'No books; it is the professional deformation always to notice books.'[85] Charles Norman and Jorgen were present and as they danced attendance Gellhorn sensed that Beryl did not care for women and found herself wishing that Beryl had been 'a game warden or paleontologist or a farm manager', affording more purpose to E. M. Forster's dictum, 'Only connect . . . Appearances deceive'.[86] Beryl seemed 'exotic'; where khaki prevailed upcountry she 'wore tight black trousers and a high necked silky pullover' showing her lean body to advantage. Gellhorn was looking at Emilio Pucci's last word in informal evening attire. Beryl bought Pucci on credit from Hetty's, Nairobi's exclusive new boutique at the rear of the New Stanley Hotel. For all the irony of having to recommend a memoir she did not like ultimately, and despite regretting not taking in more about Beryl twenty years before, Gellhorn had caught the essence of the Beryl who, 'was generally felt to be Circe in Kenya, but not your run-of-the-mill Circe. Imagine Circe casting a spell on Ulysses so she could go along on the journey, learn navigation, see the world. In passing she bewitched his company of men so that they did not resent her intrusion in their macho society, but welcomed her. It was easy to entrance the whole lot, that being her nature, and she knew what she wanted: knowledge and adventure.'[87]

Beryl was taking particular pains with her looks and her clothes at this time, conscious of her advancing years. One could say that a fear of losing Jorgen consumed her waking hours. Where most women in Kenya used Indian tailors to copy clothes, Beryl ordered pairs of slacks by the dozen from Mickey Migdoll. The former drummer had opened a shop, catering in the heyday of the Hollywood safari for stars like Sinatra, Crosby, Kelly, Gardner and William Holden at his outfitters, Esquire Ltd. Beryl got Mickey to copy in gabardine of different shades faithfully from a pair she had brought back from America.[88]

Independence for Kenya was looming, harbingers predicted the gloomiest prospects, and this is one excuse Beryl gave for emigrating to South Africa. Never explaining the real motive for leaving, Beryl found it handy to blame Kenya's Independence. The racing fraternity believed that she hankered after top stakes in South Africa, having won everything there was to win in Kenya – just what she wanted them to think. Beryl's consternation, deep down, was Jorgen's newest interest, his farm Kamwaki. His own ranch in the Loldeiga Hills was taking more and more of his time and Beryl feared most of all that her relationship with him was played out. The motivation behind her trip to South Africa was to look for some spectacular project to divert him before he became too entrenched in Kamwaki. She succeeded but, for Beryl, the choice was to prove the worst in her life.

Life in South Africa

(1964–70)

Today, Broadlands is written about in lavish terms, for its blood-stock mainly, but almost as much for its interior. Beryl's connection with it has doubled its legendary value: 'not a house but a theatre . . . that revives the spirits in a hectic bonfire of delights' and qualified 'originally discovered by Beryl Markham as a trysting place'.[1]

But Broadlands marked the onset of a downward spiral for Beryl into a vortex so bleak and lonely that no one could rescue her from it. All her life she had staved off solitude: yet as active and ambitious as she might have seemed, nothing was more reassuring to her than the presence of an agreeable companion to keep her amused. But in 1961, feeling her years, in a pre-nuptial note to Victoria she had written, 'Life is hard work and sometimes terribly lonely – no one to have a laugh with these days.'[2]

Beryl had discovered Broadlands as a broken-down property at Somerset West, dilapidated and on the market due to its owner, George Kramer, being terminally ill. Kramer, who was dying of cancer, was asking only £87,000 for what Beryl recognised as a wonderful investment. There was nothing comparable to be acquired in Kenya. The one person who could finance the project was Enid Furness.

Beryl had known Enid since 1932 but their personalities were strong and competitive, the chances of partnership working out between them would have appeared unlikely to the most optimistic of observers. But then Beryl had never found it difficult to carry off a semblance of friendship and courtesy in day-to-day living. Although there were a handful of women with whom Beryl got along and of whom she appeared fond, her motive was fundamentally selfish, for all that there had been 'a great deal of amicable hob-nobbing with other women at Nanyuki and Muthaiga'.[3]

Beryl would continue to denigrate her lack of education till the end yet she was always shrewd and intuitive and her cunning was not to be underestimated. There is no question that Beryl got Enid to emigrate to the Cape. After she had spotted that Broadlands was the magnet, she had returned to Kenya, 'to plague Enid for the next six months',[4] tactics which, remarkably, were to yield no resentment. Pat declares that it is thanks to Beryl entirely that she owns the stud today; thanks to her that the peach orchards and vineyards were made to work again, thanks to her that Enid restored the white post-and-rail paddocks to their former grandeur along its one-and-a-half-mile driveway.

Not until 1967 did the two women realise how Beryl had engineered their joint participation. She had convinced Pat that she must on no account worry her mother because of a heart condition, and then proceeded to convince Enid that *Pat's* life was endangered. Pat had given up her property at Karen, forced to move Tana, her lioness, away from Ngong where farmers had been unhappy when the lioness came into season every six weeks, calling all the males in the district. The result was that Enid built Kenmare Lodge (named at Independence) at Leopard Rock, for Pat where she could rehabilitate Tana, with a fifty-mile radius where the lioness could mate and roam without disturbing human life. But for Ted Goss, a young game ranger, Pat was entirely isolated. She found Leopard Rock idyllic but Beryl would convince Enid that this location was dangerous for Pat and that *shifta* (Somali bandits) would invade and kill her. But first, as it was well known that Enid's dream was to lead in a Derby winner, Beryl entered Lone Eagle and so as not to disappoint her future benefactress she also entered Block and Soprani's Mountie, a horse tipped to win, withdrawing Mountie at the last minute. Enid was as thrilled as punch with Lone Eagle's victory; but it caused a bitter row between Beryl, Block and Soprani.*

Beryl got to work on Jorgen, Enid and even chivvied Tubby Block over investment in Broadlands. None was more ignorant than Beryl when it came to money but Pat Cavendish is emphatic,

'Beryl was very dominant without saying much, despite her modesty and laid-back approach, never laying down the law, relying on everyone to be pleasant to her.' Tubby dropped out while the others, who questioned their sanity at the time, went ahead.

Jorgen, Charles and Enid were fused to Beryl's goal in such a way that she sensed that they would succumb and comply even when Enid had resisted Beryl; but she had listened. Then she had gone down to inspect Broadlands, weighed the prospects and could see what Beryl saw. 'Lets buy it,' Enid said to Jorgen, whose reaction was that it was a 'fantastic investment' offering security for the right person, 'in a quite different dimension from Kenya'. The drawback was that he had no wish to reside in South Africa. Like Charles Norman, Jorgen anticipated that he could fly in and out, in a 'floating involvement . . . having assessed the next development'. And he was prepared to settle Beryl in.[5]

Broadlands was purchased in equal partnership with Norman and Thrane, and Enid made the first down-payment. Her share included the main house, racing interests and the stud. Kramer could no longer look after the brood mares – these were included in the price. Norman and Thrane had the cottage which Beryl would occupy as stud manager. One of her selling persuasions to Enid was that with all those mares at livery, they had an immediate income. The men between them would undertake the running of the farm.

In January 1965, departing on a high note having won the Derby and the St Leger with Athi (with Doreen Norman's assistance), Beryl began to pack. The horses she had selected were primarily purchased from Block and Soprani, paid for by Enid, and were to be shipped along with Beryl's blue Mercedes Benz saloon from Mombasa. Jorgen dealt with the export permits for Title Deed, Lone Eagle, Mountie, Xylone, Little Dancer and some foals and yearlings and Beryl's own mare Niagara. The exercise of exporting the best horses in Kenya did nothing to endear Beryl to the Jockey Club when racing was undergoing financial difficulties in a newly independent African country.[6] The worst of it was that its finest country-breds 'were very much the worse for their Indian Ocean voyage and were never the same again.'[7] Beryl and Jorgen flew to

Cape Town taking Sun, 'the most divine and beautiful Alsatian' and another dog.[8]

Jorgen's purpose was clear in his mind; his managerial commitment was to be confined to the administrative. He was of 'enormous help . . . establishing gallops and getting an irrigation scheme installed.' Permission had to come through the Water Board in Cape Town – application alone took six months so Jorgen hired Kramer's son to look after the Jersey herd, flying back to deal with Kamwaki in the interim. Even his vitality could stretch no further.[9]

Beryl's intention was not to breed but to race. By May 1965 she was granted her licence by the Jockey Club of South Africa which she was to hold until 1967. On the racecourse, facing stiffer competition, Beryl suddenly found that in Kenya she had been 'splashing around in a very small pool'. Marie Celeste II would win the Durbanville Cup; Mountie would come third on the same day; victories with Title Deed, Lone Eagle and Kara Prince would follow, amounting to about 'fourteen wins to Enid's pleasure'.

From her cottage with its view over the mountains and the sea, Beryl had envisaged Jorgen with her. The realisation that she must tackle her future by herself turned the move from Kenya into 'a flop . . . a mess . . . chaos unprecedented. Everything went wrong,' Pat explained.[10] Beryl never stopped hoping for a *rapprochment* with Jorgen, whose uncompromising intention to stick with his dreams for Kamwaki dealt a blow to Beryl that she had not foreseen. 'She was desperately in love . . . still' but instead Jorgen's solution was to regard Broadlands not as a means to prolong the relationship, as Beryl thought, but as a haven for her where he could settle her safely and leave.

The minute he left, and each time he flew to Kenya, the atmosphere was charged with unhappiness. Beryl was accustomed to the autocracy of the farmer and the public trainer. As a private trainer in a way she was no better than Enid's servant. Cash was doled out to her like a school child receiving weekly pocket money – maybe justifiably as a precaution against her ineptitude, but its prudence was hardly dignifying. Tensions grew and grew; anyone on the sidelines could have foretold disaster. Beryl was adamant – she would have nothing to do with breeding or the mares. When the grooms went on strike, she refused to care for the mares herself, threatening to 'drive them along the road' unless Kramer, with whom she was permanently at loggerheads, fed them.

Perhaps the greatest problem was Enid. It had not occurred to Beryl that Enid would occupy Broadlands herself. Beryl had assumed that she would migrate, spending the greater part of the year at La Fiorentina, in Cap Ferrat. Beryl would then have moved into the big house and Enid would have been too far away to interfere with graduation or *carte blanche*. However Enid had become very involved with the restoration of the Cape Dutch house. Beyond the oak-shaded main house, she imagined brood mares, foals and racehorses with polished coats frisking toward Gordon Bay. Beryl's view that breeding, was 'a mug's game' had never altered.

It is doubtful if Beryl ever visited La Fiorentina; had she done so, she would have known what to expect. Enid's eye for detail went down to the last jewel in her ear. Greeting friends at Cap Ferrat on her Palladian portico, she would await them at the top of a long line of orange trees with white-washed trunks: 'In a gold *sari* roped in pearls, a scarlet parrot on her shoulder with two cheetahs with jewelled collars on a double leash.'[11] Enid was 'a splendid, magnificent woman', Jorgen recalled. And she would make Broadlands the dream it had once been.

In the eighteenth century, travellers journeying from Cape Town to South West District crossed the sandy wastes of the flats to reach the foot of the Hottentot Holland Mountains. Until the construction of Sir Lowry's Pass, this huge natural barrier, negotiated by a track, was contemplated with apprehension. Its gradients were terrifying, the rock surfaces so slippery that one false move sent ox wagon and occupants hurtling into a precipice. The last farm that the wagon track passed before the ascent, was Fortuinje, twisting between an unpretentious homestead of four rooms and the wagon-maker's shed with an equally simple dwelling on the neighbouring Gustrouw and it is these two properties that have, with 'complicated annexures and deductions over the years, combined to make up . . . Broadlands'.[12] Enid hoped to establish here the same style in which she entertained overlooking the Mediterranean. Cyril Connolly had called La Fiorentina's Italianate loggia, 'an anticipation of heaven, above a parterre of box and lavender'.[13]

Enid, during the war, had stored her Impressionists with her neighbour Somerset Maugham, entertaining guests such as Garbo, Graham Sutherland and Cecil Beaton. A stream of equally illustrious names would be invited to Broadlands.

Beryl, when thwarted, had never been easy to deal with and showed her most awkward, intransigent side. Balking at feeding the brood mares was but a useful part of a campaign to ensure that responsibility was dispensed with. All Enid saw was that Beryl meant what she said. Knowing nothing about horses herself, she sent for her daughter to sort things out. Unbeknown to Enid, meanwhile, Beryl had been getting messages through to Pat that unless she came to run the place, Enid would die of anxiety, such was her concern over Pat's exposure to *shifta* – the danger at Kenmare Lodge. Pat abandoned everything in Kenya, feeling that she could let neither her mother nor Beryl down: 'It was like going to live in the suburbs.'[14]

No one was more reluctant than Pat to be drawn into developments yet no one was more persuasive than Beryl either: 'one felt indispensible. She made one feel that if *you* let her down, it would be *terrible*.'[15] Pat was extremely tolerant. She loved Beryl dearly but would not simply let her have her own way. But in fact Pat was to be very grateful to Beryl for her singlemindedness. 'Fate deals strangely. I was the one totally opposed to leaving Kenya, relinquishing my farm, my animals, my beloved lioness – the biggest wrench, unthinkable, yet Broadlands has become my way of life, my inheritance and all this, thanks to Beryl.'[16]

The minute Pat had arrived, Beryl dispatched her to confront Kramer. She was to instruct him to get rid of the stallion, Tiger Fish, owned by Harry Oppenheimer. He was also to get rid of the brood mares. Kramer was furious.[17] This row caused great friction between Beryl and Enid, and left Beryl feeling increasingly embittered, isolated and forlorn. She swung rapidly from indications of eternal friendship with Enid, to the blackest hostility. Yet despite the head-on conflicts that were to follow, Enid was never to ask Beryl to leave.

One of their persistent rivalries came out of the fact that they were both very beautiful. Enid used her feminine mystery (and her money) to charm everybody around, whether it was her three children or any number of admirers.[18] While Enid was in a position to be generous, she also knew how to 'beat off the small beastlinesses of life . . . how to raise the temperature of the hour'.[19] Conflict was all the worse for the magnificence of the setting: Enid was recognised as one of six of the world's most beautiful women, so she and Beryl were used to queues of men lining up as escorts. Enid as Beryl's employer was a different matter from Enid as owner and friend – even when they were entertaining; and Enid invited scores of well-to-do guests to lunch or dinner, from Dukes to clergy – mealtimes could border on chaos in the two women's needs to outshine one another. Enid's pugs usually sat under the dining table. Beryl's Alsatian and her other dog growled at them, causing havoc to conversation between mouthfuls. Beryl would remark in a pained tone, 'Enid, I do wish you'd control your dogs, darling,' assuming the dominant role. By seeming not to do anything much, Beryl managed to confuse and frustrate the very European Enid, who could not get to grips with Beryl's inconsistency.

Beryl could be 'unspeakably rude' particularly after one of Jorgen's departures. She made peace impossible for Enid; doubtless she was expecting Enid to retreat to Cap Ferrat. Enid was not only disconcerted by failing health but rapidly becoming disillusioned by Beryl. On one occasion, Enid asked her if she would kindly keep her dogs out of the dining room as she was entertaining extra special VIPs. Beryl promised, charmingly, complying by not bringing them into luncheon. She had not bothered to lock them up, however; the pair leapt through the window, Anna Parnell, recalls 'All conversation stopped . . . I looked at Beryl who sat there unperturbed, continuing her meal – I thought she looked rather pleased.'[20] Meanwhile Beryl's *modus vivendi* – as it had always been – was to admit nothing, nor rationalise decisions good or bad. Pat, as a result of their quarrels was becoming emotionally drained, 'dreading . . . losing the affection of the two women I most cared for'.[21]

In June 1965, Beryl persuaded Enid that Parnell should leave Ireland to ride for them, and Enid paid for him to come out. Anna came too bringing their two children to join the *ménage*, Tina and their infant son, David to whom Beryl became godmother. Beryl's first mistake was to bring him in as an equal – whereas it was usual for jockeys to address her as 'Madam' she allowed him to call her Beryl, and Parnell, with his jumped-up ideas, used this to undermine her. Pat saw immediately that Beryl had made an error, since Parnell tended to 'take the mickey out of her, and Beryl did not like that'. Mockery was *her* prerogative.

Parnell remained until 1967 but he found the atmosphere 'intolerable' at times. None the less in 1966 the Broadlands yard acquitted itself reasonably. But one cannot help wondering if the absence of *seketet*, perhaps only to be found in Kenya, was partly responsible for fairly ordinary performances, although Mountie actually won eight races for South Africa's champion jockey, Bert Abercrombie.[22]

Beryl's crisis with Enid came at the worst time possible – the torments of having lost Jorgen had not eased; she was in a panic about her age, her looks, her past records. Defeat, as she well knew, has an odour about it. Yet, given half a chance, her fighting spirit battled on. After one particular row with Enid, Beryl was caught privately accepting training fees from Broadlands owners Annette and John Galbraith. Enid's accountant had stumbled across the evidence accidentally and 'there was a bit of a to do about it', recalled a girl groom, Shelagh McCutcheon.[23] Pat's version is that, 'It nearly landed in the law courts.' Enid, like Beryl, would do anything to avoid unpleasantness. However, hitting out in defence, Beryl went so far as to consult lawyers who advised her that she did not have a case. Pat and Beryl managed to remain friends but Beryl moved off Broadlands to live at Eerste River, taking the Galbraiths' 'not awfuly good' horses as well as Niagara, Title Deed and Kara Prince with her and one dog. The Parnells visited her occasionally: 'you had to walk for miles over sand to get to Beryl's place it was quite awful.'[24] Beryl constantly reminded Pat of her presence, claiming that she was coming back to stay; Pat found herself feeling guilty and relieved by turn for never being placed in that position. She was far too fond of Beryl ever to turn her away.[25]

Shelagh McCutcheon now became Beryl's prop, but she had had a run-in early on, and knew she meant little to Beryl. But she could no more rationalise her response to her than the others,

'Beryl would sit there, let everyone rush around. I don't know why we all did it. She *never* asked. We were all prone to the same reaction. I was a sucker for that sort of thing and so was my mother.'[26] They had sorted out their pecking order months before when an altercation over a horse-box took place and was serious enough to have damaged the relationship permanently. Shelagh was responsible for its delivery. Beryl rejected it outright, demanding that a replacement was fetched at once. Shelagh ignored her request, sensing it was important to ignore such tyranny. The next confrontation took place when Shelagh fell off a horse that had then tried to kick her. Beryl, astride Peccadillo, had stormed, 'It's no disgrace to fall off,' towering above the figure on the ground, adding, 'but it's the worst possible thing ever to let go.' Shelagh's pain as she lay recumbent cut no ice – whingeing was something Beryl would not tolerate. Days later, the performance was repeated. Shelagh in open defiance let go of the horse deliberately as Beryl watched, grim-faced but silent. 'She never uttered. Unlike me a jockey couldn't do that – she would have hammered him to death.' Beryl's psychological torment of jockeys affected her reputation so badly that by 1967 none in South Africa wanted to ride for her. She would put them on horses they could not handle 'pushing them to a point where they could only refuse, and look cowardly'.[27]

When Beryl took the house and stables at Eerste River, Shelagh agreed to help her. Eerste River was no-hoper land. Drunkards and eccentric drop-outs occupied shacks in the middle of the bush taking miles to reach over sand-flats. In a humiliating watershed, painful in its poverty, Beryl now confronted what she most dreaded – solitude, boredom and failure. Beryl's routine, which had always been based on hope, was exchanged for one of hopelessness. But Shelagh was struck by Beryl's way with horses. The quietest of horses became worked-up if she went into the box. Pat had noticed also 'a psychological charisma' so powerful and pure that its vigour affected animals and human beings alike, who could not ignore 'her singular presence'.[28] This was why she 'seldom went in with an animal'. Shelagh elaborated, 'Some were fine until she entered then they reacted strangely, they were definitely disturbed and sort of excited. Some got very agitated.' There is no doubt she exerted a certain power. On others 'her fearlessness also had a calming effect'.[29]

But Shelagh was often frustrated by the fact that Beryl appeared to be 'only interested in men and horses. She hardly ever went out. The men came to her. There was no shortage. They continually dropped in to flirt with her. One admirer was a butcher.'[30] Beryl's capacity for passion had not diminished, though her desirability had obviously lost some of its potency. Shelagh remembers a bizarre scene involving Beryl, herself and the butcher. They were taking tea when three women, a mother with two daughters drove up. 'Oh my God,' Beryl blurted, 'I don't want to talk to these people, you'd better,' delegating the obligation to Shelagh.

'What am I going to say?' Shelagh was caught off-balance.

'What difference does it make? Just talk to them.' Beryl, taking the butcher by the hand, led him toward a door leading off the room where they had been sitting.

'Where are you going?' Shelagh demanded, not quite believing her eyes.

'Into the bedroom,' said Beryl, shutting the door.

The three women advanced, demanding her whereabouts. 'She's gone to fetch the maid,' Shelagh lied.

The mother pointed to Beryl's Mercedes in the garage. 'I think friends took her,' Shelagh said, lamely offering tea. The women sat on the sofa with their backs to Beryl's bedroom door. Every so often Beryl opened it, mouthing to Shelagh, 'Talk. Talk. Talk,' ordering her to uphold the farce. Shelagh dredged up every subject possible as they sat undeterred for three-quarters of an hour when the mother stood up, followed by her daughters, and left. Shelagh was convinced they had known Beryl was there all the time. She was also furious at being put on the spot.

When the Galbraiths decamped or why they went to another trainer by mid-1967 is unclear. By November, left with nothing, Beryl relinquished her licence from the Jockey Club of South Africa.[31] She had no money and nowhere to live. Mrs McCutcheon took pity, suggesting that Beryl come to live with her for a month. She stayed for six, bringing one horse and a dog along. The dog bit their gardener. When they insisted that Beryl take the garden boy to the doctor, quite against her wishes, Beryl paid Mrs McCutcheon back by sending the bill to her. Eventually Beryl heard that Rhodesia offered opportunities to women trainers, and informed the McCutcheons that she was leaving for Salisbury.

During six miserable months of 'moseying around' Shelagh had come to know about the existence of *West with the Night* from somebody else. She had asked innumerable times to borrow Beryl's copy. She was 'most reluctant'. The usual excuse was that she had forgotten where she had put it. 'In all the time that we spent together, and she was living hand to mouth, she never had time to sit and read. Now that she was leaving and taking Niagara with her, I begged her to let me read it.' Afterwards Shelagh asked Beryl if she had been brought up by natives in Kenya, but she would not talk about it.[32] Shelagh's conclusion was as sceptical as the opinions of Enid, Pat and Jorgen. 'She would never have sat down to write it anyway . . . she would have got someone else to do it.'[33]

Raoul had been dead now for five years yet Beryl could not relinquish the role she had flirted with since the 1940s. It was not so much that the notion of being a writer was seductive. The only time it had seemed to matter was when she was competing with Tania, in return for her claim to Denys in *Out of Africa*. What was particularly tough, and it would get much tougher, was the contemplation of her own loss of face if it was to become known generally that Raoul had done all the writing. Such a blow to her ego was unthinkable. Yet as Raoul was no longer living it had nothing to do with one-upmanship. One day, as if she had definitely been toying with the idea of contemplating confessions, Beryl and Jorgen had been going through a bundle of her old snapshots; confessing to a weakness for Scandinavian men, pointing out a tanned specimen, she announced that he was a journalist with whom she had had an affair, 'who helped me write my book'. Jorgen's impression was that Beryl was merely testing him, wanting to admit that the memoir had been Raoul's. But instead of saying so, she was planting the idea of someone else having written it to see what reaction she would get.[34]

On a quite separate occasion Pat had a similar impression. She had been at Naivasha for the weekend when Beryl handed her

West with the Night, 'just gave it to me to read, without comment.
I knew straight away she hadn't written the book . . . my mother
had told me she hadn't. She couldn't string two words together. It
is obvious, knowing her, that she was totally incapable of writing
such a beautiful book.'[35] It was in 1962 that copies of the memoir
began to surface in second-hand bookshops – it could be had for
next to nothing. Its re-emergence coincided curiously with the
ghost-writer's demise.

Raoul had divorced Beryl in 1960 to marry the heiress to the
Hope fortune, Gertrude Chase Greene. Trudy, as she was called,
'had all the money on God's green earth' and Raoul never needed
to work again. Friends concluded that they were very good for
each other, notwithstanding that all that money had enabled them
to drink themselves into their graves. Scott saw Raoul one more
time only. He was in Santa Barbara to launch *Island of Blue Dolphins*,
going with his wife to meet Trudy 'at their beautiful place', Hope
Ranch. Scott saw that drink had taken hold; even so Raoul was
never 'boisterous . . . never changed . . . a controlled drunkard'.
Raoul and Trudy, 'real boozers', had tippled regularly in the dim,
narrow bar of the Hotel Miramar – with the static aura of any
artificially lit, windowless room, untouched by the cycle of day
or night. Grover Barnes, the barman, would overhear the couple
discussing Beryl's memoir, arguing over whether or not Raoul
should have received credit. He never minded that he was not
recognised. Trudy disagreed. As one of the inner circle put it, 'the
wasted talent in that crowd was enormous but the conversation
was always good.'[36] The end for Raoul came abruptly. He and
Trudy were clutching their air tickets, surrounded by luggage,
about to depart on a world tour from Santa Barbara Airport on 29
September when he collapsed. Trudy rushed him to Santa Barbara
Cottage Hospital where he died shortly afterwards from another
heart attack. He was buried in the Sunset section of Santa Barbara
Cemetery in Trudy's family plot, following a private service at El
Montecito Presbyterian Church.[37]

Had Beryl exploded the final myth she would have put an end to
the hypocrisy which was to make the last eighteen months of her
life so hellish. She was not a cheat by nature; if only she could

have stepped outside that cocoon of false authorship it could have been so different.

After Beryl quit South Africa, she settled on a farm outside Salisbury. She was whistling in the wind. She knew nobody, had no decent contacts so that others might send her horses to train. No jockeys would ride for her. She further created barriers by rowing with the Stewards. Needing funds badly, her one asset was Niagara, in foal to Ship's Bell (Doutelle-Bell of All). Beryl sold her on condition she could have Niagara's progeny. Her colt, Water Boy, was foaled in August 1969.

Beryl had one Kenya contact, Peter Leth, an acquaintance who used to cull buffalo on Soysambu. Leth rode fast work for Beryl intermittently, on indifferent horses; in his opinion 'all the odds were stacked against her'. Her Licence was restricted to Rhodesia and Malawi. The local executive had originally refused outright to licence her on the grounds that Beryl constantly gave trouble, making incorrect and late declarations.[38] It was almost as if she was setting everything against herself in order that she might be banned and never train again. Leth recalled rows between Beryl and the Stewards over the handicapping of her horses. She refused to accept their rulings, a factor which was to have endless repercussions.[39] Beryl was just beginning to show traces of the irascible old stick she would become and whose 'shocking temper' Leth discovered. That he remained fond of her is staunch indeed for a man who, after riding exercise one morning, was dismounting to find himself receiving the contents of a bucket of cold water, 'thrown over me with great passion'.[40] Beryl accused Leth of slowing the horse deliberately in front of prospective owners, blaming his riding when they failed to be impressed.

It may have been unforgivable ingratitude but it had also been an act of desperation. She was destitute. She turned to Mansfield for help, writing to him at St Peter Port, Guernsey, in the Channel Islands, where he now had interests in shipping. Without asking questions, he financed her.[41] At the end of 1969, exhausted by her need for victory, unable to be coherent in despair, Beryl returned to Kenya for good. She was totally alone, and could expect to remain so.

18

A Phoenix from the Ashes

(1970–86)

Beryl returned to the city of her first triumphs in a state of estrangement. She faced a six-year grudge held by the largely white Jockey Club of Kenya, who could not forgive that she had creamed off its best bloodstock. To black administrators, the fact that she had South Africa stamped in her passport went against her. Having broken ties a second time with Kenya's Turf, while she did establish a third career, her position was never as illustrious. Owners had died or left, loyalties had shifted – Tubby Block had gone to a new yard. Aldo Soprani alone would stand by her.

Nairobi had developed into a packed chaotic city; hidden under Governmental departments was a thriving intricate bureaucracy, within which Kikuyu and Luo struggled for supremacy. Even Beryl, whose comprehension of all things African was integral to her success, came up against ruthlessness and greed on a scale unmatched.

Old enemies in authority at the Jockey Club extended no help or encouragement. Careful study of six months' correspondence on Jockey Club files discloses antagonism; Kenya, not known for its moral standing, was fervent in disowning its ageing child, having used her in the past for its own ends. The Stewards shunted her between Ngong Racecourse and Immigration at Gill House until October.[1]

She applied on 15 May for her Trainer's Licence and until either this or a promissory note was issued, could not obtain her H permit from Immigration to work. The worst culprit was Sir Ferdinand Cavendish-Bentinck, whose tactics were both hypocritical and nothing short of victimisation. His secretary was instructed to inform Beryl that no decisions could be taken while he was in hospital. (Meanwhile his wife was inviting Beryl round for drinks and cosy chats.) He fulminated directives from his sick-bed, one of which was 'not to reply to Beryl at all'. Perhaps there were those who were fed up with her. She had certainly generated envy; rules had been waived in her favour after late declarations on the lamest of pretexts, causing resentment in rival trainers. Many were glad of the absence of competition from her since 1964, allowing 'smaller stables at least to gain more share of the spoils', not least Beryl's adversary, Vicky Jackman.[2]

Few were as brave as Beryl in a tight corner. Though she felt powerless in that she was no longer young, challenge had served her well for sixty years and she was not going to give in now. She fought with dignity. Daily she telephoned the Jockey Club. After two desperate calls on 18 May, someone with a conscience scribbled on a memo, 'I think it rather hard, not even acknowledging her letter. Shouldn't we just say that "the matter will be put before the Stewards?" But obviously CB knows best.'[3] But the Stewards were rigorously two-faced in their dealings. On 29 May, on the grounds of 'irregular immigration status', not in a professional capacity, but because Beryl was 'acting contrary to Government policy', her Licence was refused.[4]

Knowing that she had hit a wall of opposition by the end of June, Beryl turned to President Kenyatta's Minister for Co-Operativies and Social Services, the Hon. M. Muliro, for help, presenting him with her formidable *curriculum vitae* (from which authorship of *West with the Night* was significantly omitted).[5] The thongs of Jockey Club bureaucracy were loosened; Beryl was granted in August 'a restricted licence for six months' and her vital H permit was issued.

The Stewards then presented Beryl with fresh provisos; any new owner must guarantee in writing that he or she be responsible for all stable expenses.[6] When Soprani complied, she was next informed that training was to be confined to him alone.[7] To justify their over-zealous scrutiny, in October the Stewards submitted a letter to Beryl's advocates with complaints relaying earlier difficulties over refusal of her licence by the Jockey Club of South Africa.[8] Having made their presence felt again, they offered the palliative, 'this is not a reflection of Mrs Markham's character,'[9] leaving her in no doubt that she was under a magnifying glass at Ngong.

Until 1974 Beryl was based thirty miles from Nairobi on Soprani's coffee estate, Manyika, at Thika. She paid a price for throwing in her lot with him when, at best, they were incompatible by nature. At Naivasha this had not mattered – they met chiefly on the course. The distances she drove daily so as to maintain efficiency would have been physically taxing for anyone let alone a woman approaching seventy. The road between Thika and Nairobi was then notoriously narrow; increasing traffic (Kenyatta barracks was on the same stretch) created a high percentage of fatal accidents; the *murram* track of seven miles, from the main road to Manyika, was impassable during the rains. Often Beryl drove a hundred miles a day; jockeys came out by motor cycle as they could not live on the premises.

The three servants who would see out Beryl's days, joined her here: Ndungu, and the Normans' old *mpishi*, Oderu, who brought his young wife Adhiambo to work in the house. Beryl's accounting and correspondence were undertaken by two school teachers, Sue and Harry Jones, who worked in the district.[10] Soprani's faith in her in the 1971–72 season was rewarded with twenty-three winners. Heron won the coveted Kenya Triple Crown in the Kenya Guineas, Sultan won the Derby and the Kenya St Leger. But between now and 1978, in a decreasing string of entries, Beryl's wins would be fewer. According to everyone, and in particular Beryl's one solace at Thika, Freddie Nettlefold, himself an ex-trainer of steeple-chasers. 'Soprani led Beryl an impossible dance.' If Beryl predicted a win and was wrong, Soprani was 'unspeakably rude to her in public'. What he knew about horses was fatuous, so Beryl held him in contempt while as *his* trainer, Soprani wanted her to like him. The equation was simple; she could not like someone she did not respect. His male ego prevented him from showing appreciation when his runners began to display form; Soprani had the upper hand but the opportunity he gave her did not offer room for the type of dependency by which she secured further support.[11] Imbroglio notwithstanding, gradually permission was given to train for others and several wealthy Indian owners came to her. Peter Kenyatta, the President's son, and Charles Njonjo (later Kenya's defamed Attorney General) were her first African owners and, thanks to their influence, skirting restrictions in 1971, Beryl imported Water Boy, Niagara's colt, from Rhodesia.*

The period on Manyika was made bearable for Beryl, by one personality, Freddie Nettlefold, the good-natured, handsome owner of Juja, the Ruiru sisal estate which had belonged in 'Clutt's day to Northrup McMillan. 'Fweddy dahling' as she called him, was a hard-drinking bachelor somewhere in his mid-forties. His knowledge of horses was akin to hers and his company lightened her load of tribulation with Soprani. Nor was the arrangement one-sided. Freddie also led an isolated existence fifteen miles away on Juja and had put in an appearance when Beryl badly needed companionship.

On average three times a week, after work, Freddie would drive out to Manyika, rescuing Beryl from loneliness, to dine and spend the night so as to ride morning gallops, breakfasting with her before returning to Juja. With his worldly, drawling manner and his open admiration for the way she kept age at arm's length, Beryl could forget the tyrannies of the Stewards and Soprani. In Freddie's opinion, on 'all things equestrian' Beryl was 'matchless. Her physique was made to mount a horse . . . the most perfect rider and even when she was old . . . still a brilliant horsewoman.'[12] She was the mistress of illusion, especially in physical disaster. The lightness with which she bore pain, still, was astonishing. One morning, riding exercise with the string among the coffee trees, an uncut horse behind tried to mount hers, knocking Beryl off-balance with its forelegs; the jockey rushed to her assistance. Beryl refused help, picking herself up from the fall, 'I'm fine Sweetie, fine, thank you,' swinging back into the saddle. In one of seventy, such resilience illustrated a will to make men feel they were in the presence of a much younger woman, and circumstances enabled Beryl to project that same girlish charisma and vulnerability which had enslaved men in the past.

One of Freddie's appeals for her was that he never scolded her for drinking too much, and as they sipped wine by flickering candle-light Beryl began to yield secrets.[13] Perhaps after so many years of discretion, she had become weary of keeping companions in different compartments or (more realistically) perhaps alcohol loosened her tongue. Perhaps fear of age acted as a release; or perhaps she needed to show that she was still able to surprise and even shock. The maze she had always created had allowed people to wander a little, but Beryl had always held the key to their route, relying on chance that friends would never meet up in the maze. (Enid and Pat were prime examples where Beryl's strategy had misfired.) With Freddie, 'She made no pretence of her fundamental disinterest in women' and their jealousies. One evening in 1971, Freddy noticed on Beryl's mantlepiece a snapshot with curling edges that had not been there before. It showed three young men in combat dress and berets. When he asked who these were, Beryl's answer really shook him: 'Well, the middle one *was* my son.'[14] Freddie had not the slightest idea that she was a mother yet, weeks before, she had been stricken by a cable from Mansfield that Gervase was dead.

She had happened to be lunching at Muthaiga that day. Brian Jones, Beryl's red-headed jockey, had to help her bodily into the club. One witness describes Beryl as 'swept with grief', which may seem a surprisingly strong reaction given Beryl's record with Gervase. Whether her remorse was over lost chances for a relationship that could have been richer, who can say? It was all part of the enigma. Evidently regret was bleaker, hollow because there was nothing over which to be nostalgic. Mourning through guilt was an imperfect emotion, yet grieve Beryl did.[15]

Mansfield had been with Gervase when he died. Three months earlier their son had been moving furniture in a hired van, driving from Paris to a new home in Nantes, when he had a road accident and was admitted for injuries to Le Mans Hospital. Viviane alerted Mansfield who 'turned up trumps during those agonising days' and three months later wept openly as his forty-two-year-old son's life came to an end, sobbing, 'It should have been me, not him,' over and over. What Mansfield had told no one was that he himself was already the victim of an incurable blood disease.[16] For Beryl's son, it was a poignant end to an unfulfilled life. Following their visit to her in the 1950s, Gervase and Viviane had lived in London with their daughters, Fleur and Valery. Gervase had sold advertising space for the *Financial Times*. In 1967 they moved to Paris for the launch of the English weekly edition of *Le Monde* and, when Gervase fell out over advertising policy, a short spell followed with the International Chamber of Commerce; he had been unemployed at the time of the accident. Viviane observed his 'great pain but he was immensely stoic – like Beryl'. She had welcomed Mansfield's change of attitude, as a widow with two young girls to bring up, and had convinced herself that he 'died of a broken heart', three months later.[17]

Thinking to brighten Beryl's bare walls, Freddie had Gervase's photograph reshot, blown up and framed so that she could hang it appropriately. It was a kindness she could have done without.

Such frankness endowed in him a sense of privilege. He felt that he and Beryl had reached the point where he could ask questions; he learned about her Atlantic feat and, when Arthur Orchardson had a heart attack, dying that same year at his home in Riverside Drive, Beryl had elaborated on their lifelong relationship. Imagining that he knew all there was to know about this couragous, enigmatic woman Freddie was surprised when someone asked whether he had read Beryl's memoir. He had not known of the book and borrowed it. This concept Freddie refused point blank to swallow, and he confronted Beryl: 'Tell me honestly, you didn't write that book did you? You don't speak like that, you don't even use that vocabulary . . . Come on Beryl, you can't sheep's clothing me!' Throwing back her head, roaring with laughter, leaping up she said: 'Come and see the horses.'[18] She knew that he knew; it became complicity. Beryl only fell out with Freddie as his trainer. In the 1980s he sacked her for going against his orders when Supercharger had bowed tendons and was not to be ridden. In this instance Beryl's defiance was probably more of a case of 'hell hath no fury', for Freddie was now married. What had come as a surprise to his wife, Sylvia, and impressed her was how 'Beryl, who was very much in love with Freddie . . . although she did not like me, was always polite no matter how much she resented being cut out by a younger woman.'[19]

Beryl's isolation and problems were exacerbated in 1972 when she broke her leg, confining her in plaster for months. Early in

1974 Beryl had gone to live on Ololua Ridge in Karen. She was never good at administration, and now she became 'an absolute sod at declaring her jockeys' in the words of the late Robin Higgin. Kenya's furlong system had gone metric the year before; Beryl used such changes as excuses for misunderstanding. In comparison to conditions at Thika, she now lived on the doorstep of the course so that declarations could have been simplified. Horses had to be declared before 4 p.m., when entries closed, three weeks before race day. Thereafter jockeys must be declared forty-five minutes before the start of each race, otherwise the horse could not run. It was almost as if she preferred a ticking off to the indignity of losing: disqualification laid the burden with authority, rather than on herself. Any reflection that her standards were slipping she would not sanction.

Jockey Club correspondence denotes that Beryl quarrelled constantly with the Stewards from this point. She was inclined to change her mind on the morning of a race. Right up to the last minute she kept owners and Stewards in suspense; no one knew what was going on until she was ready. She still trained for Soprani but her vocation as a trainer was becoming a preoccupation that was tolerated (occasionally with amusement) because she was placed outside the sympathies and traditions of the Jockey Club. She crossed Major Collins, the Chief Steward, who found her too unorthodox in the way she broke every rule, expecting to be an exception.

Once Beryl left Thika, she occupied a series of guest houses in Karen, the district that was once Mbogani. Beryl is still a fond memory. She would park her Mercedes askew beside Anwar Patel's petrol pumps, near his provision stores and stride in to replenish her Smirnoff and red packets of Sportsman cigarettes, but she would always try to avoid paying the bill. Using one of the two *dukas* at Karen, she switched as soon as the Indian owner approached her for settlement. Poverty was only frightening when it crippled her style. She had never done anything to alleviate such encroachment. Unbanked cheques remained in her handbag.

The only people who could be certain of receiving money were her beauticians at the salon belonging to Jasmin Wali Mohammed. Beryl had been Jasmin's client since the 1950s when the Indian girl was a junior at Osa's* in the New Stanley. Jasmin kept Beryl's wardrobe up to scratch, brought her gifts – 'the latest jeans' from London – and had shirts tailored for her. 'She loved pink . . . pink jeans, pink bell-bottom trousers.' She always tipped her manicurist and hair-dresser generously, and at Christmas they received cheques.[20]

The last eight years of Beryl's life are best described as threadbare; like a Maasai nomad she would up sticks and move to another guest house seeking a lower rent or a more agreeable landlord. Pristine cleanliness always completed the overall impression of genteel shoddiness; indifferent furnishing, tatty unmatching fabrics, paintwork peeling at best, foretold the bleak future. Since Beryl chain-smoked, ashtrays tended to overflow. Otherwise, everything was neat. Piles of cotton clothes were always ironed and stacked by Adhiambo on bare wooden shelves. Tack occupied any spare room, polished and orderly, surcingles, bits and string girths hanging from nails banged directly into the wall. Commercial calendars served as reminders of the date. Her bedroom contained one bed, standing on four sawn-off logs; the other object distinctive of bygone days was her Louis Vuitton trunk.[21] The kitchen was more of a workshop; Oderu's *batterie de cuisine* sat next to spanners, a *panga*, the odd tyre, the jack for her Mercedes and dented *suferias*, identical to those in which her few horses received their mash.

Betwixt Muthaiga and Karen, Beryl at least did not lack for company; horsey friends abounded; each of a group of cronies describes the happy-go-lucky way in which Beryl would drop in, kicking off her shoes first, to stay for a 'pinkie' at midday or sundown. Shelagh Candler, Hilary and Travers Garland, Mary and Colin Hayne and the Garners were a few out of many who welcomed her and her two small Basenji crosses, Tookie and Tania (the little bitch with short legs), 'odd-looking dogs that went everywhere with Beryl'.[22] This was the steady rhythm of her life in the 1970s, interspersed with regular lunches at Muthaiga on Tuesdays and Sundays, long-standing arrangements with loyal men friends for whom she was always there.

In 1977 Beryl attended the lunch party for publication of

Denys's biography. The launch of *Silence Will Speak*, thanks to Nairobi's foremost bookseller, Dylis Rhodes, took place at Karen Club. Beryl and Tania's old *mpishi*, the celebrated Kamante, greeted one another as long-lost friends. Sitting in opposite corners of the marquee, they also signed copies of *Silence Will Speak*. Kamante pocketed twenty shillings per signature *before* painstakingly writing his name. From that afternoon, 5 November, 1977, there was to be no shaking off Beryl's link with Denys or Tania or Mbogani.

Two lots of Californian friends looked Beryl up that year – Maddie Rand and a couple, Almira and Jimmy Struthers, from Santa Barbara. The Struthers flew out to go on safari with John Alexander* the hunter, having been inspired by *West with the Night* and *Out of Africa*. They were duly enchanted, but dismayed by the change in Beryl. 'She was pretty tottery . . . almost vacant' compared to the svelte wife of Raoul. They were also surprised that she was unquestioningly referred to as the author of *West with the Night* – 'If you believe that Beryl wrote that book, then you probably believe in Santa Claus and that there are fairies at the bottom of your garden' – and suspected that this was why Beryl was not keen to meet them. Nevertheless they took her out to lunch. It proved a terrible mistake. They found her 'such a shrew, ingratitude being one of the most offensive aspects to emerge in her personality'.[23] The Struthers' unforeseen visit had plunged Beryl into panic – the terror of ridicule.

When Victoria took her daughter Nicola to Kenya to introduce her to Beryl, she too was saddened if not non-plussed when 'she came shuffling in like an old meths drinker, not so much drunk as totally disabled by not eating.' Victoria took Beryl to Muthaiga. 'I've never seen anyone eat so much, she ate like a horse.' Afterwards, they narrowly missed having a serious accident on the Thika road; Beryl had fallen asleep at the wheel, nearly plunging over a steep gulley to the left of the road.[24] Victoria knew how lovable Beryl could be, but saw that her capacity to infuriate, rather than bewitch, had taken over.

Maddie de Mott (formerly Rand) was in Nairobi to stay, working with the Flying Doctor Service at Wilson Airport, and the evening she invited Beryl for a drink she found, in place of the well groomed, stylish blonde who had beguiled Renzo Fenci, someone 'careless in her turnout ... an almost dowdy woman'. Maddie was struck by how 'uncomfortable Beryl was'. Perhaps Maddie represented the same threat as the Struthers.[25] Maddie's son Peter Rand concluded that Beryl 'was always angry at men, and the lie caught up with her'.[26] Yet Patricia Bowles, a Muthaiga friend, recognised that Beryl's unpleasantness sprang from insecurity; her defence for having let people believe she had written something she had not was to flaunt bad behaviour. It was more comfortable than losing face.[27]

Beryl's good days became impossible to predict. Drinking had really begun to affect her memory. Increasing complaints against her from owners and jockeys, with whom the Stewards were in sympathy, caused clashes of temperament, which could easily have been averted by one so clever at getting her own way. She had four horses, yet conditions for jockeys were described as 'intolerable'. She promised transport then withheld it. She made appointments, failed to turn up, offered no excuse, no apology. She would make fresh arrangements and do exactly the same. These were not new tricks by any means, but they seemed less conscious. Her finances were in a mess. A dismal stream of verbal invective from jockeys Morby, Webster, Hetherton, Little and Henry was followed by complaint in writing, painting a distressingly incompetent and degrading portrait.[28] Reverting to her tendency as a child, to outright rebellion, she convinced herself that she had been pushed beyond the limits of endurance.[29]

In June, the Jockey Club of Kenya informed her that they were not renewing her Public Trainer's Licence 'for the season 1980–81 or thereafter'. Beryl could not believe what she read. She sent a letter of protest through an advocate, before being struck down with gastro-enteritis. Baulking at hospitalisation when CB and Francis Erskine went round to insist she be admitted, as soon as Beryl heard the approach of the car, she locked her doors and windows. She refused admission to anyone for forty-eight hours.[30]

Meanwhile the Acting Senior Steward received a castigation from her advocate, for 'without warning' depriving Beryl of her only means of 'earning her livelihood', demanding that she be given 'a proper impartial consideration of her case' before further action was taken which would damage her in 'a small community where word spreads with frightening rapidity'. They also noted that she was back 'to complete fitness'. In July John de Villiers, aka 'Petersfield', racing correspondent for the *East African Standard*, who was a great fan of Beryl's, having learned what took place deplored in print the treatment of 'a leading trainer with an enviable record over the past quarter of a century', reminding her detractors 'that same Beryl Markham ... received a ticker tape welcome in New York in 1936', expressing the hope that his article was 'not a farewell tribute'.[31] Beryl's licence was re-issued almost immediately with the proviso that Ndungu be answerable to the Jockey Club for all her entries, as Head Lad.

But at the age of seventy-nine, Beryl's spirit was still undefeated. Setting off for the racecourse one morning in Marula Lane she and her Mercedes were nearly flattened when a giant eucalyptus came crashing down and they vanished beneath its foliage. Her American neighbour, Bill Purdy, a pilot and the owner of Skyline Advertising Agency, was summoned to find 'an elderly lady threading her way through the debris, two corpulent pug-type dogs, snuffled along behind ... her attire in marked contrast to her age, a soft visored cap .... at a jaunty angle, from which greying blonde hair fell to a knotted scarf at her neck.' Beryl, ignoring a gathering audience, silently inspected her car for damage. Its back seat had been removed some time ago to carry sacks of oats and bran, like a pick-up. Having looked at the scratches, a minor dent or two, she satisfied herself that things were in running order, there was not so much as a broken window. Beryl opened the driver's door: 'Come Tookie, come Tania.' She had not yet acknowledged Bill Purdy, let alone thanked him for coming to her aid. He hazarded, 'I say, that was a bloody near thing?' Without a word, Beryl reversed out of the tangle of branches and, waving briefly, drove away. This close call with disaster began their friendship. Since the blue gum had become uprooted from his property, Bill Purdy felt honour bound to contact her solicitor, Jack Couldrey,* living nearby, to offer to pay for damage.

Jack Couldrey was Jock Purves's godson. He had come across Beryl when serving a writ on behalf of one of the Karen *duka wallahs*. Appalled that a European of her background should be living as she was, a sense of obligation resulted in sorting out Beryl's tangle of insolvency. It would culminate in the handling of her considerable estate from royalties for *West with the Night*. Couldrey warned Bill Purdy, '. . . She is a flinty, ascerbic old thing and has been inseparable from that Mercedes for over twenty years. She can swear like a trooper too.'[32] From this point Bill would iron out minor domestic irritations for Beryl.

Couldrey discovered that Beryl's penury was shocking. He got her stipend increased to £750 per annum, 'which, with the greatest care, might provide for the running costs of a modest car' given the state of inflation.[33] He and a Swedish hunter, Ulf Aschan, between them organised a group of well-to-do among the flying and racing communities to set up a round robin, each contributing £10 per month. The monies were administered by Couldrey who eked out *shilingi* to Beryl in order to prevent her from squandering money on what he referred to as 'her expensive drinking habit'.[34] The Jockey Club, as if to compensate for its severity, allocated Beryl a bungalow on the course, usually reserved for jockeys. She would have no need to worry about rent.*

By now the Mercedes's engine was suffering the after-effects of short drives to the *duka* when Beryl never changed up from first gear. Lately Jasmin had come across it at sundown with 'fifteen Africans' propelling Beryl 'up the hill out of the *donga*' (the spot where in the 1920s she had the spill from the motor-bike) near Miotoni Road toward the racecourse. Jasmin offered help but Beryl waved off assistance as airily as Boadicea in her chariot: 'I'm fine sweetie, they'll get me there.' Jasmin concluded that Beryl was relishing the attention.[35] She 'hated living alone, her talent was falling off and she was impatient with the horses',[36] but people did what they could. John de Villiers brought Bing Crosby to meet her, who invited her to the Mt Kenya Safari Club for the day; highlights were scarce in her lonely routine.[37] Oderu and Adhiambo bore the brunt: 'She was exceedingly ratty with him,' Victoria observed. 'He wasn't the greatest servant, but my God, he put up with her.' After a confrontation when she had been particularly querulous, unearthing a bottle of Smirnoff which she had hidden from him, Oderu muttered good-naturedly, 'One of these days she will put it somewhere where I shan't be able to find it for her.' Africans, with their respect for the elderly, are wonderfully tolerant with ageing people and this pair proved exceptional with Beryl, sometimes with a remarkable absence of chagrin. The motions of life had returned almost to conditions of her childhood – at the mercy of Africans. As she ate less and could no longer be tempted by Oderu's 'roast chicken in a pleasant sauce, ice-cream and fresh fruit', her *mpishi's* chief role was to wash the car and ensure that her vodka supply flowed. He was to become a familiar figure traipsing to and from Karen *duka*. Beryl's friends would give him a lift, easing the walk – he was no longer young himself.

On 19 August, Ndungu found Beryl's door locked at 6.30 a.m. when he brought Moon River and her other horse round for instructions from her as usual. Oderu, washing the car, knew nothing. Ndungu dispatched him to fetch V. J. Varma, her nearest neighbour, the racecourse vet. When VJ got no response from hammering on her door, he shouted through her bedroom window, fearing she could have died in her sleep. She groaned, 'I'm in a terrible state. I can't walk. I need help.'[38] After forcing entry, they found her naked on the bed and tied; her arms were crossed, her wrists and ankles bound by telephone cord, ripped out of the wall, now cutting into her flesh after hours of constriction. Her arms were swollen, her face and neck badly contused, her hair was matted with blood. She had been robbed of everything worth taking and left for dead.[39] Her only concern was for Tookie and Tania; they were cowering under her bed. Daphne, the wife of the Jockey Club Secretary, David Bowden, and Varma administered first aid and got Beryl to hospital. Her only wish, in that appalling condition, was to return to her bungalow, 'which she accomplished in record time'.[40] Mansfield's nephew, Sir Charles Markham, a Steward at the time, commented, 'I think that beating up was a very great shock to her. She never thought that Africans would turn on her like that . . . A little while before . . . she had been [at] the christening of my grandchild and she was the life and soul of the party.'[41] There were to be two more robberies. Fortunately these were not violent.

Her robustness had been tested; but, more significantly, so had her pride. She had failed to come out on top. The experience, implanting shame and fear, was new to her; she treated her African staff shockingly afterwards, as if they were behind the attack and she must hit back at them. 'She went down hill a lot after that,' recalled Paddy Migdoll.[42] Paddy Migdoll, a staunch friend (aka Squirrel the racing correspondent and a trainer herself) now became one of a team of self-appointed women to keep an eye on Beryl for the remainder of her days. Paddy rallied round for replacements of blankets, clothes, shoes and handbags. Applications for a new passport and driving licence were necessary. The Louis Vuitton trunk had gone. The thieves had dumped on the floor Beryl's newspaper cuttings and her descriptions of childhood for Raoul for the memoir. A tin trunk was bought from the bazaar to hold the stuff she kept locked away.[43] Beryl seemed to suffer amnesia, or a mental blocking out. Her career would end 'ignominiously' eighteen months later when her last winner, ridden by jockey, Curant, broke down on the flat. Curant none the less could not help but admire her self-will in a career she had dominated.[44] Couldrey admitted, 'She stopped training only when some of us, by sleight of hand, disposed of her last horses which were costing her a fortune to maintain.'[45]

After the robbery, she became concerned over every ten cent piece for her beauty routine; indeed the first person she had contacted once the phone was reconnected was Jasmin. Under normal circumstances, she would not have come to Beryl's home (all the favours Jasmin did for Beryl were conducted at the salon) but in this instance Beryl requested that she come at once to wash her hair. The visit proved illuminating. 'She looked ghastly, arm . . . in a sling . . . face almost unrecognisable.' Jasmin tried to get Beryl to postpone the shampoo for a couple of days, to allow the dried blood to drop out of her hair. Beryl would not listen. An hour later, still trying to comb Beryl out, Jasmin asked who the glamorous pilot was in the portrait over her fireplace. Getting no reply after three futile attempts, Jasmin realised that it was not that Beryl had not heard the question. She had no intention of answering. Hobbling to the door to see Jasmin off that day, Beryl said bitterly, 'It doesn't help to have *that* hanging over my head you know.'[46]

She developed a nervous habit now, patting her hair frequently almost as if to reassure herself that it was still there. Beryl's hair became a growing obsession; she forgot that one made appointments with hairdressers, turning up expecting instant attention. If Jasmin did not drop what she was doing the minute Beryl entered the salon, she would leave. For years Jasmin had ordered, exclusively for her, L'Oreal's Golden Sable rinse; now she had to carry larger stocks to match Beryl's insistence that it be applied more and more frequently, until finally what should have been a six-weekly exercise became a weekly one. Any advice on the grounds of cost or health was met with the argument: 'It's *my* hair. I'll do what I like with it.' While her pedicure was done, she would hum to herself under the drier, breaking into song and sipping vodka (she had sent across to Anwar Patel's for a bottle), oblivious to the fact that, unlike the Gipsy Moth engine, the drier did not drown her tone-deaf ditties.[47]

There was to remain something unavoidably tragic about Beryl in that grace and favour bungalow, enshrined in her past, her photos framed by others for posterity looking down upon herself as if in scorn, turning achievement into silent burlesque. Her feistiness was intended to eclipse any chance that others might pity her.

In 1982 she had another lucky escape. She was almost killed by a jumpy *askari* when he opened fire on the old blue Mercedes during an attempted *coup* in August. She set off at the wheel for Muthaiga as usual at around 11.45 a.m., unaware that a group of airforce men had seized the radio station and announced they had overthrown the government. Beryl cut through all barriers with typical full frontal assault; she first ordered the *askari* on duty at the racecourse to open the gate when it was closed. At a road block on the roundabout near the top of Kenyatta Avenue, a soldier brandishing a gun demanded, '*Na kwenda wapi?*' Waving him out of her way, Beryl informed him that she had been lunching every Sunday at Muthaiga Club for fifty years and he was not going to stop her now. Driving on across the city unimpeded, at the Mathari roundabout road block she received a hail of bullets as she ran the gauntlet, arriving at Muthaiga, blood streaming from a nick in her chin. Young Philip Mason helped her to a seat. Beryl was so dazed that she mistook him for his father, Dickie, yet she was all for driving home. Refusing to lie down in the room allocated for her, sitting in the wicker chair near the entrance, Beryl became as gleeful as a child, realising that she could still break rules – 'They even let me bring my dogs in' – staying until law and order was restored.[48]

Before President Moi's loyal forces could put down the attempted *coup*, more than one hundred and twenty people had died and soldiers had gone on the rampage in Nairobi, raping and looting. Of the fund of *coup* stories none was more impressive than Beryl's, whose courage was on everyone's lips.

Bill Purdy insisted on putting her Mercedes into better running order. A temporary vehicle was found while her own was garaged. Requesting that Couldrey be present at the bungalow to witness the handing back of the resprayed overhauled Mercedes, they wanted Beryl to step outside to inspect the handiwork (Bill had left the bullet holes intact as testimony to her bravery). She was blunt: 'What the hell do I want to look at that effing car for?' she demanded, as if dealing with a couple of imbeciles, 'I've known it all my life.'[49]

Beryl had always held a particular fascination for Americans and, unbeknown to her, in California a restaurateur, George Gutekunst from Sausalito, had learned indirectly about her memoir through one of Hemingway's sons. Gutekunst owned Ondine's, a mecca for *gourmets* in the San Francisco Bay area; Jack Hemingway was one of them, and during a fishing trip had urged Gutekunst to read his father's recently published letters. Hemingway's praise for the author of *West with the Night*, when he more often savaged contemporary writers, prompted Gutekunst to get hold of a copy. Reading it twice in quick succession, he asked the author Evan Connell for his opinion. They shared the same enthusiasm, sending a copy to 'two men of flawless literary taste', Jack Shoemaker and William Turnball of North Point Press, who agreed to republish.

Beryl received notification of these events at Christmas in 1982 from the character she would call 'Georgie Porgy'. The paperback would be on sale by spring 1983. His letter ended, 'In appreciation of a beautiful book. I send my best regards to the woman who lived and wrote it.'[50]

So the unthinkable had occurred – the resurrection of the memoir. Consequent acclaim brought the unwelcome intrusion of strangers. People anticipated her feelings of joy. She hid her dismay. The overwhelming assumptions over republication of *West with the Night* created untold misunderstandings and pressures again, more so because she never asked for help. Circumstances made it impossible to express gratitude. It is mortifying to contemplate the effect, after the robbery and this unexpected turn of fate, that well-meaning people had upon Beryl. She had never sought such recognition. Worse, she was incapable physically of escape. There were plenty who had accused Beryl of lying. Incredible as it may seem, for someone shrouded in so much mystery, she was not. It was the mystery that was the problem. Information about her had always been propagated by gossips. Her failure to clarify and contradict was what twisted and distorted the truth.

Gutekunst was soon to sacrifice Ondine's so as to make a documentary on Beryl. In December 1980 the journalist James Fox had optioned the film rights in *West with the Night* for a nominal sum and now Couldrey inherited developments on the project. In September Fox advised him that a movie treatment was written and, when *West with the Night* went on sale, the situation had not progressed. The more enthusiastic critics compared Beryl to Dickens, the Brontës and inevitably Isak Dinesen (Karen Blixen). Martha Gellhorn, with more perception than she realised (she did not particularly admire either book) declared that Beryl's was 'a worthy companion to . . . *Out of Africa*'.[51] In fact Martha Gellhorn had no time for the purple prose and overly feminine writing. Gellhorn came to admit that if Beryl had written the book, 'it would have been superior to Raoul's offering . . . Raoul had managed to achieve the feminine effect, she [Beryl] could never have achieved.'[52] Whatever misgivings Gellhorn had privately, in her adroit handling she promoted *West with the Night*, albeit less forcefully than her former husband had done.

Re-recognition of Beryl as a writer now began to roll: the journalist James Fox flew to Nairobi to profile her for *Vanity Fair* and the *Observer Colour Magazine*. Beryl gave James a better time than most of her other interlocuters, enduring his prying as the price for charming company. An old Etonian, he could have stepped straight from Picasso's rose period so closely does he resemble a *saltimbanque*. She was much less muddled than the following year, allowing him to photocopy typewritten pages from the tin trunk. He judged these to be preparatory drafts for the memoir. Some raised questions because they bore annotations, 'in a hand not her own'. So far as is known, it was the first time she had permitted anyone to scrutinise these. Perhaps she hoped that in his chivalry, James would remove the sword of Damocles for her, bearing her responsibility. Looking back on developments, there is no doubt that Beryl was not just wary, she no longer had the energy herself to throw off the new and heavy yoke of authorship with all its humiliating possibilities. When James escorted her to the Derby, it was a new experience because she had no entry, confiding defensively, 'I wouldn't run a horse on this ground, even if I had a winner.' Beryl's last exchange with James summed up her parallel lives: 'I hear you've been married four times? Tell me, where did you get them and what tribe did they come from?'[53]

Next, in person, George Gutekunst came. From cigar to gravelly profanity, 'Georgie Porgy's persona shrieked film producer. For thirty years his glittering patrons had made Ondine's 'a kind of theatre', attracting baseball champions to celluloid cult figures – Oppenheimer, Houston, Bridges, Peckinpah, Newman and Redford. Georgie Porgy's sense of celebrity lured him to Beryl's side, an amiable companion whose taste for vodka and fun she shared. His documentary, originally titled *One Woman's Africa*, later to become *A World Without Walls*, took his crew on a stormy voyage into Beryl's past: Andrew Maxwell-Hyslop, film director, his brother-in-law, Barry Schlacter, a journalist, and Gary Streiker, the cameraman, spent from August to October coaxing information out of Beryl. They flew her back to Njoro. She refused to get out of the plane. Sometimes she would fix them with a look, and announce, 'I'm fed up with this. I'm going.'

She remained stubbornly herself. Her triumph was hers alone, as were her failings. Hardly any of the Kenya footage of her could be used. Yet the affection of the crew for her in the fight she put up was unsullied.[54] Happily Beryl forged a rewarding reciprocal bond with Georgie Porgy, who provided fleeting diversions. If he had no time to call on her in Nairobi she would resort to flirting and cajoling by telephone in the middle of the night (voices don't age), cooing 'Georgie Porgy, Beryl here. What are you doing?'

'I'm in bed. Alone.' Flirtatiously she commiserated, 'How dreadful!'

Talk of Beryl flying to New York for the release of *A World Without Walls* was countered by Georgy Porgy. She was too frail, he reasoned. Beryl argued, 'I can't see why I can't fly, when I've done it alone, with a bunch of people in a larger aircraft', teasing, 'I've still got a Maasai spear. I shall plunge it into your dark heart, if you dare set foot in Kenya again.'[55]

Overlapping, came the BBC TV *Arena* team, for Alan Yentob's Hemingway series and the documentary to mark Tania's centenary, *From an Immigrant's Notebook*. Couldrey had warned Tristram Powell, the gifted director of the latter, that Beryl's memory was failing so badly that he would be unlikely to get anything useful. He was right. Beryl hated being filmed. The lights were too bright: 'Can't you turn those bloody things off?' she demanded. 'What the hell do you need them for? Why do you keep asking the same questions?' Her compensation was the company of the predominently male crew. All her interviews ended up on the cutting-room floor. Untold pressures worsened her behaviour; she would answer in Swahili, cursing us under her breath. Few words could be interpreted, '*Siku nini? Hapana siku hizi hapana*' – obstruction, over and over again.[56]

Drink summoned her demons. She needed a second bottle of vodka to appease them. The weeping, bullying, invective side would prevail. Her only weapons were incoherance, nonsense muttered in Swahili muddled with English. Vodka blotted out the pain. One crew[57] tried to stop her drinking, not realising that without her vodka things were worse.

In 1983 critics hailed *West with the Night* as a lost masterpiece. The royalties began to roll in, but so did the journalists and accolades from new generations whose 'discovery' of her as a woman of letters raised all the old doubts as to Beryl's ability to write. In the interim, both had been forgotten. While everyone else was rejoicing on her behalf, with enthusiasm over recognition for her long-lost talent, it was merely an embarrassment to her, particularly when, immobilised by infirmity, she was unable to escape to the stables.

Beryl was beginning to show signs of senility. She was occasionally incontinent and her worst fear was that others would laugh. Adhiambo helped her to maintain her dignity, but Beryl began now to express the wish 'to go before my head goes. I should hate people to titter over my lapses; goodness knows they probably already do.'[58] Not that anyone listened, much less understood that one of her greatest phobias was the coffin. The open plain and the hyena was a cleaner death. She did not want European funeral rites: 'And if I die, do not bury me at all. Just say goodbye.'[59]

In her isolation Beryl, rather than walk to her bedroom alone at night, preferred sleeping on Joss Erroll's old sofa. It was not the sleep of exhaustion, as in the past a weariness replete from an honest day's work, but from the stringent chemicals of loneliness and drink.

By now she had taken to calling the memoir 'bloody book'. Interested visitors, taking up some point they would like to discuss, were told to read it again; 'it's all in the book. I've nothing to say.' Publication of the *Vanity Fair* and *Observer* pieces made Beryl literally front-page news again. The Gutekunst documentary *World Without Walls* was first aired with the backing of a San Francisco television station, KQED, in the Bay area in January 1986.[60] In response to ecstatic reviews, *West with the Night* was reprinted over and over again.[61] In October, the Public Broadcasting Service transmission of *World Without Walls* was to catapult the memoir on to the *New York Times* list of paperbacks where Beryl remained aloft for months, and by 1987 her book had sold 140,000 copies.

Meanwhile a corollary to events was the making of the Universal/Pollack feature film *Out of Africa*. The irony of being dominated once more by Tania's success was missed by everyone but Beryl. Journalists flew into Kenya looking for a scoop on Redford, Streep or Brandauer, only to discover *Out of Africa* was 'a closed set'. Finding themselves without a story, those who beat a path to Beryl's glass-panelled door expecting to meet an iconoclast were faced with a troubled impoverished woman who was drinking too much and rapidly losing contact with the real world. 'Bloody book' and 'Bloody women' were the last phrases of rebellion left to her.

Displays of invective made it difficult to know if she was wary of their compliments or merely disliked intrusion. Just as, fifty years before, souvenir hunters had torn fabric from the wings of the Vega Gull, they now delved into her tin trunk; even copies of bank statements and Western Union cables were collected by 'literary jackdaws'.[62] What was taking place was a magnified version of all that might have happened in 1942 if America had not been at war. The mounting interest and re-acclaim turned her into even more of an enigma as film personalities flocked to meet her. Beryl was pleased in small doses to be recognised by figures of significance again. But on the flip side of this coin was embarrassment, a deep uneasiness at the momentum gathering on the paperback. 'I didn't think it was *that* good,' she bridled at too much enthusiasm. She drank earlier each day, blotting out with half a tumbler of vodka at a time, diluted with vile-coloured orange cordial.

John Potter in Bidart, reading articles about Beryl comparing her to Karen Blixen and Hemingway, was disappointed in her heroine status. 'Surely she could have been big enough to admit that Raoul had written the memoir, now that he was dead, set the record straight . . . this would have taken moral courage yet how marvellous it would have been had she come clean and confessed.' He did not begrudge Beryl her newfound income: 'it was right and proper that she benefit, even when Raoul should have been given credit for the writing.'[63] Maddie de Mott could not believe that Beryl was 'masquerading as a writer'.[64] She would have been less troubled if so many celebrities had not converged on Nairobi to propagate the myth at top level. Warren Austin, who was drawn into the maelstrom had to admit that 'Raoul had not received his due as a ghost writer'.[65] Scott O'Dell, not wanting to embarrass Beryl as an old woman, said nothing while she was alive.

As so often down the years, the excitement over her memoir caused by well-wishers was a glamorous shell containing her kernel of private misery. She hated signing copies, resenting people 'barging in on me just so I can sign that effing book', – overheard after someone had thrust a copy under her nose while she was under Jasmin's hairdrier. Everyone on the Universal film set, if not reading the memoir, possessed it. When *Out of Africa*'s late talented art director, Stephen Grimes, wanted Beryl to sign his copy she refused initially. After a second request, swearing under her breath obscenely, she obliged. Letters – fan mail from all parts of the globe – she let others open and read to her. A sense of a hopeless struggle to remain in touch with the truth of herself was always swept aside with each new interview, and by the ground-swell of her enthusiasm for belated success.

In October on Kenyatta day, a public holiday, Oderu telephoned Paddy Migdoll summoning her urgently: '*Haraka, Haraka, memsahib ngonjwa sana.*' Beryl had suffered a thrombosis and Paddy found her lying unconscious on the floor. Beryl spent six weeks on Pioneer Ward in the Nairobi Hospital. When she was discharged, 'for an octogenerian she was pretty fit' compared to her state on admission.[66] The opportunity had been taken to remove a bilateral cataract on her right eye. Jorgen and his wife (he had not set foot on a racecourse since Broadlands), came away after visiting time, gladdened to have heard 'Beryl's fantastic laugh once more',[67] much as she resented being treated by everybody 'like a two-year old'.

Once Beryl was ready to go home, she nevertheless required the services of a nurse, full-time to begin with. Ann Addly filled the post intermittently for ten months: 'Beryl was in a bad way mentally, never thanked anyone for anything . . . could be unspeakably rude, so offensive that I considered leaving the case early on'.[68] She won Ann Addly's heart by sheer irascibility, a refusal to give in – her indominitable spirit, a triumph of determination, where now she could decide nothing for herself. Angels of mercy were not to know that they intensified Beryl's feeling of failure. 'Nobody comes to see me these days,' she would observe, flinging the words 'Bloody woman' out of Ann's earshot in her wake. Questions were rebuffed: 'I don't gossip.' The passing of time was limited to glancing through copies of *The Aeroplane* and *The Pacemaker*, 'a good racing manual' on loan from friends.[69]

People would insist that royalties could not have poured into Beryl's coffers at a better time, but she could go nowhere. Couldrey drew up Beryl's Will for her. She divided her estate in Kenya and overseas between her two grand-daughters* and George Bathurst Norman, fulfilling the promise she made when he was a lad. *West* *with the Night* has become a publishing phenomenon. At the last count it had sold over a million copies.

In April 1986 when one day Beryl went to the races, she had to be carried to the top of the grandstand (wanting the best view), and afterwards the man who brought her down missed his footing, tumbling with her to the bottom step. Luckily Beryl had no broken bones. Still the doctor insisted she go into hospital next day. The nurse whose lot it was to complete the admission form, asked Beryl's age: 'Over twenty-one,' she snapped, sharp as a blade.[70] Predictibly the ravages of old age disgusted Beryl. Where once she had walked like Mercury, with wings on her heels, now she was propelled about in a wheelchair. On her clip-board at the end of her bed were the instructions, as unorthodox as the patient, '12.30 vodka and tonic. 4.30 push her out for a walk with the dogs.'[71] Daphne Bowden made home-made tomato soup to tempt her, bringing Tookie and Tania also to see Beryl every day.

Back in her bungalow, time passed slowly. Her pleasure had never been based on adulation but now, Ann Addly noticed, if 'something made her happy, her eyes lit up', yet the relief nurse, Mollie Wilson, observed that 'Beryl was a very sad case indeed with too many people observing her decrepit state.' She became paranoid that Oderu was peering through the keyhole of her bathroom, finding her dependence on others intolerable. Difficult as those months were for Beryl in her eighty-fourth year, Ann Addly discovered 'the most stoic of patients, showing extraordinary bravery in intense pain'.[72] She refused all advice, resenting anyone telling her what to do for her own good. Mercifully the end came unexpectedly: Beryl bent down to pat Tookie and toppled off balance, shattering her femur in the fall.

She had no intention of going gently, however. At Nairobi Hospital on 29 July 'Screams, yells, curses' rent the peace of the ward with language so virulent that the other patients asked what was going on. The X-rays were being examined. Beryl was arguing violently that her femur was not broken. It was her last chance to protest and protest she did.

Adhiambo asked to look after her. A long operation lasting from 9.30 a.m. until 3.30 p.m. was performed the following day. But pneumonia set in and Beryl was moved to intensive care. Even now, Adhiambo was not turned out. Beryl was oblivious to Paddy Migdoll's visits, looking up at the ceiling as if to detach herself from the indignity of it all. On the evening of 3 August, Beryl was 'red hot, her pulse was racing, fluid was accumulating on her lungs. Yet the nurse on duty seemed optimistic for her survival.'[73] She died at 2.30 a.m. on 4 August, sinking quietly away, Adhiambo weeping in real grief by her side.[74]

In England the BBC announced the death of Beryl Markham, the 1936 conqueror of the Atlantic, on the 2 o'clock news. One memorial service took place at Karen, followed by cremation. Her ashes were later scattered near Cemetery Bend outside the race-course. Within a few days the Court Circular in the *Daily Telegraph* announced a memorial service to be held at St Clement Danes in London on 4 September 1986, the fiftieth anniversary of her epic flight.[75]

Notes

Chapter 1 The Birth of a Life (1902–4)

* p. 8: Port Florence was on Lake Victoria 582 miles from Mombasa. Now known as Kisumu, the original name thought to be after Ronald Preston's wife, Florence, was actually decided by George Whitehouse, whose wife reached the lake with him on their safari in 1898. Some believe that Lady Florence Delamere also inspired the choice of name.

Chapter 3 Life as Lakwet (1906–12)

* p. 20: Ian Quiller Orchardson, Arthur's father, the former chemist, wrote an unpublished anthropological study, KATUMET ap LAKWET, which reveals taboos and customs among the Kipsigis, from his experience as an honorary member of his Nandi wife's extended family.

Ian Orchardson Jnr, became Registrar at the School of Oriental Studies and his sister was a student there also. Upon the death of their father Ian Orchardson, in Nigeria eventually, Arthur's half brother asked Mat Matson not to reveal his father's death as it 'might cause trouble'. An attempt at litigation failed. Arthur Orchardson, 'a wonderful father and most gentle unassuming man who asked little of life' was said to be shattered to learn of the existence of two half-caste siblings at that time, (Corresp. the late A. T. Matson 15/7/86).

Chapter 4 Lessons at Home, and in the War (1913–19)

* p. 49 HQ for the Carrier Corps B called Kariokor today.

Chapter 5 Life as Beryl Purves (1919–22)

* p. 59: The late A. T. Matson, whose scholarly study, *The Nandi Rebellion*, stemmed from living at Lumbwa and Kericho, knew Arthur's father, Ian Quiller Orchardson; he also met over the years, Arthur's half-brother, Ian Jnr, the son by his common-law Nandi wife, by whom there was a daughter too (Knappert Corresp. 17/7/87). Matson also knew Beryl.

* p. 71: Major 'Wac' Conduit, well known adventurer, second husband of Lord Shrewsbury's daughter, Lady Viola, whose illustrious reputation brought Beryl new prospects in racing.

Appendix to Chapter 5 (p. 67)

SALES OF RACEHORSES AND PURCHASERS PRICES 18 DECEMBER 1920 (article published)
Ndimu Farm. Mr Clutterbuck's yard.

'This morning one of Kenya's most famous racing stables, that of Mr C. B. Clutterbuck came under the hammer and was sold up by Mr J. Beeston, the local auctioneer. Some good prices realised while at the same time one or two purchasers obtained bargains. The animals were well distributed amongst the various trainers and owners of Kenya.

Stallions:
RILLINGTON: UK 9 yrs TB. By ENGINEER out of SAVILIA by HAMPTON. Winner at Islington. Champ. Nairobi. Sire of the following winners: Rillingdale, Ringleader, Ruby, War Baby, At Last, B. P. Charlie, Miss Issippi, Lily. (Unsold)
CAMCISCAN: UK 8 yrs. By SPEARMINT. Winner Derby & Grand Prix. Out of CAMLARG by CYLLENE. Winner of Gold Cup. His first produce will be running in 1921. Subscriptions list full each season. Bought by Lord Delamere, £760
RESCO: UK 6 yrs. Bought by G. Alexander, £475
LOVED ONE: 4 yrs UK. Bought by Mr Watts, Lumbwa £65
LANGIR: 5 yrs Bought by Mr Bearcroft, £22

Brood Mares:
ORMULU: TB UK. In foal. Last served October 20. Bought by Mau Farms Ltd, £105
WINSOME: Aust. TB. In foal CAMCISCAN 20 October. Last service. Bought Maj. B. F. Webb, £55
CUDDLES: UK TB 5 yrs. Due to foal 10 March 1921. Bought by Major B. F. Webb, £130

REMEMBER: EACB 5 yrs. Accident to her knees as a foal. Never trained. Last foal died. Last service 4 October CAMCISCAN. Bought Major B. F. Webb, £160

RUBY: EACB TB 5yrs. Colt foal at foot. CAMCISCAN. In foal by again. Last service 17 September. Bought by Lord Francis Scott, £95.

KITTIWAKE: UK TB. Due to foal. CAMCISCAN 26 February. Bought by Mau Farms Ltd, £90.

NECTARITIS: TB Aust. Bred in India. Colt foal at foot. Served again last October 1. Bought by Lord Francis Scott, £105.

MRS IPPY TB UK: Aged. Due to foal 22 Feb, 1921 CAMCISCAN. Bought by Mau Farms Ltd, £105.

YORK TB UK: This year's foal died. CAMCISCAN 4 October. Bought by Mr Jenkins, Molo.

DAPHNE: TB Aust. In foal. CAMCISCAN service 28 October, 1920. £30

ROAR OF THE RING: EACB 7yrs. Filly foal at foot. CAMCISCAN. In foal AGAIN. Last Service 1 October 1920. Bought by W. G. Sewell, £155

DIAMOND STUDS: EACB. Due to foal 18 January 1921. Bought by Mr Angus, Uasin Gishu, £90

LOOT: 5 Yrs. Mare taken in GEA Campaign. Due to foal CAMCISCAN, 20 February, 1921. Bought by Mr Murton, £85

PERFECTION: Due to foal RILLINGTON, 24 January 1921. Bought by Mr Pigache, £50

REJECTED: S. A. mare. Colt foal CAMCISCAN and last service 26 September, 1920. £70

UNION JACK: S. A. Mare. CAMCISCAN. Foal due 23 February, 1921. Bought by Lady McMillan, £165

HOUSEBOAT: Unbroken. In foal CAMCISCAN. Last service October 5. Bought by Mr Murton, £100

JILTED: EACB. In foal. CAMCISCAN. Last service September 8. Bought by Townsend, Uasin Gishu, £105

LILY: EACB In foal. CAMCISCAN October 2. Bought by Mr Blach Plateau, £50

SOS: EACB In foal. CAMCISCAN September 15. Bought by Mr Watson, £75

DAMAGES: EACB In foal. CAMCISCAN. Sept 10. Bought by Mr Pigache, £35

HELP: Chestnut filly. Unbroken. Bought by Mr Pigache, £35

GOLLIWOG: Black filly. b. February 1919. Unbroken, £165

MWISHO: Bay gelding Bought by J. W. Eames, £20

CAM: Bought by Major Conduit, £95
BAR ONE: Bought by Mr Greswolde-Williams, £90
LIBERTY: Bought by Lady McMillan, £80
MY BIRTHDAY: b. 23 April, 1919. Met with an accident as foal.
Unbroken. Bought by Mr Purvis [sic], £7
CAMARGO: Bought by Lord Francis Scott, £155
REGATTA: Bought by Mr Stanning, £85
CAMILLE: Bought by Miss Collyer, £70

EACB Yearlings:
LOOTED: Bought by Mrs Hill Williams, £35
WINNIE: Bought by Mr Wheeler
BREACH OF PROMISE: Bought by Mr Purvis (sic), £40
CAST: Bought by Mr Gooch, £65
EBOR: Bought by Mr Pigache, £55
THE FIELD: b. 9 September 1919, Bought by Lady McMillan, £165
CAMBIST: Bought by Lord Francis Scott, £155
SHEM-EL-WESSEM: Bought by Mr J. Drury, £100
THANKS: Bought by Mr Pool, Thika, £55
JOHN BULL: Bought by Mr A. C. Hoey, £40
STARLIGHT: Bought by Mr Tom Lloyd, £25
AT LAST: Turned out four months – knee injury; Bought by Major Conduit
Another ten horses at present in training are to be auctioned after the next race meeting 1921 January
(*The Leader*, 18/12/20, p. 30)

Chapter 6 Life at Mbogani (1922–4)

* p. 80: A. C. Hoey, Denys Finch Hatton's farming partner. He was said to be the first European to reach the area and had been defeated by the altitude of 7 000 feet, wanting to find somewhere to retire more amenable to his blood pressure. In fact Denys found the land in 1910 and acquired it and they then went into partnership. Subsequently the district became known as Hoey's Bridge (today Moi's Bridge) and in 1947, when the Duke of Manchester came out on safari, he decided to make it his home, buying the original farm.

Chapter 7 Life (1924–7)

* p. 106:The best record for jockeys in the St Leger, out of 11 races, was shared by Arthur Orchardson and Mackorory, with 4 winners each, wrote Charles Disney, the racing correspondent to the *East African Standard* in 1964 – the year Beryl left Kenya for South Africa.

Chapter 8 Life as Beryl Markham (1927–9)

* p. 118: JC Carberry built the Maia Carberry Nursing Home in the shape of an aeroplane, in memory of his wife. Today the building houses the Kenya School of Law.
* p. 119: Passion fruit: *Passiflora subpetata*; flame vine: *Pyrostegia venusta*; morning glory: *Ipomoea pes-caprae*. The name *Markhamia lutea* was given to an indigenous shrub, later grown in the garden of Mansfield's mother in her Muthaiga property – today the residence of the Spanish Ambassador. In Abuluya= Lusiola. In Luo = Siala. It is likely that Mansfield introduced this shrub from the bush into decorative gardening in 1928.
* p. 130: Vivienne de Watteville, later author of *Out in the Blue* and *Speak to the Earth*.
* p. 130: Gladys Delamere was known as 'Glady' to friends. She was later elected Mayor of Nairobi, which is said to have 'provided a suitable outlet for her excess of energy'.
* p. 135: *Ehrengard*: gard zu ahd. gart= Slutz. In other words the first link and the second half of the word means to guard or take care of in the loyal sense of honour, rather than to stand to attention (Countess Lindi Kalnoky 22/2/89).

Chapter 9 Life with Denys (1929–31)

* p. 154: Today Ndege Road in Karen.

Chapter 10 Life as a Pilot (1931–2)

* p. 163: Louis Bleriot's crossing in 1909 of the English Channel, had inspired Denys, Tom and Florrie Wilson, who strapped herself to an umbrella, leaping from a wall in the face of a high wind, hoping to become airborne; Bleriot's historic feat inspired the Frenchman to paint the walls of his bedroom and ceiling blue, so as to waken each day to fair skies (Judy Lomax, *Women of the Air* p. 130, J. Murray, London 1986).

*p. 165: NB one inch on the map is 253440 on the ground e.g. $\frac{1}{253440}$.

* p. 170: Florrie Wilson is commemorated by Wilson airport, Nairobi, the busiest light aircraft aerodrome in the world. Today, during the peak period of Kenya's tourist season lasting for over half the year, there are 4,000 commercial light aircraft flight movements each month into the two airports of Wilson airport, Nairobi, and Moi airport, Mombasa (A. Molesworth, Executive Officer, Kenya Association of Air Operators, *Daily Nation* 6/3/92).

* p. 175 Carryl, Lord Waterpark.

Chapter 12 The Waterjump (1936)

* p. 209: Winifred Paul, in 1947 married Charles Disney, the celebrated sports editor of the *East African Standard*, who covered Beryl's racing career in his columns for over a decade.

Chapter 13 Life Without Direction (1936–8)

* p. 224: Jack Maxwell Trench, one of the sons of JC's partner, was the next and last to discover the Vega Gull. When he clambered onto a wing, it crumpled and 'went a bit further toward Africa' (Corresp. Jack le Poer Trench 20/3/87).

Chapter 15 Life as Beryl Schumacher (1942–9)

* p. 256: Blondie: The cartoon marked the longest running series in Hollywood history and the film version ran between 1938 and 1950, non-stop as well.

* p. 257: Rigel is considered the brightest and the bluest star in Orion's Belt in the Southern Hemisphere and the choice of name may have been inspired by the star or by Beryl's hated teacher Miss Rigel.

* p. 263: The Montecito Inn was built by Fatty Arbuckle and Charlie Chaplin and had inspired the song, 'There's a small hotel'.

* p. 268: Lady Mendl (Elsie de Wolfe) is said to have been responsible for making America 'antique conscious'. Her influence on Wallis Simpson was strong. It was Lady Mendl who popularised bee-stings as treatment for arthritis.

* p. 271: Renzo Fenci's work today appears vastly in private collection as well as the Santa Barbara Museum of Modern Art, Cedars Sinai Medical Center, Los Angeles. Fenci left Italy in 1938, aged twenty-three, entirely

due to the persuasions of Frederick Faust, alias Max Brand, the ghost writer. Rumour has it that Renzo was the model for Mussolini's Fascist Youth Movement poster; in spite of his powerful muscular conformation and carroty hair, this was a myth. However he had competed in throwing the discus and javelin in the Campionati di Atletica dei Fasci Giovanili (Young Fascists) leading the 1937 Athletes Parade into the stadium in Florence for the Annual Track Championship of Italy.

Having graduated as a Maestro D'Arte from the Royal Institute of Florence in 1934, Renzo won competitions, undertaking commissions with such promise that work had already been purchased by the Permanent Gallery of Modern Art in the Palazzo Pitti, Florence. (Corresp. Renzo Fenci 22/1/88; ints Wendy Foster, Santa Barbara 2/5/87; Peter Rand, New York, 12/5/87.)

* p. 272: Val Verde was owned in 1947 by Wright Ludington, but Dr Warren Austin is the owner now. Val Verde was the setting for *The Screaming Woman*, starring Joseph Cotten and Olivia de Havilland in 1971. Cotten's Cabin, within the grounds, comes from earlier days – when Raoul Scumacher was working on the radio plays, they held script conferences here.

Chapter 16 Life in Kenya Colony Once More (1950–64)

* p. 275: Lady Delamere, née Mary Ashley, was the sister of Edwina, wife of Lord Louis Mountbatten of Burma.

* p. 278: Mawingo: William Holden bought this eventually from the Block family and renamed it the Mount Kenya Safari Club.

* p. 285: Mrs O'Hea's old bungalow was acquired by the Spanish Embassy and is the residence of the Spanish Ambassador today.

* p. 289: Arthur Orchardson: Out of eleven Kenya St Legers, Arthur shared the honour of winning with jockey Mackorory, four with one tie (*East African Standard*, Charles Disney, 3/1/64). Arthur was an amateur or gentleman jockey, earning his living as an engineer with East African Railways and Harbours. He was always embittered that the railways had not released him to go to war. He discovered that Emma had cancer, during a holiday in Australia where she was living. He brought her back to Kenya to look after her and she died there in 1947. He married and had one son and was a devoted father. He always rode a bicycle, to keep himself fit.

* p. 290: Beryl Markham: trainer.

RACES WON	CLASSICS	HORSE
1960/61 (37)	The Champagne Stakes	Speed Trial
1961/62 (27)	The Kenya Guineas	Rio Grande
	The East African Derby	Speed Trial
1962/63 (38)	The East African Derby	Cutlass
	The Champagne Stakes	Mountie
1963/64 (46)	The Kenya Oaks	Blue Streak
	The Kenya Guineas	Fair Realm
	The East African Derby	Lone Eagle
	The Champagne Stakes	Spike
1964/65 (14)	The East African Derby	Athi
	The Kenya St Leger	Athi

(*The Bloodhorse In Africa* Robbin Higgin 19/3/86, (p. 2413.)

	RACES WON	STAKES
1958/59	8	£ 1,584
1959/60	15	£ 4,054
1960/61	37	£ 5,079
1961/62	27	£ 4,350
1962/63	38	£ 5,761
1963/64	46	£ 6,077
TOTAL	171	£26,905

* p. 291: *Seketet*. Latin name *Myrsine africana*; Kikuyu =*Mugaita*; Lumbwa =*Segetitich*; Kamasai and Marakwet = *Segetetwas*; Maasai= ol-*segetiti*. The Kikuyu esteem its ripe fruit as anthelminic. (Bruce Hobson, *Concrete Jungle* 27/8/89.)

Chapter 17 Life in South Africa (1964–70)

* p. 302: During this period Beryl's horses were frequently scratched from running; any entry she had left was so heavily handicapped, her few wins rendered profitability untenable. The last blow was when a Steward tried to get Beryl's licence revoked, only failing when the rest of the Jockey Club stood by Beryl. The issue was dropped. (Tel con. John de Villiers 24/8/86.)

Chapter 18 A Phoenix from the Ashes (1970–86)

* p. 317: Water Boy's sire, Ship's Bell, had done even less racing in England, because his knees had to be pin-fired as a youngster and he was sold for only 300 guineas, ending up in Rhodesia, where he had served Niagara. Ship's Bell, by Doutelle, bred by Queen Elizabeth II, beat Ballymoss in the Ormonde Stakes and also won the Two Thousand Guineas Trial Stakes, the Derby Trial Stakes and John Porter Stakes. Niagra's sire, was Messenger Boy.

* p. 321: Osa's, the salon named after Osa Johnson.

* p. 322: John Alexander; murdered in his home at Langata 1989.

* p. 324: Jack Couldrey: Beryl, as Mrs Jock Purves, trained Ruddygore for his father, Frank Couldrey, when she was living on Nakuru Racecourse. Frank Couldrey later became editor of the *Kenya Weekly News*.

* p. 325: In July 1985, the Jockey Club of Kenya made Beryl an Honorary Member.

* p. 335: Fleur and Valery Markham. The latter died in a road accident in 1989.

References

Chapter 1 The Birth of a Life (1902–4)

1 Int. the late Beryl Markham, September 1984, *World Without Walls* (hereafter *WWW*), t.v. documentary, prod. George Gutekunst, first broadcast KQED San Francisco, January 1986, later transmitted Public Broadcasting Service, that October.

2 Richard Haslam, 'Newark Park, Gloucestershire', *Country Life*, 3/10/ 85, p. 943. M. E. M. Mitchell and C. R. Hudleston (eds), *An Account of the Principal Branches of the Family of Clutterbuck*, privately printed, Gloucester, 1924; (donated by Dr Alastair Robb-Smith).

3 *Clutterbuck Diary*, notes by Rev. Robert Nott and T. E. Sanders, *Stroud News* Publishing Co. Ltd, 1935, p. 9, Glos. County Records.

4 Corresp. Major-General Richard Clutterbuck, 14/10/88.

5 Mitchell and Hudleston (eds), *An Account, op. cit.*

6 *Ibid.*

7 School Register, Repton, 17/7/87. Corresp. Old Reptonian Society, 30/7/88.

8 Ints the late Ginger Birkbeck, Likoni, 19/7/88; the late Cockie Hoogterp, Highclere, 1974; the late Bill Waudby, Bamburi 22/9/86.

9 *North Cumberland Reformer*, 2/7/1891, obituary, p. 6.

10 Mary Lovell, *Straight on Till Morning: The Life of Beryl Markham*, Century Hutchinson, London, 1987 (hereafter *SOTM*), p. 2.

11 *Evening Press*, York, 8/8/1878.

12 Royal Military Academy, Sandhurst, 6/7/87; corresp. G. Hughes, 20/3/87.

13 *Evening Press*, York, 8/8/1898.

14 *Ibid.*

15 *Ibid.*

16 *Ibid.*
17 Int. the late Beryl Markham, Nairobi, July 1979; int. the late Cockie Hoogterp, Newbury, 14/11/74.
18 Int. Jorgen Thrane, Loldiega Hills, 6/12/86; int. the Hon. Patricia O'Neill, Bletchington, 16/7/87.
19 Corresp. the Hon. Doreen Norman to Jack Couldrey, 2/4/84, *WWW*.
20 *Kelly's Yellow Directory*, 1904, p. 524, Leicester Museum.
21 Int. Diggy Spyratos, Malindi, 27/1/87.
22 *Melton Mowbray Mercury and Oakham and Uppingham Times*, 23/4/04.

Chapter 2 Africa (1904–6)

1 Int. the late Beryl Markham, Doria Block, Nairobi 1979.
2 *Truth* newspaper, Melbourne, 9/1/38; Int. the late Beryl Markham, Doria Block, Nairobi, 1979, *WWW*.
3 Corresp. Mary Gillett, April 1987.
4 Int. the late Beryl Markham, Doria Block, Nairobi, 1979.
5 Clutterbuck/Huxley 1932, MS Afr. S 782, Rhodes House, Oxford.
6 Corresp. Bonnie Miller, 16/1/89.
7 Corresp. Kit Taylor, 8/12/86; corresp. Bonnie Miller, 16/1/89.
8 Somerset Playne FRGS, *East Africa (British) 1908–1909, its History, People, Commerce, Industries and Resources*, The Foreign and Colonial Compiling and Publishing Company, pp. 125, 130, 340; Mary Gillett, *Tribute to Pioneers*, Appendix (1987), privately printed, Oxford, 1986
9 Ian Quiller Orchardson, *A Study of the Kipsigis*, unpublished MS, Afr. S 455, Rhodes House, Oxford.
10 Elspeth Huxley, *The Sorcerer's Apprentice*, Chatto & Windus, London, 1948, p. 326.
11 Clutterbuck Huxley, MS Afr. S 782, Rhodes House, Oxford.
12 Playne, *East Africa*, op. cit., pp. 125, 130, 340; *The Leader*, 1906.
13 *Ibid.*
14 *Ibid.*
15 Richard Meinertzhagen, *Kenya Diary 1902–1906*, Eland Books, London, 1983.
16 Corresp. Kit Taylor, 3/12/86, 21/2/87.
17 *African Standard*. 4/8/06.
18 *African Standard*. 1/9/06.
19 Ints Juanita Carberry, Likoni, 17/10/76; the late Ginger Birkbeck, Likoni, 24/10/86; the late Beryl Markham, Doria Block, Nairobi, 1979.
20 Int. the late Beryl Markham, Nairobi, 1984, *WWW*.

Chapter 3 Life as Lakwet (1906—14)

1 Fox/Markham/Schumacher data for *West with the Night*; (hereafter *WWTN*; reissued Virago, London, 1984).
2 *Ibid.*
3 Ints Olive Rodwell, Mtwapa, 1984; the late Ginger Birkbeck, Likoni, 30/11/86.
4 *The Leader*, Clutterbuck advertisements, 1905/1906; *The Standard*, 4/2/05.
5 Corresp. the late A. T. Matson; corresp. Muffet Bennett, 2/11/86, 10/1/87.
6 Unpub. diary, Lady Eileen Scott, 1919.
7 Ints the late Ginger Birkbeck, Likoni, 30/11/86; Petal Allen, Shanzu, 8/2/87.
8 *Ibid.*
9 Int. the late Beryl Markham/Francis Erskine, Doria Block, Nairobi, 1979, *WWW*.
10 Fox/Markham/Schumacher data for *WWTN*.
11 Int. W. K. Purdy, Tiwi, December 1985.
12 Fox/Markham/Schumacher data for *WWTN*.
13 *Ibid.*
14 *Ibid.*
15 *Ibid.*
16 *Ibid.*
17 *Ibid.*
18 *Ibid.*
19 Mary Gillett, *Tribute to Pioneers*, privately printed, Oxford, 1986.
20 Fox/Markham/Schumacher data for *WWTN*.
21 *Ibid.*
22 Int. the late Beryl Markham, Nairobi, *WWW*, 1984.
23 *Ibid.*
24 *Ibid.*
25 *Ibid.*
26 *Ibid.*
27 *Ibid.*
28 *Ibid.*
29 Harry Deacon, int. the late James Walker, Nairobi, 1978.
30 Fox/Markham/Schumacher data for *WWTN*.
31 *Ibid.*
32 Corresp. Muffet Bennett, 7/12/86.

33 Corresp. Janice Gott-Kane; Lidster family data 1978.
34 *Ibid.*
35 From Trzebinski, *The Kenya Pioneers*, Heinemann 1985 (hereafter *TKP*).
36 Corresp. A. Langley Morris, 12/12/87.
37 Int. the late Beryl Markham, Doria Block, Nairobi 1979.
38 Lord Cranworth, *Kenya Chronicles*, Macmillan, London, 1939.
39 Int. the late Kitch Morson, 1976; for *TKP*.
40 Elspeth Huxley/Lady Villiers, MS Afr. S 782, Rhodes House, Oxford.
41 *Ibid.*
42 *Ibid.*
43 Clutterbuck/Huxley, MS Afr. S 782 Rhodes House, Oxford.
44 Cranworth, *Kenya Chronicles, op. cit.*, p. 259.
45 Fox/Markham/Schumacher data for *WWTN*.
46 *Ibid.*
47 Eldoret, *EAWL Golden Jubilee Scrapbook*.
48 James Fox, 'African High Flyer', *Observer Colour Supplement*, 30/9/84.
49 Corresp. Mary Gillett, September 1987.
50 Int. the late Jimmy McQueen, Mtwapa, 11/9/86.
51 *Ibid.*
52 *Ibid.*
53 Int. Mary Mitford Barberton, Nairobi, 1979; *ibid.*, 17/12/81.
54 *Ibid.*
55 *Ibid.*; int. the late Jimmy McQueen, Mtwapa, 11/9/86.
56 Int. the late Beryl Markham, Doria Block, Nairobi, 1979.
57 Corresp. the late Doris Harries, 17/11/86.

Chapter 4 Lessons at Home, and in the War (1913–19)

1 Fox/Markham/Schumacher data for *WWTN*.
2 *Ibid.*
3 *Ibid.*
4 *Ibid.*
5 *Ibid.*
6 *Ibid.*
7 *The Leader*, 7/7/86.
8 Corresp. Muffet Benett, 17/12/86.
9 *Ibid.*
10 Fox/Markham/Schumacher data for *WWTN*.
11 Int. the late Beryl Markham, Nairobi, 1984, *WWW*.
12 *Ibid.*
13 Elkington EAWL Spring Valley extract; Elkington papers, University

of Nairobi, 1976. Unpub. MS by Margaret Elkington. Papers of Lady Francis Scott.

14 *Ibid.*
15 *SOTM*, p. 35.
16 *Ibid.*
17 Fox/Markham/Schumacher data for *WWTN*.
18 *Ibid.*
19 *Ibid.*
20 *Ibid.*
21 Corresp. the Hon. Doreen Norman/Jack Couldrey, 2/3/84; Barry Bendell, *Racing in Kenya* magazine, Nairobi 1973.
22 Fox/Markham/Schumacher data for *WWTN*.
23 Corresp. Muffet Bennett, 17/12/87.
24 Fox/Markham/Schumacher data for *WWTN*.
25 *Ibid.*
26 *Ibid.*
27 Corresp. David Christie-Miller, 14/4/92.
28 Fox/Markham/Schumacher data for *WWTN*.
29 Corresp. Professor Michael J. Smith, 15/4/91. Letter of Lady Girouard, 25/7/11.
30 Letter of Gwendoline Girouard, 3/3/11; corresp. Professor Michael J. Smith, 15/4/91.
31 *Ibid.*
32 Int. the late Beryl Markham, Nairobi, 1984, *WWW*; corresp. Doreen Norman/Jack Couldrey, 2/4/84; Fox/Markham/Schumacher data for *WWTN*.
33 Fox/Markham/Schumacher data for *WWTN*.
34 Beryl Markham, *West with the Night*, Virago, London, 1984, p. 99.
35 *Ibid.*, p. 100.
36 Corresp. Bonnie Miller, 26/3/87.
37 Corresp. Veronica Scott Mason, 7/12/86.
38 Corresp. Bonnie Miller, 16/1/89.
39 *Ibid.*
40 *Ibid.*
41 *Ibid.*
42 Fox/Markham/Schumacher data for *WWTN*.
43 Ian Orchardson papers, MS Afr. S 455, p. 110, Rhodes House, Oxford.
44 *Ibid.*
45 Int. the late Chris Langlands, Lewes, 25/6/87.
46 Int. Warren Austin/James Fox, London, July 1987.

47 Int. Warren Austin/James Fox, London, 7/8/88.
48 *TKP*, pp. 188, 189.
49 Corresp. Muffet Bennett, 7/12/86.
50 Int. the late Dickie Edmonson and corresp. 1976 for *TKP*.
51 Fox/Markham/Schumacher data for *WWTN*.
52 *Ibid.*
53 *Ibid.*
54 Int. the late Ginger Birkbeck, Likoni, 3/1/85.
55 *Ibid.*
56 *Ibid.*
57 Corresp. Muffet Bennett, 17/12/86.
58 *Ibid.*
59 Corresp. Kit Taylor, 17/11/86; Playne, *East Africa, op. cit.*
60 Int. Roland Sharpe, Mtwapa, 31/8/89.
61 Corresp. the late Margot Howard (née Hudson-Caine), 12/2/87; int. Peter Bramwell, Kilifi, 19/9/86.
62 Corresp. the late Doris Harries, 12/2/87.
63 Corresp. the late Margot Howard (née Hudson-Caine), 12/2/87; int. Peter Bramwell, Kilifi, 19/9/86.
64 Int. the late Mary Mitford Barberton, Nairobi, 1979; *TKP*.
65 Corresp. the late Doris Harries, 12/2/87.
66 *Ibid.*
67 Int. the late Dicky Edmondson, 1979. *TKP*.
68 Corresp. the late Margot Howard (née Hudson-Caine), 12/2/87.
69 Int. the late Sonny Bumpus, Watamu, 1979. *TKP*. *WWW*, 1984.
70 *Ibid.*
71 Int. Victoria Eyre, Chelsea, 2/6/87; int. the late Mary Mitford Barberton, Nairobi, 1979, *TKP*.
72 Int. the late Beryl Markham, James Fox, unpub. notes for 'African High Flyer', *Observer Colour Supplement*, 30/9/84.
73 Int. the late Beryl Markham, *WWW*, 1984.
74 Fox/Markham/Schumacher data for *WWTN*.
75 *Ibid.*
76 *Ibid.*
77 *Ibid.*
78 *Ibid.*
79 Corresp. the late Margot Howard (née Hudson-Caine) 12/2/87.
80 Corresp. the late Doris Harries, 17/11/86.
81 Int. Petal Allen, Shanzu, 7/2/87; corresp. Muffet Bennett, 7/12/86.
82 *The Leader*, 18/10/19; *East African Standard*, 18/10/19.

Chapter 5 Life as Beryl Purves (1919–22)

1 MS Afr. S 455, Rhodes House, Oxford, 1920.
2 Corresp. the late A. T. Matson, 7/7/87.
3 Int. the late Beryl Markham, Njoro, *WWW*, 1984.
4 James Fox; 'African High Flyer', *Observer Colour Supplement*, 30/9/84.
5 *Ibid.*; int. the late Beryl Markham, Doria Block, Nairobi, *TKP*, 1979.
6 Corresp. the late Doris Harries, 17/11/86.
7 Int. the late Ginger Birkbeck, 20/11/86, Likoni
8 Corresp. Muffet Bennett, 5/1/88.
9 Diary of Lady Francis Scott, 27/1/20.
10 *The Leader*, 23/10/20.
11 Fox/Markham/Schumacher data for *WWTN*.
12 Int. the late Beryl Markham, Doria Block, Nairobi, *TKP* 1979; int. the late James McQueen, Mtwapa, 11/7/86.
13 *The Leader*, 13/11/20.
14 *Ibid.*
15 Int. the late Rose Cartwright, Limuru, 22/3/74.
16 Int. the late Ginger Birkbeck, Likoni, 20/11/86.
17 Int. the late Beryl Markham, Njoro, *WWW*, 1984.
18 *Ibid.*
19 Corresp. Kathleen Fielden, 15/8/86, 28/8/80.
20 Int. C. J. McIlwain, Doria Block, Nairobi, 16/12/80.
21 Fox/Markham/Schumacher data for *WWTN*.
22 Corresp. Muffet Bennett, 10/1/87, 5/1/88.
23 Int. the late Ginger Birkbeck, Likoni, 4/4/74; *The Leader*, 18/12/20.
24 Int. the late Margaret Elkington, Masara, 1976.
25 Int. the late Cockie Hoogterp, Highclere, 14/10/74.
26 Corresp. the late Lady Diana Cooper, 1974.
27 Int. the late Ginger Birkbeck, Likoni, 5/3/74.
28 Int. the late Cockie Hoogterp, Highclere, 14/10/74.
29 Int. the late Ginger Birkbeck, Likoni, 14/3/74.
30 Corresp. the Hon. Doreen Norman to Jack Couldrey, 2/4/84.
31 Fox/Markham/Schumacher data for *WWTN*.
32 *Ibid.*
33 *Ibid.*
34 *Ibid.*
35 *Ibid.*
36 *East African Standard*, 10/12/21.

37 *The Standard*, 29/3/84.
38 *East African Standard*, 14/2/22.
39 Int. the late Ginger Birkbeck, Likoni, 5/2/89.
40 Obituary, Cockie Hoogterp, *Daily Telegraph*, 27/12/89.
41 Int. the late Cockie Hoogterp, Highclere, 14/10/74.
42 Fox/Markham/Schumacher data for *WWTN*.

Chapter 6 Life at Mbogani (1922—4)

1 Thomas Dinesen, *My Sister, Isak Dinesen*, trans. Joan Tate, Michael Joseph, London, 1975, p. 62.
2 Errol Trzebinski, *Silence Will Speak: The Life of Denys Finch Hatton and his Relationship with Karen Blixen*, Heinemann, London, 1977 (hereafter *SWS*), p. 215.
3 Int. the late Dermott Dempster, Nairobi, 20/5/75.
4 Tel. conv. the late Ginger Birkbeck, 6/6/88.
5 *Ibid.*
6 *Ibid.*
7 Int. Dolly Watts, Shanzu, 13/2/89.
8 Int. the late Cynthia Kofsky, Doria Block, Nairobi, 1978.
9 Fox/Markham/Schumacher data for *WWTN*.
10 *Ibid.*
11 *Ibid.*
12 *Ibid.*
13 *Ibid.*
14 *Ibid.*; *East African Journal* extracts, 1904—8; *Kenya Weekly News*, 13/ 12/54.
15 Genesta Hamilton, *A Stone's Throw*, Hutchinson, London, 1987, p. 60; ints Jeetu Patel, Bombay, 17/10/87; Nigel Spencer, Shanzu, 3/11/ 88.
16 Int. Ndungu Kigoli, Karen, 13/3/90.
17 Int. David Bowden, Secretary to the Jockey Club of Kenya, Nairobi, *WWW*, 1984.
18 *Ibid.*
19 *SWS*, p. 207.
20 Int. the late Ginger Birkbeck, Likoni, 20/11/86.
21 Int. the late Beryl Markham, Karen, 17/7/74.
22 Fox/Markham/Schumacher data for *WWTN*.
23 *Ibid.*
24 Int. the late Beryl Markham, Karen, 17/7/74.
25 Int. the late Cockie Hoogterp, Highclere, 14/10/74.

26 Fox/Markham/Schumacher data for *WWTN*.
27 Genesta Hamilton, *A Stone's Throw*, op. cit., p. 60.
28 Fox/Markham/Schumacher data for *WWTN*.
29 *Ibid.*
30 Elspeth Huxley, *White Man's Country*, Chatto & Windus, London, 1935, vol. 2, p. 132.
31 Judith Thurman, *Isak Dinesen: The Life of a Storyteller*, St Martin's Press, New York, 1982; Karen Blixen, *Out of Africa*, Jonathan Cape, London, 1964.
32 Extracts from the diary of Lady Eileen Scott, 1919–37; Lord Francis Scott, *Pioneers and Politics*, unpublished MS.
33 *Ibid.*
34 *Ibid.*
35 *Ibid.*
36 *Ibid.*
37 Tel. conv. Lady Maureen Fellowes, 30/6/87.
38 Ints the late Ginger Birkbeck, Likoni, 11/3/74, 21/3/74.
39 Tel. conv. Sir Osmond Williams, 21/1/92.
40 *SWS*, p. 211.
41 *SOTM*, p. 54.
42 Letter from Karen Blixen to her mother, Ingeborg Blixen, 29/4/32, *SOTM*, p. 53.
43 *Ibid.*
44 Int. Jorgen Thrane, Kamwaki Farm, 23/9/87.
45 Int. the late Beryl Markham, Karen, 17/7/74.
46 Tel. conv. the late Ginger Birkbeck, 6/6/88.
47 Int. the late Rose Cartwright, Limuru, 22/3/74.
48 *SOTM*, p. 54.
49 *Ibid.*
50 Corresp. Bonnie Miller, 16/3/87.
51 Corresp. Gillian Hughes, researcher, 28/8/87.
52 Isak Dinesen, *Letters from Africa 1914–1931*, Weidenfeld, London, 1981. ch. 8 nn. 19, 27, 29, 62, 74, 77, 80, 98, ch. 9 nn. 31, 43, 48.
53 Walt Whitman, 'Song of Myself 32', *Leaves of Grass*, introd. Gay Wilson Allen, New American Library, New York, 1955, pp. 73–4.
54 Int. the late Beryl Markham, Karen, 17/7/74.
55 *Ibid.*
56 *Ibid.*
57 *Ibid.*
58 *Ibid.*

59 *Ibid.*
60 *Ibid.*
61 *Ibid.*
62 Int. the late Cockie Hoogterp, Highclere, 14/10/74; int. the late Rose Cartwright, Limuru, 22/3/74.
63 Isak Dinesen, *Letters from Africa, op. cit.*, p. 414; int. the late Beryl Markham, Karen, 17/7/74.
64 *Ibid.*
65 *Ibid.; SWS.* p. 179
66 Corresp. the Hon. Doreen Norman, 3/12/87.
67 Isak Dinesen, *Letters from Africa, op. cit.*, pp. 170, 171.
68 Int. the late Cockie Hoogterp, Highclere, 14/10/74.
69 Int. the late Lady Eleanor Cole, Kekopey, 20/2/75.
70 Int. the late Dermott Dempster, Nairobi, 20/5/75.
71 Ints the late Lady Eleanor Cole, Kekopey, 20/2/75; the late Dermott Dempster, Nairobi, 20/5/75; the late Will Powys, Timau, 1976.
72 Int. the late Ginger Birkbeck, Mombasa Hospital, 16/5/87.
73 Int. the late Beryl Markham, Doria Block, Nairobi, 1977.
74 *SOTM,* p. 55; Karen Blixen to her mother, 29/12/23, Isak Dinesen, *Letters from Africa, op. cit.*
75 Int. the late Bill Waudby, Bamburi, 22/9/86.
76 Int. the late Rose Cartwright, Limuru, 26/3/74.
77 Karen Blixen to her mother, 21/1/24, *SOTM,* p. 57.

Chapter 7 Life (1924–7)

1 *SOTM,* p. 57; int. the late Cockie Hoogterp, Highclere, 14/10/74.
2 *Ibid.*
3 *Ibid.*
4 *SOTM,* p. 57.
5 Tel. conv. the late Hilary Hook, 28/5/87.
6 Int. the late Cockie Hoogterp, Highclere, 14/10/74.
7 *Ibid.*
8 *Daily Mail,* report on Starkie's suicide, 6/10/37.
9 Int. the late Cockie Hoogterp, Highclere, 14/10/74; *Daily Mail,* coverage of Starkie's death, 6/10/37.
10 Int. the late Cockie Hoogterp, Highclere, 14/10/74; General Medical Council Report, and minutes relating to D. Richard William Stakie 23/5/22.
11 Corresp. Cara Buxton to Desmond Buxton, May 1924.
12 *SWS,* p. 206.

13 Int. the late Cockie Hoogterp, Highclere, 14/10/74; corresp. Elspeth Huxley, 1/8/87; ints the late Ginger Birkbeck, Likoni, 11/3/74, 23/3/74.
14 *SOTM*, p. 58.
15 Int. the late Dr Gregory, Nairobi, 17/2/75.
16 *SOTM*, pp. 61, 62.
17 Mary Gillett, *Tribute to Pioneers*, privately printed, Oxford, 1986, Appendix 1987.
18 Int. the late Bill Waudby, Bamburi, 22/9/86; corresp. Doreen Norman to Jack Couldrey, 2/4/84.
19 Corresp. Cara Buxton to Desmond Buxton, Lumbwa, 1924.
20 Corresp. Molly Ryan, 5/4/88; Molly Ryan, *Over My Shoulder*, Grange Press, Dublin, 1987, p. 22; Wedgewood corresp. 1988.
21 Corresp. Doreen Tryon 30/12/86.
22 Fox/Markham/Schumacher data for *WWTN*.
23 *Ibid*.
24 Hjalmar Frisell, *Sju Aritalt-Bland Vita och Svarta*, Lars Hockerbergs, Stockholm, 1937, p. 285, provided and translated by Tonni Arnold.
25 Judith Thurman, *Isak Dinesen: The Life of a Storyteller, op. cit.*, p. 208.
26 Fox/Markham/Schumacher data for *WWTN*.
27 *Ibid*.
28 Corresp. the Jockey Club of Kenya, 15/1/88.
29 Int. the late Sonny Bumpus, James Fox for 'African High Flyer', *Observer*, 1984.
30 *East African Standard*, 7/8/26.
31 Int. the late Sonny Bumpus, James Fox, *op. cit.*; *WWW* 1984.
32 *East African Standard*, 15/1/27.
33 M. F. Hill, 'Beryl Markham', *Kenya Weekly News*, July/August 1964.
34 Int. Joan Bagehot, Shanzu, 9/11/86.
35 Tel. conv. the late Ginger Birkbeck, 30/12/86.
36 *East African Standard*, 19/3/27.
37 Tel. conv. the late Ginger Birkbeck, 30/12/86.
38 *Ibid*.
39 Int. the late Sonny Bumpus, *WWW*, 1984.
40 Ints Jorgen Thrane, Kamwaki Farm, 1987–8.
41 Tel. conv. the late Ginger Birkbeck, 6/6/88; int. G. F. Webb, 5/12/77.
42 *Ibid*.
43 Corresp. Annabel Maule, 21/4/92.
44 Corresp. Sir Charles Markham, 3rd Bt, 16/9/86.
45 Tel. conv. Michael Markham, 23/10/90.
46 Corresp. Sir Charles Markham, 3rd Bt, 8/10/87.

47 *Ibid.*, 16/9/86.
48 Int. the late Ginger Birkbeck, Likoni, 12/11/86.
49 James Fox, *White Mischief*, Jonathan Cape, London, 1982, p. 49.
50 Int. the late Ginger Birkbeck, Likoni, 12/11/86.
51 *Ibid.*
52 *Ibid.*
53 *SOTM*, p. 72.
54 *Ibid.*, pp. 69, 70.
55 *SWS*, p. 230.
56 *SOTM*, p. 72.
57 *East African Standard*, 3/9/27.
58 *SOTM*, p. 70.
59 *East African Standard*, photograph, 27/8/27.
60 Karen Blixen to her mother, 28/8/27, *SOTM*, p. 70.
61 *SOTM*, p. 72.
62 *Ibid.*, Karen Blixen to her mother, 9/9/27.
63 *Ibid.*, p. 73.
64 *Ibid.*, pp. 72, 73.
65 Fox/Markham/Schumacher data for *WWTN*.

Chapter 8 Life as Beryl Markham (1927–9)

 1 Corresp. Christian de Pange, 27/11/91; Louis Vuitton Archive, 27/8/27.
 2 Int. the late Cockie Hoogterp, Highclere, 14/10/74.
 3 Fox/Markham/Schumacher data for *WWTN*.
 4 *Ibid.*
 5 *Ibid.*
 6 *Ibid.*
 7 *Ibid.*
 8 *Ibid.*
 9 Int. the late Sonny Bumpus, Watamu, *WWW*, 1984.
10 Fox/Markham/Schumacher data for *WWTN*.
11 *Ibid.*
12 Int. the late Captain H. W. C. 'Jimmy' Algar, Ringwood, 1977.
13 Int. Elizabeth Arden, 'The Beauty Queens' ITV documentary, 4/1/89.
14 Corresp. Annabel Maule, 11/3/92.
15 Fox/Markham/Schumacher data for *WWTN*.
16 Int. Sir Charles Markham, 3rd Bt, Nairobi, *WWW*, 1984.
17 Int. the late Ginger Birkbeck, Likoni, 12/11/86.
18 Karen Blixen to her mother, 18/3/28, *SOTM*, p. 74.

19 Isak Dinesen, *Letters from Africa 1914–1931*, University of Chicago Press, Chicago, 1991, p. 352, Karen Blixen to her mother, 18/3/28.
20 Ints the late Ginger Birkbeck, 1974–88.
21 Olga Pelensky, *Isak Dinesen: The Life and Imagination of a Seducer*, Ohio University Press, Athens, Ohio, 1991, p. 125.
22 *SWS*, p. 217.
23 Ints the late Ingrid Lindstrom, 26/3/74; the late Cockie Hoogterp, the late Rose Cartwright, and the late Ginger Birkbeck, 1974–86.
24 Fox/Markham/Schumacher data for *WWTN*.
25 Tel. conv. the late Ginger Birkbeck, 6/6/88.
26 Int. Sir Charles Markham, 3rd Bt, *WWW*, 1984.
27 Isak Dinesen, *Letters from Africa, op. cit.*, p. 361, Karen Blixen to her mother, 20/5/28.
28 *SOTM*, p. 78, Karen Blixen to her mother, 27/7/28.
29 Isak Dinesen, *Letters from Africa, op. cit.*, p. 381.
30 *Ibid.*; int. the late Ingrid Lindstrom, 26/3/74.
31 *Ibid.*; *SWS*, pp. 302, 303; Judith Thurman, *Isak Dinesen: The Life of a Storyteller*, St Martin's Press, New York, 1982, p. 232.
32 Int. the late Ginger Birkbeck, Likoni, 20/11/86; *ibid.*, Mombasa Hospital, 17/5/89.
33 *Sport and Travel in East Africa, an Account of Two Visits, 1928 and 1930, compiled from the private diaries of HRH the Prince of Wales* by Patrick Chalmers, Dutton & Co., New York, n. d., pp. 27, 31.
34 Philip Ziegler, *Edward VIII: The Official Biography*, Collins, London, 1990, p. 190.
35 *Ibid.* p. 112.
36 Int. the late Ginger Birkbeck, Mombasa Hospital, 17/5/89.
37 Int. Sir Charles Markham, 3rd Bt, *WWW*, 1984.
38 The late Sir Derek Erskine, unpublished memoir.
39 Elspeth Huxley, *Out in the Midday Sun: My Kenya*, Chatto & Windus, London, 1985, p. 46.
40 Int. the late Ginger Birkbeck, Mombasa Hospital, 17/5/89.
41 Int. Bunny Allen, Lamu, *WWW*, 1984.
42 Ziegler, *Edward VIII, op. cit.*, p. 190; int. the late Beryl Markham, *WWW*, 1984.
43 Ziegler, *Edward VIII*, op. cit., pp. 222, 316.
44 The late Sir Derek Erskine, unpublished memoir, p. 49.
45 Int. Bunny Allen, Lamu, *WWW*, 1984.
46 Int. Steve Miller, Likoni, 4/2/87.
47 *Ibid.*
48 Int. Bunny Allen, Lamu, *WWW*, 1984.

49 Int. Steve Miller, Likoni, 4/2/87.
50 Int. John Carter, Nairobi, 13/3/90.
51 Int. the late Jacko Heath, Mtwapa, 27/2/74; int. the late Gertrude Alexander, York, 9/11/78.
52 *Ibid.*
53 Int. the late Beryl Markham, *WWW*, 1984.
54 Corresp. Bunny Allen, 20/4/89.
55 The late Sir Derek Erskine, unpublished memoir; int. Bunny Allen, *WWW* 1984.
56 Int. Bunny Allen, Lamu, *WWW*, 1984.
57 Noble Frankland, *Prince Henry, Duke of Gloucester*, Weidenfeld & Nicolson, London, 1980, p. 118.
58 Int. Bunny Allen, Lamu, *WWW*, 1984.
59 By kind permission of William Kilpatrick Purdy.
60 Tel. conv. the late Ginger Birkbeck, 20/1/86.
61 Corresp. Bunny Allen, 20/4/89.
62 Isak Dinesen, *Letters from Africa, op. cit.*, p. 384, Karen Blixen to her mother; Judith Thurman, *Isak Dinesen, op. cit.*, p. 234.
63 *Ibid.*
64 *Ibid.*
65 *Sport and Travel, op. cit.*, p. 89.
66 Int. Hilda Tofte, Bamburi, 14/8/86.
67 Duff Hart Davis (ed.), *In Royal Service: The Letters and Journals of Sir Alan Lascelles 1920–1936*, Hamish Hamilton, London, 1989, p. 97.
68 Int. Hilda Tofte, Bamburi, 14/8/86.
69 Int. the late Ginger Birkbeck, Mombasa Hospital, 16/5/89.
70 *Ibid.*
71 *Ibid.*
72 *In Royal Service, op. cit.*, p. 101.
73 *Ibid.*
74 Isak Dinesen, *Letters from Africa*, op. cit., pp. 385–6.
75 *Ibid.*
76 *Sport and Travel, op. cit.*, p. 78
77 Isak Dinesen, *Letters from Africa, op. cit.*, pp. 286–7, Karen Blixen to her mother, 11/11/28.
78 The late Sir Derek Erskine, unpublished memoir; int. the late Cockie Hoogterp, Highclere, 27/4/74.
79 *Ibid.*
80 Isak Dinesen, *Letters from Africa, op. cit.*, pp. 387–8.
81 Int. the late Ginger Birkbeck, Mombasa Hospital, 17/5/89.
82 *SWS*, p. 264.

83 *In Royal Service, op. cit.*, p. 109.
84 *Ibid.*
85 *Ibid.*
86 *Ibid.*
87 *Ibid.*, pp. 111–12; A. V. Croom, *Edward the Eighth Our King*, Allied Newspapers, London, 1936.
88 Ints the late Ginger Birkbeck, Likoni, 10/11/86, Mombasa Hospital, 17/5/89.
89 *Ibid.*
90 *Ibid.*; int. Mr Meakin, the Grosvenor Hotel, 15/8/88.
91 Int. the late Ginger Birkbeck, Likoni, 20/11/86, tel. conv. 30/12/86.
92 Ints the late Ginger Birkbeck, Likoni, 20/11/86, Mombasa Hospital, 17/5/89.
93 Fox/Markham/Schumacher data for *WWTN*.
94 *SOTM*, p. 83.
95 Int. the late Ginger Birkbeck, Likoni, 20/11/86.
96 Corresp. Sir Charles Markham, 3rd Bt; int. Professor George Fegan, Lamu, 21/8/87; int. the late Ginger Birkbeck, Likoni, 20/11/86.
97 Int. Professor George Fegan, Lamu, 28/8/87.
98 Isak Dinesen, *Letters from Africa*, op. cit., p. 379.
99 David Creaton, *Winds of Change*, Allen & Unwin, London, 1960; Fox/Markham/Schumacher data for *WWTN*.
100 Int. the late Ginger Birkbeck, Likoni, 20/11/86.
101 *SOTM*, p. 84, Karen Blixen to her mother, 17/3/29.
102 Isak Dinesen, *Ehrengard*, Michael Joseph, London, 1963, p. 36.
103 Ints the late Ginger Birkbeck, the late Cockie Hoogterp; int. the late Chris Langlands, Lewes, 25/6/86.
104 Frankland, *Prince Henry, Duke of Gloucester, op. cit.*, p. 86.
105 Corresp. Hugh Barclay, 31/8/86.
106 Obituary, Duke of Gloucester, *The Times*, 11/6/74.
107 *SOTM*, p. 129.
108 Corresp. Sir Charles Markham, 3rd Bt, 23/3/84.
109 Int. Sir Charles Markham, 3rd Bt, *WWW*, 1984.
110 Corresp. Lord Chamberlain's Office, St James's Palace, 12/8/87.
111 Int. the late Ginger Birkbeck, Likoni, 20/11/86.
112 Corresp. Lord Chamberlain's Office, St James's Palace, 12/8/87.
113 James Fox, 'African High Flyer',*Observer Colour Supplement*, 30/9/84.
114 *SOTM*, p. 88.
115 Corresp. Sir Charles Markham, 3rd Bt, 27/8/90.
116 *SOTM*, pp. 90, 91.

117 *Ibid.*

Chapter 9 Life with Denys (1929–31)

1 Ints the late Jacko Heath, Mtwapa, 8/2/74, 27/2/74.
2 *Ibid.*
3 *Ibid.*
4 Philip Ziegler, *Edward VIII: The Official Biography*, Collins, London, 1990, p. 248.
5 Int. the late Cockie Hoogterp, Highclere, 14/10/74.
6 Int. the late Beryl Markham, Nairobi, *WWW*, 1984.
7 *SWS*, p. 120.
8 Corresp. the late Lady Diana Cooper, 1975.
9 Int. the late Beryl Markham, *From an Immigrant's Notebook*, Arena, BBC1, 3/9/84.
10 *The Times*, 1/10/29, 20/11/29; Finch Hatton papers 1928–9 (Trzebinski collection); *The Times*, 26/6/29; Denys Finch Hatton, 'Stalking Game with a Camera', *The Times*, 20/7/29, 23/7/29, 27/7/29; *Daily Mirror*, 25/8/29; *The Field*, 30/4/29.
11 Ints the late Cockie Hoogterp, Malmesbury, 7/3/80, Highclere, 14/10/75.
12 Int. the late Ginger Birkbeck, Mombasa Hospital, 17/5/89.
13 Ints the late Rose Cartwright, *From an Immigrant's Notebook, op. cit.*, Limuru, 22/3/74.
14 Int. the late Ginger Birkbeck, Likoni, 20/11/86.
15 *SWS*, p. 284.
16 *Ibid.*, pp. 279, 280.
17 Tel. conv. Sir Osmond Williams, 2/5/92.
18 *SWS*, pp. 296, 297.
19 Int. the late Ginger Birkbeck, Mombasa Hospital, 17/5/89.
20 *SWS*, pp. 296, 297.
21 Int. the late Ginger Birkbeck, Likoni, 20/11/86.
22 *Sport and Travel in East Africa, an Account of Two Visits, 1928 and 1930, compiled from the private diaries of HRH the Prince of Wales* by Patrick Chalmers, Dutton, New York, n.d., p. 169.
23 *SWS*, p. 295.
24 *Ibid.*
25 Int. the late Jacko Heath, Mtwapa, 22/2/74; int. Peter Bramwell, Takaungu, 27/5/89; int. Bunny Allen, Lamu, *WWW*, 1984.
26 *Ibid.*
27 Denys Finch Hatton, 'Stalking Game with a Camera: The New African "Sport"', *The Times*, 29/6/29.

28 Int. Peter Bramwell, Takaungu, 27/5/89.
29 *Ibid.*
30 Int. Penelope Birkbeck, Mombasa Hospital, 17/5/89.
31 Karen Blixen to her mother, 2/3/30, Isak Dinesen, *Letters from Africa 1914–1931, op. cit.* pp. 401, 402.
32 Ziegler, *Edward VIII, op. cit.*, p. 197.
33 Int. the late Cockie Hoogterp, Highclere, 14/10/74.
34 Letter from the Prince of Wales to Denys Finch Hatton, 13/11/29.
35 Ints the late Ginger Birkbeck, Mombasa Hospital, 17/5/89; the late Jacko Heath, Mtwapa, 27/2/74.
36 Film clip from the Royal Archive, Windsor, *An Immigrant's Notebook, op. cit.; SWS*, p. 290.
37 Barbara Goldsmith, *Little Gloria, Happy at Last*, Macmillan, London, 1980, p. 163.
38 H. W., *Something New Out of Africa*, Pitman, London, 1933, p. 33. *Sport and Travel, op. cit.*, p. 202; Gloria Vanderbilt and Thelma, Lady Furness, *Double Exposure*, Frederick Muker, USA, 1959, pp. 261, 263.
39 *SOTM*, pp. 92, 93, Karen Blixen to her mother, 30/4/30.
40 Int. the late Chris Langlands, Lewes, 25/6/87.
41 Int. the late Ginger Birkbeck, Mombasa, 17/5/89.
42 Int. the late Chris Langlands, Lewes, 25/6/87.
43 *Karen Blixen: Letters from Africa, op. cit.*, p. 407.
44 *SWS*, p. 297.
45 Int. the late Ginger Birkbeck, Mombasa Hospital, 20/11/86.
46 *Ibid.*
47 Corresp. Capt. Hugh Barclay, 31/8/86.
48 *Karen Blixen: Letters from Africa, op. cit.*, p. 411.
49 Int. the late Beryl Markham, Karen, 17/7/74.
50 Karen Blixen, *Out of Africa*, Jonathan Cape, London, 1937, p. 373.
51 Int. the late Beryl Markham, Karen, 17/7/74.
52 Olga Pelensky, *Isak Dinesen: the Life and Imagination of a Seducer*, Ohio University Press, Athens, Ohio, 1991, p. 128.
53 Judith Thurman, *Isak Dinesen: The Life of a Storyteller*, St Martin's Press, New York, 1982, p. 246; *SWS*, p. 352.
54 Int. the late Dr Gregory, Nairobi, 17/2/75; *SWS*, p. 303.
55 Ints the late Cockie Hoogterp, Highclere, 15/10/75; the late Bill Waudby, Bamburi, 22/9/86; The late Ginger Birkbeck, Likoni, 20/11/86.
56 Int. Vicky Nancarrow, Nairobi, 1977.
57 Int. the late Beryl Markham, Karen, 3/9/84.
58 *Ibid.*

59 *Ibid.*
60 Judith Thurman, *Isak Dinesen, op. cit.*, p. 245; int. the late Beryl Markham, *An Immigrant's Notebook, op. cit.*, sound roll no. 3.
61 Denys Finch Hatton to Michael Williams, May 1931.
62 Int. the late Beryl Markham, *An Immigrant's Notebook, op. cit.*
63 *SWS*, p. 303.
64 Int. the late Joan Waddington, Nyeri, 20/5/75.
65 *Ibid.*; int. the late Jacko Heath, Mtwapa, 27/2/74.
66 Fox/Markham/Schumacher data for *WWTN*.
67 *Ibid.*; Florence Desmond, *By Herself*, Harrap, London, 1953.
68 Fox/Markham/Schumacher data for *WWTN*.
69 Int. the late Ginger Birkbeck, Mombasa Hospital, 17/5/89.
70 *SWS*, p. 310.
71 Corresp. John Cole, 8/5/86.
72 Int. the late Beryl Markham, Karen, 17/7/74.
73 Corresp. David Laws, Civil Aviation Authority, 1987.
74 Int. the late Beryl Markham, Karen, 17/7/74.
75 *Ibid.*
76 *Ibid.*
77 *Ibid.*
78 *Ibid.*
79 *Ibid.*
80 *The Times*, 16/5/31; *WWTN*, p. 193.

Chapter 10 Life as a Pilot (1931–2)

1 Fox/Markham/Schumacher data for *WWTN*.
2 *Ibid.*
3 *Ibid.*
4 Obituary, Tom Campbell Black, *Daily Mail*, 21/9/36.
5 Int. The late Ginger Birkbeck, Likoni, 5/3/74.
6 Corresp. Sir Charles Markham, 3rd Bt, 27/8/90.
7 Int. the late Ginger Birkbeck, Likoni, 5/3/74.
8 *Women of the Air*, p. 130. Judy Lomax, J. Murray, London 1986.
9 Fox/Markham/Schumacher data for *WWTN*.
10 *Ibid.*
11 *Ibid.*
12 *Ibid.*
13 *Ibid.*
14 *Ibid.*
15 *Ibid.*

16 *Ibid.*
17 *Ibid.*
18 *Ibid.*
19 *Ibid.*
20 Corresp. Christian de Pange, 4/9/91.
21 Corresp. the Hon. Robin Finch Hatton, 27/4/90.
22 Fox/Markham/Schumacher data for *WWTN*.
23 *Ibid.*
24 H. W., *Something New Out of Africa*, Pitman, London, 1933, p. 121.
25 Fox/Markham/Schumacher data for *WWTN*.
26 *Ibid.*
27 Hugo Dunkerly, 'Aviation in East Africa', *East African Annual 1930–31*, p. 47.
28 Fox/Markham/Schumacher data for *WWTN*.
29 *Ibid.*
30 Corresp. Sir Charles Markham, 3rd Bt, 27/8/90.
31 James Fox, *White Mischief*, Penguin, London, 1987, p. 103.
32 Ints the late Cynthia Kofsky, Nairobi, 1974; Jacko Heath, Mtwapa, 8/2/74, 27/2/74.
33 Genesta Hamilton, *A Stone's Throw*, Hutchinson, London, 1987, p. 103.
34 Dominic Dunne, 'Memento Mori', *Vanity Fair*, March 1991.
35 Lin Sampson, 'Bright Mischief', *Style*, December/January 1989.
36 *Ibid.*
37 Fox/Markham/Schumacher data for *WWTN*.
38 *Ibid.*
39 *SOTM*, p. 125.
40 *Daily Sketch*, May 1932; *East African Standard*, May 1932. See p. xvi. Cape-Cairo route.
41 *Daily Express*, 17/5/32.
42 *Ibid.*
43 Fox/Markham/Schumacher data for *WWTN*.
44 Int. Group Captain Christopher Clarkson, 13/11/86; G. D. Fleming, *Blue is the Sky*, William Earl, London, 1945.
45 Fox/Markham/Schumacher data for *WWTN*.
46 Ints the late Cockie Hoogterp, Highclere 14/10/74; the late Ginger Birkbeck, Likoni, 12/11/86.
47 *The Field*, 2/11/35.
48 Corresp. Humphrey Cottrill, 1/6/87.
49 *Ibid.*
50 Corresp. the Hon. Patricia O'Neill, 6/9/86.

51 *Ibid.*
52 Ints the late Rose Cartwright, Limuru, 1/3/74, 4/11/79.
53 *Ibid.*; Ronald Seth, *Sir Archibald McIndoe*, Cassell, London, 1942; tel. conv. the late Sir Michael Wood, Nairobi, 1979.
54 Corresp. the Hon. Patricia O'Neill, 12/12/87.
55 Corresp. Doreen Tryon 13/12/86.
56 Corresp. Royston Powell, 7/6/89.
57 Int. Sylvia Richardson, Kilifi, 13/10/86; corresp. the late Dan Trench, 10/6/88.
58 *SOTM*, p. 128.
59 Int. Sylvia Richardson, Kilifi, 13/10/86.

Chapter 11 An Ocean Flyer in Embryo (1932–5)

1 Int. Sylvia Richardson, Kiganjo, 3/10/87.
2 Corresp. Jeremy Langlands, 30/5/87.
3 Int. Sylvia Richardson, Kilifi, 13/10/87.
4 James Fox, *White Mischief*, Penguin, London, 1984, p. 68.
5 Corresp. Sylvia Richardson, 28/3/90.
6 Corresp. Royston Powell, 7/6/89.
7 Fox, *White Mischief, op. cit.*, p. 67.
8 Int. Juanita Carberry, Mombasa, 1989.
9 Corresp. Wing Commander 'Flip' Fleming, 31/12/89.
10 Int. Maddie de Mott, Nairobi, 27/9/87.
11 Wendy Boase, *The Sky's the Limit – Women Pioneers in Aviation: The Women's Decade*, Osprey, London, 1879, p. 130.
12 Corresp. Jeremy Langlands, 30/5/87.
13 Int. the late Chris Langlands, Lewes, 25/6/86.
14 Int. Sylvia Richardson, Kilifi, 13/10/87.
15 *Ibid.*
16 Int. the late Chris Langlands, Lewes, 25/6/86.
17 Int. Sylvia Richardson, Kilifi, 13/10/87.
18 Fox/Markham/Schumacher data for *WWTN*; int. Jorgen Thrane, Kamwaki Farm, 6/12/86.
19 Corresp. Royston Powell, 7/6/89; int. the late Chris Langlands, Lewes, 25/6/86.
20 Int. Jack Trench, *WWW*, 1984.
21 *Daily Express*, 18/9/36.
22 *Mombasa Times*, 19/9/33.
23 Int. the late Chris Langlands, Lewes, 25/6/86.
24 Corresp. Jane Stanton, 24/8/89.

25 Int. Sylvia Richardson, Kiganjo, 3/12/86.
26 *Ibid.*
27 *Ibid.*
28 Corresp. the late Dan Trench, 10/6/88.
29 Int. Sylvia Richardson, Kilifi, 13/10/86.
30 Ints Jorgen Thrane, Sylvia Richardson, the late Ginger Birkbeck, Warren Austin.
31 Int. the late Chris Langlands, Lewes, 25/6/86.
32 *Ibid.*
33 *Ibid.*
34 *Ibid.*
35 Int. the Hon. Patricia O'Neill, Bletchington, 16/7/87.
36 Int. the late Chris Langlands, Lewes, 25/6/86.
37 Corresp. Group Captain Christopher Clarkson, 13/11/86.
38 Int. the late Chris Langlands, Lewes, 25/6/86.
39 Corresp. Wing Commander 'Flip' Fleming, 13/12/86; letters of Arnold Paice, 4/2/26.
40 *Ibid.*
41 James Fox, 'African High Flyer', *Observer Colour Supplement*, 30/9/84.
42 Corresp. Royston Powell, 30/6/89.
43 James Fox, 'African High Flyer', *Observer Colour Supplement*, 30/9/84.
44 Int. Maddie de Mott, Nairobi, 27/9/87.
45 James Fox, 'African High Flyer', *Observer Colour Supplement*, 30/9/84.
46 Corresp. Royston Powell, 7/6/86.
47 Int. the late Chris Langlands, Lewes, 25/6/86.
48 Int. the late Rose Cartwright, Limuru, 1979.
49 *Ibid.*
50 Letter from Tom Campbell Black to Beryl Markham, 23/3/34; Fox/Markham/Schumacher data for *WWTN*.
51 *Ibid.*
52 Int. Jack Trench, Nairobi, *WWW*, 1984; *Aero Club of East Africa 1927–1977: Golden Jubilee Commemorative Review*.
53 *Daily Express*, 19/8/36.
54 Int. the late Sir Malin Sorsbie, Claridge's, 17/7/86; log-book entry, the late Captain Malin Sorsbie, 20/4/34; corresp. and int. Lady Sorsbie, August 1986; int. the late Chris Langlands, Lewes, 25/6/86.
55 *Ibid.*
56 *Ibid.*
57 Int. the late Beryl Markham, Nairobi, *WWW*, 1984.
58 *Evening Standard*, 9/12/33.
59 E. H. to Charles Scribner, *Ernest Hemingway: Selected Letters*, ed. Carlos Baker, Scribner, New York, 1981, p. 665.

60 Int. the late Beryl Markham, Karen, 17/7/74.
61 E. H. to Maxwell Perkins, 27/8/42, *Ernest Hemingway: Selected Letters*, ed. Carlos Baker, Panther, London, 1985, p. 541.
62 *Bror Blixen: The African Letters*, ed. and introd. G. F. V. Kleen, St Martin's Press, New York, 1988, p. 157.
63 *Ibid.*
64 Int. the late Beryl Markham, Karen, 17/7/74.
65 Int. Bunny Allen, Lamu, *WWW*, 1984; Bunny Allen, *The First Wheel*, p. 66, privately printed USA 1985.
66 Int. the late Beryl Markham, Karen, 17/7/74.
67 Int. the late Chris Langlands, Lewes, 25/6/86.
68 *Ibid.*
69 Jan Hemsing, *Ker & Downey Safaris: The Inside Story*, Seapoint Publicity, Nairobi, 1989, p. 116
70 Corresp. Diana Guest Manning, 10/4/87.
71 Int. Roland Sharpe, Mtwapa, 31/8/87.
72 Int. Veronica Scott Mason, 27/12/86.
73 *Ibid.*
74 Int. the late Rose Cartwright, Limuru, 14/11/85.
75 Int. Mickey Migdoll, Malindi, 1/9/86.
76 Int. Robin Long, Kalifi, 31/7/90
77 *East African Standard*, 27/10/34.
78 *SOTM*, p. 195
79 Int. the Hon. Patricia O'Neil, Bletchington, 16/7/87.
80 *SOTM*, p. 171
81 Corresp. Royston Powell, 30/6/86; *Daily Express*, 18/8/36.
82 *SOTM*, p. 151.
83 Corresp. Wing Commander 'Flip' Fleming, 2/5/86.
84 G. D. Fleming, *Blue is the Sky*, William Earl & Co, London, 1946, p. 189.
85 *WWTN*, p. 12.
86 *SWS*, p. 211.
87 Bror von Blixen, *The Africa Letters [Brev fran Afrika]* Sweden, 1942, p. 189.
88 Int. the late Jimmy Algar, Ringwood, 1977.
89 *The Africa Letters op. cit.*, pp. 237, 238.
90 *Ibid.*

Chapter 12 The Waterjump (1936)

1 David Beaty, *The Waterjump: The Story of Transatlantic Flight*, Secker & Warburg, London, 1976, pp. 74–5; corresp. Betty Beaty, 8/7/86; tel. conv. Betty Beaty, 14/7/86.
2 *Ibid.*
3 James Fox, 'African High Flyer', *Observer Colour Supplement*, 30/9/84.
4 Corresp. Sir Charles Markham, 3rd Bt, 27/8/90; corresp. Patrick Hemingway, 13/1/87; int. the late Ginger Birkbeck, Mombasa Hospital, 17/5/87.
5 Duchess of Windsor, *The Heart Has its Reasons*, Michael Joseph, London, 1969, p. 239.
6 Ints the late Ginger Birkbeck, Likoni, 1974–9; int. the late Cockie Hoogterp, Highclere, 14/10/74.
7 *Ibid.*
8 James Fox, 'African High Flyer', *Observer Colour Supplement*, 30/9/84; Raleigh Gilbert, 'Beryl Markham, the Unorthodox', *Sunday Post*, 15/5/60.
9 Florence Desmond, *By Herself*, Harrap, London, 1953, p. 107.
10 *Ibid.*
11 Corresp. Sir Peter Masefield, 9/12/88.
12 Corresp. Group Captain Christopher Clarkson, 29/1/87; corresp. Lord Carbery, 11/2/88.
13 Beaty, *The Waterjump*, *op. cit.*, p. 74; corresp. Royston Powell, 28/3/87.
14 *Daily Express*, 18/8/36.
15 *Daily Express*, 19/8/36.
16 Corresp. Sir Charles Markham, 3rd Bt, 23/9/87, 27/8/90.
17 *Ibid.*
18 Corresp. Annabel Maule, 11/3/92.
19 Int. the late Beryl Markham BBC1 *Arena*, Hemingway documentary, 1984.
20 Int. the late Beryl Markham, Karen, 17/7/74; corresp. Doreen Norman to Jack Couldrey, 2/4/84, *WWW*.
21 Georgina Howell, *In Vogue: Sixty Years of Celebrities and Fashion from British Vogue*, Allen Lane, London, 1975.
22 Int. the Hon. Patricia O'Neill, Bletchington, 16/7/87; ints Jorgen Thrane, 1987–90.
23 Int. Mickey Migdoll, Malindi, 1/9/86.
24 Int. Air Commodore H. W. Mermagen CB, CBE, AFC, Painswick, 2/8/86.
25 *Daily Sketch*, 2/9/36.

26 *News Chronicle*, 3/9/36.
27 *Daily Express*, 5/9/36.
28 Corresp. Winifred Disney, 7/1/87.
29 *Ibid*.
30 *SOTM*, p. 173.
31 Corresp. Royston Powell, 28/3/87.
32 Beaty, *The Waterjump, op. cit.*, p. 74.
33 'Beryl Markham's Triumph', Aero Club of East Africa, Tribute to Beryl Markham, 28/9/86, p. 3.
34 James Fox, 'African High Flyer', *Observer Colour Supplement*, 30/9/84; corresp. Wing Commander 'Flip' Fleming, 17/1/87.
35 *Sunday Express*, 5/9/36.
36 Corresp. Wing Commander 'Flip' Fleming, 9/2/89; corresp. Michael Shyne, 6/12/89.
37 *Daily Express*, 7/9/36.
38 *New York Times*, 6/9/36.
39 *Daily Express*, 7/9/36.
40 Fox/Markham/Schumacher data for *WWTN*.
41 *New York Times*, 6/9/36.
42 *East African Standard*, 18/9/36.
43 Berle/Markham, film clip, 1936, *WWW*, 1984.
44 *Sunday Dispatch*, 6/9/36.
45 *Daily Express*, 7/9/36.
46 *East African Standard*, 10/9/36; Int. Steve Miller, Likoni 4/2/87.
47 *Daily Mail*, 21/9/36.
48 *New York Times*, 23/9/36.
49 *The Times*, 21/9/36; *Daily Express*, 21/9/36; *Daily Mail*, 21/9/36.
50 *Daily Mail*, 29/9/36.
51 *Daily Sketch*, 29/9/36.
52 *Ibid*.

Chapter 13 Life without Direction (1936–8)

1 Corresp. the Hon. Doreen Norman, 15/11/87.
2 *Daily Mail*, 29/9/36.
3 Florence Desmond, *By Herself*, Harrap, London, 1953, p. 149.
4 *Ibid*.
5 Corresp. Sir Charles Markham, 3rd Bt, 27/8/90; *SOTM*, pp. 199, 100.
6 Tel. conv. the late Florence Desmond/James Fox, July 1987.
7 Corrresp. Julian Phipps, 23/4/87.
8 Corresp. Joyce Raw, 15/12/86.

9 Int. the late Beryl Markham, Karen, 12/3/75.
10 *STOM*, p. 282.
11 Corresp. Jeri Allen, 6/1/87.
12 Florence Desmond, *By Herself, op. cit.*, p. 150.
13 *SOTM*, p. 200.
14 *Daily Telegraph*, 15/10/36.
15 Int. the late Ginger Birkbeck, Mombasa Hospital, 15/6/89.
16 Tel. conv. the late Ginger Birkbeck, 30/12/86.
17 *Daily Express*, 18/10/36.
18 *New York Times*, 10/10/36.
19 *Women of the Air*, Judy Lomax, J. Murray, London, 1986, p. 133.
20 Ints the late Beryl Markham, *WWW*, 1984; the late Ginger Birkbeck, Mombasa Hospital, 17/5/89.
21 *Ibid.*, corresp. Jack le Poer Trench, 20/3/87; *ibid.*, *WWW*; int. the late Tom Lockhart-Mure, Shanzu, 18/9/87, 21/1/88.
22 Florence Desmond, *By Herself, op. cit.*, p. 150.
23 *Memoirs of Princess Alice, Duchess of Gloucester*, Collins, London, 1983, p. 82.
24 Int. the late Chris Langlands, Lewes, 25/6/86.
25 Duff Hart Davis (ed.), *In Royal Service: The Letters and Journals of Sir Alan Lascelles 1920–1936*, Hamish Hamilton, London, 1989, vol. 2, p. 200.
26 *Ibid.*, p. 210.
27 *SOTM*, Mary Lovell, Century Hutchinson Ltd, London, 1987, p. 199.
28 Int. the late Ginger Birkbeck, Mombasa Hospital, 16/5/89.
29 Michael Taub, *Jack Doyle: Fighting for Love*, Stanley Paul, London, 1990, p. 157.
30 *Ibid.*, p. 294.
31 *Ibid.*
32 *Ibid.*, p. 158.
33 *Ibid.*
34 *Ibid.*, p. 159.
35 *Ibid.*, p. 188.
36 Corresp. Julian Phipps, 23/4/87.
37 Corresp. Bunny Allen, 20/10/87; int. Jeri Allen, Mombasa Hospital, 6/1/87.
38 Taub, *Jack Doyle, op. cit.*, p. 236.
39 Corresp. Bunny Allen, 20/10/87.
40 Ints Warren Austin, Santa Barbara, 5/5/87; W. K. Purdy, Tiwi, July 1987.
41 *Ibid.*

42 *Ibid.*; int. David M. Mathias, Thomson's Falls, 20/3/87.
43 AP caption. Acme Betteman picture, 19/6/37; *New York Times*, 17/6/37.
44 Reuters; *Sunday Nation*, Nairobi, 14/7/91.
45 *Los Angeles Times*, 19/7/37.
46 Reuters; *Sunday Nation*, Nairobi, 14/7/91.
47 Corresp. Elizabeth Hall O'Dell, 7/1/90.
48 Int. the late Scott O'Dell, New York, 15/5/87.
49 Ints the late Scott O'Dell/James Fox, New York, April 1987; ET/O'Dell, New York, 15/5/87.
50 Corresp. the late Scott O'Dell, 2/1/88.
51 *Ibid.*
52 *Ibid.*
53 Tel. convs Elizabeth Hall O'Dell, 7/1/90; Lucile Flagg, 20/4/90; corresp. Elizabeth Hall O'Dell, 7/1/90; int. the late Scott O'Dell, New York, 15/5/87.
54 *Ibid.*
55 Int. the late Scott O'Dell/James Fox, New York, April 1987.

Chapter 14 West with the Night (1938–42)

1 Int. the late John Potter, Bidart, 17/4/87.
2 Int. the late Scott O'Dell/James Fox, New York, April 1987; int. Haley Fiske, Santa Barbara, 7/5/87.
3 Anon. Corresp. 2/3/87.
4 Int. Teddy Baring-Gould, Santa Barbara, 10/5/87.
5 Corresp. the late John Potter, 4/1/90.
6 Tel. conv. Alex White, Montecito, 10/5/87.
7 Int. Almira Struthers, Santa Barbara, 5/5/87.
8 Corresp. the late John Potter, 4/1/90.
9 Raoul Schumacher, 'The Whiphand', *Colliers*; 'The Week's Work', 24/6/44, p. 36.
10 Ian Hamilton, *Writers in Hollywood 1915–1951*, Heinemann, London, 1990, p. 74.
11 Melbourne Public Library, Shipping Lists 1938, SS *Mariposa*.
12 Corresp. the Hon. Roddy Ward, 19/5/39, to Beryl Markham.
13 *SOTM*, p. 211.
14 Int. the late Beryl Markham, James Fox for *Vanity Fair*, 1984; tel. conv. the late Ginger Birkbeck, 12/7/89.
15 Int. the late Patricia Bowles, Kilifi, 7/9/89.
16 *New York Times*, 22/6/39.

17 *Ibid.*
18 Scott O'Dell, letter, *Vanity Fair*, March 1987; int. the late Scott O'Dell/James Fox, New York, April 1987; int. Haley Fiske, Montecito, 8/5/87.
19 *Ibid.*
20 Ints Maddie de Mott, Nairobi, 17/9/86; the late John Potter, Bidart, 17/4/87.
21 Int. the late Scott O'Dell, New York, 15/5/87; int. the late Scott O'Dell/James Fox, New York, April 1987; Scott O'Dell, letter, *Vanity Fair*, March 1987.
22 *WWTN*, p. 198.
23 Adele Breaux, *Saint Exupéry in America 1942–43 A Memoir*, Farleigh Dickinson University Press.
24 James Fox, 'Beryl Markham', *Vanity Fair*, 1984.
25 Fox/Markham/Schumacher data for *WWTN*.
26 Ints Almira and the late James Struthers, Santa Barbara, 8/5/87; int. Haley Fiske, Montecito, 7/5/87.
27 Int. the late Scott O'Dell/James Fox, New York, April 1987; int. the late Scott O'Dell, New York, 15/5/87; Scott O'Dell, letter, *Vanity Fair*, March 1987.
28 Paul Brooks, inter-office memo, 20/6/41.
29 R. N. Linscott, 25/6/41.
30 *SOTM*, p. 200.
31 Int. Warren Austin/James Fox, London, 1987.
32 *Ibid.*
33 Letter from Beryl Markham to Lee Barker, 26/6/41.
34 Houghton Mifflin corresp., Houghton Mifflin Library, B. MS Am. 125 1198.
35 E. H. to Maxwell Perkins, 27/8/42, *Ernest Hemingway: Selected Letters*, ed. Carlos Baker, Panther, London, 1985, p. 541.
36 *Ibid.*
37 Scott O'Dell, letter, *Vanity Fair*, March 1987.
38 Corresp. the late Scott O'Dell, 25/10/88; tel. conv. 8/9/88.
39 Corresp. Elspeth Huxley, 23/11/87.
40 Corresp. Wing Commander 'Flip' Fleming, 19/10/86.
41 *Ibid.*
42 Corresp. Sir Charles Markham, 3rd Bt, 23/9/87.
43 Scott O'Dell, letter, *Vanity Fair*, March 1987.
44 *New York Times*, 22/6/39; *ibid.*, 18/6/42; corresp. Anthony Levintow, 8/10/86.
45 *Ibid.*

46 *New York Times*, 6/10/42.
47 Int. the late John Potter, Bidart, 17/4/87; *ibid.* corresp. 6/10/42.
48 *New York Times*, 16/10/42.

Chapter 15 Life as Beryl Schumacher (1942–9)

1 Corresp. Sir Charles Markham, 3rd Bt, 27/8/90.
2 Int. Warren Austin, Santa Barbara, 5/5/87.
3 Corresp. Cloete to Gremslet, 2/9/42; Stuart Cloete to Dale Warren, filed 16/2/43.
4 *Ibid.*, 25/2/43.
5 Scott O'Dell, letter, *Vanity Fair*, March 1987.
6 Scott O'Dell, letter, *Vanity Fair*, March 1987.
7 Fox/Markham/Schumacher data for *WWTN*.
8 Scott O'Dell, letter, *Vanity Fair*, March 1987.
9 Int. the late Scott O'Dell, New York, 15/5/87.
10 *Ibid.*
11 Int. the late Beryl Markham, Karen, 17/7/74.
12 Int. Almira Struthers, Santa Barbara, 6/5/87.
13 Scott O'Dell, letter, *Vanity Fair*, March 1987.
14 *Ibid.*
15 *Ibid.*
16 *Ibid.*
17 Int. the late Scott O'Dell, New York, 15/5/87; *ibid.*, James Fox, New York, April 1987.
18 Amy Porter, 'Beryl Markham', 'The Week's Work', *Collier's*, 29/1/44, p. 54; Raoul Schumacher, *ibid.*, 24/6/44, p. 36.
19 *SOTM*, p. 254.
20 Gloria Vanderbilt, *Black Knight, White Knight*, Knopf, New York, 1987, p. 219.
21 *Truth* newspaper, Melbourne, 9/1/38.
22 Int. Warren Austin, Santa Barbara, 5/5/87.
23 Ints Almira Struthers, Santa Barbara, 6/5/87; Haley Fiske, Montecito, 8/5/87; the late John Potter, Bidart, 19/4/87; Maddie de Mott, Nairobi, 18/9/87.
24 Corresp. Douglas Hall, 2/4/89.
25 *Ibid.*
26 Int. Maddie de Mott, Nairobi, 18/9/87.
27 Int. Douglas Hall, Montecito, 8/5/87; corresp. 2/4/89.
28 Peter Rand, *A Renegade from the Golden Ghetto*, Avenue Publishers, New York, 1989, pp. 231–235.

29 Int. Nancy Brown, Coral Casino, Montecito, 6/5/87.
30 Maria Churchill, 'A Private Oasis, the Coral Casino and Cabana Club'. *Montecito Magazine*, May, 1987.
31 Corresp. Warren Austin, 5/2/90.
32 Corresp. Audrey Palmer Neville, Montecito, 9/5/87.
33 *Ibid.*
34 Int. Peter Rand, New York, 12/5/87.
35 Int. Maddie de Mott, Nairobi, 27/9/87.
36 Int. Peter Rand, New York, 12/5/87.
37 Int. the late Scott O'Dell, New York, 15/5/87; tel. conv. 11/5/87; int. Scott O'Dell/James Fox, New York, April 1987.
38 Int. the late Scott O'Dell, New York, 15/5/87.
39 Tel. conv. the late Scott O'Dell, 11/5/87.
40 Int. the late Scott O'Dell/James Fox, New York, April 1987.
41 Scott O'Dell, letter, *Vanity Fair*, March 1987; int. the late Scott O'Dell, New York, 15/5/87.
42 *Ibid.*
43 Corresp. Huntington Memorial Hospital, 15/6/87, 23/6/87.
44 Corresp. the late Scott O'Dell, 25/10/88.
45 *Ibid.*
46 *Ibid.*; ints Almira Struthers, Santa Barbara, 5/5/87; Haley Fiske, Montecito, 8/5/87; the late John Potter, Bidart, 17/5/87; Vicky Needham-Clark, Kilifi, 13/8/87.
47 Scott O'Dell, letter, *Vanity Fair*, March 1987.
48 Int. the late Scott O'Dell, New York, 15/5/87.
49 *Ibid.*
50 *Ibid.*
51 Fox/Markham/Schumacher data for *WWTN*.
52 Int. Warren Austin, Santa Barbara, 5/5/87; corresp. Warren Austin, 5/2/90.
53 Int. the late James Struthers, Santa Barbara, 6/5/87.
54 Int. Warren Austin, Santa Barbara, 5/5/87.
55 *Ibid.*
56 *Ibid.*
57 *Ibid.*
58 *Ibid.*
59 *Ibid.*
60 Int. Almira Struthers, Santa Barbara, 5/5/87.
61 Int. Warren Austin/James Fox, London, June 1987.
62 Int. Warren Austin, Santa Barbara, 5/5/87.
63 Int. the late John Potter, Bidart, 18/4/87; tel. conv. Alex White, 10/5/87.

64 Tel. conv. the late John Potter, 31/7/86.
65 Tel. conv. Lady Maureen Fellowes, 30/6/87.
66 Corresp. Sir Charles Markham, 3rd Bt, 27/8/90.
67 Int. the late Viviane Markham, Angers, 21/4/87.
68 Corresp. Annabel Maule, 11/3/92.
69 Int. the late Viviane Markham, Angers, 21/4/87; corresp. Sir Charles Markham, 3rd Bt, 8/9/87, 10/9/87, 23/9/87.
70 *Ibid.*
71 Tel. conv. Anna Cataldi, 1990; corresp. Sir Charles Markham, 3rd Bt, 23/10/87.
72 *Ibid.*
73 Int. Warren Austin/James Fox, London, June 1987; int. Warren Austin, Santa Barbara, 5/5/87.
74 *SOTM*, p. 250.
75 *Ibid.*; tel. conv. Warren Austin, 18/3/87.
76 Tel. conv. the late John Potter, 31/7/87.
77 Int. Warren Austin 5/5/87.
78 *Ibid.*
79 *Ibid.*; int. Warren Austin/James Fox, London, June 1987.
80 Int. Warren Austin, Santa Barbara, 5/5/87.
81 *Ibid.*
82 Int. Warren Austin/James Fox, London, June 1987; int. Jorgen Thrane, Kamwaki Farm, 6/12/86.
83 Corresp. Warren Austin, 5/2/90.
84 Corresp. Renzo Fenci, 10/1/88.
85 Corresp. Renzo Fenci, 18/11/87.
86 Int. Teddy Baring-Gould, Santa Barbara, 9/5/87.
87 Int. Warren Austin, Santa Barbara, 5/5/87.
88 Int. the late John Potter, Bidart, 18/4/87.
89 Corresp. the late John Potter, 26/3/90.
90 *SOTM*, p. 257.

Chapter 16 Life in Kenya Colony Once More (1950–64)

1 Ints Jeremy and Vicky Needham-Clark, Kilifi, 8/9/89; Jorgen Thrane, Kamwaki Farm, 6/12/86; Alan Bobbe, transcript, Cable & Wireless broadcast, 'Nairobi Becoming a City', 21/3/50.
2 *The Times*, 30/3/50.
3 Int. Warren Austin, Santa Barbara, 5/5/87.
4 Int. Sir Charles Markham, 3rd Bt, Nairobi, *WWW*, 1984.
5 *SOTM*, p. 261.

6 Int. Roland Sharpe, Mtwapa, 31/1/89.

7 Int. Sylvia Richardson, Kilifi, 13/10/86.

8 Nanyuki Sports Club.

9 Int. Victoria Eyre, Chelsea, 2/6/87.

10 Corresp. Dora Stevens, 15/4/88; corresp. Kit Taylor, 30/10/86; int. Olive Rodwell, Mtwapa, 10/2/88; corresp. Bonnie Miller, 26/3/87.

11 Int. Victoria Eyre, Chelsea, 2/6/87.

12 *Ibid.*

13 Corresp. Victoria Eyre, 8/9/87.

14 Int. Victoria Eyre, Chelsea, 2/6/87.

15 *Ibid.*

16 Int. Jorgen Thrane, Muthaiga, 28/2/87

17 Int. Jorgen Thrane, Kamwaki Farm, 13/9/87.

18 *Ibid.*

19 *Ibid.* 10/3/90.

20 *Ibid.* 13/3/90.

21 *Ibid.*

22 *Ibid.* 13/9/87.

23 *Ibid.*

24 Ints the Hon. Patricia O'Neill, Bletchington, 16/7/87; Jorgen Thrane, Kamwaki Farm, 13/9/87; int. Victoria Eyre and corresp., 2/11/87, 27/3/90.

25 Int. Victoria Eyre, Chelsea, 2/6/87.

26 Corresp. Sir Charles Markham, 3rd Bt. 30/9/87; int. the Hon. Patricia O'Neill, Bletchington, 16/7/87.

27 Corresp. the late Viviane Markham, 24/9/86.

28 *Ibid.*

29 *Ibid.*

30 Int. the Hon. Patricia O'Neill, Bletchington, 16/7/87.

31 Int. the late Viviane Markham, Angers, 21/4/87.

32 Corresp. Dora Stevens, 15/8/88; Doreen Norman to Jack Couldrey, 2/4/84.

33 Ints Victoria Eyre, Chelsea, 2/6/87; Jorgen Thrane, Kamwaki Farm, 13/9/87.

34 The late Lady Diana Delamere to Leda Farrant, Nairobi, 1987.

35 Corresp. Raleigh Gilbert, 21/6/87; int. Jorgen Thrane, Kamwaki Fram, 13/9/87.

36 Robin Higgin, *The Blood Horse in Africa*, 29/3/86, pp. 2411–13.

37 Int. Jorgen Thrane, Kamwaki Farm, 13/9/87.

38 Raleigh Gilbert, 'Beryl Markham, the Unorthodox', *Sunday Post*, 15/5/60.

39 Int. Ndungu Kigole, Kingscliff Stud, 15/3/90.
40 Int. Jorgen Thrane, Kamwaki Farm, 13/9/87.
41 Int. Petal Allen, Shanzu, 8/2/87.
42 Corresp. Muffet Bennett, 13/12/86; int. Petal Allen, Shanzu, 8/2/87.
43 Int. Jorgen Thrane, Kamwaki Farm, 13/9/87; *East African Standard*, 4/8/59.
44 *East African Standard*, 4/3/84.
45 Ints Francis Erskine, Gerry Alexander, *WWW*, 1984.
46 Int. Ndungu Kigole, Karen, 15/3/90.
47 Fox, Markham/Schumacher date for *WWTN*; Raleigh Gilbert, 'Beryl Markham', *op. cit.*
48 David Read, *Barefoot over the Serengeti*, Cassell, London, 1979, p. 55; int. Lucy W. Mbugua, Bamburi, 18/9/89.
49 Ints Jorgen Thrane, Kamwaki Farm, 13/3/90; the Hon. Patricia O'Neill, Bletchington, 16/6/87.
50 Corresp. Veronica Scott Mason, 18/10/86, 27/12/86.
51 Int. Paddy Migdoll, 1/9/86.
52 Diary entry, 29/9/86.
53 Corresp. the Hon. Patricia O'Neill, 12/12/86; M.F. Hill, *Kenya Weekly News*, July/August 1964.
54 Corresp. Peter Hughes, 2/2/87.
55 Int. Jorgen Thrane, Kamwaki Farm, 13/3/90.
56 Int. Roland Sharpe, Mtwapa, 31/8/89.
57 *Ibid.*
58 *Ibid.*
59 *Ibid.*
60 *Ibid.*
61 *Ibid.*
62 Int. Jorgen Thrane, Kamwaki Farm, 13/9/87.
63 *Ibid.*
64 *Ibid.*; Barry Bendell, *Kenya Racing*, Kenya Derby issue, 1976, p. 7
65 Int. the Hon. Patricia O'Neill, Bletchington, 16/7/89; int. Jorgen Thrane, Kamwaki Farm, 16/12/86; Owners, Breeders and Trainers Society.
66 Int. Jorgen Thrane Kamwaki Farm, 16/12/86.
67 *SOTM* p. 283.
68 Ints Jorgen Thrane, Kamwaki Farm, 13/9/87; Vicky and Jeremy Needham-Clarke, Kilifi, 8/9/89.
69 *SOTM*, p. 283
70 Corresp. the Hon. Patricia O'Neill, 16/7/86.

71 *East African Standard*, 14/8/61.
72 Int. Tubby Block, *WWW*, 1984; corresp. Pip Thorpe, 13/8/86.
73 Ints the Hon. Patricia O'Neill, Bletchington, 16/7/86; Victoria Eyre, Chelsea, 2/6/87.
74 Int. Jorgen Thrane, Kamwaki Farm, 13/9/87.
75 Int. the Hon. Patricia O'Neill, 20/9/87.
76 Corresp. Pip Thorpe, 13/8/86.
77 *Sunday Post*, 15/10/86.
78 Corresp. Sir Charles Markham, 3rd Bt, 15/9/87.
79 Int. Jorgen Thrane, Kamwaki Farm, 13/9/87.
80 *Ibid.*, 6/12/86.
81 *SOTM*, p. 287
82 Corresp. Pip Thorpe, 13/8/86.
83 Int. the Hon. Patricia O'Neill, Bletchington, 16/7/89.
84 Beryl Markham, *West with the Night*, Virago, London, 1984, Intro. Martha Gellhorn, pp. viii–ix.
85 *Ibid.*
86 *Ibid.*
87 *Ibid.*
88 Int. Paddy and Mickey Migdoll, Malindi, 1/9/86.

Chapter 17 Life in South Africa (1964–70)

1 Lin Sampson, 'Bright Mischief', *Style*, December/January, 1989, p. 106.
2 Letter from Beryl Markham to Victoria Eyre, 20/9/61.
3 Corresp. Victoria Eyre, 1989.
4 *Ibid.*
5 Tel. Conv. Jorgen Thrane, 25/1/87; int. Jorgen Thrane, Kamwaki Farm, 13/3/90.
6 Corresp. the Hon. Patricia O'Neill, 12/12/86; ints Tubby Block, *WWW*, Jorgen Thrane, Kamwaki Farm, 13/3/90.
7 Ints the Hon. Patricia O'Neill, Bletchington, 16/6/87; Jorgen Thrane, Kamwaki Farm, 13/3/90; Victoria Eyre, Chelsea, 2/6/87.
8 Letter from Beryl Markham to Victoria Eyre, 20/9/61.
9 Ints Jorgen Thrane, 13/6/87; the Hon. Patricia O'Neill, Bletchington, 16/7/87.
10 *Ibid.*
11 Lin Sampson, 'Bright Mischief', *op. cit.*
12 Viney, Graham, 'Broadlands, Sir Lowry's Pass,' *Colonial Houses of South Africa*, Struik, Cape Town, 1987.

13 Lin Sampson, 'Bright Mischief', *op. cit.*
14 Int. the Hon. Patricia O'Neill, Bletchington, 16/7/87.
15 *Ibid.*
16 *Ibid.*
17 Int. Jorgen Thrane, Kamwaki Farm, 13/3/90.
18 Corresp. Betty Kiggan, 7/1/88.
19 Lin Sampson, 'Bright Mischief', *op. cit.*
20 *SOTM*, p. 305.
21 Corresp. the Hon. Patricia O'Neill, 3/1/89.
22 *Ibid.*, 25/12/88.
23 Int. Shelagh McCutcheon/Betty Kiggan, Broadlands, 15/10/87.
24 *SOTM*, p. 306.
25 Corresp. the Hon. Patricia O'Neill, 27/9/86.
26 Int. Shelagh McCutcheon/Betty Kiggan, Broadlands, 15/10/87.
27 *Ibid.*
28 Corresp. the Hon. Patricia O'Neill, 16/7/86.
29 Int. the Hon. Patricia O'Neill, Bletchington, 16/7/87; int. Shelagh McCutcheon/Betty Kiggan, Broadlands, 15/10/87.
30 *Ibid.*
31 Corresp. Jockey Club of Kenya, 18/7/72–20/2/84.
32 Int. Shelagh McCutcheon/Betty Kiggan, Broadlands, 15/10/87.
33 *Ibid.*
34 Int. Jorgen Thrane, Kamwaki Farm, 13/9/87.
35 Int. the Hon. Patricia O'Neill, Bletchington, 16/7/89.
36 Ints Hilbert Lee, Montecito, 4/5/87; Haley Fiske, Montecito, 10/5/87.
37 Corresp. Sally Christiensen, 1988.
38 Corresp. Jockey Club of Kenya, 18/7/72–20/2/84.
39 *SOTM*, p. 308.
40 *Ibid* pp. 107, 108; *WWW* int. Leth 1984
41 Corresp. Sir Charles Markham, 3rd Bt, 18/11/87.

Chapter 18 A Phoenix from the Ashes (1970–86)

1 Corresp. the Jockey Club of Kenya, 16/5/70–9/10/70; int. Richard Chew, Stipendiary Steward, Jockey Club of Kenya, 26/9/86.
2 Int. Paddy Migdoll, Malindi, 1/9/86.
3 Corresp. the Jockey Club of Kenya, 16/5/70; memos 18/5/70, 25/5/70.
4 Corresp. the Jockey Club of Kenya, 29/5/70.
5 Corresp. the late Beryl Markham to Hon. Mrs M. Muliro, 26/6/70.

6 Corresp. the Jockey Club of Kenya, 12/7/70.
7 *Ibid.*
8 *Ibid.*
9 *Ibid.*
10 Int. Freddie Nettlefold, Watamu, 23/1/87.
11 Int. Paddy Migdoll, Malindi, 1/9/87.
12 Int. Freddie Nettlefold, Watamu, 23/1/87.
13 *Ibid.*; int. Paddy Migdoll, Malindi, 1/9/87; corresp. Paddy Migdoll, 23/8/87; int. Vicky Needham-Clark, Kilifi, 8/9/89.
14 Int. Freddie Nettlefold, Watamu, 23/1/87.
15 Corresp. Diana Cadot, 23/8/87.
16 Corresp. Sir Charles Markham, 3rd Bt, 27/8/90; int. the late Viviane Markham, Angers, 21/4/87.
17 *Ibid.*
18 Int. Freddie Nettlefold, Watamu, 23/1/87.
19 Int. Sylvia Nettlefold, Watamu, 23/1/87.
20 Int. Jasmin Wali Mohammed, Nairobi, 29/9/86.
21 Int. the late Beryl Markham, Karen, 17/7/74.
22 Int. Freddie Nettlefold, Watamu, 23/1/86.
23 Int. the late James Struthers and Almira Struthers, Santa Barbara, 6/5/87.
24 Int. Victoria Eyre, Chelsea, 2/6/87.
25 Int. Maddie de Mott, Nairobi, 27/6/87.
26 Int. Peter Rand, New York, 14/5/87.
27 Int. the late Patricia Bowles, Kilifi, 7/8/87.
28 Corresp. Jockey Club of Kenya, 18/7/72–20/2/84.
29 *Ibid.*
30 *SOTM*, pp. 316. 317.
31 Int. John de Villiers, Mombasa, 1989.
32 Ints. W. K. Purdy, Tiwi, 17/10/86, 7/11/87; unpublished story 'The Aviatrix', 14/6/88
33 *SOTM*, pp. 90, 91.
34 Int. the late Sir Malcolm Sorsbie, Claridge's, London, 1986; W. K. Purdy, 'The Aviatrix', unpub. story, 1988.
35 Int. Jasmin Wali Mohammed, Nairobi, 29/9/86.
36 Int. Francis Erskine, *WWW*, 1984.
37 Int. John de Villiers, Nairobi, 26/9/86.
38 Int. V. J. Varma, *WWW*, 1984.
39 *Ibid.*; corresp. Paddy Migdoll, 24/9/86.
40 *Ibid.*
41 *East African Standard*, August 1982.

42 Int. Paddy Migdoll, Malindi, 24/9/86.
43 Ints Paddy Migdoll; tel. conv. 12/8/86; int. the late Beryl Markham, James Fox for *Vanity Fair*, 1984.
44 Corresp. Humphrey Cottrill, 28/7/88.
45 *SOTM*, p. 342.
46 Int. Jasmin Wali Mohammed, Nairobi, 29/9/86.
47 *Ibid.*
48 Int. Philip Mason, Kilifi, 21/8/88.
49 Purdy, 'The Aviatrix', *op. cit.*
50 *SOTM*, p. 327.
51 James Fox, 'African High Flyer', *Observer Colour Supplement*, 30/9/84.
52 Tel. conv. Martha Gellhorn, Mombasa, 6/3/88.
53 James Fox, 'African High Flyer', *Observer Colour Supplement*, 30/9/84.
54 Complete transcription of *WWW* ints with Beryl Markham, 1984.
55 Int. Paddy Migdoll, 25/9/86.
56 BBC1, *Arena*, ints for *From an Immigrant's Notebook* and *Hemingway*, 1985.
57 *WWW*, 1984, reel 57.
58 Mirella Ricciardi, 'Staying on in Kenya', *Harpers & Queen*, November 1985, p. 165.
59 *WWW*, 1984.
60 Corresp. Andrew Maxwell Hislop, 11/5/84.
61 James Hamilton, 'Sausalito to Nairobi: The Beryl Markham Connection', *California Magazine*, January 1987.
62 Corresp. Jack Couldrey, 20/8/86; James Fox, 'African High Flyer', *op. cit.*
63 Tel. conv. the late John Potter, 31/7/86.
64 Int. Maddie de Mott, Nairobi, 27/9/86.
65 Tel. conv. Warren Austin, 18/4/87.
66 Corresp. Ann Addly, 12/11/86.
67 Int. Jorgen Thrane, Kamwaki Farm, 6/12/86
68 Corresp. Ann Addly, 12/11/86.
69 Corresp. Paddy Migdoll, 24/9/86; int. Beryl Markham, 8/9/84; corresp. Ann Addly, 7/10/86, 12/11/86.
70 Corresp. Ann Addly, 7/10/86.
71 Int. Philippa Corse, Kilifi, 13/8/89.
72 Corresp. Ann Addly, 7/10/86.
73 Int. Paddy Migdoll, Malindi, 24/9/86.
74 Corresp. Ann Addly, 12/8/86.
75 Court Circular, *Daily Telegraph*, 13/8/86.

Bibliography

Aero Club of East Africa 1927–1977: Golden Jubilee Year Commemorative Review.

Baker, Carlos (ed.), *Ernest Hemingway: Selected Letters*, Scribner, New York, 1981.

Best, Nicolas, *Happy Valley*, Secker & Warburg, London, 1979.

Blixen, Karen, *Out of Africa*, Jonathan Cape, London, 1937.

Chalmers, Patrick (ed.), *Sport and Travel in East Africa, an Account of Two Visits, 1928 and 1930, compiled from the private diaries of HRH the Prince of Wales*, Dutton & Co., New York, n.d.

Country Life, English Country Houses Open to the Public, Country Life, London, 1951.

Dinesen, Isak, *Ehrengard*, Michael Joseph, London, 1963.

Dinesen, Isak, *Letters from Africa 1914–1931*, Weidenfeld & Nicolson, London, 1981.

Fitzgeorge-Parker, Tim, *Training the Racehorse*, Pelham Books, London, 1973.

Fox, James, *White Mischief*, Penguin, London, 1984.

Frankland, Noble, *Prince Henry: Duke of Gloucester*, Weidenfeld & Nicolson, London, 1980.

Frisell, Hjalmar, *Sju Aritalt-Bland Vita och Svarta*, Lars Hockerbergs, Stockholm, 1937.

Gillett, Mary, *Tribute to Pioneers*, privately printed, Oxford, 1987.

Hamilton, Ian, *Writers in Hollywood 1915–1951*, Heinemann, London, 1990.

Huxley, Elspeth, *White Man's Country*, Chatto & Windus, London, 1935.

Huxley, Elspeth, *The Sorcerer's Apprentice*, Chatto & Windus, London, 1948.

Huxley, Elspeth, *Out in the Midday Sun: My Kenya*, Chatto & Windus, London, 1985.

Lambton, The Hon. George, *Men and Horses I Have Known*, Thornton Butterworth, London, 1924.

Lomax, Judy, *Women of the Air*, J. Murray, London, 1986.

Lovell, Mary, *Straight on Till Morning: The Life of Beryl Markham*, Century Hutchinson, London, 1987.

Markham, Beryl, *West with the Night*, Virago, London, 1984.

Mitchell, M. E. M. and Hudleston, C. R. (eds), *An Account of the Principal Branches of the Family of Clutterbuck*, privately printed, Gloucester, 1924.

Pelensky, Olga, *Isak Dinesen: The Life and Imagination of a Seducer*, Ohio University Press, Athens, Ohio, 1991.

Playne, FRGS, Somerset, *East Africa (British) 1908–1909, its History, People, Commerce, Industries and Resources*, ed. Holderness Gale, The Foreign and Colonial Compiling and Publishing Company.

Read, David, *Barefoot Over the Serengeti*, Cassell, London, 1979.

Richards, Mark, *The Cotswold Way*, Penguin, London, 1984.

Rose, Phyllis, *Jazz Cleopatra: Josephine Baker and Her Time*, Vintage, London, 1991.

Ryan, Molly, *Over My Shoulder*, Grange Press, Dublin, 1987.

Taylor, Helen, *Scarlett's Women*: Gone with the Wind *and its Female Fans*, Virago, London, 1989.

Thurman, Judith, *Isak Dinesen: The Life of a Storyteller*, St Martin's Press, New York, 1982.

Trzebinski, Errol, *The Kenya Pioneers*, Heinemann, London, 1985.

Trzebinski, Errol, *Silence Will Speak: The Life of Denys Finch Hatton and his Relationship with Karen Blixen*, Heinemann, London, 1977.

Vanderbilt, Gloria, *Black Knight, White Knight*, Knopf, New York, 1987.

Ziegler, Philip, *Edward VIII: The Official Biography*, Collins, London, 1990.

Index

The names printed in italics are those of horses

Abercrombie, Bert 308
Adamson, Tommy 280
Addly, Ann 335, 336
Adhiambo 316, 321, 325–6, 333, 336–7
Adley, Mary Ellen (later Mrs Mansfield Markham) 236, 247, 267, 285
'Afghan Princess' see Temple, Sylvia
Africans in Kenya 13, 76
Afrikaners and Kenya 32
Air Cruises 200–1
Aird, Major John H. 122, 146
Aldenham, Lord 207, 208
Alexander family of County Carlow 2
Alexander, Gerry 71, 98, 103, 163
Alexander, John 322, 346
Alexander, Josiah William (grandfather) 5, 6
Alexander, Sir Ulick 137, 151, 200
Algar, Jimmy 197
Allen, Bunny 124, 125, 147, 193, 228
Alouette 291
Aschan, Ulf 325
Astor family 141
Athi 290, 291, 303
Atlantic crossings by air 199
Austin, Dr Warren 263–70, 275, 334

Bage, A. A. 203
Baldwin, Stanley 131, 132, 141, 225
Baring-Gould, Teddy 234
Barker, Lee 243
Barrymore, John 231, 234
Batey, William and Lucile 231–2
Baudet, G. F. 183

Berle, Milton 214
'Beryl bloom', on horses 291–2
Birkbeck, Major Benedict 67, 71, 73, 75, 80, 93, 106, 109, 121, 123, 132–3, 153
Birkbeck, Cockie (Jaqueline, née Alexander, later Baroness von Blixen, later Hoogterp) 67, 71, 72, 73, 81, 84, 101–2, 113, 151, 161, 163
  and Bror Blixen 74, 193
  and Denys Finch Hatton 94, 100–1
  in England 97–101
  and the Prince of Wales 131, 149
Birkbeck, Penelope 'Ginger' (née Mayer) 67, 68, 74, 75, 75, 84, 85, 94, 107, 128, 132, 133, 137, 144, 146, 151, 153, 200, 223, 226
  and the Markhams' marriage 108, 109, 116
  and Denys Finch Hatton 177, 152, 159, 161, 165
Blixen Finecke, Baron Bror von ('Blix') 73, 74, 109
  and BM 190–1, 192–3, 194, 197–8
  and Prince of Wales 131, 146
Blixen Finecke, Baroness Cockie von see Birkbeck, Cockie
Blixen Finecke, Baroness Karen von ('Tania') 67, 68, 72, 73, 81, 85, 95, 134
  and Denys Finch Hatton 73, 80, 82, 85–6, 87, 89, 91, 92–3, 117, 120, 142, 143–4, 145, 152–5
  and DFH's death 159, 161
  and BM 81, 83, 84–5, 101, 104–5, 116, 117–18, 126, 129, 151

Blixen Finecke – *cont'd.*
  on BM 85, 86, 102
  and BM's pregnancy 134–5
  rivalry with BM 142–3, 152
  BM's view of 92–3, 96
  and Mrs Kirkpatrick 86, 87
  and Mansfield Markham 110, 110–11
  receives bed from BM 111–12
  and Prince of Wales visits 119, 120–1,
    127, 129, 130, 149
  Ehrengard 135
  Out of Africa 152, 154, 161, 239, 330,
    333
  financial troubles 152, 154
  leaves Kenya 167–8
  and Bror Blixen 192–3
  BM's dog named after 221
Block, Abraham 278, 295
Block, Jack 295
Block, Tubby 278, 295, 196, 197, 298, 302,
  314
Blue Bird Flying Circus 184–94
Blue Coat Boy 20
Blue Streak 290
Bowden, Daphne 336
Bowden, David 326
Bowles, Patricia 323
Bowring, Sir Charles 58
Bramwell, Frank 77
Broad, Captain Hubert 222, 236
Broadlands, BM at 300–8
Brook, Edward 122, 126
Brooks, Paul 241, 243
Bruno, Harry 204, 212, 214, 216
Bumpus, Sonny 53, 105, 106, 114, 122
Burkitt, Dr 107

Cam 71
Camargo 71
Cambrian 122–3, 127
Camciscan 93, 105
Cameo 71
Cameron, Jock 209
Camiknickers 106
Campbell Black, Frank 163
Campbell, Black, Tom 103, 150, 160,
  163–4, 195, 208
  BM's flying instructor 146, 147, 158,
    162–3, 166, 168
  relations with BM 163, 168, 188–9, 201,
    202, 220–1
  and Lord Furness 170–1, 173–4, 188–9
  in England 173–4, 177
  and Florence Desmond 195–6, 201
  death 215, 216

Candler, Shelagh 321
Carberry, J. C. (John Evans-Freke, Baron
  Carbery) 87, 118, 163, 187
  and BM 177–8, 178–9, 180–1, 199,
    200, 202, 224
  and BM's flight 187–8, 196, 207, 212,
    213
Carberry, June (née Weir Mosley) 180,
  181, 188, 207, 212, 213
Carberry, Maia 118, 180, 342
Cardale Luck, Mr and Mrs 103, 105
Cardross, Lord 13
Cartwright, Algy 65, 68, 73, 102, 144
Cartwright, Rose (née Buxton) 65, 68, 72,
  73, 144, 151, 176, 195, 215
Cavendish, Carryll 175
Cavendish, Enid 170–1; *see also* Furness,
  Enid
Cavendish, Patricia, later O'Neill 175, 285,
  286, 293, 297, 311–12
  and Broadlands 302, 304, 306, 307, 308
Cavendish-Bentinck, Sir Ferdinand 105,
  314–15, 323
Charlatan 106
Cholmley family 5–6, 15–16
Cholmondeley, Tom 12, 65, 94, 95, 149
  as 4th Baron Delamere 275, 287
Cloete, Evangeline 246
Cloete, Stuart 248, 276
Clutterbuck family 2–3, 134
Clutterbuck, Annie (aunt) 29
Clutterbuck, Charles Baldwin (father)
  'Clutt'
  birth 4
  relations with BM 1, 2, 16–17
  horseman 4, 7, 8, 9
  military career 4–5
  inheritance 5
  marriage 5
  cashiered 6
  farming 7
  to Africa 1, 9, 10
  and Ndimu Farm 10, 14
  dairy manager to Lord Delamere 11, 12,
    13–14
  attitude to Africans 13
  buys Brickfields 14
  training Delamere horses 14, 25, 62, 64
  riding 15, 36
  and Emma Orchardson 20–1
  and BM's upbringing 21, 26–7, 36, 40,
    44
  as boss 40–1
  and World War I 48, 49, 50
  and BM's first wedding 57, 58

bankruptcy 62–4
farm sold 66–7
sale of horses 339–41
to Cape Town 67
back training in Kenya 120, 132
BM sees 148, 150, 236, 275–6
and BM as flyer 168–9, 215
death 286
Clutterbuck, Clara Agnes (mother), née
Alexander, later Mrs Kirkpatrick
horsewoman 5–6, 7, 8
marriage 5
children 6–7
abandonment of BM 1, 2, 16
in Africa 11–12
and Major Kirkpatrick 14–15
back to UK 16
see also Kirkpatrick, Clara
Clutterbuck, Henry Baldwin (uncle) 4, 29
Clutterbuck, Jasper (cousin) 29
Clutterbuck, Mary Rose (née Baldwin),
grandmother 4
Clutterbuck, Richard 'Dickie' (brother) 7,
12, 16
in Africa 12, 61–2, 71, 87
death 98
Clutterbuck, Richard Henry (grandfather)
3–4, 5
Cohen, Jack 228
Cole, Berkeley 14, 42, 69, 70, 73, 92, 94,
187
Cole, Florence *see* Delamere, Florence, Lady
Cole, Galbraith 14, 42, 74, 94
Cole, Hilda 159, 160
Cole, John 160
Cole, Vernon 159, 160
Colliers magazine 252, 257, 263
Collins, Major 320
Colman, Ronald 234, 256
Colvile, Lady 121
Colvile, Diana, later Lady Delamere 287,
294
Colvile de Preville, Gilbert 287
Conduitt, Major Wac 71
Connell, Evan 329
Connolly, Cyril 305
Coquette 54, 133
Coryndon, Sir Robert 81
Cosmopolitan magazine 265
Cotten, Joseph 234, 256, 265
Cottrill, Henry 174–5
Cottrill, Humphrey 174–5
Couldrey, Jack 324–5, 327, 329, 330, 332,
335, 346
Cowie, Dudley and Mervyn 118

Craven, Charles and Rupert 8, 14
Crosby, Bing 325
Culley, Mary Lou 272
Cunard, Emerald 141, 176
Cunard, Nancy 141
Curant, jockey 327
Cutlass 290, 291

'D' *see* Delamere, Hugh Cholmondeley
Daily Express 204, 209, 212, 223
Daily Mail 216
Daily Sketch 216
Damfine 15
Darling, Fred 116
de Mott, Maddie (formerly Rand) 334
de Villiers, John 'Petersfield' 324, 325
de Wolfe, Elsie (Lady Mendl) 271, 343
Del Rio, Dolores 231
Delamere, Diana Cholmondeley, Lady
(formerly Colvile) 287, 294
Delamere, Florence Cholmondeley, Lady
(née Cole) 11–12, 28, 42–3
help to BM 29–30, 31
Delamere, Hugh Cholmondeley, 3rd Baron
('D') 30–1, 49, 63, 116
and Clutterbuck 11, 12, 13–14
attitude to Africans 13
and BM 30, 58, 58, 75, 93, 110, 168
social life 69, 73, 80–1, 94
at Soysambu 75–6
leader of community 76, 81–2, 149
Vigilance Committee 76, 81
and Jock Purves 95
death 170
Delamere, Tom Chomondeley, 4th Baron
275, 287
as the Hon. Tom 12, 94, 95, 149
Delves Broughton, Jack 287
Dempster, Dermott 'Dempey' 74, 94
Desmond, Florence (Mrs Campbell Black)
195–6, 201–2
after husband's death 219–22, 224, 226
Diamond 280
Dinesen, Isak *see* Blixen, Karen
Dinesen, Thomas 84, 104, 152
Dixon, Eva 193
Doyle, Jack 227–8, 231
Drury, John 103
Drury, Nina 242–3, 265
Dupré, François 200–1

Earhart, Amelia 230
East African Turf Club 48, 62, 70
East African Airways 190, 196
East African Derby 106, 295

East African Protectorate (EAP) 8–9
Eastleigh racecourse, Nairobi 77–8
Edmondson, Captain 48
Edmondson, Dickie 53
Edward VIII, later Duke of Windsor 200,
    202–3, 224, 225–6
  in Bahamas 242, 263, 264–5
  see also Wales, Edward Prince of
Elburgon, BM training at 118–19
Eliot, Sir Charles 8–9
Elkington, Jim 8, 29, 38, 102
Elkington, Margaret 29, 67
Emergency, Kenyan 278
Erroll, Josslyn Hay, 22nd Earl of 169, 185,
    287
Erroll, Molly 169
Erskine, Derek 123, 125
Erskine, Francis 323

Fair Realm 290
Farah 73, 91
Fenci, Renzo 271, 323, 343–4
Finch Hatton, Denys 80, 84, 88–9, 146,
    152, 322
  and BM 67–8, 83, 89–90, 94, 95, 101
  and Karen Blixen 73, 80, 82, 85–6, 87,
    89, 91, 92–3
  and Muthaiga Club 79
  flying career 87, 91, 126, 142–3, 145
  and Africans 91–2
  possible father of BM's child 99
  in London 100–1
  back in Kenya 102
  cool to Karen Blixen 104–5, 117,
    120–1, 142, 144
  and the Prince of Wales trips 118,
    119–22, 126–7, 128–9, 131, 132,
    146–7, 148, 150
  still sought by BM 107, 110
  in London again 141–2, 146
  crusade for Serengeti 143
  other women 143
  breakup with Karen 143–4, 152–3,
    154–5
  view of marriage 144
  affair with BM 154–6
  photographs destroyed 157
  death and dispersal of effects 158–60,
    167–8
Finch Hatton, Guy Montagu George 'Toby',
    Viscount Maidstone, later 14th Earl
    of Winchilsea 100, 145, 146
Fitzgerald, F. Scott 235, 256
Fleming, 'Flip' 196, 211, 244–5
Forster, Brigadier 278

Foster, Varick 271
Fox, James 181, 330–1
  and BM's writing 239, 241
Frisell, Hjalmar 104
Furness, Averill 175, 188–9
Furness, Marmaduke, Viscount Furness
    ('Duke') 147, 150, 164, 176, 188–9
  and Tom Campbell Black 170–1, 173–4
Furness, Enid Lady Furness (née
    Lindeman, formerly Cavendish, later
    Countess of Kenmare) 170–1,
    175–6, 305–6
  friend of BM 175, 176–7, 195–6, 229, 298
  and Broadlands 301, 302, 303, 304, 305,
    306–7
Furness, Thelma Lady Furness (née
    Morgan) 139, 140, 141, 146, 148,
    150, 200, 225, 227
Furse, David 103

Galbraith, Annette and John 308, 310
Garbo, Greta 253, 255
Garland, Hilary and Travers 321
Garten, Roy 185
Gay Warrior 127
Gellhorn, Martha 299, 330
George V 131, 132, 141, 153
  death 200, 225
George VI (Prince George) 143
Gilbert, Raleigh 288
Gladys 105
Gloucester, Alice, Duchess of 200, 224
Gloucester, Prince Henry, Duke of 118,
    122, 123, 124, 125–6, 131
  and possible paternity of Gervase 134–5
  and BM in London 136, 141, 144, 153,
    173, 174, 224
  threatened by Markhams 136–7
  in Japan 136
  trust fund for BM 137–8
  flying 143, 145
  married 200
  kissed by BM in Kenya 274
Goddard, Theodore 164
Gooch, Eric 105, 129, 248
Gooch, Gladys 105, 106, 129, 170, 221,
    248
  rival trainer, as Gladys Graham 288–9
Grant, Nellie 81
Gravesend, home of Vega Gull 201, 202,
    203, 207
Greswolde-Williams, Ann 71
Greswolde-Williams, Frank 100, 102, 125
Grigg, Sir Edward, later Lord Altrincham,
    'Uncle Ned' 121

Grigg, Joan, Lady Grigg 123, 125, 130, 147, 148, 149
Griggs, Dr Joseph 260
Grimes, Stephen 334
Grogan, Quentin 117
Grosvenor Hotel 132–3, 135, 136, 153, 199
Guest, Diana 193, 194, 197, 198
Guest, Captain Freddie 191, 197
Guest, Raymond 193
Guest, Winston 'Wolfie' 191, 192, 193, 194, 197
Gutekunst, George 329, 330, 331–2

Hamilton, Ian 236
Hamlin (jockey) 111
Happy Valley set 102
Hayne, Mary and Colin 321
Heath, Wing Commander 'Jacko' 124, 139–40, 149, 185
Hellman, Lillian 235
Hemingway, Ernest 191–2, 194, 235, 244
Hemingway, Jack 329
Henry (jockey) 323
Heron 316
Heston 202
Hetherton (jockey) 323
Hewlett, Ray 147–8
Higgin, Robin 320
Hindlip, Lord 13
Hoey, A. C. 80, 111, 128, 341
Hook, Hilary 98
Houghton Mifflin 241–2, 243, 258, 259, 262
Hughesdon, Charles 222
Hunter, J. A. 159–60
Huntingdon Memorial Hospital, Pasadena 260
Huxley, Elspeth 81, 239, 244
Hyland, Alfred and Hannah 75

Indian question, in Kenya 76
Ingram (Rex) Films 174
Ives, Burl 272–3, 284

Jackman, Vicky 315
Jebbta 49–50
Jockey Club of Kenya 314, 315, 320, 323–4, 325
Johnson, Amy 153, 200, 202, 204, 205, 206
  divorce from Jim Mollison 223
Johnson, Evie and Van 256
Johnson, Martin and Osa 127, 184, 321
Jones, Brian 318
Jones, Sue and Harry 316

Kamante 322
Kamau 156, 157–8, 159
Kara Prince 304, 308
Kavirondo tribe 44
Kekopey estate 74
Kell, Ivan, pseudonym *see* Schumacher, Raoul
Kenya
  economic crisis 63
  growth after World War II 276–7
  independence 300
  photographic craze 143, 145, 147, 149–50
  politics of development 76, 294–5
  racing in 286–7
  and World War I 56–7
  after World War I 64–5
  politics of development 76
  Uhuru (freedom) 294–5
Kenyatta, Jomo 278, 295
Kenyatta, Peter 317
Kibii 19, 22, 24, 27, 32, 35–7, 43–7, 49–50, 99, 289, 290
  see also arap Ruta
Kigole, Ndungu 288, 290, 316, 324, 326
Kikuyu tribe 46, 277
Kipsigis tribe 18, 19, 24, 27, 45, 47, 134
Kirkpatrick, Alex (James Alexander), half-brother 86, 87, 278–9
Kirkpatrick, Clára, formerly Clutterbuck (mother)
  in Kenya 86–7, 106, 111, 215, 279
  death 286
  for earlier years see Clutterbuck, Clara
Kirkpatrick, Major Henry Fearnley ('Harry') 14–15, 15–16, 87
Kirkpatrick, Ivonne (half-brother) 86
Kramer, George 301, 303, 305, 306

La Guardia, Fiorella 212, 214
La Mont, Lenore 256
Ladies Home Journal, BM's stories in 248, 249, 265
Lambton, The Hon. George 292
Langlands, Cecil and Charles 182
Langlands, Christopher 47, 179–80, 182, 184, 185, 186, 190, 193, 195, 277
  and BM's sense of money 193, 194–5
Langlands, Walter 182
Lascelles, Sir Alan 'Tommy' 122, 123, 125, 127, 128–9, 131, 132, 145, 149, 153, 225
Lavender, Captain 57
Le May, Miss, governess 25–7

Legh, Colonel Piers 'Joey' 122, 131, 146, 147
Lenare, photographer 229
Leth, Peter 313
Lidster, Edward 28
Lidster, Wilhelmina 'Billie' 28–9
Lindbergh, Charles 212
Lindeman, Charles 176
Lindstrom, Gilles 117
Lindstrom, Ingrid 117, 121, 161
Linscott, Robert N. 242
Little (jockey) 323
Little Dancer 287, 288, 290, 303
Lone Eagle 290, 298, 302, 303, 304
Long, 'Boy' 69, 94, 95, 97, 207
   and BM 75, 185, 195
Lowe, Blanche 51, 53, 54
Ludington, Wright 272

Maasai tribe 13, 27, 30, 37, 148–9
McAleer, Alec 294
McCutcheon, Shelagh 308–9, 310
MacDonald, Ramsay 141
McIndoe, Archibald 176
McMillan, Sir Northrup 77, 317
McMillan, Lady 157, 159
McQueen, Jimmy 'Syrup' 33
arap Maina 27, 35–7, 49, 99, 116
Manyika, BM training at 314–27
Marie Celeste II 304
Markham family 116
   racing colours 3, 191
Markham, Sir Arthur, 2nd bt 108
Markham, Beryl
   book: *West with the Night* 18, 44, · 238–41, 243–5, 249, 261, 276–7, 284, 289, 299, 311–12, 312–13, 319, 322, 325, 329–30, 332, 333, 334, 335–6
   characteristics 152
      Africanism 1, 18–34, 47, 59, 78
      beauty and attractiveness 32, 33, 85, 146, 201
      bitchiness 221–2
      competitiveness 40, 78–9, 218
      dislike of funerals 161
      dislike of women 19, 25
      dogs 31–2, 221, 256–7, 281, 307, 321, 326, 336
      domesticity, lack of 86, 268, 272
      expressionlessness 47, 54
      fatalism 19, 166–7
      flying 143, 145, 146, 162–7, 168–9, 171–2, 183, 187, 188–92, 196, 199–212

fortitude 21–2, 26–7, 27–8
humour, laughter 221
insecurity, vulnerability 1–2, 54, 322, 323
money, attitude to 41–2, 193, 194–5, 292–3
racing successes in Kenya 345
self-control 20–7
sexuality 45–6, 53–4, 85, 95, 107, 115, 185–6, 269, 310
strength 24, 34
life
   birth, as Beryl Clutterbuck 1, 7
   and horses 4, 7, 19
   to Africa 10, 12
   importance of Africa to 1, 59
   and Africans 12, 16, 19, 24, 35–6
   as *Lakwet* in Africa 18–34
   Swahili speaker 18
   and Emma Orchardson 21, 22
   and Arthur Orchardson 21
   under governesses 25–7, 28
   learns about horses from father 25, 27–8
   trauma of learning Emma not her mother 29
   help from Lady Delamere 29–30, 42
   dog Buller 31–2
   pony *Wee MacGregor* 30, 32
   to school in Nairobi 32–4
   and wildlife 23, 36–7
   surrounded by men 35
   and the lion Paddy 37–8
   and the stallion *Camciscan* 38–9
   superior runner 39–40
   as rider 40
   isolated by Lady Delamere's death 42–3
   night-time adventures 43–4
   friendship with Kibii 43–7, 53, 55
   early sexual experience 44–8
   at Miss Seccombe's school 51–4
   foals *Pegasus* 54–5
   marriage to Jock Purves 56, 57–8
   to India 60–1
   failure of marriage 61, 65
   relations with brother Dickie 61–2
   relations with Emma Orchardson 62
   father's problems 62, 64, 67
   sexual relations 65
   and Kibii (now *arap* Ruta) 62, 64, 66
   pursues Denys Finch Hatton 67–9, 74
   trains at Soysambu 70–2, 74, 75, 77–9
   social life 73, 79–81

affair with 'Boy' Long 75
friendship with Karen Blixen 81, 83–5
affair with Denys 83, 94, 95
beauty at seen by Karen 85
mother's return to Kenya 86–7
and Denys 89–90
on Karen 92–3
training still 93–4
to England 95–6, 97–101
shortage of money 97–9
pregnancy and abortion 99–100
back to Kenya, training at Westerland 102–3
learns to drive 103–4
at Nakuru stables 104–6
engaged to Bobby Watson 106–8
still pursuing Denys 107, 110
illness 107
and Mansfield Markham 108, 110–11
marriage to Markham 111
rare photo with mother 111
gives bed to Karen Blixen 111–12
educated by Markham 113
sleeps around 115
still pursuing Denys 116–18, 124, 132
and Karen 116–17
training again 119
and Prince of Wales 119, 122–3, 126, 127–8, 130–1, 132
pregnant again 120, 132–3
and Henry, Duke of Gloucester 124, 125–6
to London 132
gives birth to Gervase 133
problems with sick son 133–4, 152
presented to Queen Mary 136–7
royal trust fund for 137
royal mistress 139–40
social life 141
rivalry with Karen Blixen 142–3, 143–4, 156
and flying 143, 145, 146
hunting 144
visit to Sherfield Manor 145
racing abandoned for flying 145, 162
in Kenya with Prince of Wales 146–7, 149, 150
and Denys Finch Hatton 150, 151
and Karen 151
rents bungalow at Muthaiga 154
affair with Denys Finch Hatton 154–6
hears of Denys' death 158–9
and Denys' funeral 160–1
learning to fly 162–7

and Tom Campbell Black 164, 168
flying 168–9
links forged with lovers 170
maiden flight to England 171–2
at the Grosvenor again 173
abandoned by Tom Campbell Black 174
relations with Mansfield Markham 174
and with Duke of Gloucester 174
never sees son 174
and the Furnesses 175–7
nose alteration 176–7
meets John Carberry and St Barbe 177–8
flies to Kenya 178–80
proposal from Christopher Langlands 179–80
stays with Carberry 178–83
a trained mechanic 183
qualifies with B licence 184, 187
challenged to fly Atlantic 188
false start 190
in Aerial Derby 190
ill with malaria 190
elephant scouting 190–2
sleeps with Bror Blixen 192–3
rival to Karen 192–3
and Guest family 193–4
money earned for Blue Bird 193, 194–5
the Atlantic challenge 196, 199
flies to Paris with Blix 197–8
in London 199–207
Air Cruises 200–1
press coverage 203–6, 208
the flight 208–12
in USA 212–16
return to UK 216–17
low after flight 218
need for a man to push her 218–19
and Florence Desmond 219–20, 224, 226
dog Tania 221
price of fame 224–5, 226
affair with Jack Doyle 227–8
screen test 228–9, 230, 231
photo by Lenare 229
to USA 228, 229–30
and Raoul Schumacher 231, 232, 233–4
to Melbourne 232
to Cape Town to see father 236
cited in divorce 237
Markham tries to divorce 236–7

Markham, Beryl – *cont'd.*
  life – *cont'd.*
    to USA again 237
    writes *West with the Night* with
      Schumacher 238–41
    work on *Safari* film 238
    in Bahamas 242–3
    West with the Night published 243,
      249, 261
    reactions to it 244–5
    divorces Mansfield Markham 245
    married Raoul Schumacher 245
    reputation as a writer 247, 248, 254
    stories by BM 248, 249, 251–2, 257,
      263, 265, 271
    ranch Elsinore 248, 250
    life with Raoul 247, 249, 250–2
    possible book on Tod Sloan 250, 258,
      259, 262
    living in Montecito 251, 252, 253
    acrimony with Raoul 252, 258
    at The Monastery 252–6
    social life 256
    dogs 256–7
    work on African novel 250–1, 257
    promiscuity again 258, 261, 270, 271
    dumps Raoul 259–60
    reconciliation 262–3
    affair with Warren Austin 263–6,
      268–70
    poverty 263–4
    left by Raoul 266
    and Gervase 267
    possible pregnancy 271–2
    vengeance against Austin 270
    and against Raoul 272
    and Burl Ives 272–3
    leaves USA for Kenya 273, 274
    meets Duke of Gloucester in Kenya
      274
    bad health 274–5
    non-use of contraceptives 275
    makes use of Cloete's stories 276
    accused of not writing *West with the
      Night* 276–7
    fiftieth birthday 278
    training again, on Forest Farm 279,
      283
    hysterectomy 280
    dog Caesar 281
    and Jorgen Thrane 282–4
    grows pyrethrum 283
    life in the cottage 284–5
    West with the Night 284, 289, 299
    and Kipling 284

    visit from Gervase and wife 285–6
    will in favour of George Norman 286
    training career 286–95, 345
    and Africans 288
    training methods 290–2
    use perhaps of *seketet* 290–1
    and Buster Parnell 293–4, 307–8
    Forest Farm takeover 295
    new premises 296
    quarrel with Jorgen 296
    drinking 298–9
    meets Martha Gellhorn 299
    dress 299–300
    worry about Jorgen 299–300
    move to South Africa 300
    at Broadlands 300–8
    racing in South Africa 304
    and the brood mares 304–5, 306
    rivalry with Enid Kenmare 306–7
    dogs 307, 321, 326
    accepts fees from owners 308
    quarrel with Enid 308
    poor relations with jockeys 309
    moves to Eerste River 308–9
    loneliness 309
    difficult relations with horses 309–10
    still enjoying sex 310
    licence relinquished 310
    West with the Night 311–12, 312–13,
      319, 322, 325
    to Rhodesia 311, 313
    licence to race in Rhodesia and Malawi
      313
    back to Kenya 313
    training at Manyika 314–27
    still a horsewoman 317
    an irritating trainer 320, 323
    poverty 320, 325
    last eight years 321–37
    drinking too much 323, 332
    licence problems 323–4
    ill 323
    accident 324
    attacked and robbed 326–7
    last racing win 327
    and the coup in Kenya 328–9
    West with the Night republished 329–30,
      332, 333, 334, 335–6
    James Fox interview 330
    film of *West with the Night* 331
    television *Arena* film 332
    a degree of senility 333
    journalistic pieces 333
    thrombosis and other illnesses 335–6
    will 335–6

visit to races 336
death 337
ashes 337
Markham, Sir Charles, 3rd bt 108, 109, 136–7
Markham, Sir Charles, 4th bt 245, 326
Markham, Fleur 318, 335
Markham, Gervase 133–4, 204–5, 266, 285
  rumours about paternity 135, 174, 266
  visit to California 266–8
  visit to Kenya 285–6
  death 318
Markham, Lingar 'Gar', Lady Markham (later Mrs O'Hea) 108, 109, 112
  and Gervase 134, 136–7, 205, 206
  and BM 115, 136–7, 223, 285
Markham, Mansfield (husband) 68, 108, 285
  marriage to BM 110–11, 113–16
  buys property 117, 118
  criticism of Prince of Wales 123
  to London 132
  row over Royal princes 136–7
  seeking divorce 164, 169, 236–7
  relations with Gervase 205, 266, 285, 318
  divorced by BM 245, 247
Markham, Mary Ellen (née Adley) 236, 247, 267, 285
Markham, Valery 318, 335
Markham, Viviane 285, 318–19
Marshall Field, Mr & Mrs 154
Martin, Flo 96
Martin, Hugh 155, 167
Mary, Queen 123, 136, 140, 141, 199–200, 225
  meets BM 136–7
Masefield, John 216
Mason, Philip 328
Matson, 'Mat' 59
Mau Mau 277, 278, 281, 286
Maxwell-Hyslop, Andrew 331
Mbogani estate 73, 85–6, 104, 117
  Denys Finch Hatton leaves 154–6
Melhuish, Jack 155, 157
Melton Pie 105, 106
Mendl, Sir Charles 268, 271
Mendl, Elsie, Lady Mendl (Elsie de Wolfe) 271, 343
Meredyth, Bess 231
Merlin 125
The Messenger (plane) *see* Vega Gull
Messenger Boy 116, 118, 257
Migdoll, Mickey 207, 299–300
Migdoll, Paddy 'Squirrel' 327, 335, 337

Miles, Tich 70, 73, 80, 81, 124
Milne, Alison and Dr 100
Milne, Elizabeth 58, 100
Moffat, Curtis 141
Mohammed, Jasmin Wali 320–1, 325, 327–8
arap Moi, President Daniel
Mollison, Jim 188, 202–3, 205, 207, 209, 222, 226, 227
  divorce from Amy Johnson 223
Moon River 326
Morby (jockey) 323
Morris, Francis 28, 29
Morris, Langley 29
Mostert, M. C. P. 'Mossie' 185, 189, 277
Mountie 290, 298, 302, 303, 304
Movita (actress) 231
Mulholland, Joey 71
Muliro, Hon. M. 315
Muthaiga Country Club 79, 85, 123, 124

Nairobi 48–9, 77–8, 274, 276, 314
  races 14
  see also Nakuru; Ngong
Nakuru 48, 49, 104–6
Nandi tribe 13, 46
Naro Moru 277, 283, 292
Ndimu farm 62–3, 64, 66
Ndungu *see* Kigole, Ndungu
Nettlefold, Freddie 316, 317–18, 319
Ngong racecourse 78, 315
Niagara 288, 289–90, 303, 308, 313
Niven, David 256
Njongo, Charles 317
Njoro 11–13
Noonan, Fred 230
Norfolk Hotel, Nairobi 11, 14, 57–8
Norman, Charles Bathurst 278, 279, 281, 282, 295, 297, 299, 303
Norman, the Hon. Doreen 278, 279, 280, 281, 285, 303
Norman, George 278, 279, 280, 281, 284, 286
Norman, Victoria 278, 279, 280, 281, 284, 322, 325
Norman and Thrane Ltd 282, 283
Northey, Sir Edward 57, 63, 81
Northey, Evangeline, Lady Northey 81

O'Dell, Scott 230–1, 234, 236, 237, 238, 239, 240, 241, 244, 245, 248–9, 250–1, 334
  BM dumps Raoul on 259–60
  and Raoul 261, 312

Oderu 316, 321, 325–6, 335, 336
Ogilvie-Boyle, E. 105
O'Hea, Gar *see* Markham, Lingar
O'Hea, Colonel James 108, 138
O'Neill, Dr Freeman 211
O'Neill, the Hon, Patricia *see* Cavendish
Oppenheimer, Harry 306
Orchardson, Arthur 19, 20, 21, 22, 27, 28,
	62, 67
	to school 32–3, 34, 49
	good rider 40, 67, 218, 297, 342, 344
	'Clutt's bastard' allegation 152
	and BM after World War II 279, 282
	special relationship with BM 289, 319
	death 319
Orchardson, Emma 16, 18, 20, 28
	and BM 21, 22, 52–3, 56, 62
	shown not to be BM's mother 29
	and World War I 48, 49, 50
	no longer with Clutt 67
Orchardson, Gordon 20
Orchardson, Ian 20, 28, 338
Out of Africa, book 152, 154, 161, 239, 330,
	333
Out of Africa, film 333, 334

Parnell, Anna 293, 294, 307
Parnell, Ryan 'Buster' 293–4, 307–8
Patel, Anwar 320, 328
Paul, Winifred 209, 343
Payne, Maurice 292
Peccadillo 309
Pegasus 19, 54–5, 65, 68–9, 70, 77, 79,
	102, 106
Percival, Edgar 203, 207–8, 209, 210, 216,
	222
Percival, Philip 191
Perkins, Maxwell 244
Pfeiffer, Pauline 191
Phillips, Captain Gray 265
Photography, replacing hunting 143, 145,
	147, 149–50
Pitt, Mary 33
Porter, Amy 252
Potter, John 239, 268, 271, 272, 334
Poulton, Billy and Pearl 103
Powell, Tristram 332
Powys, Will 94
Preston, Kiki 237
Price, George 294
Prudhomme, Gabriel 181, 185, 188, 190,
	255, 278
Prudhomme, Rhoda 181, 252, 255–6, 266,
	278
Purdy, Bill 324, 325, 329

Purves, Captain Alexander Laidlaw 'Jock'
	(husband) 50–1, 56
	marriage to BM 57–8, 60, 61, 65, 69, 70
	problems 65–6, 71–2, 74, 75, 94–5
	perhaps divorced 102

Rand, Chris 257
Rand, Maddie (later de Mott) 322–3, 334
Rand, Peter 257, 323
Rattray, Andrew 175, 176, 188–9
Referee 105
Repton, Guy 185
Rhodes, Dylis 322
Rhodesia, BM in 311–13
Richardson, Derek 276
Richardson, Sir Philip 172
Richardson, Sylvia (formerly Temple) 'The
	Afghan Princess' 182–3, 184, 276,
	277
Rift Valley (Happy Valley) 102
Rigel, Miss, teacher 33–4
Rio Grande 290, 292, 297
Ritchie, Archie 125, 149, 150
Rollo, lawyer 137
Roosevelt, Kermit and Belle 141
Ropner, Colonel Leonard 191, 192
Rothschild, Louis 184, 190
Royal Aero Club 139–40
Ruark, Robert 279
Rundgren, Eric 281, 282, 283
arap Ruta 62, 64, 66, 71, 163, 190, 197
	working with horses 77, 102, 105
	in London 113–15
	back in Kenya 118, 119
	at the Muthaiga bungalow 154, 158
	and aeroplanes 169
	reunion with BM after World War II
		277, 279, 282
	dismissed 288
	for his earlier life see Kibii

St Barbe, Sydney 177–8, 179, 182–3, 185,
	190
Saint-Exupéry, Antoine de 162, 240
Saturday Evening Post 257
Schlachter, Barry 331
Schlesinger Air Race 202, 203
Schumacher, Raoul Cottereau 44, 234–6
	and BM 230–66
	working on *West with the Night* 238–41,
		244–5
	BM's literary reputation 248, 250–1
	buys ranch Elsinore 248
	to write an African novel 250–1, 257
	own writing 251, 265–6, 271

living at The Monastery 252, 253–4, 256
ghost writer 257, 261–2, 263, 312, 334
and the Tod Sloan book 252, 258
dumped by BM, ill 259–60
illness 260, 261
leaves BM post-adultery 266
relationship with Mary Lou Culley 272
divorces BM 312
marriage to Gertrude Chase Greene 312
death 311, 312
Scott, Charles W. A. 189, 195
Scott, Lord Francis (and Lady Eileen) 82–3, 93, 106, 128, 170, 200, 224
Scott-Mason, Veronica 291
Seccombe, Blanche, school 44, 51
Seketet (drug *Kaita*) 290–1, 292, 308, 345
Seremai, flying centre 179–83
Serengeti game reserve 143
Sewell, W. G. 28, 29
Sharpe, Roland 292
Sherfield Manor (Buckfield House) 145
Shoemaker, Jack 329
Simpson, Mrs Wallis 140, 200, 224, 225–6
Duchess of Windsor in Bahamas 242, 264, 265
Sloan, Tod 191, 250, 258, 259
Soames, Jack 185, 242
Soden, Mongoose 277
Sofer-Whitburn family 154
Soprani, Aldo 295, 297, 298, 314, 314, 316, 320
Sorsbie, Malin 190
South Africa, BM in 300–10
Soysambu 71–2, 74, 75–6
Speed Trial 297
Spiers, Mrs Kay 287
Spike 290, 291, 297, 298
Spurling, Milton 256
Stanning Brothers 103
Stansfield, Derek 294
Stanton, 'Silver' Jane 190
Starkie, Dr Richard 100
Stokowski, Evangeline 253, 254, 255
Stokowski, Leopold 252–3, 254–5, 263
Streiker, Gary 331
Struthers, Almira and Jimmy 322
Sultan 316
Supercharger 319
Swahili
BM as speaker of 18
glossary xiv–xv
Swanson, Gloria 231

Tarlton, Henry 148
Temple, Commander Grenville 182
Temple, Sylvia 'The Afghan Princess' 182–3, 184
later Mrs Richardson 276, 277
Thomas, Tony 290, 294
Thomson, Christopher Birdwood, Lord 143
Thorpe, Pip and Barbara 298
Thrane, Jorgen 281, 282–3, 286, 288, 289, 293, 295, 298, 311
problems with BM 296
BM's worries over 299, 300
and Broadlands 303–4
last visit 335
Thurman, Judith 129, 152
Tiger Fish 306
Title Deed 287, 290, 297, 303, 304, 308
Totem 40
Tree, Iris 141, 157
Trench, Dan 185
Trench, John Maxwell 343
Trotter, Brigadier General G. 122, 124, 127, 146
Tryon, Spencer 71, 125
Turnball, William 329

Uganda Railway 8–9, 10–11
Ulysses 287, 288

Valentino, Rudolph 231
Vanderbilt, Alfred 191, 192, 194
Vanderbilt, Gloria (later Stokowski) 141, 253
Vanity Fair magazine 240
Varma, Dr V. J. 326
Vega Gull, '*The Messenger*' (VP-KCC) 188, 196, 201, 202, 203, 207, 214
the flight 208–11
off loaded in London 223–4
model, in Africa 284
Velvet Glove 116
Vincent, Alan 231
Vorbeck, General bon Lettow 55–6,
Vuitton, Louis, trunk by 113, 167, 239, 327

Waddington, Joan 157
Wakefield, Charles Cheers, Viscount Wakefield 163
Wales, Edward Prince of 140–1, 190
in Kenya 118, 119–23, 128–30
and BM 122–3, 124, 125, 126, 127, 130
and BM in London 132–3, 136, 139–40
flying 143, 145
and Serengeti 143

Wales, Edward Prince of – *cont'd.*
  new safari in Kenya 146–50
  see also Edward VIII *for later life*
Walters, Harry 70, 71, 111
Wangmweze tribe 13
Ward, Freda Dudley 139, 200
Ward, Roddy 185, 195
Water Boy 313, 317, 346
'Waterjump' *see* Altantic crossings
Waterman, Doris 'Dos' 52–3, 56, 60
Watkins, Ann 241, 243
Watkins, Archie 171, 172, 173
Watson, Robert Fraser, engagement to BM
  106–8, 123
Watteville, Vivienne de 130, 153
Webb, B. F. 'Bertie' 71, 105, 106
Webster (jockey) 323
Wee Macgregor 28, 30, 32
Weingan, Al 256
Weir-Mosley, Mrs 188, 207, 213, 217
Welsh Guard 106
West with the Night see Markham, Beryl:
  book
Weston, Harry 38

White Rhino, Nyeri 187
Whitman, Walt, poem 89–90
Wild life 23, 36–7
Wilson, Florrie 163, 170, 171, 189, 342, 343
Wilson, Mollie 336
Wilson Airways 162, 163, 170, 189
Winchilsea, Ann Jane Finch Hatton,
  Countess of 100–1
Winchilsea, Margaretta Finch Hatton,
  Countess of 141, 143
Winchilsea, Henry Stormont Finch Hatton,
  13th Earl of, and 8th Earl of
  Nottingham 72, 104
Windsor, Duke of *see* Edward VIII
Wise Child 53, 105–6, 133, 248, 288, 289
Wood, Captain George 'Woody' 81,
  184–5, 187, 190, 196, 242, 243, 265
World War I 48
Wrack 103, 105

Xylone 303

Yentob, Alan 332